FROM EMPEROR TO CITIZEN

W. J. F. JENNER was a translator at the Foreign Languages Press in Beijing (1963–5) after reading Chinese at Oxford. From 1965 he was a lecturer at the University of Leeds until his appointment as Professor of Chinese at the Australian National University beginning in 1988. He has written and translated widely on Chinese history and literature.

SIMON WINCHESTER is the Pacific region correspondent for the *Guardian* and travels throughout the area from his base in Hong Kong.

FROM EMPEROR TO CITIZEN

The Autobiography of Aisin-Gioro Pu Yi

TRANSLATED WITH NEW GENERAL AND
CHAPTER INTRODUCTIONS BY
W. J. F. JENNER

AFTERWORD BY
SIMON WINCHESTER

Oxford New York
OXFORD UNIVERSITY PRESS

Oxford University Press, Walton Street, Oxford OX2 6DP

Oxford New York Toronto
Delhi Bombay Calcutta Madras Karachi
Petaling Jaya Singapore Hong Kong Tokyo
Nairobi Dar es Salaam Cape Town
Melbourne Auckland

and associated companies in
Berlin Ibadan

Oxford is a trade mark of Oxford University Press

Published in the United States by Oxford University Press, USA

General and chapter introductions © W. J. F. Jenner, 1987
Afterword © Simon Winchester, 1987

This translation was first published in 1964 and 1965 by
Foreign Languages Press, Peking,
and is republished here with their agreement. This paperback edition with
new introductions and afterword was first published in 1987
by Oxford University Press
Reprinted 1988 (twice)

British Library Cataloguing in Publication Data
Pu Yi
From emperor to citizen: the autobiography
of Aisin-Gioro Pu Yi.
1. Pu Yi   2. China—Kings and rulers—
Biography   3. China—History—20th century
I. Title
951'.03'0924   DS773
ISBN 0–19–282099–0

Library of Congress Cataloging in Publication Data
P'u-i, 1906–1967.
From emperor to citizen.
Translation of: Wo ti ch'ien pan sheng.
Includes index.
1. P'u-i, 1906–1967. 2. China—Kings and rulers—
Biography. I. Jenner, W. J. F. (William John Francis)
II. Title.
DS773.C51513 1987   951'.03'0924 [B]   87–18652
ISBN 0–19–282099–0 (pbk.)

Printed in Great Britain by
Richard Clay Ltd.
Bungay, Suffolk

Contents

vi

List of Illustrations

General Introduction to the 1987 Edition

W. J. F. Jenner

It is at first sight a remarkable thing to have the autobiography of a man who was twice emperor of China and once the emperor of a part of China, and was then so successfully remoulded in the prisons of a Communist government that he ended as a contented citizen leading an ordinary life and earning his living like anyone else. When this book was first published in Chinese (in a deliberately restricted edition) in 1964, the general public were so eager to see it that the few available copies were read round the clock as people took their turn to have it in their hands for a few hours. For over ten years after that the book was, like so many others in China, banned for being a reactionary, counter-revolutionary, poisonous weed. Since being available again in recent years it has sold well over a million copies.

And yet this book was first issued, by a publishing house that makes no secret of being a part of the Ministry of Public Security, as a work of propaganda designed to show the imperial regimes of the past in a bad light and the rule of the Communist Party in a good one. Whether it succeeds in those aims for foreigners is one that can be left to the readers of this translation to judge. My own impressions when making the translation and re-reading it over twenty years later is that the supposedly bad old days are much more interesting than the tale of remoulding.

During the radical year of 1968 an unofficial publication in Canton came out with a characteristic Cultural Revolution blast against *From Emperor to Citizen*. The authors of this diatribe start from the judgement that the book was

> written from the standpoint of feudalism and imperialism to distort history, express hatred for the revolution, eulogize imperialism and vilify the revolutionary mass movement. It publicizes the extravagant and corrupt life in the imperial court and beautifies and honours the arch war criminal and

traitor who betrayed the motherland. . . . It advocates the theory of the dying out of class struggle, composes the class contradictions, distorts the socialist system and the policy of remoulding criminals. . . . It is a big poisonous weed against the Party, socialism and Mao Tse-tung thought . . . a book used by Liu Shao-ch'i to create public opinion for counter-revolutionary restoration . . .

They go on to give what purports to be a detailed account of how and by whom the 'big poisonous weed' was written. It was, we are told, 'actually written by someone else on behalf of the author in 1955', and this first version was printed in a small secret edition for the highest officials. A team was then set up under Li Wen-ta, who according to other sources was and is an editor in the Ministry of Public Security's publishing house, to collect information and rewrite the book.

The draft of this second version, the pamphlet continues, was then submitted to a panel of luminaries by the Communist Party's United Front Department, the body that has the job of 'uniting' non-Communists under Communist Party leadership. (One of the bodies under its control is the Chinese People's Political Consultative Conference in whose Institute of Literature and History the survivors of earlier regimes compile records of the past.) The process of revision lasted four years, and involved a number of leading historians. Other sources attribute much of the final polish of the text to the most distinguished of Manchu writers, the novelist Lao She (Lau Shaw). It was the Central Committee's Propaganda Department that authorized publication, originally intended to be open and in a large edition. It was only later that the decision was made to bring out instead the smaller and more discreet edition in which it actually appeared in 1964. In Hong Kong and elsewhere in the Chinese-speaking world Peking encouraged the publication of very big editions. Here the political purpose of the book was very clear: if even a former emperor, traitor, and war criminal such as P'u Yi could become an honoured citizen of the People's Republic happy to bask in the glow of the Communist Party's benevolence, what did any other Chinese have to fear from returning to the embrace of the motherland? The Chinese world outside the People's Republic was almost certainly the book's main target all along.

Non-Chinese foreigners were also intended to read the memoirs that were so hard to obtain inside China in the original. According to the Canton leaflet, foreign-language publication was first suggested by Hu Ch'iao-mu, then a member of the Communist Party's secretariat with responsibility for propaganda, in the winter of 1960/61. Early in 1964 the translation was entrusted to me by the English Section of the Foreign Languages Press in Peking. It was made clear that this was an important assignment, and that we had to get the book out quickly in order to beat into print any unauthorized translation abroad. Because of the urgency of the job I worked from the proofs of the Chinese text before the book was published; and the translation was split into two volumes so that the first one, going up to Chapter Five and covering P'u Yi's life in the Forbidden City and then in Tientsin, could appear as soon as possible after the original was published in Peking and Hong Kong. It came out in the autumn. The pace of publishing the second volume slackened, and though ready by winter it did not appear till a year later.

The text I worked from was a somewhat shortened version of the original. Most of the cuts were made in the earlier chapters, deleting some of the anecdotes and details about palace life. Little of importance was lost. The later chapters were, unfortunately, hardly cut at all. This reprint includes all of the English edition first published by the Foreign Languages Press in 1964 and 1965. As it has not been reset, it was not possible to revise the translation or to change the spelling of the Chinese names to the Hanyu Pinyin versions that are now standard. We are thus left with the simplified version of the Wade-Giles romanization that was the Foreign Languages Press's house style until the late 1970s. Readers may find the Empress Dowager Tzu Hsi, for example, called either Tz'u Hsi or Ci xi in other books. In the brief introductory notes to each chapter that have been specially written for this edition, I have made the Wade-Giles less inaccurate, so that Pu Yi becomes P'u Yi.

The book in English has been made much use of since then by all sorts of people, from one who used it wholesale in what purported to be a different translation to film-makers looking for something exotic. The translator should no doubt be gratified that his work has been so profitable to others. It may even have worked quite well as propaganda.

A question that must be asked but cannot readily be answered is how far the original is P'u Yi's own work. The Canton pamphlet denies him authorship altogether, and in more recent years the argument has been advanced—or so it is said—that the rights to the book belong to the Ministry of Public Security's publishing house, as they wrote it. Nobody claims that it was his unaided work. His widow, for example, refers to all the help he had with it. Nor can the book be seen as anything but a very public statement of the orthodox view of the world at the time it was written. It may be relevant that when I was doing the translation in Peking in 1964 and I had queries about the text that Chou Chia-ts'an, the excellent Foreign Languages Press editor who was checking my version, could not answer he consulted P'u Yi's very capable younger brother P'u Chieh rather than the supposed author himself. On the only occasion I met P'u Yi, a rather formalistic occasion laid on for the benefit of my parents who were visiting Peking in September 1964, he was not very impressive: a tall, shambling figure whose conversation was notable more for the slurred, thick, Peking accent in which he spoke than for anything useful he had to say about the contents of, or background to, the book.

Does this all lead us to treat the book as fabrication? I would not go that far. The writing of autobiographies, sometimes over and over again, is a big part of Chinese prison life, and P'u Yi would certainly have been required to put a lot about himself on paper during his years in the Fushun and Harbin gaols. He would also have been questioned at great length, and his answers written down. It is not inconceivable that the 1955 first draft referred to in the Canton pamphlet was an edited version of such material, containing many of P'u Yi's words even if written up by other hands. Much of the book may have drawn on things he wrote either when still in gaol or after his release. After all, the main function of the institute where he spent his last years was to be a place where people wrote their memoirs. It is unlikely that he contributed as much to the first chapter, with all its detail on Ch'ing history, as to the later ones.

Even if he had written every word of the book himself I do not think that he would have told a very different story. Throughout his life he had a pattern of doing what was expected of him by whoever dominated him at the time. Unkind though it is to make such a statement, one has the impression that he never became a person in his own right. As child emperor, both before and after the abdication, he was in effect a motherless prisoner of the palace, controlled by an army of stepmothers, tutors, and eunuchs. As he grew a little older he learned to adapt to the expectations of his Scottish tutor R. F. Johnston. After the expulsion from the Forbidden City in 1924, the dominant influences were the Ch'ing elder statesmen and, increasingly, the Japanese army. Once he went to the Northeast (Manchuria) to become the puppet ruler of a Japanese client state he was almost completely Japan-oriented. Then came the years in the Soviet Union, where once again he learned to adapt, trying hard to be allowed to stay. On his return to China to spend nearly ten years in gaol he became a model prisoner in his attitudes. I see no reason to doubt that P'u Yi tried to please his masters at every stage of his life; and as this book is what was wanted in the early 1960s, I am sure that he would have written it all by himself had he been capable of it.

As to whether he was a different person underneath, that is harder to say. *From Emperor to Citizen* does not disguise a tendency to be cruel to underlings who disobeyed or offended, and the trait continued, as was shown by the way he snubbed his fourth wife when she offered to see him after she obtained a divorce in 1957. This is consistent with a toadying approach to those who had power over him. His bleak childhood found no compensation in adult relationships: his marriages all appear to have been in form only as he was unable to perform sexually, and he never seems to have had a real friendship on the basis of equality in his life.

We may even doubt how far he was ever 'remoulded'. He never learned to look after himself, as was obvious to me when he could not smoke a cigarette without covering himself with ash. After his release from prison he lived a very privileged but also powerless life, right up to his death in 1967. He was protected even from the violence of the Cultural Revolution, but he never knew the satisfaction of ordinary life.

In the end it is pity as much as anything else that P'u Yi's story, whether told here or in the accounts of those who knew him, evokes. Pity for his victims certainly, but also pity for the weak and helplessly dependent personality he was. He is probably seen at his best in the descriptions that his fourth and fifth wives have written of him showing, however clumsily, affection and a need for their uncritical company.

As the book was written for Chinese readers familiar with the general historical background I have added brief introductions to each chapter.

Twenty years ago Chou Chia-ts'an, the original editor of this translation, was left to die in a field, a victim of the factional struggles of the Cultural Revolution. Though it is too late now, I would like to thank him. His work editing this probably contributed to his death.

Postscript. China's State Copyright Bureau have ruled that the secret 1960 edition of this book was written as self-criticism in gaol by P'u Yi and P'u Chieh. The 1964 version translated here was a *new* book written by Li Wen-ta and revised by P'u Yi and others. Li and P'u Yi are therefore co-authors and share Chinese copyright.

∗   ∗   ∗   ∗

P'u Yi has had quite a lot written about him over the years. An excellent biography that is both informative and entertaining is Henry McAleavy's *A Dream of Tartary: The Origins and Misfortunes of Henry P'u Yi* (London: George Allen and Unwin, 1963). A more awestruck approach to the dragon throne pervades his former tutor Sir Reginald F. Johnston's *Twilight in the Forbidden City* (London: Victor Gollancz, 1934; Hong Kong: Oxford University Press, 1986).

McAleavy lists in his acknowledgements the principal sources in Chinese and Japanese available in 1963. Of the P'u Yi literature since then, the original of this book, *Wo-te ch'ien pan sheng* (Peking: Ch'ün-chung ch'u-pan-she, 1964), and the volume of memoirs by close associates including his last two wives, *P'u Yi li-k'ai Tzu-chin-ch'eng i-hou* (*After P'u Yi Left the Forbidden City*) (Peking: Wen-shih tzu-liao ch'u-pan-she, 1985), are probably the most important. The Red Guard pamphlet on which I draw in the introduction is translated in *Survey of the China Mainland Press* no. 4177, 14 May 1968.

There are several general histories of China during P'u Yi's lifetime, of which one of the most informative is Immanuel C. Y. Hsü, *The Rise of Modern China* (New York: Oxford University Press, 1970 and later editions). Other views of 'remoulding' in prison can be had from Robert Jay Lifton's *Thought Reform and the Psychology of Totalism* (New York: W. W. Norton, 1961), from Amnesty International's *Political Imprisonment in the People's Republic of China* (London: Amnesty International Publications, 1978), and from Allyn and Adele Rickett, *Prisoners of Liberation* (New York: Cameron Associates, 1957).

The Pedigree of the Ching House

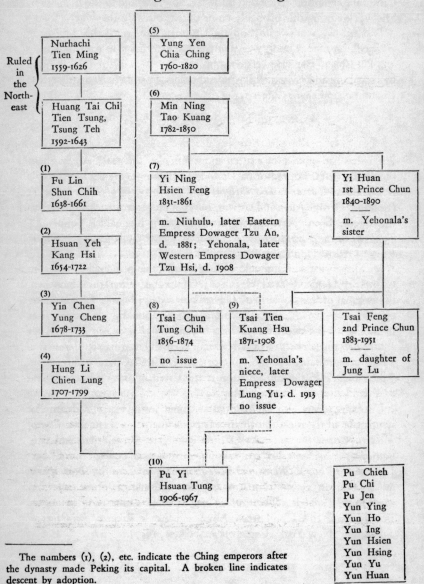

The numbers (1), (2), etc. indicate the Ching emperors after the dynasty made Peking its capital. A broken line indicates descent by adoption.

CHAPTER ONE

□□□□□□□□□□□□□□□□□□□□□□□□□□□□□□□□□□□□□□

MY FAMILY

The first chapter, which goes into the palace politics of the last sixty years of the Ch'ing dynasty, may confuse at first reading as it provides no clear overall narrative to hold together the fascinating anecdotal detail. It may be helpful to start with a highly condensed summary here.

Briefly, one of the great uncertainties of Chinese dynastic politics, to which the Manchu conquerors who imposed their Ch'ing dynasty on the Han Chinese in the seventeenth century were no exception, was the perennial problem of succession. In the absence of primogeniture or any other certain principle to determine which member of the imperial clan should succeed to the throne, this was always a matter for intrigue and conflict. And as a woman could not rule in her own right, an empress with ambitions for power would almost inevitably try to ensure a succession that left her in control.

The Hsien Feng emperor, who reigned from 1851 to 1861, took for one of his many wives a girl of the Yehonala clan. She saw to it that she bore his only surviving son, got herself promoted to full empress, and became the Empress Dowager Tz'u Hsi after his death. When the new emperor, T'ung Chih, came to the throne as a mere child of six (five by the Western count*) she organized a coup that got rid of the eight-man regency council her husband had appointed on his deathbed. This was the Su Shun affair described on pp. 4–6. For almost all of the rest of his reign she was in power as empress dowager. When the T'ung Chih emperor died in 1874,

---

* The traditional Chinese method of counting age is to regard a child as one year old at birth.

conveniently sonless, she ensured that the successor would be another child, her nephew Kuang Hsu. This guaranteed her continued control until her death in 1908, interrupted only briefly by Kuang Hsu's attempt to take power and impose reforms that she ended with a coup in 1898, after which Kuang Hsu was a prisoner. When Kuang Hsu died shortly before her death she chose as successor P'u Yi, another infant descended from her Yehonala clan (P'u Yi's grandmother was her sister). His father Prince Ch'un could be expected to cause her no trouble as nominal regent. But as it was she died the next day, and just over three years later the dynasty collapsed.

My Grandfather Prince Chun

I was born in Peking in the mansion of Prince Chun on February 7, 1906. My grandfather Yi Huan, the seventh son of Emperor Tao Kuang (reigned 1821-50), was the first Prince Chun. Although my father was only his fifth son he inherited the title as the eldest, third and fourth sons died in childhood and the second son was taken into the palace to become the emperor Kuang Hsu (reigned 1875-1908). I was the eldest son of the second Prince Chun. I was nearly three when on November 13, 1908 the empress dowager Tzu Hsi suddenly decided to make me the heir to the throne as she and the emperor Kuang Hsu lay seriously ill. I became the adopted son of Emperor Tung Chih (reigned 1862-74) and the ritual heir of his cousin Kuang Hsu. Within two days of my entering the palace both Kuang Hsu and the Empress Dowager were dead. On December 2 I ascended the imperial throne as the tenth ruler of the Ching Dynasty[1] and the last emperor of China. Before three years were out the 1911 Revolution against the Ching Dynasty broke out and I abdicated.

My earliest memories are of the time of my abdication, but to make things clearer it would be best to start with my grandfather and my family.

In that blackest of eras, the late Ching Dynasty, the family of Prince Chun were for half a century the faithful servants of the empress dowager Tzu Hsi, and my grandfather in particular devoted his life to her service.

My grandfather was born in 1842 and died in 1890. Looking through the records of the imperial family one can see that he received few honours during the eleven-year reign of his brother, Emperor

---

[1] (1644-1911), a dynasty set up by the Aisin-Gioro clan of the Manchus, a people who originated in the Northeast of China.

Hsien Feng (reigned 1851-61), but that in the six months or so after Hsien Feng's death, when Tzu Hsi had just been made Empress Dowager, he was suddenly loaded with titles and positions.

The obvious reason why a young man of twenty was able to attain such eminence was that his wife's sister had become an empress dowager; but it was not the only reason. I remember that when I was young I heard an anecdote about how during a theatrical performance at home an uncle of mine, then six years old, was so terrified by one scene that he started to cry. My grandfather shouted at him in front of everybody, "What disgraceful behaviour! When I was twenty I captured Su Shun with my own hands, but if you go on like that you'll never be able to handle affairs of state." The capture of Su Shun had been the real beginning of his meteoric rise.

The Su Shun affair took place in 1861. The Second Opium War[1] had ended with a series of humiliating treaties and the emperor Hsien Feng lay mortally ill in his refuge in Jehol. He summoned to his deathbed three Ministers of the Presence and five Grand Councillors who had accompanied him in his flight, and having made his six-year-old son Tsai Chun heir to the throne, he appointed them as a regency council. The next day Hsien Feng died, and in accordance with his wishes the eight princes and high officials put Tsai Chun on the throne with the reign title Chi Hsiang and took all power into their own hands.

The most important of the eight regents were two princes and Su Shun, an Assistant Grand Secretary and President of the Board of Revenue who had earned the hatred of the Manchu nobility by promoting many officials of Han nationality and had a reputation for ruthlessness. A more basic reason for Su Shun's later disastrous fall was that his group underestimated the strength of Prince Kung (Yi Hsin), who had made the most of the unpleasant assignment of negotiating peace after the Second Opium War: in concluding the

---

[1] From 1856 to 1860 Britain and France jointly carried on a war of aggression against China. The Ching government was then devoting all its energy to suppressing the peasant revolution of the Taiping Heavenly Kingdom and adopted a policy of passive resistance towards the foreign aggressors, with the result that China suffered a disastrous defeat.

unprecedentedly humiliating Treaty of Peking he had won the admiration of the foreigners. As an uncle of the emperor with foreign support he was not prepared to take second place to Su Shun and his party, and he was encouraged by the Manchu nobility and other high officials who had long been Su Shun's political enemies. Just at this moment an edict was brought in secret from the two dowagers in Jehol.

One of the dowagers was the lady Niuhulu, who had been the empress of Hsien Feng and was later given the title Empress Dowager Tzu An; she was also known as the Eastern Dowager. The other was Empress Dowager Tzu Hsi, or the Western Dowager. Tzu Hsi had originally been a palace concubine. When pregnant she had been promoted to be a Secondary Consort, and as her child Tsai Chun was the only son of Emperor Hsien Feng she became an empress dowager when he succeeded to his father's throne. I do not know how it was managed, but as soon as she was made an empress dowager one of the censors memorialized requesting that the two dowagers should act as joint regents. This proposal met with the fiercest opposition from Su Shun and his fellow-regents on the grounds that there was absolutely no precedent for anything of the kind in the history of the dynasty. This did not worry the dowager Tzu An, who was completely without ambition, but it aroused Tzu Hsi's bitter resentment. First she persuaded Tzu An that the eight regents were untrustworthy conspirators and then she got Tzu An's consent to a secret letter being sent to Prince Kung summoning him to the palace in Jehol to discuss how to deal with them. To consolidate their newly gained power the eight regents tried every method to keep Prince Kung in Peking and the dowagers in Jehol apart.

There are a number of different stories about how the dowagers managed to dodge Su Shun's agents and make contact with Prince Kung. Some say that the dowagers' decree was secretly carried by a cook to Peking, while others maintain that Tzu Hsi had a favourite eunuch, An Te-hai, given a public thrashing and then sent to Peking to be dealt with by the court, thus enabling him to take the edict to the capital. Anyhow, the edict reached Prince Kung, and as soon as he received it he submitted a memorial asking for an audience with the emperor. Su Shun's party tried to block this with an "imperial edict" saying that it was "most important" that he should "stay in his post", but they did not succeed. Su Shun then attempted to prevent him from meeting the dowagers by invoking the old rule of behaviour that a man should not meet his sisters-in-law, but this too failed.

There are many different accounts of how Prince Kung and the dowagers met. One story is that Prince Kung disguised himself as a *shaman* (a kind of wizard) and another is that he checkmated Su Shun by saying to him that it would be proper for him to meet his sisters-in-law if Su Shun were present to supervise the occasion; Su Shun was completely nonplussed and had to abandon his attempts at obstruction. Yet another story is that when Prince Kung went to sacrifice to the memorial tablet of the late emperor the dowager Tzu Hsi had a trusted eunuch bring him a bowl of noodles in which was hidden an edict written by Tzu Hsi. Whatever method was in fact used, the result was that Prince Kung and the dowagers were able to discuss everything.

When the dowagers returned to the capital Prince Kung was given a new title and the eight regents were arrested. The two princes among them were allowed to commit suicide, Su Shun was decapitated, and the others among them were either sent into exile or imprisoned. The new emperor's reign title was changed to Tung Chih and the forty-seven years of rule by Tzu Hsi had begun. My grandfather's great achievement in this *coup* was to arrest Su Shun at Panpitien as he was escorting the coffin of the dead emperor back to the capital, and this was why he received so many honours.

During the reign of Emperor Tung Chih he was further elevated until, when Kuang Hsu came to the throne, he was given an additional honour by which his title of prince could be inherited by his successors in perpetuity when normally titles went down one grade with each generation. During the reign of Kuang Hsu, Prince Kung lost favour a number of times but my grandfather continued to be heaped with honours until he seemed to have reached the very pinnacle of human glory.

In the Chun mansion I saw many scrolls of moral maxims in my grandfather's own handwriting hanging in the rooms of each of his sons and grandsons. There was one pair of scrolls which read

> Wealth and Fortune breed more Fortune
> Royal Favours bring more Favours.

At the time I thought that my grandfather must have been a very contented man, but now I see things differently and even think that he meant something else when he scolded his son during the theatricals.

If the twenty-one-year-old Prince Chun had been rather raw and inexperienced the Prince Chun who had lived through the thirteen years of the Tung Chih reign should certainly have learnt enough. As a member of the royal family he must have known a lot more than outsiders did about the deaths of the emperor Tung Chih and his empress and must have been more deeply affected by it.

In popular romances it is said that Tung Chih died of venereal disease, but from what I have heard the cause of his death was smallpox, and the diary of an eminent official of the time confirms this. Smallpox is not an incurably fatal disease, but while he was suffering from it Tung Chih received a shock which "made the pustules burst inwards" so that his condition became hopeless and he died. One day Tung Chih's empress went to visit him on his sickbed and burst into tears as she asked him why her mother-in-law, the dowager Tzu Hsi, was always scolding her. Tung Chih begged her to put up with it patiently, saying that some time in the future she would have her day. Tzu Hsi, who had never liked this daughter-in-law of hers, had long ago set informers to watch over her son and her daughter-in-law, and when she heard that the empress had gone to visit Tung Chih she herself went and stood outside his room to eavesdrop on them. Unaware of the disaster their few words of private conversation had brought about, they saw Tzu Hsi rush into the room in a flaming temper. She grabbed the empress by the hair and started to beat her mercilessly, and shouted instructions for palace officials to prepare rods. Tung Chih fainted from horror, and so Tzu Hsi did not have to carry out the beating. Once Tung Chih was dead Tzu Hsi put all the blame for his decease onto the empress and gave orders that her consumption of food and drink should be restricted. Two months later the empress died of her privations.

During Tung Chih's life it was an open secret that he got on very badly with his mother, Tzu Hsi. When I lived in the palace an old eunuch told me that when Tung Chih went to pay his respects to the eastern dowager Tzu An he used to stay there and talk with her for a while, but that to his own mother he said nothing. Even during the period when Tung Chih was himself ruling the Eastern Dowager took little interest in affairs of state whereas Tzu Hsi had already built up her own group of trusted supporters at court; the emperor could get hardly anything done without first consulting her. This was the real reason for the bad relations between mother and son. Tzu Hsi had a very highly developed lust for power and was most unwilling to abandon any power that came into her hands. From her point of view the principles of moral conduct and the ancestral code existed to suit her needs, and she was certainly not prepared to let them inhibit her. Whether it was her own flesh and blood, her in-laws or palace officials, the same principle applied: those who obeyed her flourished and those who crossed her were doomed. After the death of the emperor Tung Chih she revealed her true nature even more clearly; and it was because my grandfather had understood her character well that he almost went out of his wits with terror at the news that his son was being summoned to the palace to be emperor. An official who was present at that imperial council meeting wrote in his diary that when Tzu Hsi proclaimed Tsai Tien as the future emperor Kuang Hsu, my grandfather "beat his head on the floor and wept bitterly before falling to the ground in a faint. He was unable to rise even with support. . . ."

According to the ancestral code, a close relation of the generation below Tung Chih's should have been his heir, but this would have ended Tzu Hsi's regency as she would no longer have been the emperor's mother, so she overruled all protests and appointed her nephew Tsai Tien, although he was of the same generation as Tung Chih, adopting him as her son.

From then on my grandfather had the curious experience of having honours showered on him by Tzu Hsi while he declined them, and when his son the emperor Kuang Hsu entered the palace he resigned all his offices, though he was unable to renounce his rank of hereditary prince. For several years after that his only duty was to supervise the emperor's studies. After Prince Kung fell from favour he was entrusted with very important offices by Tzu Hsi, but he remained exceedingly cautious, filling his house with inscriptions, scrolls and other objects to remind himself and his family of the dangers of being too great. In 1876, the second year of the reign of his son Kuang Hsu, he submitted a memorial as a counterplea to a hypothetical proposal in which he said that someone might in the future cite precedents from history to suggest giving him very great honours as the father of the sovereign. He was afraid that such honours would arouse Tzu Hsi's jealousy and put him in a dangerous position. A few years later this did in fact happen, and the empress dowager Tzu Hsi was so angry that the proposer retired from politics for three years.

There can be no doubt that from the time Kuang Hsu entered the palace onwards my grandfather must have got to know the character of his sister-in-law Tzu Hsi even better. During Kuang Hsu's reign (1874-1908) her temper became even more unpredictable. Once a eunuch who was playing chess with her said, "Your slave is killing this knight of the venerable ancestor." At this she flew into a rage and, announcing that she would kill his whole family, she had him dragged out and beaten to death. She treasured her hair very greatly; one day a eunuch who was combing it for her found a strand of it in the comb. In his panic the eunuch tried to conceal it but she saw what he was doing in a mirror and he too was beaten. The eunuchs who used to serve Tzu Hsi told me that all of them except her favourite Li Lien-ying used to be frightened when their turn came to be in attendance on her. As Tzu Hsi grew older she developed a facial tic and she hated people to notice it. When one eunuch had been looking at it for a little too long she

9

asked him what he was staring at; he could find no answer and was given several scores of strokes of the heavy rod. Another eunuch who had heard about this did not dare so much as to look up when he went on duty but she flared up at this too: "Why are you keeping your head down?" He could not think of anything to say either and suffered a similar punishment. Apart from the eunuchs, the palace women were often beaten as well.

For eunuchs to be flogged and even to die of it was nothing unusual in Peking's princely households and affairs of this sort were quite possibly not very shocking to my grandfather, but the sudden death of the eastern dowager Tzu An in 1881 must have seemed certainly something out of the ordinary even to him. It is said that Emperor Hsien Feng was worried before he died that when his Secondary Consort Yi (the future Tzu Hsi) was made an empress dowager as the mother of the next emperor she would make the most of her position to wield power and that his empress, later the Eastern Dowager, would be no match for her. He therefore left a special edict written in vermilion ink giving his empress the authority to control Tzu Hsi when necessary. The inexperienced Eastern Dowager, who had been brought up in a noble family and lacked worldly wisdom, once casually revealed this to Tzu Hsi. From then on Tzu Hsi spent all her time making up to her until the Eastern Dowager finally burnt Hsien Feng's testament before her eyes.

Shortly after that the Eastern Dowager died a sudden death in the palace. Some say that she ate some cakes sent her by Tzu Hsi and others that she drank some soup that Tzu Hsi had prepared with her own hands. There can be no doubt but that it was a great shock to Prince Chun as after this he was even more cautious than ever, regarding winning the trust and favour of Tzu Hsi as his sole duty.

When he was made responsible for the founding of a navy my grandfather misappropriated a large part of the funds to build the Summer Palace as a pleasure park for the Empress Dowager. The busiest stage in the building of the Summer Palace coincided with exceptionally heavy floods around Peking and in what is now Hopei Province, but a censor who suggested that work should be temporarily suspended to avoid provoking the flood victims into making trouble was stripped of his office and handed over to the appropriate authorities to be dealt with. Prince Chun, however, said nothing and worked his hardest to get the job finished. When the Summer Palace was completed in 1890 he died. Four years later the so-called navy he had created came to a disastrous end in the Sino-Japanese War, and the marble boat in the Summer Palace was the only one left of all the vessels on which so many tens of millions of taels (ounces of silver) had been spent.

My Maternal Grandfather Jung Lu

My paternal grandfather Prince Chun had four wives, who bore him seven sons and three daughters. Three sons and one daughter survived him, of whom the oldest was my father who inherited his title at the age of eight. From then onwards my family received new "fortune and favour", and these, like the hardships and humiliations suffered by the Chinese people, were all connected with Tzu Hsi.

One major event was the marriage that Tzu Hsi arranged for my father, an event that could be regarded as a product of the *coup* of 1898 and the Yi Ho Tuan[1] affair of 1900. In the first place, it was an honour conferred on her loyal servant Jung Lu for the great services he had done her in 1898, a year in which he played a large part in defeating the attempts of a group of reformers to eliminate the influence of Tzu Hsi and modernize the monarchy.

Jung Lu, my maternal grandfather, was a Manchu bannerman who was an expert political climber who would use any means to win the favour and confidence of Tzu Hsi. He was a close friend of her favourite eunuch Li Lien-ying, and his wife ingratiated herself

---

[1] The Yi Ho Tuan (Righteous Harmony Corps) were generally known as "Boxers" in the West.

with the dowager so successfully that she was often called to the palace to keep her company and chat with her; he was therefore able to get an even more expert knowledge of the workings of her mind. Aware as he was of the bad relations between Tzu Hsi and Kuang Hsu he fully understood how this could affect his own future and was naturally more willing than ever to advise Tzu Hsi.

When Emperor Kuang Hsu issued a series of edicts in 1898 ordering political reforms, others who had been dismissed from office or were afraid that they were going to be squeezed out were reduced to helpless tears, but Jung Lu had already worked out a plan for Tzu Hsi. Jung Lu was the head of the group known as the "dowager's party" that was in power while Weng Tung-ho, the emperor's former tutor, headed the "emperor's party" that had no real power. It was through Weng Tung-ho's privileged position as an imperial tutor that the reformers were able to make contact with the emperor. Tzu Hsi followed the pre-arranged plan and forced Kuang Hsu to send Weng Tung-ho into retirement, and within a few days of his departure from Peking Jung Lu was given a grand secretaryship and made Viceroy of the metropolitan province of Chihli with command over the armies round the capital.

With the Reform Movement of 1898 Jung Lu finally got the chance he had been waiting for to strip the emperor Kuang Hsu of his power and put the country back into the hands of Tzu Hsi. Previously he had made a plan to carry out a *coup* when Tzu Hsi and Kuang Hsu inspected the new Peiyang (Northern) Army at Tientsin. When Kuang Hsu learnt of this plot he sent a secret message to the reformers asking them to think of a way to save him.

The reformers and the emperor foolishly put their trust in a subordinate of Jung Lu's named Yuan Shih-kai, an official who was in control of the New Army, an up-to-date military force, and brought him into their plot to execute Jung Lu and imprison Tzu Hsi when they went to inspect his troops at Tientsin. Yuan Shih-kai agreed to co-operate with them and then betrayed them by going straight to Jung Lu and telling him the whole story. On hearing the news Jung Lu took a train back from Tientsin and hastened to the Summer Palace to report to Tzu Hsi. The result was that the emperor was imprisoned, Tan Sze-tung and five other reformers were executed, their leader Kang Yu-wei fled to Japan, and the brief hundred days of reform was over. As another of the reformers, Liang Chi-chao, wrote, my maternal grandfather Jung Lu "combined in his person the highest civil and military offices and his power was greater than that of the court itself." In the words of the *Draft History of the Ching Dynasty*, "he had won the Empress Dowager's trust and devotion and he had no peer at that time. Everything, whether great or small, was decided by his word."

In the calamitous year of 1900, when Tzu Hsi used the Yi Ho Tuan to kill the foreigners and then used the foreigners to kill the Yi Ho Tuan, Jung Lu went even further in showing his loyalty to her. After the 1898 *coup* Tzu Hsi wanted to be rid of Kuang Hsu, and when one attempt to kill him under pretext of an invented illness was uncovered she decided first to appoint a successor to the previous emperor, Tung Chih, before deposing Kuang Hsu. She invited all the foreign envoys to come and offer their congratulations and show their support. They refused to come, and it is now quite clear that this refusal was not based on any personal disapproval of Tzu Hsi's character; it was because the ministers of Britain, France, America and Japan did not want to see an inordinate growth in the power of the pro-Tsarist Russia "dowager's party". Before this Tzu Hsi had never dared to provoke the foreigners. When they had slaughtered the Chinese people or seized the country's wealth it had meant little to her, but now that they were protecting the leading reformer Kang Yu-wei and blocking her plans to depose the emperor and appoint a new heir to the throne they were directly opposing her rule. This was more than she could possibly tolerate. Jung Lu advised her not on any account to provoke the foreigners but rather to think things over very calmly: it would be best not to be too explicit about the new heir's title. She followed his suggestion and changed his title to "Ta-ah-ko". The heir's father, wanting to see his son become emperor, joined with some other princes and high officials to propose another plan to Tzu Hsi: to use the anti-foreign Yi Ho Tuan to crush the foreigners and thus kill two birds with one stone.

The Yi Ho Tuan were the Ching court's biggest headache. Mistreated and oppressed by the foreign churches, the common people had received no protection from the court, which even joined with the foreigners in repressing them. Armed struggle had therefore broken out and Yi Ho Tuan were formed in various parts of the country under the slogan of "Eliminate the foreigners". In the course of their struggles the Yi Ho Tuan became a powerful armed force which was able to rout all the troops which the court sent against them. The question facing Tzu Hsi was whether to "exterminate" or whether to "conciliate" them. One group at court, including the father of the heir, advocated conciliating them for a time so that they could be used to drive out the foreigners who were interfering in the question of the succession. Another group, completely opposed to this in the belief that it would be bound to have disastrous consequences, urged that the Yi Ho Tuan should be exterminated.

Just when the supporters of the two policies were deadlocked Tzu Hsi received an urgent but unconfirmed intelligence report that the violent actions of foreigners in different parts of the country were intended to force her to hand power back to the emperor. This put an end to her hesitations as in a terrible rage she ordered that the Yi Ho Tuan were to be "won over" and that the foreign legations in Peking were to be attacked. Money from the imperial privy purse was given to the Yi Ho Tuan and rewards were offered for the heads of foreigners. As an additional earnest of her determination she had the leading advocates of exterminating the Yi Ho Tuan decapitated.

When the attack on the legations had failed, the coastal defences at Taku and the city of Tientsin had fallen and the allied armies of the foreigners were approaching Peking, Tzu Hsi changed her tactics. She started communicating secretly with the foreigners and sent emissaries to make contact with the legations while the fighting was still going on. When Peking fell she fled to Sian, and in order to show that she had not been the one to initiate resistance to the foreigners she had some of the leading supporters of the policy of "conciliating" the Yi Ho Tuan beheaded.

Throughout these changes of policy Jung Lu did all he could to keep himself out of trouble. Taking his cue from Tzu Hsi's behaviour he never went against her wishes and at the same time he prepared a line of retreat for her. When obeying her command to send soldiers to attack the barracks of the foreign troops in the Legation Quarter he did not issue them with artillery shells and even discreetly sent fruit to the foreigners as a token of his concern. After the armies of the eight foreign powers had entered Peking and Tzu Hsi had fled, Jung Lu proposed the single principle to which the officials responsible for negotiating the peace were to hold: any conditions could be accepted provided that Tzu Hsi was not held responsible for the affair and the emperor was not returned to power. Thus a treaty was signed in 1901 by which China had to pay an indemnity of a billion taels (including interest) and the foreign powers were allowed to station troops in the capital. Jung Lu was rewarded for these services with many fresh honours among which was the marriage Tzu Hsi arranged between his daughter and the second Prince Chun.

I was told later by some older members of the household that the marriage between my parents was very deliberately planned by Tzu Hsi. She had been rather suspicious of the family of Prince Chun ever since the *coup* of 1898 and someone suggested to her that the growth of a tall gingko tree on the tomb of the first Prince Chun implied, through a kind of wordplay on the name of the tree and the Chinese word for "prince", that his family would produce an emperor. On hearing this Tzu Hsi at once gave orders for the tree to be felled. But the real reason for her suspicion of the family was the interest shown by the foreigners in Kuang Hsu and his brothers. Before the events of 1900 she felt that in being partial to Kuang Hsu the terrible foreigners were extremely impolite to her. After 1900 the commander of the allied armies asked the emperor's brother to go to Germany as representative to apologize for the killing of the German minister during the troubles. The splendid reception accorded my father by the German Kaiser caused the Empress Dowager considerable uneasiness and strengthened her suspicions. Connecting her faithful henchman Jung Lu with the family of Prince Chun through marriage was the solution she eventually found to this dangerous problem. Tzu Hsi was a person who would devote the greatest pains to dealing with any situation that posed the slightest threat to her security: she had Kuang Hsu's Pearl Consort drowned in a well before her flight in 1900 out of fear that she might cause trouble for her later. In any circumstances, her first consideration was always the protection of her own rule. Thus it was that my father received the edict arranging his marriage almost as soon as he came back from Germany and reported on the "courteous reception" he had received there.

Tzu Hsi's Decision

After 1900 the father of the heir to the throne was one of those held responsible for the troubles of that year and his son was therefore stripped of the title. The question of the succession was not openly raised for another seven years.

In November 1908 Tzu Hsi contracted dysentery while celebrating her seventy-third birthday at the Summer Palace. After lying ill for ten days she suddenly made the decision to appoint a new heir, and in the course of the next two days the emperor Kuang Hsu and she herself both died. The day before the emperor died my father was summoned to court and appointed Prince Regent and I was taken into the palace. The next day, November 14, I became emperor-designate, and Tzu Hsi announced in an edict that my father was to consult her in his administration of all state affairs.

In the previous few years Tzu Hsi had been putting ever increasing power into the hands of Yuan Shih-kai, the unscrupulous Han official who had played such a vital role in the defeat of the reformers in 1898, but at the same time his control of the modern Peiyang Army and his opportunism caused her a great deal of concern. She was also worried by the close relationship that existed between Yuan

Shih-kai and Prince Ching (Yi Kuang), an ambitious Manchu who had started as a low-ranking noble and become a prince of the first rank and the leading Grand Councillor. In an attempt to curb their power she tried unsuccessfully to dismiss Prince Ching and in 1907 gave Yuan Shih-kai a nominal promotion that made him give up his command over the Peiyang Army.

Tzu Hsi fully understood that she could not end Yuan Shih-kai's actual control over the Peiyang Army at once and that the relations between Yuan and Prince Ching could not be broken in a moment. She herself fell ill just when she was planning her next move, and on her sickbed she received a piece of shocking news: Yuan Shih-kai was planning to depose Kuang Hsu and install the son of Prince Ching in his place. Despite Prince Ching's skill in dealing with foreigners and in flattering her, despite all that Yuan Shih-kai had done for her, and despite the fact that the target of their plan was the emperor Kuang Hsu whom she hated so deeply, she was at once aware of the threat that this plot posed to the Aisin-Gioro dynasty and to herself. She made up her mind very quickly. She sent Prince Ching on a mission outside the capital and moved one unit of the Peiyang Army out of Peking, replacing it with a more reliable one. By the time Prince Ching came back to Peking I had already become heir to the throne and my father had been made Prince Regent. To keep the loyalty of Prince Ching, who had so many foreign friends, she made his title of prince hereditary in perpetuity.

I once heard from an old eunuch about the suspicious circumstances of Kuang Hsu's death. According to his story Kuang Hsu was fairly well on the day before his death and what made him seriously ill was a dose of medicine he took. Later it was discovered that this medicine had been sent by Yuan Shih-kai. The normal practice when an emperor was ill was for copies of the prescriptions and diagnoses of the Grand Physicians to be given to each of the senior officials of the Imperial Household Department or, in the case of a serious illness, to all the members of the Grand Council. I was later told by a descendant of one of the Household Department officials that before his death Kuang Hsu was only suffering from an ordinary case of flu; he had seen the diagnosis himself, and it had said that Kuang Hsu's pulse was normal. Moreover he had been seen in his room standing and talking as if he were healthy, so that people were very shocked to hear that he was seriously ill. What was even stranger was that within four hours of this came the news of his death. All in all, Kuang Hsu's death was very suspicious. If the eunuch's story is true it is further proof that there was a conspiracy, and a deep-laid one at that, between Yuan Shih-kai and Prince Ching.

Another tradition is that when Tzu Hsi realized that her illness was fatal she murdered Kuang Hsu rather than die before him. This is possible, but I do not believe that she thought herself fatally ill on the day she proclaimed me successor to the throne. Two hours after Kuang Hsu's death she commanded my father, the Prince Regent, "You shall administer all affairs of state in accordance with my instructions." It was not till the next day that she said, "Now my condition is critical and I fear that I may never recover. In future all affairs of state are to be decided by the Regent. When there are important matters on which he requires direction from the Empress Dowager [Kuang Hsu's empress, a niece of Tzu Hsi's], the Prince Regent shall appear before her and ask her instructions before dealing with them." The reason why she chose such a regent as my father and such a successor to the throne as myself was that she did not realize at the time that she was going to die as soon as she in fact did. As Grand Empress Dowager (the title given to the grandmother of an emperor) she would not have been able to rule on the emperor's behalf, but with a docile Prince Regent between herself and the child emperor she could still have had everything her own way.

Of course, she can have been under no illusions that she was going to live for ever, and she must have regarded making this choice as doing all she could to protect the throne of the Aisin-Gioro clan. She may even have thought that her choice was right because the regent she chose was a brother of Kuang Hsu. It would have been quite natural to think that only a man in his position would not be hoodwinked by Yuan Shih-kai.

My Father's Regency

It was only during the last of the three years during which I was emperor and my father was regent that I got to know him, when he came to inspect my lessons shortly after I had begun to study. When a eunuch came in to report that "His Royal Highness" was coming, my tutor became very tense and hastily tidied the desk while explaining to me how I should behave with him. Then he told me to stand up and wait. A moment later a beardless stranger wearing a peacock feather in his hat appeared in the doorway of the study and stood stiffly before me. This was my father. I greeted him in the standard way and we sat down together. I picked up my book and started to read aloud as my tutor had instructed me.

I got stuck after the first two sentences as I was feeling flustered, but fortunately my father was even more nervous than I was and he kept nodding his head and mumbling:

"Good, good, very good, Your Majesty. Study hard, study hard!" He nodded a few more times then got up and went. He had only spent two minutes with me.

So now I knew what my father looked like: unlike my teacher he had no beard, his face was unwrinkled and the peacock feather at the back of his head was always shaking. He used to make a visit every two months, but he never stayed longer than two minutes. I also discovered that he had something of a stutter and realized that the reason his peacock feather shook was that he was always nodding his head. He said very little, and apart from "good, good, good" it was very indistinct.

My brother once heard my mother say that when my father resigned his regency after the 1911 Revolution[1] he went straight home from the palace and said to her, "From today onwards I can

---

[1] On October 10 of that year, a section of the New Army, at the urging of the revolutionary societies of the bourgeoisie and petty bourgeoisie, staged an uprising in Wuchang. This was followed by uprisings in other provinces, and the Ching Dynasty soon collapsed.

stay at home and hug my children." My mother was so angry at his light-hearted mood that she was reduced to tears; later she said to my brother, "Don't be like your father when you grow up!" This story and a couplet that my father once wrote out — "To have books is real wealth, to be at leisure is half-way to being an immortal" — show that while he did not have any genuine wish to "withdraw from the world" he did find his three years as regent a great strain. Those three years could be regarded as the three most unsuccessful years of his life.

From his own point of view his most fundamental failure was that he was unable to do away with Yuan Shih-kai. There is a story that his brother Kuang Hsu told him of his heartfelt wish and gave him an edict with the four words "Kill Yuan Shih-kai" written in vermilion ink, but as far as I know this meeting never took place. Although the Prince Regent wanted to kill Yuan to avenge his brother, he was prevented from doing so by a group of Grand Councillors with Prince Ching at their head. There is no way of knowing the details about this, but there was one remark of Prince Ching's which discouraged my father: "There would be no problem about killing Yuan Shih-kai, but what would happen if the Peiyang Army mutinied?" The result was that the new empress dowager, Lung Yu, let Yuan off by sending him home to nurse his "foot ailment".

At that time many people offered my father conflicting advice on how to deal with Yuan Shih-kai, some doing their utmost to defend him and others trying to eliminate him. The question of whether to kill or to support Yuan was not a struggle between reformers and conservatives or between the former "emperor's party" and "dowager's party"; nor was it one between Manchus on the one side and Hans on the other it was rather a power struggle between two groups of nobility and senior officials. The cabinet of the time, which was composed mostly of the members of the royal family, was divided into one faction headed by Prince Ching and another headed by Tsai Tse, a duke. It was principally this latter group that suggested policies to my father and wanted to win power. Caught in the middle of the fighting my father would take the advice first of one side then of another, agree with both and do nothing, thus satisfying nobody.

The people he found it hardest to deal with were Prince Ching and Tsai Tse. Before Tzu Hsi's death Prince Ching had been the leading Grand Councillor and after her death he became premier of the newly organized cabinet to the great indignation of Tsai Tse, the President of the Board of Revenue and Finance, who took every opportunity to denigrate his rival before the regent. But if Tzu Hsi had been incapable of removing Prince Ching, what chance did the Prince Regent stand? So although my father often agreed with Tsai Tse's suggestions he was incapable of acting on them and Prince Ching always came out on top. Yet Tsai Tse's defeats were really defeats for himself while Prince Ching's victories were really triumphs for Yuan Shih-kai living in his hometown in mock retirement. Although my father was aware of this there was nothing he could do about it.

In 1911 the Wuchang rising[1] suddenly erupted and the armies under a Manchu commander sent to put it down were defeated. Under irresistible pressure from Prince Ching and his associates my father had to call Yuan Shih-kai back from his retirement and give him the supreme military command.

My father was not a complete fool. One lesson he had learnt from the Kaiser during his trip to Germany was that the royal family had to control the army and that its members had to become army officers. He accordingly put his brother in charge of the palace guard, founded a special army under the royal family, and put other relations in charge of the navy and the army general staff. It is said that my father intended to eliminate Yuan Shih-kai whether he succeeded in putting down the rising or not. Whatever happened, he was not going to leave the armed forces in Han hands, least of all those of Yuan Shih-kai. But my father's plans were too impractical, and even his own brothers shook their heads over his incompetence.

When my grandmother was suffering from an ulcer of the breast which Chinese traditional doctors had been unable to cure he called

---

[1] The rising that sparked off the 1911 Revolution.

in a French doctor on his brothers' advice. The doctor wanted to operate, but as this was opposed by the whole family the only thing he could do was to apply ointment. Before doing so he lit a spirit lamp to sterilize his instruments. This gave my father a terrible fright and he asked the interpreter:

"Wha . . . what's he doing? Is he going to burn the old lady?"

Seeing how ignorant he was an uncle of mine signalled to the interpreter not to translate this question.

The doctor left some medicine for her and went. He was surprised to discover on a later visit that the old lady's condition had not improved at all and asked to see the box of ointment that he had left the previous time. My father fetched it himself: the original seal was unbroken. Once again, my uncles could not help shaking their heads and sighing.

After the death of Tzu Hsi everyone in my father's household called themselves reformers. From the details of my father's daily life one can see how in some ways he opposed superstition and was if favour of modernization. He did not reject the things that the old officials regarded as strange and improper contraptions. He was the first of the princes to have a motor-car or to install a telephone in his house. His household were the first to have their queues cut off, and he was the first of the princes and the nobility to wear Western clothing. But how far his real understanding of things Western went can be illustrated by the way he wore Western clothes. When he had been wearing them for a number of days he asked a brother of mine sadly: "Why do your shirts fit so well while mine are always longer than my jacket?" When my brother had a look he found that he was wearing his shirt outside his trousers and that he had been putting up with this discomfort for days.

He drove out some witches who had come to cure an illness of my grandmother's, and once kicked a hedgehog, an animal which the servants held in superstitious awe, into the gutter — though after doing so his face went deathly pale. He was against worshipping the gods and Buddhist chanting, but every time a new year or a festival came round he would be very conscientious about burning incense and making offerings.

I looked through my father's diary in the hope of understanding more about his three years of regency. There was not much useful material in it, though there were two interesting types of entries. One referred to conventional behaviour; for example, every May it would always say "Had my hair cut short as usual" and every August "Started to let my hair grow as usual." There were also entries about the different kinds of clothes he wore at different times of year in accordance with custom and the kinds of fresh food he ate. The other interesting kind of entry was detailed records of the movements of the heavenly bodies and summaries of what the newspapers carried on astronomy. There was a strong contrast between his jejune daily life and the enthusiasm he had for astronomy. Had he been a man of the present age he might have become an astronomer; but as it was he lived in that family and in that society and became a prince of the royal clan at the age of nine.

A Prince's Household

I had four grandmothers altogether. The principal wife of the first Prince Chun, the lady Yehonala, who was not my real grandmother, died ten years before I was born. I was told that this old lady was not at all like her sister, the empress dowager Tzu Hsi; she adhered rigidly to the conventional morality. When Tzu Hsi continued to watch theatricals as usual after the death of the emperor Tung Chih she would have nothing to do with it. Although she obeyed the summons to go to the palace for the performances she kept both of her eyes shut tight as she sat in front of the stage. When Tzu Hsi asked her why, she replied without even opening her eyes, "This is a time of national mourning; I cannot watch drama." Tzu Hsi was nonplussed. Many words were taboo to her and the members of her household had to be very careful in their speech, particularly with such words as "finished" or "dead". Throughout her life she was a devout Buddhist and would not go into the garden in the summer, saying that she was afraid of trampling any ants to death. Yet although she was so benevolent towards ants she was merciless when it came to beating servants. It was said that the incurable facial tic of one of the family's eunuchs was the result of a flogging she once had him given.

She had five children altogether, of whom the only daughter and the eldest son died in childhood within twenty days of each other. Her second son was the emperor Kuang Hsu, and he was taken from her at the age of four. After he went into the palace she gave birth to another son who did not live two days. When her fourth son was born she fussed over him terribly, frightened that he was not wearing enough and would freeze or that he would eat too much and suffer from a surfeit. My grandmother believed in the practice of going without food for a whole day sometimes, and she never allowed her children to eat their fill, even cutting up a prawn into three pieces before giving it to them. The result was that this fourth son died of malnutrition before reaching the age of five. As one old eunuch remarked, if my grandmother had not killed her children with misplaced kindness my father would never have inherited my grandfather's title.

Although my father was not her own child, she was responsible for bringing him up. Although she did not control the diet of my father and his younger brothers, she dominated them psychologically. The eunuch I mentioned above said that they even had to be careful when smiling, because if their smiles turned into laughs the old lady would shout at them: "Why are you laughing? Have you no manners?"

My grandfather's first secondary wife died young and his second one was my real grandmother. After the death of my father's first wife she was in charge of the household, and although she was not as bigoted as her predecessor, she was mentally unstable, a condition that was brought on by the fate of her children and grandchildren. She lost a daughter at the age of two, but what first deranged her was having her young sons adopted. She bore three sons altogether, of whom my father was the oldest. Her third son, Tsai Tao, had been brought up very close to her and when he was eleven she received an edict from the empress dowager Tzu Hsi ordering that he was to become the adopted son of Yi Mo, a cousin of my grandfather's. The receipt of this document made her weep till she was seriously ill, and the shock left her rather unbalanced.

The childless Yi Mo was naturally overjoyed at being given a son and he gave a great feast to celebrate the event, just as if a son had been born to him. He had not, to Tzu Hsi's displeasure, been much of a man for ingratiating himself with her, and when she learnt how overjoyed he was she was even more angry with him and determined that his good fortune would not be allowed to last. There was a famous saying of hers that "if anyone causes me a moment's sorrow I shall give him a lifetime's misery." After some injury he suffered from her Yi Mo vented his feelings by painting a picture which simply consisted of a foot. This foot implied by a play on words that Tzu Hsi specialized in making trouble and that she had got the affairs of both her family and the country into a mess. On the picture he had written a verse of doggerel:

> Poor me, I tried to dodge the foot's dread power,
> And so I built a foot-avoiding tower.
> But though I built the tower very high,
> The foot still chased me up into the sky.

Somehow Tzu Hsi got to hear of this, and so to spite him she issued without warning another decree ordering that the boy Tsai Tao, who had then been adopted by Yi Mo for over five years, should be adopted once again by yet another relation. The shock made both Yi Mo and his wife sick, and when Yi Mo died soon afterwards Tzu Hsi deliberately sent Tsai Tao, the son who had been snatched away from him, as her representative to offer sacrifices for him. Acting in this capacity my uncle could not kneel before his memorial tablet. Yi Mo's wife also died within the year.

When Tzu Hsi ordered Tsai Tao to be adopted for the second time she also arranged to have his brother Tsai Hsun adopted by another cousin of my father's. It was indeed a case of

> Although I built the tower very high,
> The foot still chased me up into the sky.

The sudden loss of yet another son was an unexpected shock to my grandmother.

It was not long before she received a third blow. Just when she had arranged a match for my father an edict came from Tzu Hsi ordaining that he should marry someone else. Of course, she did not bother about obtaining the consent of the couple concerned or of the heads of their families, and nobody dared to utter a word of comment on anything that she had arranged. My grandmother was terrified on the one hand of incurring the displeasure of the Empress Dowager and on the other of what her son's original fiancée might do to herself if the engagement were broken off. If anything did happen it would be tantamount to resisting an edict of the Empress Dowager and the girl's family and her own might be held responsible. Although people tried to calm her fears by explaining that there could be no difficulty about cancelling a betrothal on orders from the Empress Dowager, my grandmother would not be soothed and she became deranged again.

Six years later she had another breakdown when a Grand Councillor came with an edict ordering that I be sent into the palace. I had been brought up from my earliest days by my grandmother and she doted on me. According to my nurse, she used to get up once or twice every night to come over and look at me; she did not even put shoes on for fear that the noise of their wooden soles would disturb me. Having reared me like this for more than two years she fainted at the news that Tzu Hsi was taking me into the palace. For the rest of her life she was very liable to fits of insanity. She died in 1925 at the age of 58.

After losing his father when he was seven, the second Prince Chun was brought up by the two old ladies in accordance with the instructions left by the first Prince Chun, and he led a traditional noble's life. When he was Prince Regent he had an enormous income, his mother ran his household, there was a special office to look after his property and entertain visitors and he had a host of guardsmen, eunuchs and servants to wait on him, to say nothing of the body of retainers to advise and amuse him. Thus he did not have to worry about household affairs and had no need for any useful knowledge. He had little contact with the outside world and had no social life apart from the exchange of formal visits.

My father had two wives, and they bore him four sons and seven daughters of whom all but two are alive today. My father died in 1951 and my own mother in 1921.

My father and my mother were completely different types. It is said that Manchu women are often far more capable than their husbands, and this may well be true. My wife Wan Jung and my mother were far more knowledgeable than myself or my father, particularly when it came to enjoying themselves or buying things. One explanation for the way in which Manchu girls were able to run their households and were treated with respect by their elders in their generation was that they all had the chance of being chosen for service in the palace and becoming imperial consorts; but my own opinion is that as the men were either idling or busy with official business, household management and financial affairs tended to fall on their sisters' shoulders so that the women naturally became rather more able. My mother was a favourite in her mother's home, and Tzu Hsi once said of her: "That girl isn't even afraid of me." Her extravagance was a big headache for my father and grandmother, but there was nothing they could do about it. Excluding his land-rents, prince's stipend and "Money for the Nurture of Incorruptibility" (a form of payment to officials that was supposed to prevent them from accepting bribes), my father had an income of 50,000 taels a year which was always paid in full even during the Republic, but it was never long after he received it before my mother spent it all. Later he tried all sorts of solutions including giving her a fixed allowance but none of them worked. He even tried smashing vases and other crockery to show his anger and determination. As he could not bear to lose all this porcelain he replaced it with unbreakable vessels of bronze and lead. My mother soon saw through his tricks and in the end my father would give her more spending money as usual. She spent so much that my grandmother would weep and sigh over the bills sent over by the counting house and my father had no option but to tell his stewards to sell more antiques and land.

My mother often used to sell on the sly the jewellery that she had brought with her at her marriage, and I later discovered that she secretly spent the money thus obtained on political activities as well as on her everyday luxuries. But the money that she and the other imperial consorts spent to try and realize their dreams of restoration was all pocketed by the eunuchs and others.

From earliest childhood my brothers and sisters were never frightened of my father and grandmother but were terrified of my mother. Of course, the servants were even more scared of her. One day my father came home to find that the doors and windows had not yet been shut, so he asked a eunuch why. The eunuch replied that as madam was not back there was no hurry. My father lost his temper and punished him by making him kneel on the ground. A maid remarked to him that "if it had been the master you would ·have been beaten black and blue." By "the master" she meant my mother who, like Tzu Hsi, loved being referred to as if she were a man.

I went into the palace when I was nearly three and did not meet my own mother and grandmother again till I was ten, when they were summoned to the palace. When I met them I felt a complete stranger and not at all close to them, but I do remember that my grandmother's eyes were fixed on me all the time and that they seemed to be glistening with tears. My mother left quite a different impression on me: I found her frightening as well as distant. Whenever she saw me she would say with a severe expression: "Your Majesty must study diligently the precepts of your ancestors," or "Your Majesty must not be greedy; Your Majesty's body is a sacred body, Your Majesty must get up early and go to bed early. . . ." I still have that very stiff impression of her when I think of her today. What a difference of character there was between my grandmother, who was of humble origin, and my mother, brought up as she was in a grand family.

CHAPTER TWO

□□

CHILDHOOD

The next two chapters tell P'u Yi's story from his accession in 1908 as a child of two till his expulsion from the Forbidden City in 1924 with the rest of the Ch'ing court. His reign ended with his abdication in 1912; but for over twelve years after that he was allowed by the new Republic to remain in the palace, retaining his imperial title and receiving a substantial annuity of 4 million taels (5.3 million ounces) of silver. This made it possible for him to continue the life of a boy emperor, surrounded by palace women, eunuchs, princes, officials, and tutors, until he was driven out at eighteen.

The crisis that brought down the dynasty began with a mutiny by republican revolutionaries among the Ch'ing troops in the city of Wuch'ang (part of modern Wuhan) in October 1911. The Ch'ing called their most powerful former official, Yuan Shih-k'ai, out of retirement to command the loyalist forces; and Yuan, playing the revolutionaries against the court, ended by forcing the dynasty's abdication on very favourable terms (pp. 33–8) while he, not any of the revolutionary leaders, became first president of the Republic. P'u Yi was of course much too young to have played any part in these events; but the dynasty's collapse owed something to the short-sighted and ineffective leadership shown by his father, the prince regent, who did not push ahead fast or firmly enough with the drastic reforms by which the Empress Dowager Tz'u Hsi had been trying to save the monarchy, through sharing some of its powers with the officials and the provincial gentry.

The strange politics of the deposed Ch'ing court living on in its own palace, constantly hoping or even scheming for the overthrow of the

Republic, will be described in some detail in Chapter Three. Most of Chapter Two is about P'u Yi's life in the palace as a young emperor without an empire, a most unnatural form of upbringing. His relations with his own parents, excluded from the Forbidden City, were very distant; he describes his mother's suicide with a chilling detachment. He was required to treat four wives of two dead emperors as his mothers, but got little warmth from them. The only person who really mothered him as a boy was his wet-nurse, who suckled him till he was eight years old and was then expelled by the stepmothers.

Both victim and tyrant, P'u Yi found satisfaction from an early age in having his eunuch servants flogged. This had already begun by the time he was seven (not eleven as wrongly translated on p. 70). Fortunately the Ch'ing court was no longer allowed, after the abdication, to accept new volunteers for the castration that permitted them to live in the inner quarters of the palace among the emperor's women; but many of these unfortunates were still in the court's service. There is no need to add to P'u Yi's own account of them; nor to his description of the Chinese part of his education. By his time the Manchu language of his martial ancestors was virtually dead, and he learned next to nothing of it.

Accession and Abdication

On the evening of November 13, 1908 the mansion of Prince Chun was in chaos. My grandmother fainted before hearing the end of the Dowager's decree that had been brought back by the new Prince Regent. Eunuchs and serving women were pouring ginger tea and sending for doctors while on the other side of the room a child was crying and adults were trying to pacify it. My father, the regent, was rushing all over the place: entertaining the Grand Councillor and the eunuchs who had come with him from the palace; telling people to get the child dressed; forgetting that the old lady had fainted; being called in to see her; and then forgetting that the Grand Councillor and eunuchs were waiting to take the future emperor into the palace. During this confusion the old lady came round and was helped into an inner room where the future emperor was still "resisting the edict", howling and hitting the eunuchs as they tried to pick him up. The palace eunuchs were forcing themselves to smile as they waited for the Grand Councillor to tell them what to do next while the Councillor was helplessly waiting for the Prince Regent to deal with the situation. But all the regent could do was to nod. . . .

Some of the older members of the household described this scene to me later; my memory of it disappeared long ago. They said that the confusion was ended by my wet-nurse who gave me the breast and thus ended my cries. This action of hers brought my father and the Councillor to their senses: they decided that she should take me to the palace before handing me over to the eunuchs who would carry me in to see Tzu Hsi.

I still have a dim recollection of my meeting with Tzu Hsi, the shock of which left a deep impression on my memory. I remember suddenly finding myself surrounded by strangers, while before me was hung a drab curtain through which I could see an emaciated and terrifyingly hideous face. This was Tzu Hsi. It is said that I burst into loud howls at the sight and started to tremble uncontrollably. Tzu Hsi told someone to give me a string of candied haws, but I threw it on the floor and cried, "I want nanny, I want nanny", to Tzu Hsi's great displeasure. "What a naughty child," she said. "Take him away to play."

Two days after I entered the palace Tzu Hsi died, and on December 2, the "Great Ceremony of Enthronement" took place, a ceremony that I ruined with my crying.

The ceremony took place in the Hall of Supreme Harmony (Tai Ho Tien). Before it began I had to receive the obeisances of the commanders of the palace guard and ministers of the inner court in the Hall of Central Harmony (Chung Ho Tien) and the homage of the leading civilian and military officials. I found all this long and tiresome; it was moreover a very cold day, so when they carried me into the Hall of Supreme Harmony and put me up on the high and enormous throne I could bear it no longer. My father, who was kneeling below the throne and supporting me, told me not to fidget, but I struggled and cried, "I don't like it here. I want to go home. I don't like it here. I want to go home." My father grew so desperate that he was pouring with sweat. As the officials went on kotowing to me my cries grew louder and louder. My father tried to soothe me by saying, "Don't cry, don't cry; it'll soon be finished, it'll soon be finished."

When the ceremony was over the officials asked each other surreptitiously, "How could he say 'It'll soon be finished'? What does it mean, his saying he wanted to go home?" All these discussions took place in a very gloomy atmosphere as if these words had been a bad omen. Some books said that these words were prophetic as within three years the Ching Dynasty was in fact "finished" and the boy who wanted to "go home" did go home, and claimed that the officials had a presentiment of this.

What really gave them forebodings, of course, was much more than a couple of chance sentences. The records of the time show that the rising anti-Manchu storm, serious enough in the last years of

Kuang Hsu, became ever more menacing during my reign. Later, the increasing power of Yuan Shih-kai was another headache for some high officials and members of the royal clan who saw that outside the government they had to reckon with the revolutionaries while inside they had to reckon with Yuan Shih-kai; they regarded my reign as one of the most ill-omened in history.

After making a very poor show as emperor for three years I made a very poor show of abdicating. One incident of those last days stands out clearly in my memory. The empress dowager Lung Yu was sitting on a *kang*[1] in a side room of the Mind Nurture Palace (Yang Hsin Tien) wiping her eyes with a handkerchief while a fat old man knelt on a red cushion before her, tears rolling down his face. I was sitting to the right of the Dowager feeling rather bewildered and wondering why the two adults were crying. There was nobody in the room besides us three and it was very quiet; the fat man was sniffing loudly while he talked and I could not understand what he was saying. Later I learnt that this fat man was Yuan Shih-kai. This was the only time I ever saw him and his last meeting with the Dowager. If what I have been told is right, this was the occasion on which Yuan directly brought up the question of abdication. After this meeting Yuan Shih-kai used the pretext of an attempt that had been made on his life not to come to court again.

The Wuchang rising sparked off responses all over the country, and when the Manchu commander-in-chief of the imperial forces proved incapable of directing the Peiyang Army against the Republican forces the Prince Regent had no choice but to bring back Yuan Shih-kai. Yuan, who knew how to wait for his price and was kept well informed of developments in the capital, repeatedly declined the offers of reinstatement until he was offered the premiership and supreme military command. Only then did he accept the imperial edict and order the Peiyang Army to advance on the Republicans. After recapturing Hanyang he halted his troops and

---

[1] A *kang* is a low brick platform on which people sit or sleep; it can be heated in winter, and is very common in north China.

returned to Peking for audiences with the Prince Regent and the empress dowager Lung Yu.

Yuan Shih-kai was no longer the Yuan Shih-kai of before. In addition to his political and military power he had obtained some things even more valuable: some foreigners, including the British minister at Peking, were interested in him and he also had friends on the Republican side, including Wang Ching-wei[1] who had been captured after his unsuccessful attempt to assassinate the Prince Regent but whose life had been spared through the intercession of some Japanese who made it clear that Japan would be displeased to see him executed. Wang was released from jail after the Wuchang rising and served as a link between Yuan Shih-kai and some of the Republican leaders; he also kept him well-informed on developments in the revolutionary camp, and some of the constitutional monarchists were beginning to feel well disposed towards Yuan.

With all his new and old friends and his clear intelligence picture Yuan's position was stronger than ever. Within a month of his return to Peking he used Prince Ching to get the regent dismissed. Then he took over the palace treasury of the empress dowager Lung Yu on the pretext that it was needed to meet military expenses, and at the same time made the members of the royal family and the nobility hand over funds for the army. With political, military and financial power in his hands he went on to arrange for the Chinese diplomatic envoys in Russia and other countries to telegraph the Ching court requesting the emperor's abdication, while at the same time he presented the Empress Dowager with a secret memorial in the name of the whole cabinet saying that a republic was the only solution. He must have presented the memorial on the occasion when I saw him, and this would explain why Lung Yu was weeping so copiously as the memorial said that there was no hope for the

---

[1] Wang Ching-wei later became a notorious Kuomintang leader and pro-Japanese traitor. He openly surrendered to the Japanese invaders in December 1938 when he was vice-chairman of the Kuomintang and chairman of its People's Political Council. In March 1940 he became president of the puppet central government then formed in Nanking. He died in Japan in November 1944.

dynasty even in flight and that delay in abdicating might lead to a fate similar to that suffered by Louis XVI and his family in the French revolution.

The terror-struck Dowager called an emergency meeting of the imperial council to hear the opinions of the members of the royal family. When they were told of the secret memorial and of what Yuan Shih-kai had said they were very alarmed, not by the reference to Louis XVI but by the sudden change in Yuan's loyalties.

At first Yuan Shih-kai had opposed the setting up of a republic and had advocated a constitutional monarchy in the negotiations with the Republican side. Later the Ching and Republican sides had agreed in principle that the question of the state structure should be decided by a provisional national assembly; but obstruction from the Ching side had prevented agreement on its composition, time and place. With these questions still unresolved the Republicans set up a Provisional Government at Nanking and elected Sun Yat-sen as Provisional President. This prompted Yuan Shih-kai to withdraw the credentials of his delegate in the negotiations and to deal directly with the Republican representatives by cable. The suggestion of Yuan's cabinet that the dynasty should abdicate at a time when the structure of the state was still undecided naturally came as a severe shock to the royal house.

Yuan Shih-kai already had foreign support and he now had enough friends on the Republican side to be able to influence its actions. Those among the revolutionaries who had originally been constitutional monarchists had for some time been aware that Yuan was their hope, and their attitude had infected some of the more naive of the Republicans. Thus it was that the Republican side decided that if Yuan consented to it a republic could be rapidly achieved and that Yuan should be invited to be the first president. This was just what Yuan wanted; he knew, moreover, that the former Prince Regent was surrounded by a group implacably hostile to himself who intended to eliminate him whether he succeeded in defeating the revolutionaries or not. He had decided to accept the Republican offer and was considering how to deal with the Ching house when the unexpected news that Sun Yat-sen had taken office as Provisional

President in Nanking made a solution to the question much more urgent. If the Republicans went on to set up a national assembly in the south it would be impossible for him to get rid of it; he decided therefore to put pressure on the imperial house by frightening the empress dowager Lung Yu while at the same time offering her the bait of the Articles of Favourable Treatment. In this way he hoped that she would announce the abdication voluntarily and give him full powers to organize a provisional government. This, then, was the explanation for Yuan Shih-kai's sudden volte-face.

Although Yuan had betrayed the Ching house one would never have guessed it from his tearful countenance at his private audience with the empress dowager Lung Yu. But even the members of the royal house who had trusted Yuan Shih-kai before knew that they had been betrayed.

Some of the princes and nobles who had always been anti-Yuan were in favour of putting up a desperate last-ditch fight and of avenging the slaughter of Manchu bannermen that had taken place in some parts of the country, and when the empress dowager Lung Yu called the first meeting of the imperial council the atmosphere was charged with anger. A proposal by Yuan Shih-kai's old ally Prince Ching and others that the court should agree to abdicate was fiercely attacked. Prince Ching did not come to court the next day and his chief supporter in the council changed his tune.

This situation did not last long. From various accounts one can tell that one of the long series of imperial council meetings went approximately as follows. Having established that all present were in favour of the monarchy and opposed to a republic the Dowager went on to say that she had been told by Prince Ching that the imperial forces were incapable of defeating the Republicans and that the foreigners would come to the help of the Ching government after the Prince Regent resigned.

Pu Wei, a leader of the anti-Yuan group among the nobility, protested that this was obviously a lie as the regent had already resigned and the foreigners had done nothing to help them. He and others then said that the rebels were nothing to be afraid of and reported that Feng Kuo-chang, a Peiyang general, maintained that three months' military funds would be enough to defeat them. But, as the Dowager pointed out, Yuan Shih-kai had taken over the funds of the Palace Treasury so that she had no money. "Besides," she went on, "what if we lose? Surely we won't be able to fall back on the Articles of Favourable Treatment then?"

Pu Wei objected that the Articles were a trick, but when the Dowager asked about the state of the army she only got a non-committal reply.

As one inconclusive meeting of the imperial council followed another the advocates of fighting it out became fewer and fewer. Tuan Chi-jui, another Peiyang general, sent a telegram requesting the abdication of the Ching emperor. Two leaders of the war party in the royal family left Peking. One hastened to German-occupied Tsingtao and the other to Japanese-held Lushun, but they were prevented from going on to plead the imperial case in Germany and Japan by the local officials of the two countries.

On February 12, 1912 the empress dowager Lung Yu proclaimed my abdication. Some of the royal family and the nobility fled to the Legation Quarter while Prince Ching took his family and his valuables to the foreign concessions in Tientsin. My father, who had said not a word throughout the imperial council meetings, returned home to "hug his children". Yuan Shih-kai meanwhile was organizing a provisional Republican government as he had been ordered to by the Empress Dowager while at the same time he acted on an agreement with the revolutionaries and changed from premier of the cabinet of the Great Ching Empire to Provisional President of the Republic of China. And I became the President's neighbour as I started my life in the "Little Court" according to the articles providing for the favourable treatment of the Ching house.

These articles, the "Articles providing for the Favourable Treatment of the Great Ching Emperor after his Abdication", were as follows:

1. After the abdication of the Great Ching Emperor, his title of dignity is to be retained and not abolished. The Republic of China will treat him with the courtesy due to a foreign sovereign.

2. After the abdication of the Great Ching Emperor he shall receive an. annual allowance of four million taels, or four million dollars after the minting of the new currency. This allowance shall be paid by the Republic of China.

3. After the abdication of the Great Ching Emperor he may live temporarily in the Imperial Palace; later he shall move to the Summer Palace. He may retain his usual bodyguard.

4. After the abdication of the Great Ching Emperor the sacrifices at his ancestral temples and the imperial tombs shall be maintained for ever. The Republic of China shall provide guards to ensure their protection.

5. The uncompleted tomb of Te Tsung (Emperor Kuang Hsu) shall be finished according to the original plan. The funeral ceremonies shall be observed in accordance with the ancient rites. The actual expenses shall be borne by the Republic of China.

6. All the persons of various grades working in the palace may continue to be employed as before; with the provision that no further eunuchs be engaged.

7. After the abdication of the Great Ching Emperor his existing private property shall receive the special protection of the Republic of China.

8. The existing Palace Guard shall be incorporated into the Army of the Republic of China; its numbers and salary shall be continued as before.

Living as an Emperor

The "Articles for Favourable Treatment" stipulated that I could live temporarily in the Imperial Palace without fixing any definite time limit. Apart from three large halls that were handed over to the Republic, the rest of the Forbidden City continued to belong to the Imperial Palace. It was in this tiny world that I was to spend the most absurd childhood possible until I was driven out by the soldiers of the National Army in 1924. I call it absurd because at a time when China was called a republic and mankind had advanced into the twentieth century I was still living the life of an emperor, breathing the dust of the nineteenth century.

Whenever I think of my childhood my head fills with a yellow mist. The glazed tiles were yellow, my sedan-chair was yellow, my chair cushions were yellow, the linings of my hats and clothes were yellow, the girdle round my waist was yellow, the dishes and bowls from which I ate and drank, the padded cover of the rice-gruel saucepan, the material in which my books were wrapped, the window curtains, the bridle of my horse . . . everything was yellow. This colour, the so-called "brilliant yellow", was used exclusively by the imperial household and made me feel from my earliest years that I was unique and had a "heavenly" nature different from that of everybody else.

When I was ten my grandmother and mother started to come and visit me on the orders of the High Consorts[1] and they brought my brother Pu Chieh and my first sister to play with me for a few days. Their first visit started off very drearily: I and my grandmother sat on the *kang* and she watched me playing dominoes while my brother and sister stood below us very properly, gazing at me with a fixed stare like attendants on duty in a yamen. Later it occurred to me to take them along to the part of the palace in which I lived, where I asked Pu Chieh, "What games do you play at home?"

"Pu Chieh can play hide-and-seek," said my brother, who was a year younger than me, in a very respectful way.

"So you play hide-and-seek too? It's a jolly good game." I was very excited. I had played it with the eunuchs but never with children younger than myself. So we started to play hide-and-seek and in the excitement of the game my brother and sister forgot their inhibitions. We deliberately let down the blinds to make the room very dark. My sister, who was two years younger than me, was at the same time enraptured and terrified, and as my brother and I kept giving her frights we got so carried away that we were laughing and shouting. When we were exhausted we climbed up on to the *kang* to get our breath back and I told them to think of some new game. Pu Chieh was thoughtful for a while, then started to gaze at me wordlessly, a silly smile on his face.

---

[1] Dowager Consorts of the first degree, widows of the emperors Tung Chih and Kuang Hsu.

"What are you grinning at?"

He went on grinning.

"Tell me! Tell me!" I urged him impatiently, thinking that he must certainly have thought out some new game. To my surprise he came out with, "I thought, oh, Pu Chieh thought that Your Majesty would be different from ordinary people. The emperors on the stage have long beards. . . ." As he spoke he pretended to be stroking his beard.

This gesture was his undoing. As he raised his hand I noticed that the lining of his sleeve was a very familiar colour. My face blackened.

"Pu Chieh, are you allowed to wear that colour?"

"But . . . bu . . . but isn't it apricot?"

"Nonsense! It's imperial brilliant yellow."

"Yes, sire, yes, sire. . . ." Pu Chieh stood away from me, his arms hanging respectfully by his sides. My sister slipped over to stand with him, frightened to the point of tears.

"It's brilliant yellow. You have no business to be wearing it."

"Yes, sire."

With his "yes, sire" my brother reverted to being my subject. The sound "yes, sire" died out long ago and it seems very funny when one thinks of it today. But I got used to it from early childhood, and if people did not use the words when replying to me I would not stand for it. It was the same with kneeling and kotowing. From my infancy I was accustomed to having people kotow to me, particularly people over ten times my own age. They included old officials of the Ching Dynasty and the elders of my own clan, men in the court robes of the Ching Dynasty and officials of the Republic in Western dress.

Another strange thing which seemed quite normal at the time was the daily pomp.

Every time I went to my schoolroom to study, or visited the High Consorts to pay my respects, or went for a stroll in the garden I was always followed by a large retinue. Every trip I made to the Summer Palace must have cost thousands of Mexican dollars: the

Republic's police had to be asked to line the roads to protect me and I was accompanied by a motorcade consisting of dozens of vehicles.

Whenever I went for a stroll in the garden a procession had to be organized. In front went a eunuch from the Administrative Bureau whose function was roughly that of a motor horn: he walked twenty or thirty yards ahead of the rest of the party intoning the sound "chir ... chir ..." as a warning to anyone who might be in the vicinity to go away at once. Next came two chief eunuchs advancing crabwise on either side of the path; ten paces behind them came the centre of the procession — the Empress Dowager or myself. If I was being carried in a chair there would be two junior eunuchs walking beside me to attend to my wants at any moment; if I was walking they would be supporting me. Next came a eunuch with a large silk canopy followed by a large group of eunuchs of whom some were empty-handed and others were holding all sorts of things: a seat in case I wanted to rest, changes of clothing, umbrellas and parasols. After these eunuchs of the imperial presence came eunuchs of the imperial tea bureau with boxes of various kinds of cakes and delicacies, and, of course, jugs of hot water and a tea service; they were followed by eunuchs of the imperial dispensary bearing cases of medicine and first-aid equipment suspended from carrying poles. The medicines carried always included potions prepared from lampwick sedge, chrysanthemums, the roots of reeds, bamboo leaves, and bamboo skins; in summer there were always Essence of Betony Pills for Rectifying the Vapour, Six Harmony Pills for Stabilizing the Centre, Gold Coated Heat-Dispersing Cinnabar, Fragrant Herb Pills, Omnipurpose Bars, colic medicine and anti-plague powder; and throughout all four seasons there would be the Three Immortals Beverage to aid the digestion, as well as many other medicaments. At the end of the procession came the eunuchs who carried commodes and chamber-pots. If I was walking a sedan-chair, open or covered according to the season, would bring up the rear. This motley procession of several dozen people would proceed in perfect silence and order.

But I would often throw it into confusion. When I was young I liked to run around when I was in high spirits just any child does. At first they would all scuttle along after me puffing and panting with their procession reduced to chaos. When I grew a little older and knew how to give orders I would tell them to stand and wait for me; then apart from the junior eunuchs of the imperial presence who came with me they would all stand there waiting in silence with their loads. After I had finished running around they would form up again behind me. When I learnt to ride a bicycle and ordered the removal of all the upright wooden thresholds in the palace so that I could ride around without obstruction the procession was no longer able to follow me and so it had to be temporarily abolished. But when I went to pay my respects to the High Consorts or to my schoolroom I still had to have something of a retinue, and without it I would have felt rather odd. When I heard people telling the story of the last emperor of the Ming Dynasty who had only one eunuch left with him at the end I felt very uncomfortable.

The type of extravagant display that wasted the most effort, money and material was meals. There were special terms to refer to the emperor's eating and it was absolutely forbidden to fail to use them correctly. Food was called not "food" but "viands"; eating was called "consuming viands"; serving the meal was "transmitting the viands"; and the kitchen was the "imperial viands room". When it was time to eat (and the times of the meals were not set but were whenever the emperor felt like eating), I would give the command "Transmit the viands!" The junior eunuchs of the presence would then repeat "Transmit the viands" to the eunuchs standing in the main hall of the palace in which I lived and they would pass it on to the eunuchs standing on duty outside the hall; these would in turn call it out to the eunuchs of the "imperial viands room" waiting in the Western Avenue of the Forbidden City. Thus my order went straight to the kitchens, and before its echoes had died away a procession rather of the sort that used to take a bride's trousseau to her groom's house had already issued from the "viands room". It was made up of an imposing column of several dozen neatly dressed eunuchs hurrying to the Mind Nurture Palace with seven tables of various sizes and scores of red-lacquered boxes painted with golden dragons. When they reached the main hall they handed their burdens over to young eunuchs wearing white sleeves who laid out the meal in an eastern room of the palace.

Usually there were two tables of main dishes with another one of chafing-dishes added in winter; there were three tables with cakes, rice and porridge respectively; and there was another small table of salted vegetables. All the crockery was imperial yellow porcelain with dragon designs and the words "Ten thousand long lives without limit" painted on it. In winter I ate from silver dishes placed on top of porcelain bowls of hot water. Every dish or bowl had a strip of silver on it as a precaution against poison, and for the same reason all the food was tasted by a eunuch before it was brought in. This was called "appraising the viands". When everything had been tasted and laid out and before I took my place a young eunuch would call out "Remove the covers". This was the signal for four or five other junior eunuchs to take the silver lids off all the food dishes, put them in a large box and carry them out. I then began to "use the viands".

And what was the food laid out "ten cubits square"? The empress dowager Lung Yu would have about a hundred main dishes on six tables, an extravagance inherited from the empress dowager Tzu Hsi. I had about thirty. But these dishes which were brought in with such ceremonial were only for show. The reason why the food could be served almost as soon as I gave the word was that it had been prepared several hours or even a whole day in advance and was being kept warm over the kitchen stoves. The cooks knew that at least since the time of Kuang Hsu the emperor had not eaten this food. The food I ate was sent over by the Empress Dowager, and after her death by the High Consorts. She and each of the High Consorts had kitchens of their own staffed by highly skilled chefs who produced twenty or more really delicious dishes for every meal. This was the food that was put in front of me, while that prepared by the imperial kitchens was set some distance away as it was only there for the sake of appearances.

To show how they loved and cared for me the High Consorts also sent a responsible eunuch to report on how I had "consumed viands". This too was a pure formality. No matter what I had really eaten, the eunuch would go to the quarters of the High Consorts, kneel before them and say:

"Your slave reports to his masters: the Lord of Ten Thousand Years consumed one bowl of old rice viands (or white rice viands), one steamed breadroll (or a griddle cake) and a bowl of congee. He consumed it with relish."

At Chinese New Year and other festivals and on the birthdays of the High Consorts my kitchen sent a spread of food to the Consorts as a mark of my filial piety. This food could be described as expensive and showy without being good, and was neither nutritious nor tasty.

According to the record of one month of the second year of my reign, the empress dowager Lung Yu, the four High Consorts and myself used up 3,960 catties of meat (over two tons) and 388 chickens and ducks every month, of which 810 catties of meat and 240 chickens and ducks were for me, a four-year-old child. In addition there was a monthly allocation for the numerous people·in the palace who served us: members of the Grand Council, imperial bodyguards, tutors, Hanlin academicians, painters, men who drew the outlines of characters for others to fill in, important eunuchs, *shaman* magicians who came every day to sacrifice to the spirits, and many others. Including the Dowager, the Consorts and myself, the monthly consumption of pork was 14,642 catties at a cost of 2,342.72 taels of silver. On top of this there were the extra dishes we had every day which often cost several times as much again. In the month in question there were 31,844 catties of extra meat, 814 catties of extra pork fat and 4,786 extra chickens and ducks, to say nothing of the fish, shrimps and eggs. All these extras cost 11,641.07 taels, and with miscellaneous items added the total expenditure came to 14,794.19 taels. It is obvious that all this money (except what was embezzled) was wasted in order to display the grandeur of the emperor. This figure, moreover, does not include the cost of the cakes, fruit, sweets and drinks that were constantly being devoured.

Just as food was cooked in huge quantities but not eaten, so was a vast amount of clothing made which was never worn. I cannot now remember much about this, but I do know that while the Dowager and the High Consorts had fixed yearly allocations there were no limits for the emperor, for whom clothes were constantly made throughout the year. I do not know what exactly was made, but everything I wore was always new. I have before me an account from an unspecified year headed "List of materials actually used in making clothes for His Majesty's use from the sixth day of the tenth month to the fifth day of the eleventh month". According to this list the following garments were made for me that month: eleven fur jackets, six fur inner and outer gowns, two fur waistcoats, and thirty padded waistcoats and pairs of trousers. Leaving aside the cost of the main materials and of the labour, the bill for such minor items as the edgings, pockets, buttons and thread came to 2,137.6335 silver dollars.

My changes of clothing were all laid down in regulations and were the responsibility of the eunuchs of the clothing storerooms. Even my everyday gowns came in twenty-eight different styles, from the one in black and white inlaid fur that I started wearing on the nineteenth of the first lunar month to the sable one I changed into on the first day of the eleventh month. Needless to say, my clothes were far more complicated on festivals and ceremonial occasions.

To manage all this extravagant pomp there was, of course, a suitable proliferation of offices and personnel. The Household Department, which administered the domestic affairs of the emperor, had under its control seven bureaus and 48 offices. The seven bureaus — the storage bureau, the guard bureau, the protocol, the counting house, the stock-raising bureau, the disciplinary bureau and the construction bureau — all had storerooms, workshops and so on under them. The storage bureau, for example, had stores for silver, fur, porcelain, satin, clothes and tea. According to a list of officials dating from 1909, the personnel of the Household Department numbered 1,023 (excluding the Palace Guard, the eunuchs and the servants known as "sulas"); in the early years of the Republic this number was reduced to something over 600, and at the time I left the Imperial Palace there were still more than 300. It is not hard to imagine an organization as large as this with so many people in it, but the triviality of some of its functions was almost unthinkable.

One of the forty-eight offices, for example, was the As You Wish Lodge (Ju Yi Kuan). Its only purpose was to paint pictures and do calligraphy for the Empress Dowager and the High Consorts; if the Dowager wanted to paint something the As You Wish Lodge would outline a design for her so that all she had to do was to fill in the colours and write a title on it. The calligraphy for large tablets was sketched out by the experts of the Great Diligence Hall or else done by the Hanlin academicians. Nearly all late Ching inscriptions that purport to be the brushwork of a dowager or an emperor were produced in this way.

The buildings all around me and the furniture of the palace were all a part of my indoctrination. Apart from the golden-glazed tiles that were exclusively for the use of the emperor, the very height of the buildings was an imperial prerogative that served to teach me from an early age that not only was everything under heaven the emperor's land, but that even the sky above my head belonged to nobody else. Every piece of furniture was "direct method" teaching material for me. It was said that the emperor Chien Lung once laid it down that nothing in the palace, not even a blade of grass, must be lost. To put this principle into practice he put some blades of grass on a table in the palace and gave orders that they were to be counted every day to see that not a single one of them was missing. This was called "taking the grass as a standard". Even in my time these thirty-six withered blades of grass were still preserved in a cloisonné canister in the Mind Nurture Palace. This grass filled me with unbounded admiration for my ancestor and unbridled hatred for the Revolution of 1911.

There is no longer any way of calculating exactly the enormous cost of the daily life of an emperor, but a record called "A comparison between the expenditure of the seventh year of Hsuan Tung (1915) and the past three years" compiled by the Household Department shows that expenditure in 1915 topped 2,790,000 taels, and that while it dropped in each of the following three years it was always over 1,890,000 taels. Thus it was that with the connivance of the Republican authorities we continued our prodigious waste of the sweat and blood of the people in order to maintain our former pomp and continue our parasitic way of life.

Some of the rules in the palace were originally not simply for the sake of show. The system by which all the food-dishes had strips of silver on them and the food was tasted before the emperor ate it, and the large-scale security precautions whenever he went out were basically to protect him against any attempt on his life. It was said that the reason why emperors had no outside privies was that one emperor had been set upon by an assassin when going out to relieve himself. These stories and all the display had the same effect on me: they made me believe that I was a very important and august person, a man apart who ruled and owned the universe.

Mothers and Son

When I entered the palace as the adopted son of the emperors Tung Chih and Kuang Hsu all their wives became my mothers. Strictly speaking, I became the adopted son of Tung Chih while only "continuing the sacrifices" to Kuang Hsu. This meant that I was now primarily the son of Tung Chih and only secondarily the son of Kuang Hsu. But Kuang Hsu's empress, the empress dowager Lung Yu, ignored this and used her authority as dowager to push the three high consorts of Tung Chih into the background for daring to argue this point with her. For the rest of her life they were not really numbered among my mothers, and Kuang Hsu's Chin Consort did not get the treatment of a secondary mother as she should have done either: when we ate together she had to stand while Lung Yu and I sat. After the death of Lung Yu the three consorts of Tung Chih combined with Kuang Hsu's consort to put their case to the princes and members of the nobility and succeeded in getting the titles of High Consorts. From then on I addressed all of them as "August Mother".

47

Although I had so many mothers I never knew any motherly love. As far as I can remember today the greatest concern they ever showed for me was to send me food at every meal and hear the report of the eunuch that I had "consumed it with relish".

In fact I was unable to "consume it with relish" when I was small as I had a stomach ailment, a condition that was probably caused by their "motherly love". Once when I was five I stuffed myself with chestnuts and for a month or more afterwards the empress dowager Lung Yu only allowed me to eat browned rice porridge; and although I was crying with hunger nobody paid any attention. I remember that one day when I was going for a walk by the side of one of the lakes in the palace the Dowager told them to take some stale steamed breadrolls for me to feed to the fish. I could not restrain myself from cramming one of them into my mouth. So far from feeling any regret at my display of hunger, Lung Yu actually tightened up her restrictions; but the tighter they got the stronger grew my desire to steal food. One day I noticed that the tribute food sent by the princes to the Dowager had been put down in the Western Avenue of the palace, so I made straight for one of the food containers, opened it, and saw that it was full of cold pork. I grabbed a piece and sank my teeth into it. The eunuchs with me turned pale with horror and rushed up to snatch it from me. I put up a desperate resistance, but as I was small and weak the delicious morsel was snatched away almost as soon as I had put it into my mouth.

Even after I was allowed to eat normally again I still got into trouble. Once a senior eunuch observed that I had downed six pancakes and, afraid that I had overeaten, thought up a way of helping me digest them. He had two other eunuchs pick me up by the arms and bring me hard down on to the floor as if they were ramming earth with me. Later they were very pleased with themselves and said that it was thanks to their cure that I had suffered no ill effects from the pancakes.

This may seem rather unreasonable, but there were other things more unreasonable still. Whenever I got impatient or lost my temper before I was seven or eight the chief eunuch would make the following diagnosis and prescription: "The Lord of Ten Thousand Years has fire in his heart. Let him sing for a while to disperse it." I would then be shut into some small room, usually the room in the schoolroom palace where my commode was kept. Once I was in there by myself it made no difference how much I cursed, kicked the door, implored or wailed: nobody would pay any attention. Only when I had finished howling, or, as they put it, finished "singing" and "dispersed the fire" would they let me out.

This strange cure was not an invention of the eunuchs nor, for that matter, of the dowager Lung Yu: it was a family tradition from which my brothers and sisters also suffered in my father's house.

When I was seven the empress dowager Lung Yu died. All I can remember about her "motherly love" is what I have related above.

I lived rather longer with the four High Consorts. Normally I saw very little of them and I never sat and talked with them in an ordinary, friendly way. Every morning I would go to pay them my respects. A eunuch would put down a hassock covered with yellow silk for me to kneel on, and after kneeling to them for a moment I would get up and stand to one side waiting for them to make their usual remarks. At this time of day they were having their hair combed by eunuchs and they would ask me, "Did the emperor sleep well?" or advise me to dress warmly as the weather was cold, or inquire how far I had got in the book I was studying. It was always the same — a few dry and stereotyped remarks; sometimes they would give me a few clay toys or something of the kind and then they would say, "Go away and play now, Emperor." This would be the end of our meeting and I would not see them again for the rest of the day.

The Dowager and the four High Consorts addressed me as "Emperor", as did my real parents and grandmother. Everyone else called me "Your Majesty". Although I had an ordinary name as well as a "milk name"[1] none of my mothers ever used them. I have heard others saying that when they think of their "milk names"

---

[1] "Milk name" is a name used in childhood.

they are reminded of their childhood and their mother's love. Mine has no such associations. I have also been told by some people that whenever they fell ill when studying away from home they would think of their mothers and of how their mothers comforted them when they were ill as children. I have often been ill in my adult life, but the thought of the visits I had from the High Consorts when I was sick as a child has never made me feel at all nostalgic.

I always caught colds or flu when the weather turned chilly. Whenever this happened the High Consorts would come to see me one after another. Each of them would ask the same question: "Is the emperor at all better? Have you had a good sweat?" and before two or three minutes were up she would be off again. I have a rather stronger memory of the swarms of eunuchs who accompanied them and crowded into my little bedroom. They would come and go again all within the space of a few minutes, thus disturbing the atmosphere in my room. As soon as one High Consort had gone another one would arrive and the room would be packed again. With four visits in a single day the atmosphere would be disturbed four times. Fortunately I always got better on the following day, and my bedroom would be quiet again.

When I was ill my medicines were made up by the dispensary in the palace of the high consort Tuan Kang, who after the death of the dowager Lung Yu managed, with the help of Yuan Shih-kai, to be made the senior of the four High Consorts and thus my chief mother.

Thus I grew to the age of twelve or thirteen under the "care" of my four mothers. Like any other child I was very fond of new toys, and some of the eunuchs tried to please me by buying me amusing things from outside. Once a eunuch had a replica of the ceremonial uniform of a general of the Republic made for me with a plume in its cap like a feather duster and a military sword and belt. When I put it on I felt very pleased with myself, but when the senior high consort Tuan Kang heard of this she was furious. She ordered an investigation, which also revealed that I had been wearing foreign stockings bought outside the palace by one of the eunuchs. She regarded all this as intolerable and summoned the two eunuchs responsible to her quarters, had each of them given two hundred strokes of the heavy rod and demoted them, sending them to the cleaning office to work as menials. Having dealt with them she sent for me and lectured me on the disgracefulness of the Great Ching Emperor wearing the clothes of the Republic and foreign stockings. I had no choice but to put away my beloved uniform and sword, take off my foreign stockings and change back into court clothes and cloth socks embroidered with dragon designs.

If the high consort Tuan Kang had limited her control over me to uniforms and foreign stockings, I would not have rebelled against her later. After all, such control as this only made me even more aware of my uniqueness and reinforced the lessons I was learning in my schoolroom. I think that it was for the sake of my education that she had the eunuchs beaten and gave me that scolding.

Tuan Kang took the empress dowager Tzu Hsi as her model and strove to emulate her, although Tzu Hsi had been responsible for the death of her own sister. The lessons she learnt from Tzu Hsi did not end with the savage flogging of eunuchs: she also sent eunuchs to spy on the emperor. After dealing with some eunuchs of mine she sent over a eunuch of her own to wait on me. He would go to her daily and report on my every action. This was just how Tzu Hsi had treated Kuang Hsu. Whatever her motive was, it hurt my pride, and my tutor Chen Pao-shen, who was very indignant about it, explained to me the theory about the difference between first wives and secondary wives, the category into which Tuan Kang fell. I seethed with repressed anger.

The explosion came not long later when one of the Imperial Physicians was dismissed by Tuan Kang. The affair really had nothing to do with me as the doctor in question was one of those attending to Tuan Kang, but I had heard some inflammatory suggestions such as the remark of my tutor, "Although she is only a consort, her high-handed behaviour is going too far." And one of the eunuchs had said to me, "Is not the Lord of Ten Thousand Years becoming another Kuang Hsu? The affairs of the College of Physicians should only be settled by the Lord of Ten Thousand Years. Even your slave cannot bear to see such things happen." Raging with fury I stormed over to the palace of Tuan Kang. As soon as I saw her I shouted, "Why did you dismiss that doctor? You're too highhanded. Aren't I the emperor? Who gives the orders? You've gone too far."

I did not wait for Tuan Kang, whose face had gone white from anger, to reply and went straight out again with a flick of my sleeve. When I returned to my schoolroom my tutors covered me with praises.

The furious Tuan Kang sent for my father and several other princes and with tears and sobs asked for advice, which none of them ventured to give her. When I was told that they had come I called them to my study and said to them with great spirit:

"Who is she? She's only a consort. Never in the history of our house has an emperor had to call a consort 'mother'. Are we to maintain no distinction between principal and secondary wives? If not, why doesn't my brother call the prince's secondary wives 'mother'? Why must I call her 'mother'? Why should I obey her?"

The princes received my tirade in silence.

Another of the High Consorts, who was on bad terms with Tuan Kang, came over specially to tell me that Tuan Kang was inviting my real mother and grandmother to come and see her, and so I had better be careful. They did in fact come, and where Tuan Kang had got nowhere with the princes her rantings had some effect on them: my grandmother in particular was terrified and ended up kneeling on the ground with my mother imploring Tuan Kang to desist from her wrath and promising to persuade me to apologize. I saw my mother and grandmother in a wing of the Lasting Peace Palace (Yung Ho Kung) in which Tuan Kang lived and heard that the High Consort was still raging in the main hall. I had orginally wanted to go and have it out with her, but unable to hold out against the tears and desperate entreaties of my mother and grandmother I relented and promised that I would apologize to Tuan Kang.

I resented making that apology. I went and greeted Tuan Kang without even looking at her, mumbled, "August Mother, I was wrong", and went away again. Her face restored, Tuan Kang stopped weeping. Two days later I heard that my mother had killed herself.

My mother had never before been scolded in her life. She had a headstrong personality and this shock was too much for her: when she returned from the palace she swallowed a fatal dose of opium. For fear that I might go too thoroughly into the circumstances of my mother's death Tuan Kang changed her treatment of me completely: she no longer restricted my activities in the least and became very accommodating. With this my family life in the Forbidden City was peaceful again and the High Consorts and myself were once more mothers and son. But for this my mother's life had to be sacrificed.

Studying in the Yu Ching Palace

When I was five the empress dowager Lung Yu chose a tutor for me and ordered an astrologer to select an auspicious day for me to begin my studies. This day was September 10, 1911.

My first schoolroom was on an island in one of the palace lakes but later I changed to the Yu Ching Palace (Palace of the Cultivation of Happiness), a rather small building inside the Forbidden City. It contained two studies which were furnished more simply than most other rooms in the palace. Under the southern window was a long table on which stood hat-stands and vases of flowers. By the west wall was a *kang* on which I studied at first with the low *kang* table for a desk. Later I sat at a table. There were two more tables by the north wall with books and stationery on them. On the walls hung scrolls that my grandfather, the first Prince Chun, had written out for his son the emperor Kuang Hsu. The most eye-catching thing in the room was a huge clock about two metres in diameter whose hands were longer than my arms. Its mechanism was on the other side of the wall, and to wind it up you had to go into the next room and use a thing like the starting handle of a car.

Where this strange and enormous object came from or why it was there I cannot remember, nor can I recall what sort of sound it made or how loud were the chimes at the hour.

But despite the colossal size of the clock in the Yu Ching Palace the boy who studied there had no idea of time, as could be guessed from the books I read. My principal texts were the Thirteen Classics, and I also read such books as the maxims and exploits of my ancestors and histories of the foundation of the Ching Dynasty. When I started English at thirteen the only two texts I used apart from an English reader were *Alice in Wonderland* and an English translation of the Chinese classical *Four Books*. I had some basic lessons in Manchu, but before I was even able to use the alphabet my teacher Yi Ko Tan died and my lessons stopped. So from 1911 to 1922 I learnt nothing of mathematics, let alone of science. As for my own country, I read only about such events as the "Tung Chih and Kuang Hsu Restoration"; my knowledge of foreign countries was limited to my trip with Alice to Wonderland. I was totally ignorant of George Washington, Napoleon, Watt's invention of the steam engine, and Newton and his apple. All I knew about the universe was that "the great Pole produced the two Forms, the two Forms produced the four Symbols, and the four Symbols produced the eight Trigrams."[1] If my tutors had not been prepared to chat with me about things that were not in the texts and had I not read more widely myself I would not even have known where Peking was in relation to the rest of China or that rice grew in the ground. In history no one dared to explode the myths about the origins of the ancestors of the Ching house, and as for economics, I had no idea of the price of a catty of rice. So for a long time I believed that my earliest ancestor was born after the goddess Fokulun swallowed a red fruit, and that the common people always had a table covered with dishes at every meal.

As I read a considerable number of ancient books over quite a long period of time I should have known classical Chinese very well. In fact I did not as I was not in the least conscientious. Apart from

---

[1] A quotation from the ancient classic, *Book of Changes*.

using minor illnesses as pretexts, I would sometimes tell a eunuch to inform my tutors that they were to take a day's holiday if I was not feeling like studying and had no better excuse. Up to the age of ten I was far more interested in a big cypress tree that grew outside the Yu Ching Palace than in my books. In summer there were always ants crawling up and down this tree. I got very interested in them and would often squat by their tree so absorbed in watching them or feeding them crumbs of cake and helping them to move their food that I would forget my own meals. Later I developed an interest in crickets and earthworms, so I had many an ancient porcelain bowl and urn brought over for me to keep them in. I was never very keen on my schoolbooks, and when reading them became intolerably tiresome my only thought was of going out to see those friends of mine.

In my early teens I began to understand that my textbooks had something to do with me and grew interested in how to be a "good emperor", in why an emperor was an emperor, and in what heavenly significance there was in this. It was the content rather than the language of the books that held my attention, and the content was far more concerned with the emperor's rights than with his duties. One of the sages did, it is true, say, "The people are important, the spirits of the land and grain come next and the sovereign is unimportant", "If the sovereign regards his subjects as so much grass the subjects will regard the monarch as their enemy", and other things of the kind. Far more of their admonitions, however, were directed at the ministers and common people. An example of this is the saying, "The ruler should be a ruler, the subjects should be subjects, the fathers should be fathers and the sons should be sons." The very first textbook, the *Classic of Filial Piety*, laid down the moral principle that one should "start by serving one's parents and end by serving one's sovereign". Before I started to read about this morality which seemed so delightful to me I had heard about it from the conversation of my tutors and later on they had even more to say about it than the texts. Ancient literature did not make nearly so deep an impression on me as their ancient talk.

Many of the people who studied in old-fashioned schools had to learn books by heart, and the great efforts involved are said to have had some good results. I never enjoyed any of these benefits as my tutors did not make me memorize my texts, being content with making me read them through a few times.

Perhaps it was to help me remember what I had read that they decided that I should read my text aloud to the dowager Lung Yu when I went to pay my respects to her and that the chief eunuch should stand outside my bedroom when I got up in the morning and read out the previous day's lessons several times. Nobody was interested in how much I remembered or in whether I wanted to remember it or not.

My teachers never examined me on my work and set me no compositions to write. I remember that I wrote some couplets and verses but the tutors would never comment on them, let alone correct them. Yet I was very keen on writing things when I was a child. As the tutors did not think much of such trifles I wrote them secretly for my own amusement. From the age of twelve or thirteen I read a lot for pleasure. I read most of the books of essays and the unofficial histories of the Ming and Ching Dynasties, the historical romances, tales of knights and fighters with magic powers and detective stories of the late Ching and early Republican period and the series of novels published by the Commercial Press. When I was a little older I read some English stories. Imitating all these works, Chinese and Western, ancient and modern, I concocted and illustrated many romances out of my daydreams just for my own enjoyment. I even submitted them for publication under assumed names, but I was nearly always disappointed. I remember that I once copied out a poem by a Ming writer and sent it to a small newspaper under the pseudonym of "Teng Chiung-lin". The editor was taken in and printed it. He was not the only person to be deceived: my English tutor Reginald Johnston translated it into English and put it into his book *Twilight in the Forbidden City* as evidence of his pupil's "poetic gifts".

The subject at which I was worst was Manchu: I only learnt one word in all the years I studied it. This was *yili* (arise), the reply

I had to make when my Manchu ministers knelt before me and said a set phrase of greeting in the language.

When I was eight they thought of another way of making me study better: I was provided with some fellow-students. Each of them received a stipend of the equivalent of eighty taels of silver a month and was granted the coveted privilege of being allowed to ride a horse in the Forbidden City. Although it was the time of the Republic this was still regarded as a great honour by the young men of the imperial clan. The three recipients of these favours were my brother Pu Chieh, Yu Chung (a son of my cousin Pu Lun), and Pu Chia, the son of my uncle Tsai Tao. Yet another honour conferred on these three was that of being scolded on behalf of their emperor in the schoolroom: when I made a mistake in reading out my lessons the teacher would tell one of my fellow-students off. As Pu Chieh was my brother the victim was nearly always Yu Chung, whose studies naturally suffered when he found himself being scolded whether he read well or badly.

When I had no fellow-students I was very naughty. If I felt like it I would take my shoes and socks off while I was reading and put the socks on the table. The tutor had to put them back on for me. Once I took a fancy to the long eyebrows of my tutor Hsu Fang and told him to come over so that I could stroke them. When he came obediently with his head bowed I suddenly plucked a hair from them. When he died later the eunuchs all said that this was because the "Lord of Ten Thousand Years" had pulled out his eyebrow of longevity. Another time I made my tutor Lu Jun-hsiang so angry with me that he forgot the distinction between ruler and subject. I was refusing to read my text as I wanted to go out into the garden and watch my ants. At first Lu tried to persuade me to pay attention by quoting such classical tags as "One can only be a true gentleman when one has both polish and substance", but I could not understand what he was talking about and went on fidgeting and looking around the room. Seeing that I was still unsettled my tutor went on to cite another classical saying: "If the gentleman is not serious he carries no authority; his learning will not be solid", but I naughtily got up and was about to go away from the table when suddenly he lost his temper and roared at me, "Don't move!" I started with fright and did in fact behave a little better, though it was not long before I was thinking of my ants and fidgeting again.

When I had some fellow-students, things were rather better and I was able to bear sitting in the schoolroom. My teachers had ways of reproving me when I misbehaved: I remember one occasion when I came scampering into the classroom and the teacher said to Yu Chung, who was sitting there like a good boy, "Look how frivolous you are."

I studied Chinese every day from eight to eleven in the morning and English in the afternoon from one to three. At eight o'clock every morning I would be carried in a yellow-canopied sedan-chair to the Yu Ching Palace. At my command of "Call them" a eunuch would go and call out the tutor and the fellow-students from a waiting room. They always went into the schoolroom in a set order: first a eunuch carrying books, then the tutor for the first lesson, and finally my fellow-students. Once through the door the tutor would stand and gaze at me as a form of greeting. By the rules of protocol I was not obliged to return his salutation as although he was my teacher he was still my subject, and although I was his pupil I was still his sovereign. Then Pu Chieh and Yu Chung would kneel and pay their respects to me. These formalities over, we would all sit down. I sat by myself at the north side of the table, facing south, the teacher faced west and my fellow-students sat beside him. The eunuchs arranged the others' hats on the hat-stands and filed out. With that the lesson began.

I came across some pages of my diary dating from 1920, when I was fourteen. An excerpt may serve to give an idea of the life I led while I was studying.

27th. Fine. Rose at four, wrote out eighteen sheets of the character Prosperity in a large hand. Classes at eight. Read *Analects, Chou Ritual, Record of Ritual,* and Tang poetry with Pu Chieh and Yu Chung: listened to Tutor Chen lecturing on the *General Chronological History with Comments by Emperor Chien Lung.* Finished eating at 9:30, read *Tso Commentary, Ku Liang Commentary,* heard Tutor Chu on the *Explanation of the Great Learning,* wrote couplets.

Lessons finished at 11, went to pay respects to four High Consorts. Johnston did not come today as he had mild flu, so returned to Mind Nurture Palace and wrote out thirty more sheets of characters Prosperity and Longevity. Read papers, ate at four, bed at six. Read *Anthology of Ancient Literature* in bed: very interesting.

My tutor Lu Jun-hsiang, a Kiangsu man, was a former Grand Secretary who died before he had been teaching me for a year. Yi Ko Tan, who taught me Manchu for over nine years, was a Manchu of the Main White Banner who had qualified in the palace examination as a translator of Manchu. Chen Pao-shen, a Fukienese who came at the same time as Lu Jun-hsiang and Yi Ko Tan, had been a sub-chancellor of the Grand Secretariat and Vice-President of the Board of Rites; of all my tutors he was the one who was with me longest. After the death of Lu Jun-hsiang I had three more teachers of Chinese: the deputy head of the imperial academy Hsu Fang, Hanlin academician Chu Yi-fan, and Liang Ting-fen who became famous for planting trees at the tomb of Kuang Hsu.

The tutor who had the deepest influence on me was Chen Pao-shen; the next most influential was my English tutor Reginald Johnston. Chen had a considerable reputation as a scholar in his native Fukien. On passing the palace examination during the Tung Chih period he had been appointed a Hanlin academician at the age of nineteen, and after entering the Grand Secretariat he made a name for himself with his remonstrances to the empress dowager Tzu Hsi. As he did not show Chang Chih-tung's willingness to trim his sails to the political winds he was demoted five grades in 1891 and on a pretext of incompetence returned home to live in retirement for twenty years. On the eve of the 1911 Revolution he was reinstated and was appointed governor of Shansi, but before he left to take up his post he was kept at Peking as my tutor From then until I went to the Northeast he never left me. He was regarded as the most stable and careful of the Ching veterans in my entourage, and at the time I thought him the most loyal to myself and the "Great Ching". Before I regarded his caution as too much of an encumbrance to me he was the one and only authority to whom I referred all matters whether great or trivial for decision.

"Although the king is small he is a worthy Son of Heaven," was a phrase that Chen Pao-shen often quoted in approval of me, smiling till his eyes became slits behind his spectacles and stroking his thin, white beard.

I always found his conversation interesting. As I began to grow up I asked him almost every day to tell me the latest news about the Republic. When he had finished discussing this he would nearly always go on to talk about "the Tung Chih and Kuang Hsu restoration" and "the Golden Age of Kang Hsi and Chien Lung". He was, naturally enough, particularly fond of telling stories about how he had remonstrated with the empress dowager Tzu Hsi. Whenever he referred to former Ching officials who were now serving the Republic it was always with indignation as he regarded them as turncoats. He spoke as if the Revolution and the Republic were the roots of all evil, and the people associated with them were no better than brigands. "Those who defy the sages have no law; those who defy filial piety have no parents: this is the source of great disorder" was his general conclusion about everything that displeased him. He told me the story of the king of the defeated state of Yueh who slept on firewood and frequently tasted gall to remind himself of his humiliation, and explained the principle of retiring from public affairs and waiting for one's opportunity. After explaining the current situation he would almost invariably come up with this opinion: "The Republic has only been in existence for a few years, but both heaven and the people have from the beginning been angry and dissatisfied with it. Because of the great goodness and bounty of the dynasty over more than two hundred years the people think of the Ching in their hearts: heaven and the people will inevitably end by returning it to power."

Of my other tutors Chu Yi-fan liked to play mahjong all night with the result that he tended to lethargy during the day, and Liang Ting-fen was fond of telling stories about himself. I used to find the bookish air of my tutors intolerable at times; they showed nothing of the scholar's ignorance of profit, however, when I invited them to choose themselves presents from the palace's collections of antiques and art treasures. They were also expert at fishing for honours, and knew how to wheedle congratulatory scrolls out of me.

All these tutors received posthumous titles after their deaths that were the envy of the other Ching survivals. One might almost say that they got whatever they wanted out of me and that they gave me whatever they wanted to in return. My achievements under their coaching were never tested in any examination, but there was one matter — a judgement on "loyalty" — in which I gave them great satisfaction when I was eleven.

The year Prince Ching died his family submitted a request that he be granted a posthumous title, and the Household Department sent me a list of suggestions. Normally such a matter should have been discussed with the tutors, but as I was ill with flu at the time I had not gone to class, so I had to make a decision by myself. As I found the Household Department's list completely unsatisfactory I tossed it aside and wrote out a list of very offensive titles which I sent back. This brought my father over to see me, and in his stammering voice he begged me to remember that the prince belonged to the imperial family. I adamantly refused on the grounds that Prince Ching had been a traitor to the dynasty.

When I went to the schoolroom the next day and told Chen Pao-shen about the affair he was so delighted that he smiled until his eyes were mere slits, and expressed his whole-hearted approval of the way I had stood up to my father. The title finally chosen for Prince Ching was one which I originally thought insulting but which, as I found out too late, implied that I had pardoned him.

Eunuchs

No account of my childhood would be complete without mentioning the eunuchs. They waited on me when I ate, dressed and slept; they accompanied me on my walks and to my lessons; they told me stories; and had rewards and beatings from me. There were times when other people did not have to be with me, but they never left my presence. They were the main companions of my childhood; they were my slaves; and they were my earliest teachers.

While I am not sure when the employment of court eunuchs began, I do know exactly when it ended: the day on which I was dethroned for the third time at the victorious conclusion of the Second World War. This was perhaps the time when the eunuchs were fewest as there were only about ten of them left. It is said that they were most numerous during the Ming Dynasty (1368-1644), when they reached a strength of 100,000. Although there were limits set to their numbers and functions during the Ching Dynasty, there were still over three thousand at the time of the empress dowager Tzu Hsi. Most of the eunuchs fled after the 1911 Revolution, and although the Articles of Favourable Treatment specified that no more eunuchs were to be engaged the Household Department continued to take them on secretly. According to a list dating from 1922 there were still 1,137 then. Two years later, after I had ordered a mass expulsion of the eunuchs, there were about 200 left, of whom the great majority were in the service of the High Consorts and my wives (who also had nearly a hundred maids). From that time on the palace staff was made up of members of the greatly depleted palace guard or else genuinely male servants known as "attendants".

In the past there was a time of day after which there were no true males apart from the guards on duty and the men of the emperor's own family left in the Forbidden City. The duties of the eunuchs were very extensive. In addition to being in attendance at all hours, carrying umbrellas and stoves, and other such jobs their tasks, according to the *Palace Regulations,* included the following: transmitting imperial edicts, leading officials to audiences, and receiving memorials; handling official documents of the various offices of the Household Department, receiving money and grain sent by treasuries outside the palace, and keeping a fire watch; looking after the books of the library, the antiques, calligraphy, paintings, clothing, fowling-pieces, bows and arrows; keeping the ancient bronzes, the *objets de vertu,* the yellow girdles granted to meritorious officials, and fresh and dried fruit; fetching the Imperial

Physicians to attend in the various palaces, and obtaining the materials used in the palace by outside builders; burning incense before the records and precepts of the emperor's ancestors, their portraits, and the gods; checking the comings and goings of the officials of various departments; keeping the registers of the attendance of the Hanlin academicians and of the watches of the officers of the guard; storing the imperial seals; recording the actions of the sovereign; flogging offending eunuchs and serving women; feeding the various living creatures in the palace; sweeping the palace buildings and keeping the gardens tidy; checking the accuracy of the chiming clocks; cutting the emperor's hair; preparing medicine; singing opera; reciting classics and burning incense as Taoist monks in the City Temple; becoming lamas in the Yung Ho Kung as substitutes for the emperor; and many other duties.

The eunuchs in the palace fell into two main categories: Those in attendance on the empress dowager, the emperor, the empress and the imperial consorts on the one hand, and all the rest of the eunuchs on the other. They were very strictly graded and could be divided roughly into chief eunuchs, head eunuchs and ordinary eunuchs. There were chief and head eunuchs in the service of the empress dowager and the empress: the consorts only had head eunuchs. The highest rank normally ever reached by a eunuch was the third grade, but Li Lien-ying, the favourite of the empress dowager Tzu Hsi, had created a precedent for a eunuch being accorded the even higher second grade, so that Chang Chien-ho, the chief eunuch in my service, was given this honour. Other eunuchs were placed in the third to the ninth grade, and below them came the ordinary, ungraded eunuchs, of whom the very lowest in rank were those who had been sent as a punishment to work as menials in the cleaning office. The official salaries of the eunuchs were rather low, with the very highest being eight taels of silver, eight catties of rice and one string plus three hundred copper cash a month; with various legal and illegal "extras", however, their actual incomes were much higher, particularly those of the senior ones. Juan Chin-shou, for example, the deputy chief of my entourage, was so rich that he could wear a different fur gown every day in the winter, and although these gowns included a number of different sables he never wore the same one twice. The sea otter cloak that he wore on New Year's Day alone would have represented a lifetime's expenditure for a petty official. Nearly all the other chief eunuchs and many of the head eunuchs had their own private kitchens, and some even had their own "families" complete with serving women and maid-servants.

The life of the humbler eunuchs on the other hand was extremely hard; they ate poorly, had to endure beatings and other punishments and were left with nobody and nothing to support their old age. They had to live on a very meagre imperial "bounty", and if they were driven out for making some mistake they could only expect a future of begging and starvation.

The eunuchs with whom I was in the closest contact were those of the Mind Nurture Palace, particularly the junior eunuchs of the presence who dressed me and waited on me at mealtimes. They lived in two alleyways behind the Mind Nurture Palace, each of which was under a head eunuch. The eunuchs responsible for cleaning this palace were under another head. All of these eunuchs came under the control of the chief eunuch Chang Chien-ho and the deputy chief eunuch Juan Chin-shou.

When the empress dowager Lung Yu was alive she sent one of her chief eunuchs to be my *anda,* a post in which his duties included looking after me and instructing me in the palace etiquette. But I felt for him nothing of the trust and warmth that I did for Chang Chien-ho, my first teacher in fact if not in name, who was at the time an older man of about fifty with a slight hunchback. On the orders of Lung Yu he taught me to recognize characters printed large on cards and then read through elementary texts with me: the *Three Character Classic* and the *Hundred Surnames*. After I started my formal schooling he used to stand outside my bedroom and read aloud the previous day's lessons to help me to remember them. Like the chief eunuch of any emperor, he would take every opportunity to show his loyalty to me. I could often tell about the developments in the external situation from the changes of his mood, and could even judge from the tone of his voice as he read my lessons to me in the morning whether he was anxious or happy about my prospects.

Chang Chien-ho was my first travelling companion. He used to play at racing me, though of course I always won easily. I also remember that one New Year when the high consort Ching Yi invited me to go over and play dice he was banker; the number I staked my money on always won until I cleaned out the bank. He did not mind — the money was all the High Consort's.

Just like any other child I was fond of being told stories. The stories that Chang Chien-ho and many other eunuchs told me could be divided into two sorts: ghost stories about the palace and myths about "all the spirits helping the sacred Son of Heaven". According to them everything in the palace — bronze cranes, golden jars, trees, wells, stones and so on — had at some time turned into a spirit and shown its magic powers, not to mention the clay images of Kuan Yu, the god of war, and of the Taoist gods. Through these stories, which I never tired of hearing, I believed that all the ghosts and spirits tried to win the emperor's favour and that there were even some that did not succeed, which all went to show that the emperor was the most exalted creature in existence.

The eunuchs said that a bronze crane in one of the halls of the palace had a dent in its left leg because when it had turned itself into a spirit to protect the emperor Chien Lung during a trip to the south of China it had been hit by an arrow from the emperor's bow. It had been so disappointed that it had slipped back to stand in its original position in the palace. The rusty dent on its left leg was supposed to be the arrow wound. They also said that an ancient pine that grew by the Western Fish Pond in the Imperial Garden had shaded Chien Lung throughout one of these southern tours; after his return he had written a poem to it to be inscribed on a nearby wall. What this poem said was something about which the illiterate eunuch did not concern himself.

There was even a myth about the big pearl in the imperial hat. It was said that one day when Chien Lung was strolling beside a stream in the Yuan Ming Yuan Palace he noticed something gleaming in the water which disappeared when he shot at it with a fowling-piece. He had the stream dragged, and a large clam was found with this huge pearl inside. After it became a hat pearl it would often fly away by itself until a hole was bored through it on imperial orders and it was given a golden mount; then it stayed put.

When I was a child I believed all these stories implicitly, as can be seen from the following incident. Once when I was ill at the age of about seven or eight Chang Chien-ho brought me a purple pill to take. When I asked him what sort of medicine it was he said, "Your slave has just had a dream. An old man with a white beard held a pill in his hand and told me that it was a pill of immortality that he had especially brought as a humble present to the Lord of Ten Thousand Years." I was so pleased to hear this that I forgot about my own illness and, remembering the stories of the twenty-four filial sons, I took the pill to the quarters of the four High Consorts to share it with them. Chang Chien-ho must have made some sign to my four mothers as they all looked overjoyed and praised my filial piety. When I happened to go to the Imperial Dispensary to get some medicine some time later I noticed some ordinary pills which looked just like the "pill of immortality". Believe it or not, although I was a little disappointed I still believed the story about the old man with the white beard.

While making me inordinately proud of myself these stories also made me afraid of ghosts from an early age. According to the eunuchs there were ghosts and spirits in every corner of the palace. The lane behind the Lasting Peace Palace was where ghosts grabbed people by the neck; the well outside the Ching Ho Gate was the home of a swarm of she-devils, and had not a piece of iron over the gate kept them in they would have come out every day; every three years a ghost would come and drag a passer-by off one of the bridges in the lakes in the palace grounds. The more I heard such stories the more frightened I got, and the greater my fear the keener my appetite for them. From the age of about eleven I became an addict of books of stories of the supernatural (which the eunuchs bought for me) and these, combined with the incessant sacrifices to gods and Buddhist worship, the spirit dances of the *shaman* wizards and so on, made me even more afraid of ghosts and spirits, of the dark, of thunder and lightning, and of being alone in a room.

Every evening at dusk when all the people who came to the palace on business had gone away a spine-chilling call came from the Chien Ching Palace (Palace of Cloudless Heaven), the still centre of the Forbidden City: "Draw the bolts, lock up, careful with the lanterns." As the last drawn-out sounds of this died away there arose waves of ghostly responses from the eunuchs on duty in all the corners of the palace. This practice, which had been instituted by the emperor Kang Hsi to keep the eunuchs alert, filled the palace with an eerie atmosphere. I did not dare to go out of doors for the rest of the evening and felt as if all the ghosts and demons in the stories were gathered around the windows and doors.

It was not just with the intention of frightening me and pandering to me that the eunuchs used to feed me with such stories, they were extremely superstitious themselves. Chang Chien-ho was no exception, whenever he was faced with some problem he would always consult the *Record of the Jade Box* before making a decision. The ordinary eunuchs were very devout in their offerings to the "palace gods": snakes, foxes, weasels and hedgehogs. There was a great variety of other forms of worship in the palace that were carried out by the imperial house; the palace gods, however, were the protectors of the eunuchs and were not included in the offerings made by the royal family. According to the eunuchs the palace gods had been made immortals of the second grade by some emperor. A eunuch once told me that one evening when he was standing on the steps outside the Palace of Cloudless Heaven a man wearing a hat button of the Second Grade and official robes and insignia had grabbed him and thrown him down the steps: this had been one of the palace gods. The eunuchs would not eat beef, and one of them told me that if they offended this taboo the palace gods would punish them by making them rub their lips against the bark of a tree until they bled. Whenever a eunuch went into an empty hall they would shout in a loud voice "Opening the palace" before they opened the door: thus they avoided being punished for accidentally meeting a palace god. On the first and fifteenth of every month, at New Year and at other festivals they would make offerings to them, usually of eggs, dried bean curd, spirits, and cake; at the New Year and other festivals, they would also offer whole pigs and sheep as well as large quantities of fruit. For the poorly paid eunuchs of the lowest ranks their share in all this was a burden, but it was one which they gladly undertook as they hoped that the palace gods would protect them from the beating and other forms of ill-treatment from which they often suffered.

The eunuchs had many ways of augmenting their incomes. There are descriptions in plays and novels of how the emperor Kuang Hsu had to give money to Li Lien-ying, the chief eunuch of the palace of the empress dowager Tzu Hsi, as otherwise he would make things difficult for him and refuse to announce him when he went to pay his respects to Tzu Hsi. While such things as this could not have happened I did hear a great deal about how the eunuchs used to extort money from high officials. At the time of Emperor Tung Chih's marriage the Household Department missed out one part of the palace in a distribution of bribes. On the wedding day the eunuchs of the section that had been overlooked sent for an official of the Household Department saying that a pane of glass in one of the windows of the palace in question was cracked. As a Household Department official he was not allowed to mount the terrace of the palace unless he had been specially summoned, so he could only see the crack from a distance. He was terrified, as he would be in very deep water if Tzu Hsi heard that there was something as ill-omened as a broken window on the wedding day. The eunuchs then said that there was no need to go and look for a workman as they could discreetly change the pane themselves. Although he realized that this was a racket the Household Department man had no option but to send over a sum of money; and as soon as this was done the window was repaired. This was not very difficult as the "crack" in the glass was only a strand of hair stuck on to it.

When Chung Lun, the father of Shih Hsu, was comptroller of the Household Department he once failed to distribute enough bribes. One of the eunuchs who was dissatisfied with his portion lay in wait for him one day when he was going to an audience with the Empress Dowager and deliberately threw a basinful of water out of a room and drenched his sable jacket. The eunuch pretended to be distraught and begged to be punished. Chung Lun, knowing that he was in no position to make a scene as the Dowager was waiting to see him, desperately begged the eunuch to think of some way out. The eunuch produced another sable jacket, saying, "This humble place of ours would be very grateful to be able to share in your good fortune; we know you will be very bountiful." The eunuchs always kept a complete range of court clothing to be hired out at short notice to officials. Chung Lun had no choice but to submit to this extortion and pay a very considerable "rental".

A former official of the Household Department told me that when I got married my chief eunuch Juan Chin-shou (who had replaced Chang Chien-ho) extorted a sizable sum of money from them. As the Department had been ordered by me to keep the expenses of the wedding within a limit of 360,000 taels there had been little left over above the actual costs for the eunuchs, so that the chief eunuch blocked the whole plan. One of the officials of the Household Department had to go to Juan Chin-shou's quarters to intercede with him, but his pleas and flattery were of no effect until he accepted Juan's way of doing things.

But I believe that Chang Chien-ho and Juan Chin-shou were no comparison with Chang Yuan-fu, the chief eunuch of the empress dowager Lung Yu. When I was in Tientsin he was living there too in a magnificent mansion in the British concession in the style of a warlord with several concubines and a host of servants. One of his concubines fled to the police station of the British concession to escape his cruelty; but such was the miraculous power of his wealth that so far from protecting her the police station sent her back to that hellish household. He had her beaten to death, but nobody dared touch him.

My Nurse

In the journal of my actions and utterances kept by my tutor Liang Ting-fen there is an entry for February 21, 1913:

His Majesty frequently beats the eunuchs; he has had seventeen flogged recently for minor offences. His subject Chen Pao-shen and others remonstrated but His Majesty did not accept their advice.

That goes to show how by the age of eleven flogging a eunuch was a part of my daily routine. My cruelty and love of wielding my power were already too firmly set for persuasion to have any effect on me.

Whenever I was in a bad temper or feeling depressed the eunuchs would be in for trouble; and their luck was also out if I was in high spirits and wanted some sort of amusement. In my childhood I had many strange tastes, and apart from playing with camels, keeping ants, rearing worms, and watching fights between dogs and bulls I took the greatest delight in playing unkind tricks on people. Long before I learnt how to make the Administrative Bureau beat people many a eunuch came to grief through my practical jokes. Once when I was about seven or eight I had a brainwave: I wanted to see whether those servile eunuchs were really obedient to the "divine Son of Heaven". I picked on one of them and pointed at a piece of dirt on the floor. "Eat that for me," I ordered, and he really knelt down and ate it. Another time an aged eunuch almost died as a result of my soaking him with a fire pump.

Growing up as I did, with people pandering to my every whim and being completely obedient to me, I developed this taste for cruelty. Although my tutors tried to dissuade me from it with their talk about the "way of compassion and benevolence", at the same time they acknowledged my authority and taught me about that authority. No matter how many stories they told me about illustrious sovereigns and sage rulers of history I still remained the emperor and "different from ordinary people", so that their advice had little effect.

The only person in the palace who could control my cruelty was my nurse Mrs. Wang. Although she was completely illiterate and incapable of talking about the "way of compassion and benevolence" or illustrious sovereigns and sage rulers of history, I could not disregard the advice she gave me.

Once I was so pleased with a puppet show given by one of the eunuchs that I decided to reward him with a cake; then an evil inspiration came to me. I opened up a bag filled with iron filings that I used for doing exercises and put some of them into the cake. When my nurse saw what I was doing she said to me, "Master, who will be able to eat those filings?"

"I want to see what he looks like when he eats the cake."

"But he'll break his teeth. If he breaks his teeth he won't be able to eat anything, and if he can't eat anything then where will he be?"

I could see that she was right, but I did not want to miss my fun, so I said, "I just want to see him breaking his teeth this once." Nurse then suggested that I put dried lentils in instead as it would be great fun when he bit them. Thus she saved that eunuch from disaster.

One time when I was playing with an air-gun, shooting lead pellets at the eunuchs' quarters and making little holes in the paper of their windows, I was really enjoying myself. Then somebody sent for my nurse to come to the eunuchs' rescue.

"Master, there are people in there. You'll hurt someone, if you shoot into the house!"

Only then did it occur to me that there might be people in the room and that they might get injured. My nurse was the only person who ever told me that other people were just as human as myself. I was not the only person to have teeth: other people had them too. Mine were not the only teeth not made for biting iron filings. Just as I had to eat so did others get hungry when they did not eat. Other people had feelings; other people would feel the same pain as I would if they were hit by air-gun pellets. This was all common knowledge which I knew as well as anybody; but in that environment I found it rather hard to remember it as I never would consider others, let alone think of them in the same terms as myself. In my mind others were only my slaves or subjects. In all my years in the palace I was only reminded by my nurse's homely words that other men were the same as myself.

I grew up in my nurse's bosom, being suckled by her until I was eight, and until then I was as inseparable from her as a baby from its mother. When I was eight the High Consorts had her sent away without my knowledge. I would gladly have kept her in exchange for all four of my mothers in the palace, but no matter how I howled they would not bring her back. I see now that I had nobody who really understood humanity around me once my nurse had gone. But what little humanity I learnt from her before the age of eight I gradually lost afterwards.

After my wedding I sent people to find her and sometimes had her to stay with me for a few days. Towards the end of the "Manchukuo" period I brought her to Changchun and supported her there until I left the Northeast. She never once took advantage of her special position to beg any favours. She had a mild nature and never quarrelled with anybody; on her comely face there was always a slight smile. She did not talk much and was often silent. If someone else did not take the initiative in talking with her she would just smile without saying a word. When I was young I used to find these smiles of hers rather strange. Her eyes seemed to be fixed on something far, far in the distance, and I often wondered if she had seen something interesting in the sky outside of the window or in a picture hanging on the wall. She never spoke about her own life and experiences. After my special pardon I visited her adopted son and found out what suffering and humiliation the "Great Ching Dynasty" had inflicted on this woman who suckled a "Great Ching Emperor" with her own milk.

She was born in 1887 to a poor peasant family named Chiao in a village of Jenchiu County in Chihli (now Hopei Province). There were three other people in her family: her parents and a brother six years older than herself. The fifty-year-old father rented a few *mou* of low-lying land which was parched when it did not rain and flooded when it did. What with rents and taxes they did not get enough to eat even in good years. In 1890 there were disastrous floods in northern Chihli and her family had to leave their village as refugees. Her father thought of abandoning her several times during their wanderings, but he always put her back into one of the baskets slung from his carrying pole. The other basket contained the tattered clothes and bedding that was all the property they had in the world. They did not have a single grain of food. When she later told her adopted son about how she had been in such danger of being abandoned she had not a word of complaint against her father; she only repeated that he had been hungry for so long that he could no longer carry her. He had not been able to beg a scrap of food on their journey as everyone they met had been reduced to more or less the same state.

Finally the two parents with their son of nine and daughter of three managed to drag themselves to Peking. They had originally planned to take refuge in the house of a eunuch who was a relative of theirs, but when he refused to see them, they had to drift round the streets as beggars. Peking was full of tens of thousands of refugees who slept in the streets moaning with hunger and cold. At this very time the court was carrying out large-scale building at the Summer Palace and my family was spending money like dirt on my grandfather Prince Chun's funeral. Meanwhile the victims of the floods, whose sweat and blood had provided that money, were on the brink of death and selling their own children. The Chiao family wanted to sell their daughter but could find no buyer. The prefect of Shuntienfu opened a congee kitchen as a measure to prevent disturbances and so they were able to stay for a while. A barber took on the nine-year-old boy as an apprentice, and this enabled them to last out the winter, albeit with difficulty.

With the coming of spring the refugees thought of their land and faced the prospect that the congee kitchen would soon close, so they drifted off home again. Back in the village the Chiaos spent several more cold and hungry years, and in 1900 the allied armies of the foreign powers devastated the district. The daughter of the family was now a girl of thirteen, and she fled again to Peking where she stayed with her brother the barber. But he was unable to support her, so when she was sixteen she was half sold and half married to a yamen runner named Wang. Her husband developed tuberculosis, but lived a rather loose life. After three years as a downtrodden slave she gave birth to a daughter, shortly after which her husband died, leaving his wife, daughter and parents destitute.

This was just about the time that I was born, and the household of Prince Chun was looking for a wet-nurse for me. She was chosen from among twenty applicants for her healthy and pleasant appearance and the richness of her milk. For the sake of the wages with which she could support her parents-in-law and her daughter she accepted the most degrading conditions: she was not allowed to return home or to see her own child, she had to eat a bowl of unsalted fat meat every day, and so on. For two ounces of silver a month a human being was turned into a dairy cow.

In the third year in which she was my nurse her own daughter died of malnutrition, but my family kept this news from her lest it should affect the quality of her milk.

In the ninth year a woman servant quarrelled with a eunuch and the High Consorts decided to expel them and my nurse as well. This docile and long-suffering woman, who had borne everything in those nine years with a slight smile and a set stare, only then discovered that her own child had long been dead.

CHAPTER THREE

□■□

FROM THE FORBIDDEN CITY TO THE JAPANESE LEGATION

Chapter Three covers the first thirteen years after the dynasty lost power in 1912. Until 1924 the charades described in the previous chapter went on being played while the Republic ran its undistinguished course. Its first regular president, the Yuan Shih-k'ai who had organized the Ch'ing abdication, was never a convinced republican. The Ch'ing had hoped that he would restore them to power; but it gradually became clear that he wanted the throne for himself. Yuan's imperial dreams were cut short by his death in 1916, and the next year Ch'ing hopes of a restoration were briefly fulfilled when a loyalist general, Chang Hsun, used his troops to stage a restoration that lasted only a few days, but probably meant rather more to the eleven-year-old P'u Yi than he admits in these pages.

Chang Hsun's fiasco was not the end of the Ch'ing court's hopes that one or other of the Republic's succession of presidents and premiers, most of whom had served in the Ch'ing army or civil service, would bring P'u Yi back to power. Given the mess that the Republic was in, a restoration was not unthinkable. It was with such hopes still alive that P'u Yi took an empress and a consort in five days of magnificent but empty ceremony late in 1922. Other sources allude to an unspecified physical deficiency that prevented these, like the rest of his marriages, from being consummated. A more important change in his life came with the arrival in 1919 of Reginald Johnston, the district officer and magistrate of the British-leased territory of

Weihaiwei in Shantung, who was seconded by the Colonial Office to be P'u Yi's tutor. Even from the carefully worded account that follows on pp. 108–16 it is obvious that P'u Yi felt both respect and affection for his Scottish teacher; and Johnston gives the impression in his book Twilight in the Forbidden City that he held his pupil in high esteem.

When Feng Yü-hsiang, a war-lord with some revolutionary pretensions, changed sides in one of the squalid civil wars and occupied Peking in 1924, he cancelled all the Ch'ing court's privileges and expelled them from the palace. P'u Yi, no longer the protégé of the Republic, moved first to his father's house (the Northern Mansion) and then to the Japanese Legation, thus beginning twenty-one years under the patronage, later to become the control, of Japan.

The Yuan Shih-kai Period

It was a peculiarity of morning in the Forbidden City that deep in the palace one could sometimes hear the sounds of the outside world. You could make out the cries of pedlars quite distinctly, as well as the rumbling of the wooden wheels of heavy carts and, at times, sounds of soldiers singing. The eunuchs used to call this phenomenon the "city of sounds". After I left the Forbidden City I often used to recall the "city of sounds" and the strange images it conjured up for me. What made the deepest impressions were the military bands that sometimes could be heard playing in the neighbouring palace of the President of the Republic. "Yuan Shih-kai has been eating," the chief eunuch Chang Chien-ho said to me once. "He has music at mealtimes, which is even grander than Your Majesty."

From the way he screwed his face up it was clear that he felt very indignant. Even though I was only about eight at the time I could detect the touch of sadness in his voice. The sound of the bands brought the most humiliating picture to my mind: Yuan Shih-kai sitting there with even more dishes spread in front of him than the Empress Dowager, and an army of servants waiting on him, making music for him and fanning him.

There was another "city of sounds" in which I became more and more interested as I grew older, and which I heard about from my tutors: the rumours about my restoration.

Restoration, in the language of the Forbidden City, was "recovery of the ancestral heritage"; in the language of the former officials of the Ching it was "the glorious return of the old order" or "returning government to the Ching". Activities with this aim in view did not begin with my brief restoration in 1917, nor did they end with my flight to the Japanese Legation in 1924. One would be safe in saying that they did not cease for a day from the abdication proclamation in 1912 to the establishment of the "Empire of Manchukuo" in 1934.[1] At first I played my role under the direction of adults, but later I was able to act on my own initiative, guided by my class instincts. In my childhood my tutors were my directors, and behind them there were of course the senior officials of the Household Department and my father, who supervised the affairs of the imperial house with the consent of the President of the Republic. Although their fervour was not a whit less than that of anyone outside the palace, I gradually came to understand that they had not got the real power to bring about a restoration; they even realized this themselves. Comical though it may seem, the Forbidden City pinned its hopes on the very men who ruled the country in place of the Ching. The first object of these illusions was President Yuan Shih-kai, for all that he did to arouse the palace's resentment.

On December 31, 1912 my tutor Chen Pao-shen came into the schoolroom, sat down, and, instead of taking up his red brush to punctuate our text, looked at me for a moment with a quizzical smile before saying:

"Tomorrow is New Year's Day by the Western calendar, and the Republic is going to send someone over to convey greetings to Your Majesty. He will be the representative of their president."

I cannot remember whether this was the first time that he acted as my political director, but it was the first time I had seen him in one of the rare moments when he looked pleased with himself. He told me that when I received this formal visitor from the Republic I should treat him as I would the minister of a foreign country. I would not have to say anything and Shao Ying, the Comptroller of the Household Department, would be there to look after everything; all I would have to do would be to sit behind the dragon table and observe the proceedings.

---

[1] Strictly speaking, the restoration movement did not come to an end then as some people worked for the establishment of a "Later Ching" after the Japanese invasion of north China. As their Japanese masters did not approve, their efforts came to nothing.

The next day I was dressed in the full imperial regalia of golden dragon coat and gown, hat with a pearl button, pearl necklace, and I sat solemnly on the throne in the Cloudless Heaven Palace. A Minister of the Presence stood on either side of me, and beside them were Companions of the Presence and sword-bearing imperial bodyguards. Chu Chi-chien, the envoy of President Yuan, entered the hall and bowed to me from a distance, advanced a few more steps, bowed again, came up to my throne dais, made a third and very low bow; then he delivered his congratulatory address. When he had finished Shao Ying ascended the throne dais and knelt before me. I took the reply that had been written out beforehand from a wooden box covered with yellow silk and handed it to Shao Ying, who stood up to read it to the envoy. Then he gave it to Chu Chi-chien, who bowed once again and withdrew. The ceremony was over.

The change in the atmosphere was even more marked the next morning. Chang Chien-ho's voice rang clear as he read the previous day's lessons to me, and in the schoolroom my tutor Chen Pao-shen twirled his white beard into a ball and wagged his head as he said, "The Articles of Favourable Treatment are stored in the national archives and recognized by all the powers. Even that president of theirs can't flout them."

Not long after this the President sent envoys to convey his congratulations on my birthday, which falls on the 13th of the first month in the Chinese calendar. These attentions from Yuan Shih-kai encouraged those princes and former Ching officials who had been lying low throughout the first year of the Republic to put on their robes with official insignia and to wear their red hat buttons and peacock feathers; some of them even went so far as to revive the practice of having outriders to clear the way and a retinue crowding around them when they went through the streets. The northern gate of the palace and the Forbidden City were bustling with activity for a while. In the first year of the Republic these people had nearly all come to the palace in ordinary clothes and only changed into court dress after their arrival, but from the beginning of the second year they dared to go along the street in full imperial costume.

The birthday and then the death of the empress dowager Lung Yu in 1913 were the occasions when the splendour of the old days was fully restored. Lung Yu's birthday was on March 15 and she died seven days later. Yuan Shih-kai sent Liang Shih-yi, the head of his secretariat, to congratulate her on her birthday; in his official letter he wrote solemnly, "The President of the Great Republic of China writes to Her Majesty the Great Ching Empress Dowager Lung Yu." After this envoy had gone Chao Ping-chun, the prime minister, arrived with the whole of the cabinet to pay his respects.

Yuan Shih-kai's reaction to the death of Lung Yu was even more impressive: he himself wore a black armband; he ordered that flags were to be flown at half-mast throughout the country and that civil and military officials were to wear mourning for 27 days; and he sent the whole cabinet to pay their last respects to her. A so-called National Memorial Assembly was held in the Palace of Supreme Harmony with the Head of the Senate as master of ceremonies, and a similar meeting conducted by the army at which another of Yuan's trusted henchmen, General Tuan Chi-jui, presided. In the Forbidden City men in black court robes and Western dress came and went side by side to the sound of the wails of the eunuchs. The members of the royal family and the nobility, who had been ordered to wear mourning for 100 days, were beaming with delight. What gave them most pleasure was the presence of Hsu Shih-chang from Tsingtao and his acceptance of the honour conferred on him by the Ching house of wearing a peacock feather. After the Ching abdication this Grand Tutor of the Ching house had fled to the German-occupied Tsingtao as a refugee. I shall have something to say later about the significance of his arrival in Peking.

Before the obsequies for Lung Yu were over the expedition against Yuan Shih-kai that was known as the "second revolution" started in the south of China and ended not many days later in Yuan's victory. After this Yuan surrounded the National Assembly with his military police and forced it to elect him as full president (instead of acting president as he had been before). He sent a report to me saying that he had previously organized a provisional Republican government in obedience to the edict of the empress dowager Lung Yu and that he had now been elected full president, thanks to the regard for the common good of the "Great Ching Empress Dowager Lung Yu" and the "Great Ching Emperor". He was going to lead the people to good government and order, and strictly observe the Articles of Favourable Treatment to console Lung Yu's spirit in heaven.

Many of the veteran officials changed their views on Yuan Shih-kai. They said that Yuan had only agreed to a republic as a trick to defeat the South, that the term used for my abdication might really only mean a temporary retirement, and that when he referred to "running" a republic it meant that it was only an experiment. Indeed, such was the mood of the time that when the cabinet came to the funerals of the emperor Kuang Hsu and the empress dowager Lung Yu the Republican premier changed into court mourning robes and performed the ninefold kotow before the coffins. When my tutor Liang Ting-fen saw that the Republic's foreign minister, who had been a Ching official, was still in Western dress he upbraided him to his face and made him admit that he was less than nothing.

When 1914, the third year of the Republic, began there was a feeling that this was to be the year of restoration. One thing after another made the Ching loyalists more and more excited: Yuan Shih-kai sacrificed to Confucius, reverted to using feudal administrative titles, established an institute to write an official history of Ching, and promoted former officials of the Ching. What most dazzled them was the appointment of Chao Erh-sun, a former Ching Viceroy of the Northeastern Provinces, as head of the Institute for Ching History. My tutor Chen and others regarded him as a turncoat, but he said of himself, "I am a Ching official, I edit the Ching history, I eat the Ching's rice, and I do the Ching's business." Lao Nai-hsuan, a former vice-minister of education and chancellor of the Metropolitan College under the Ching who had taken refuge in Tsingtao, openly advocated in an article that government should be handed back to the Ching and urged Hsu Shih-chang in a letter to persuade Yuan Shih-kai to do this. Hsu Shih-chang, then both a

Grand Tutor of the Ching house and Secretary of State of the Republic, showed Lao Nai-hsuan's article to Yuan Shih-kai, and Yuan invited Lao to come to Peking as an adviser. Other writers too were advocating a Ching restoration, and there was even said to be a bandit in Szechuan known as Thirteenth Brother who wore Ching court dress and rode in a green wool-covered litter with all the airs of an elder statesman of the late dynasty, waiting to enjoy his share of the fruits of restoration.

In the Forbidden City there was no more talk of moving out to the Summer Palace as there had been shortly after the abdication. To be on the safe side, Shih Hsu, the cautious head of the Household Department, went to see Yuan Shih-kai, who was his sworn brother, and brought back some even more exciting news. Yuan had said to him, "Don't you see, brother, that these articles were just made to cope with the southerners? The imperial ancestral temple is in the Forbidden City, so how could it do for His Majesty to move? Besides, who could live in the palace if His Majesty didn't?" I was told about this a long time later by a man who had worked in the Household Department; in those days Shih Hsu and my father never discussed such matters with me directly, and would only do so through my tutor Chen Pao-shen when it was necessary. My tutor's line at the time was, "By the look of things that president of theirs still gives special treatment to the Great Ching. The Articles of Favourable Treatment are stored in the national archives. . . ."

Chen Pao-shen always seemed to leave something unsaid. Looking back on it now, it would seem to be an indication of his "cautious" attitude. The optimism in the Forbidden City in those days was undoubtedly cautious and reserved compared with that of some of the veterans of the Ching outside the palace. Of course, many of Yuan Shih-kai's actions — from his open references to not forgetting Lung Yu's "spirit in heaven" to his secret assurance that "His Majesty" would not have to leave the imperial palace and ancestral temple — gave rise to a number of illusions inside the Forbidden City; but this was as far as they expected him to go, so that the excitement of the palace had to be partly concealed.

The change in the political climate in Peking at the end of what had at first been called the "year of restoration" showed that this reserve had been justified.

The change in the political climate started when an official of the Republic's Inspectorate proposed that the rumours about a restoration should be investigated. Yuan Shih-kai instructed the Home Ministry to "examine and deal with" the case, and as a result Sung Yu-jen, one of the advocates of the Ching restoration, was sent back to his hometown under an escort provided by the army command. This news caused a panic in some circles: no more was heard about returning the Ching to power, and Lao Nai-hsuan decided not to leave his refuge in Tsingtao and come to Peking to take the post as adviser that Yuan had offered him. But there was still considerable confusion: on the document about the investigation of restoration activities Yuan had written the enigmatic words "Rumours about a restoration are severely prohibited, but do not go into them too thoroughly", and when Sung Yu-jen was sent back to his hometown Yuan sent him 3,000 Mexican dollars and arranged that all the government yamens on his route should feast him; thus it was not clear whether Sung was being punished or rewarded. In 1915, the fourth year of the Republic Frank J. Goodnow,[1] an American adviser in the office of President Yuan, published an article in which he maintained that a Republican system was not suited to Chinese conditions. After this came the appearance of the Chou An Hui (Society for the Preservation of Peace), an organization entirely under the control of Yuan Shih-kai which recommended that Yuan should become the emperor of China. The type of restoration that Yuan had in mind was now clear for everyone to see, and now that this was so obvious the atmosphere in the Forbidden City changed markedly.

It was at this time that I heard military bands playing in the presidential palace. The three great halls in the southern part of

---

[1] Goodnow had been a professor of Columbia University in America. This article of his, entitled "On Republic and Monarchy", laid the theoretical foundation for Yuan Shih-kai's monarchy by asserting such nonsense as "a monarchy is better suited than a republic to China".

the imperial palace were then being renovated and one could get a clear view of the painters at work on their scaffolding from the top of the steps of the Mind Nurture Palace in which I lived. The eunuch Chang Chien-ho told me that these were preparations for Yuan Shih-kai's accession to the throne. Later Pu Lun, a member of the royal clan, submitted a petition to Yuan in the name of the imperial house and the eight banners requesting him to take the throne. Pu Lun was rewarded with the title of prince of the first rank and sent to the palace to demand the weapons carried in imperial processions and the imperial seals from the High Consorts. This news was both mortifying and frightening to me as although my tutor Chen Pao-shen would not say so in as many words I knew the old saying that "there are neither two suns in the sky nor two rulers in the country". When Yuan made himself emperor he was not likely to tolerate my continued existence as a superfluous sovereign. There were too many historical examples pointing the other way: had not the Grand Historian of antiquity counted that "in the Spring and Autumn Period (770 to 475 B.C.) there were thirty-six cases of monarchs being killed."

Everyone in the palace was passionately concerned about the activities in the three great halls. Whenever people walked across the courtyard they would take an anxious look in that direction to see whether the work of painting and renovation with which their fate was so closely bound was finished yet. The High Consorts would burn incense and pray every day to the tutelary god of the Ching Dynasty to lend them aid. The processional weapons were hastily handed over but the imperial seals were not taken away as they were inscribed in both the Han and the Manchu languages and thus unsuitable for Yuan's purposes.

The big change in the schoolroom was that the tutors became very polite to my fellow-student Yu Chung as he was the son of Yuan Shih-kai's protégé Pu Lun. One day when Yu Chung was out of the schoolroom on a visit to the High Consorts' quarters, Chen Pao-shen looked out of the windows to make sure that there was not anybody outside, produced a piece of paper, and said to me furtively:

"Your subject made a divination last night. Please look at what it omened, Your Majesty."

I took the paper, which read "My enemy has a sickness; he is not able to approach me. Auspicious." Chen explained that it meant that my enemy Yuan Shih-kai faced a bleak future and would be unable to endanger me. This was a good omen. In addition to making this divination by the trigrams of the *Book of Changes* he had scorched the tortoise shell and consulted the milfoil and they had given favourable omens too. He told me this so that I could stop worrying. The old fellow had used all the methods of divination of the primitive society of antiquity to ascertain my fate. He announced his happy conclusion that the nefarious Yuan could not come to a good end and that the Articles of Favourable Treatment were inviolable.

Activity by my tutors, my father and the Household Department to protect my position and the Articles of Favourable Treatment was not confined to consulting the oracles, and though I was told nothing about it officially I was not completely in the dark. They made a deal with Yuan Shih-kai by which the Ching house would support Yuan as emperor and he would observe the Articles. Documents to this effect were exchanged, including an assurance in Yuan's own handwriting that he would observe the Articles and incorporate them into his constitution. It was even arranged that I would take one of his daughters as my empress, but before any of these agreements could be put into effect Yuan died in June 1916, after only 83 days as emperor, with a storm of opposition ringing in his ears.

The Restoration of 1917

The news of Yuan Shih-kai's death was received with great rejoicing in the Forbidden City. The eunuchs rushed hither and thither spreading the news, the High Consorts went to burn incense to the tutelary god, and there were no lessons that day in the Yu Ching Palace.

New opinions were expressed in the palace.

"Yuan died because he wanted to usurp the throne."

"It's not that a monarchy is impracticable, it's just that the people want their old sovereign."

"Yuan Shih-kai was different from Napoleon III: he had no such ancestry on which to rely for support."

"It would be much better to return things to the old sovereign than to have a Mr. Yuan as emperor."

All these voices were in tune with the saying of my tutor that "because of the great goodness and rich benefit conferred by our dynasty the people of the whole country are thinking of the old order."

I was now old enough to be interested in the papers, and it was not many days after Yuan's death before they were full of reports of "Failure of Rising by Imperial Clan Party" and "Mongol and Manchu Bandit Threat". From these news items I learnt that four Manchu noblemen who had been open opponents of the Republic from the beginning still were acting on my behalf. Of these four one had taken refuge in a foreign concession in Tientsin and the others were staying in the Japanese-leased Lushun and Talien and, acting through Japanese *ronin,* were co-operating with Japanese militarists and financiers in armed activities for a restoration. The most important of these was Shan Chi, Prince Su, who had got a million yen from the financier Ohira Kihachiro and had Japanese officers training an army of several thousand Manchu and Mongol bandits. They started making trouble after the death of Yuan Shih-kai. One group of them under the Mongol noble Babojab came close to Changchiakou (Kalgan) and was quite dangerous until Babojab was killed by one of his subordinates. Even at the height of the crisis, while "loyalist" and Republican troops were fighting in various places in the Northeast, the Republic and the "little court" continued their exchanges of courtesy visits. The rising excitement in the Forbidden City after the death of Yuan Shih-kai was not influenced by Babojab and Shan Chi's armed rising, and neither was it affected by their defeat.

After Yuan's death, Li Yuan-hung succeeded him as president with Tuan Chi-jui as premier. The palace sent a representative to congratulate President Li and Li Yuan-hung returned to the palace the imperial processional weapons that Yuan had taken. Some of the Ching princes, nobles and senior officials were even given Republican decorations, including a few who had been in hiding during Yuan Shih-kai's time. The Household Department was busier than ever conferring such honours as posthumous titles, the permission to ride a horse in the Forbidden City or wear a peacock's feather; bringing girls for the High Consorts to select ladies-in-waiting from; and secretly recruiting more eunuchs despite the prohibition in the Articles of Favourable Treatment. And of course there were all sorts of contacts being made that I did not know about, from private dinners to public banquets for the members of the Republic's parliament.

In short, the Forbidden City was as active as it had been in the old days; and with Chang Hsun's audience with me in 1917 the restoration movement reached a climax.

I had not received many people in audience before then and they had all been Manchus. Those parts of my day that were not devoted to studying in the Yu Ching Palace or reading newspapers in the Mind Nurture Palace I mostly spent playing. I was very excited to see how many people wearing court clothes were always coming and going in the palace; the news of the rising of the "loyalist" troops of Prince Su and Babojab thrilled me even more, and their defeat naturally depressed me. But generally speaking I soon forgot about such matters; and while I could not help worrying about the flight of Prince Su to Lushun and his uncertain fate, the highly amusing sight of a camel sneezing was enough to make me forget all about his predicament. With my father, my tutors and my ministers to look after things what need was there for me to concern myself? When my tutors told me about any matter it meant that everything had already been discussed and agreed. So it was on June 16, 1917.

Chen Pao-shen, who had recently been granted the title of "Grand Guardian", and Liang Ting-fen, a newly appointed tutor, came into the schoolroom together that day; and before they had sat down Chen Pao-shen said, "Your Majesty will have no lessons today. A high official is coming for an audience with Your Majesty, and a eunuch will be here to announce him very shortly."

"Who is he?"

"Chang Hsun, the Viceroy of Kiangsi, Kiangsu and Anhwei and Governor of Kiangsu."

"Chang Hsun? The Chang Hsun who won't cut his queue off?"

"Yes, that's the man," said Liang Ting-fen, nodding in approval. "Your Majesty's memory is very good." Liang missed no opportunity to flatter me.

This had in fact been no feat of memory as Chen Pao-shen had told me the story of Chang Hsun not long before. From the beginning of the Republic he and his troops had kept their queues. Yuan Shih-kai owed his successful crushing of the "second revolution" in 1913 to the capture of Nanking by his pigtailed soldiers. When in the sack of the city Chang Hsun's men had mistakenly injured some of the personnel of the Japanese consulate he went and apologized to the Japanese consul in person and promised to pay full damages. He announced national mourning for the death of the empress dowager Lung Yu in a telegram of condolences and went on to say that "all we Republican officials are the subjects of the Great Ching". After the death of Yuan Shih-kai another telegram of Chang's was published in the press in which he made known his political position. Its first item was "I attach the greatest importance to all of the Articles of Favourable Treatment of the Ching house". I believed that he was a loyal subject and was interested to see what he looked like.

According to the practice of the Ching house nobody else could be present when a high official was received in audience by the emperor. For this reason my tutor would have to give me some coaching and tell me what to say before I received anyone who did not come regularly. This time Chen Pao-shen told me very seriously that I must praise Chang Hsun's loyalty, that I should remember that he was the High Inspecting Commissioner for the Yangtse River and had sixty battalions of troops in the region of Hsuchow and Yenchow; I could ask him about the military situation in Hsuchow and Yenchow and was to make it very clear that I was interested in him. Finally Chen repeated two or three times, "Chang Hsun is bound to praise Your Majesty. You must remember to reply modestly so as to display Your Majesty's divine virtue."

I had tried to form a picture of what Chang Hsun looked like from the picture magazines that the eunuchs bought for me, but I had not yet succeeded when I got down from my carrying chair. Soon after I reached the Mind Nurture Palace he arrived. As I sat on the throne he knelt before me and kotowed.

"Your subject Chang Hsun kneels and pays his respects. . . ."

I waved to him to sit on a chair as the court had ended the practice of having officials report in a kneeling position. He kotowed again to thank me and then sat down. I dutifully asked him about the military situation in the Hsuchow and Yenchow area, but I did not pay any attention to his reply. I was somewhat disappointed at the appearance of this "loyal subject" of mine. He was dressed in a thin silk jacket and gown, his face was ruddy and set with very bushy eyebrows, and he was fat. The sight of his short neck made me think that but for his whiskers he would have looked like one of the eunuch cooks: he was far from perfect. I looked carefully to see if he had a queue and indeed he did: a mottled grey one.

Then he started to talk about me and, as Chen Pao-shen had expected, spoke in very respectful terms.

"Your Majesty is truly brilliant," he said.

"I am not up to much," I replied. "I am young and I know very little."

"Emperor Sheng Tsu of this dynasty (Kang Hsi) acceded to the throne when of tender years. He was only five."

"How can I be compared with my august ancestor? He was my ancestor, after all. . . ."

This audience was not much longer than an ordinary one, and he went after five or six minutes. I found his speech rather coarse and reckoned that he was probably not a second Tseng Kuo-fan:[1] I was not very excited by him. But when Chen Pao-shen and Liang Ting-fen came to me the next day beaming with smiles to tell me that Chang Hsun had praised my modesty and intelligence I was very pleased with myself. I did not ask myself why Chang had come for an audience, or why my tutors were so visibly excited, or why the Household Department had given him such lavish presents, or why the High Consorts had held a banquet for him.

About a fortnight later, on July 1, my tutors Chen Pao-shen, Liang Ting-fen and the newly arrived Chu Yu-fan came to the schoolroom together with very grave faces. Chen Pao-shen spoke first.

"Chang Hsun is here. . . ."

"Has he come to pay his respects?"·

"No, he has not just come for that. All preparations have been made and everything has been settled. He has come to bring Your Majesty back to power and restore the Great Ching."

Seeing that I was startled he went on to say, "Your Majesty must allow Chang Hsun to do this. He is asking for a mandate on behalf of the people; heaven has complied with the wishes of the people."

I was stunned by this completely unexpected good news. I stared at Chen Pao-shen in a daze, hoping that he would go on to tell me a little about how to be a "true emperor".

"There is no need to say much to Chang Hsun. All you have to do is to accept." Chen Pao-shen spoke with great confidence. "But it wouldn't do to accept at once; you must refuse at first and only finally say, 'If things are so then I must force myself to do it.' "

I returned to the Mind Nurture Palace and received Chang Hsun in audience again. What Chang Hsun said was much the same as had been written in his memorial requesting a restoration, except that it was less elegantly expressed.

------

[1] Tseng Kuo-fan (1811-72), a Han landowner and bureaucrat from Hunan, played a major role in suppressing the revolutionary Taiping Heavenly Kingdom, thus helping to save the Ching Dynasty from well-deserved destruction.

"The empress dowager Lung Yu was not prepared to inflict a disaster on the people for the sake of one family's illustrious position, so she issued a decree ordering that a republic be organized. But who would have thought it, it was run so badly that the people have no way to make a living. . . . A republic does not suit our country. . . . Only Your Majesty's restoration will save the people."

When he had finished gabbling I said, "I am too young; I have neither talent nor virtue. I could not undertake so great an office." He lavished praises on me and droned on about how Emperor Kang Hsi had come to the throne at the age of five. While he talked I thought of a question: "What about their President? Will we give him favourable treatment?"

"Li Yuan-hung has already memorialized asking that he be allowed to resign. All that is necessary is for Your Majesty to grant his request."

"Ah. . . ." Although I did not understand what was going on I thought that my tutors must have settled everything and that I had better end this audience quickly. "If things are so I must force myself to do as you say." With this I regarded myself as the emperor of the "Great Ching Empire" again.

After Chang Hsun's departure hosts of people came to kotow to me, some to pay their respects, some to thank me, and some both to thank me and pay their respects. After this a eunuch brought in a pile of nine "imperial edicts" that had already been written out. The first of these proclaimed my return to the throne, and another created a board of seven regents, including Chang Hsun and Chen Pao-shen.

Old Pekinese remember how on that morning the police suddenly told all the households in the city to hang out imperial dragon flags; the people had to improvise them with paper and paste. Then Ching clothes that had not been seen for years reappeared on the streets worn by people who looked as if they had just stepped out of their coffins. The papers brought out special issues for the restoration at a higher price than usual, so that amid the strange sights one could hear news-vendors shouting as they sold the "Edicts of Hsuan Tung", "Antiques, six cash only! This nonsense will be an antique in a few days — six cash for an antique — dead cheap."

Some of the shops outside the Chien Men Gate did a booming trade in those days. Tailors sold Ching dragon flags as fast as they could make them; the second-hand clothes shops found that newly appointed officials were struggling to get hold of Ching court dress; and theatrical costumiers were crowded with people begging them to make false queues out of horsehair. I still remember how the Forbidden City was crowded with men wearing court robes with mandarins' buttons and peacock feathers on their hats. From the back of everyone's head dangled a queue. When later the Army to Punish the Rebels approached Peking one could pick up real queues all over the place: these were said to have been cut off by Chang Hsun's pigtailed soldiery as they fled.

If those visitors to the Forbidden City had shared any of the foresight of the news-vendors about the fate of "imperial edicts" and queues they would not have got so excited in the first days of the restoration.

The princes and nobles of the royal clan were very disappointed in those few days as they did not see their personal ambitions realized. On the morrow of the restoration an "imperial edict" was issued banning them from interfering in state affairs. My father became the leader of a group of nobles who were opposed to this, and he wanted to argue this point with Chang Hsun and myself. When my tutor Chen heard this he hurried over to tell me to refuse them as it was their extreme incompetence that had brought about the abdication in 1912. I followed his advice, and before the princes had time to do anything about it the early collapse of the restored monarchy paradoxically saved them from being held responsible for its establishment.

Chen Pao-shen, who was normally a stable and sensible man, was quite carried away by the restoration, surprising me with his opposition to the princes and the violence of his views on how to deal with President Li Yuan-hung who had refused to resign when urged to by one of my tutors. The three tutors came into the Yu Ching

Palace and Chen, his face livid with anger, had burst out uncontrollably:

"Li Yuan-hung has actually dared to refuse to accept the order. Will Your Majesty please instruct him to commit suicide at once."

I was startled to hear so extreme a suggestion. "It wouldn't do at all for me to tell Li Yuan-hung to kill himself so soon after my return to the throne. Didn't the Republic give me favourable treatment?"

This was the first time that Chen Pao-shen had been openly rebuffed by me, but he was so carried away by his hatred for the President that, oblivious to everything else, he went on, "Li Yuan-hung is not only refusing to resign, he is even hanging on to the Presidential Palace, the rebellious brigand and traitor. How could you mention him in the same breath as yourself, Your Majesty?"

Seeing how determinedly I refused to follow his advice he had to drop his proposal. When an emissary went to make another attempt at persuading Li Yuan-hung he found that Li had already fled with his seals of office to the Japanese Legation.

In the first few days of the restoration I spent half of my time in the Yu Ching Palace. Although my lessons were suspended I was obliged to see my tutors as I had to follow their directions in whatever I did. For the rest of my time I looked over the "imperial edicts" that were to be issued, read the official papers of the cabinet, and received homage and salutations; apart from this I would watch ants crawling from one hole to another or tell the eunuchs of the Imperial Stables to bring out some camels for my entertainment. But before five days of this kind of life were up the bombs dropped by the aircraft of the Army to Punish the Rebels changed things completely. Nobody came to kotow to me any longer, there were no more "imperial edicts", and all my regents had disappeared except for Chen Pao-shen and one other, Wang Shih-chen.

On the day of the air-raid I was sitting in the schoolroom talking to my tutors when I heard an aeroplane and the unfamiliar sound of an explosion. I was so terrified that I shook all over, and the colour drained from my tutors' faces. With everything in chaos eunuchs hustled me over to the Mind Nurture Palace as if my bedroom were the only safe place. The High Consorts were in an even worse state, some of them lying in the corners of their bedrooms, and some of them hiding under tables. The air was filled with shouts and the whole palace was in confusion. This was the first air-raid in Chinese history and the first time a Chinese air force was used in civil war. Here are the first air-raid precautions, for what they may be worth: everyone lay down in their bedrooms and the bamboo blinds in the corridors were let down. As far as the knowledge of the eunuchs and the palace guard went, these were the wisest measures they could take. Fortunately the pilot did not mean business and gave us nothing worse than a fright, dropping only three tiny bombs about a foot long. One of them fell outside the Gate of Honouring the Ancestors (Lung Tsung Men) wounding one of the carriers of sedan-chairs; one fell into a pond in the Imperial Garden, damaging a corner of the pond; and the third fell on the roof of one of the gateways in the Western Avenue of the palace striking dread into the hearts of a crowd of eunuchs who were gambling there although it failed to explode.

Soon after this the sound of approaching gunfire was heard in the Forbidden City. Wang Shih-chen and Chen Pao-shen did not come to court and the palace had no more contact with the outside world. A little later a false report was brought from the commander of the palace guard that Tuan Chi-jui's Republican army had been defeated by Chang Hsun's men, but the next morning the news of Chang Hsun's flight to the Dutch embassy swept away the smiles of the day before.

My father and Chen Pao-shen now appeared, dejection written all over their drooping faces. Reading the abdication edict that they had drafted both frightened and saddened me, and I wept out loud. The decree ran like this:

> On the twentieth day of the fifth month of the ninth year of Hsuan Tung the Cabinet receives this Imperial Edict: Formerly we followed the memorials of Chang Hsun and others who, saying that the nation was in a state of fundamental disorder and that the people longed for the old way, advised us to resume the government. As our years are tender and we live deep in the Forbidden City we have heard

nothing about the people's livelihood and the affairs of the nation. Remembering with reverence the great benevolence and the instructions of the late August Empress Hsiao Ting Ching (Lung Yu) who yielded the government out of pity for the people, we had not the least intention of treating the world as our private property; it was only because we were asked to save the nation and the people that we forced ourselves to accede to the requests made of us and assume power.

Now yesterday Chang Hsun reported armed risings in every province, which may lead to military insurgencies in a struggle for power. Our people have been suffering hardships for years, and their state is as desperate as if they were being burned or drowned. How could we then compound their miseries with war? Thinking upon this we were disturbed and unable to rest. We therefore resolved that we would not keep this political power for ourselves and thus besmirch the living soul of the August Empress Hsiao Ting Ching by turning our back on her abundant virtue.

Let Wang Shih-chen and Hsu Shih-chang inform Tuan Chi-jui at once, that the transfer of power may be arranged and the present troubles brought to an end, so calming the people's hearts and avoiding the calamity of war.

By the command of the Emperor.

The Chieftains of the Peiyang Clique

This abdication edict was never issued. All that was published at the time was a statement of the Household Department that was quoted in an order of the President of the Republic.

By order of the President:

The Home Ministry reports that it has received the following communication from the Household Department of the Ching house:

"This day the Household Department received an Edict:

"'Formerly on the twenty-fifth day of the twelfth month of the third year of Hsuan Tung a Decree was issued by the August Empress Dowager Lung Yu in which, recognizing that the whole people were inclined towards a republic, she and the Emperor returned sovereign power to the whole country. She ordained that there should be a republic and settled that the Articles of Favourable Treatment for the Ching house should be adhered to for ever; for the past six years the Ching house has been very well treated and has never had any intention of using the political power for its own ends; what cause could it have had for going back on its word?

" 'But contrary to expectation Chang Hsun led his soldiery to occupy the palace on July 1. He fraudulently issued edicts and decrees and altered the state structure, thus disobeying the instructions of the Empress Dowager of the former dynasty. I, a child living deep in the Forbidden City, had no choice in the matter; in these circumstances I should have allowances made for me by the whole world. The Household Department has been instructed to request the Government of the Republic to make this generally known both within the country and abroad.' "

When the Ministry received this letter they thought it right to report this matter.

As it is common knowledge that Chang Hsun the traitor and usurper was the originator of the disturbances, let the details of this document be speedily proclaimed.

For general information,

Issued by the Prime Minister Tuan Chi-jui

July 17, sixth year of the Republic of China

It was through the collaboration of the three bosses of the Peiyang clique and the Forbidden City that the admission in the abdication edict that I had decided to "assume power" was changed in the Household Department's statement into Chang Hsun occupying the palace and the "child" having no choice in the matter. The man who thought out this clever formulation was the Grand Tutor Hsu Shih-chang, and it was carried out by President Feng Kuo-chang and Premier Tuan Chi-jui. The role of the Forbidden City in the restoration was glossed over, and its new activities after the failure of this attempted restoration received little attention.

As the palace was able to draw a veil over its role in the restoration public attention was focused on its unsuccessful supporters outside the Forbidden City. I was able to get a picture of what had really happened from articles I read in the press and what I was told by my tutors.

After the failure of Yuan Shih-kai's usurpation in 1916 Hsu Shih-chang and Chang Hsun had agreed that a restoration of the Ching monarchy was their only chance of resisting the southern Republicans. After Yuan's death Chang Hsun called a conference of warlords at his headquarters in Hsuchow (the "Second Hsuchow Conference") at which it was decided that the first thing was to get foreign support, particularly from Japan. When their plan met with the approval of the commander of the Japanese garrison in Tientsin, Chang Hsun established contact with the "loyalist" troops led by Babojab and Prince Su in Inner Mongolia and the Northeast. He arranged with some other warlords that they would march on Peking on the pretext of defending the capital against the "loyalist" army, but this scheme fell through when Babojab was killed by one of his subordinates.

The other leader of the restoration conspiracy, Hsu Shih-chang, tried to win the support of the Japanese cabinet for his plans, but when Chang Hsun realized that Hsu was trying to make himself regent he was furious, and the monarchist movement was split.

Meanwhile a power struggle was going on in Peking between Peiyang warlord Tuan Chi-jui, who was prime minister at the time, and President Li Yuan-hung. When Tuan was dismissed from his premiership and went to Tientsin, Chang Hsun, who had been promised the support of various other warlords and the Peiyang leaders Tuan Chi-jui and Feng Kuo-chang at his fourth Hsuchow Conference, saw this as his opportunity to lead his troops north. He tricked Li Yuan-hung into inviting him to come and mediate between him and Tuan Chi-jui. Having contacted the Peiyang chiefs in Tientsin he entered Peking and enacted his restoration on July 1.

Most of the press attributed Chang Hsun's failure to the way he monopolized power and to two other major blunders: giving only an empty title to Hsu Shih-chang and underestimating Tuan Chi-jui. Thinking that he had the Peiyang leaders in his pocket, he was astounded to hear that Tuan Chi-jui had administered an oath to his troops in Tientsin that they would "punish the rebels" and that the other local warlords had all changed sides and become "supporters of the Republic". This volte-face paid Tuan Chi-jui and

Feng Kuo-chang handsomely as the former became premier once more and the latter won the presidency.

But although the blame for the restoration was put on Chang Hsun, he was treated very leniently by the new Republican authorities as he told them that he possessed a case of incriminating documents that proved that they had originally supported his monarchist schemes. When Hsu Shih-chang became president the following year the warrant for his arrest was withdrawn.

What interested me about all these revelations was that all the chiefs of the Peiyang clique and some other leading figures in the Republic had been enthusiastic monarchists, and that they were now making Chang Hsun the scapegoat so as to protect me. They explicitly stated that the palace had been blameless. Feng Kuo-chang in his telegram announcing his support for the Army to Punish the Rebels even went so far as to say, "I was not a supporter of Republicanism in the former Ching Dynasty but the pressure of events created a republic at the time of the Revolution of 1911." Why were they covering up for the Forbidden City and announcing their own monarchist sympathies so frankly? The only conclusion I could draw was that these men were not really opposed to a restoration and that the only problem at issue was the question of who was to lead it.

From the point of view of the Forbidden City all cats whether tabby or white were good cats provided they caught mice. It made no difference to us whether a Mr. Chang or a Mr. Tuan restored the monarchy. Thus it was that when Feng Kuo-chang and Tuan Chi-jui came to power the hopes of the monarchists were focussed on these two new strong men. But the palace's schemes came to nothing when the Peiyang group split into a Chihli clique led by Feng Kuo-chang and an Anhwei one with Tuan Chi-jui at its head. In the friction between the two factions Feng lost his presidency. Although Tuan hinted to the palace through Shih Hsu, the head of the Household Department, that a restoration was still perfectly possible, Shih Hsu was now too cautious to attach much importance to the word of a man who had come to power by leading an expedition against a restoration.

Feng Kuo-chang was succeeded as president by Hsu Shih-chang. A commentary in the Shanghai *Hsin Wen Pao* shortly after the collapse of the 1917 restoration had contained a passage that made a big impact in the Forbidden City:

> Had the restoration been managed by Hsu Shih-chang it would certainly not have been so clumsily handled; had it not been the work of Chang Hsun the commanders of the Peiyang clique would have soon acknowledged themselves the emperor's subjects. . . .

Thus it was that not only I, who had satisfied my craving to be emperor for only a few brief days, but other monarchists as well were very excited at the beginning of Hsu Shih-chang's presidency. A sixty-year-old Manchu resident of Peking has told me: "When Hsu Shih-chang became president in 1918 many Manchu carriages and women's hairstyles appeared in the streets of Peking, and the houses of the nobility became very lively with noisy birthday parties, theatrical performances, and feasts. There were even amateur nobles' drama groups and clubs. . . ."

Another old gentleman of Han race explained to me, "There were three occasions after the founding of the Republic when we had 'walking ancestors'[1] in the streets of Peking. The first time was the days after the death of the empress dowager Lung Yu, the next was the period of Chang Hsun's restoration, and the last was from when Hsu Shih-chang became president to the 'Great Nuptials'.[2] This last time was when things really bustled. . . ."

Hsu Shih-chang had been a friend of Yuan Shih-kai's in the days before Yuan made his name and later became the adviser Yuan consulted before making almost any important move. It was said that Yuan and Hsu Shih-chang had held a discussion with Feng Kuo-chang, Tuan Chi-jui and others before they made the empress dowager Lung Yu give up state power in 1912. At this meeting they had agreed that as the Republican Army would have to be dealt with by cunning rather than by force they should first accept

---

[1] So called because they wore Ching court dress which made them look like the figures in ancestral portraits.

[2] My wedding.

the terms of the revolutionaries and found a republic, then wait for the revolutionary army to disintegrate and bring the emperor back to power. Hsu Shih-chang was none too pleased when Yuan Shih-kai proclaimed himself emperor in 1916. A relation of mine was once told by a nephew of Hsu Shih-chang's that Yuan came to see Hsu the very day his monarchy was abolished. When Yuan entered the reception room this nephew was in the smoking room next door and did not dare come out. From what he could catch of the conversation Hsu Shih-chang was advising Yuan to "keep to the original agreement", but he could not make out Yuan's reply. As later developments showed, Yuan either did not follow this suggestion or else died before he could put it into effect. It was, however, virtually an open secret that Hsu Shih-chang never abandoned his idea of a Ching restoration.

When Hsu became president in September 1918 he announced that he could not live in the presidential palace of his predecessors (which had originally been a part of the imperial palace) and would therefore live in his own home until a new presidential palace was built. He pardoned Chang Hsun, advocated the study of the Confucian classics, honoured Confucius, sacrificed to heaven, and gave civil and military office to members of the royal family. He referred to the Ching as the "present dynasty" in public as well as in private and spoke of me as if I were the reigning emperor.

The Household Department had helped to provide Hsu with discreet financial backing in his bid for the presidency, and after it was clear that he would get it he announced at a private dinner given for him by the senior officials of the Department that his only purpose in taking office was to "act as regent on behalf of the young monarch". He also presented Shih Hsu with a pair of scrolls inscribed with a couplet in his own handwriting which implied loyalty to me.

The people around me told me nothing at the time of these events. All I knew was that Hsu's name was always mentioned in a very hopeful way. From Hsu's coming to power onwards the Forbidden City was alive with activity: posthumous titles and permission to ride a horse in the palace seemed to have become far more desirable, and officials of the previous dynasty both true and false flocked to the palace. Although my tutors never said much about the negotiations that were going on between the palace and the president, Chen Pao-shen once remarked contemptuously in the course of a conversation, "Hsu Shih-chang still wants to be Prince Regent: it's asking a bit much. A dukedom would be enough for him." On another occasion he commented, "He originally proposed that the daughter of a senior Han official should be made empress: what was the motive behind that? You can see what sort of person he really is from the fact that he has taken office under the Republic although he is a Grand Tutor of the Ching."

From this time onwards the Forbidden City never spoke about Hsu Shih-chang again with the old enthusiasm. He was not in fact in a very strong position a year after coming to power. With the Peiyang group split into two factions he could no longer achieve much in his capacity as a chief of the Peiyang clique; he was on increasingly bad terms with Tuan Chi-jui; and in 1919 the May 4th Student Movement that shook the whole of China made them devote all their energies to trying to maintain themselves in power. No matter how loyal a monarchist he had been, there was nothing Hsu could have done to bring about a restoration. But although the palace heard less and less from Hsu it never despaired of its future completely.

Undying Hope

One day as I was riding my bicycle in the Palace Garden I nearly ran into somebody as I turned a corner. For such a thing to happen in the palace was a gross solecism, but I did not care. I turned round and was about to ride off when I saw that the man was kneeling on the ground and saying, "Your humble servant pays his respects to the Lord of Ten Thousand Years."

He was wearing a dark-coloured waistcoat of the sort the eunuchs wore, but when I looked at him more closely I noticed stubble on his chin and knew he could not be a eunuch. Riding round in circles I asked him what he was doing.

"Your servant is seeing to the electric light."

"Hm, so that's your job. You were lucky not to be knocked over just now."

"Your servant's luck is very good; today I have been able to see the true dragon, the Son of Heaven. I beg the Lord of Ten Thousand Years in his celestial bounty to grant his humble servant a title."

I was amused by his absurd request and thought of the nickname that the eunuchs had told me was given in Peking to the beggars who squatted at the ends of bridges.

"Very well, I enfeoff you as the Marquis Guarding the Bridge,"[1] I said, roaring with laughter. Little did I imagine that this title-crazy fellow would take my joke seriously and go along to the Household Department to ask for a "patent of nobility". Unfortunately I never heard what the outcome of this was.

I was often told by my tutors and the eunuchs in those days that people in the countryside used to ask "How is the Hsuan Tung Emperor?" or "Who is on the throne nowadays?" or "Would the world be at peace if the true dragon, the Son of Heaven, were sitting on the throne?" My English tutor Reginald Johnston told me that according to an article in some journal even the most deeply anti-monarchical people were disappointed in the Republic, so that it was clear that even they were changing their minds. The real reason why some people were talking about the "former Ching" was, of course, that they were sick of the disasters inflicted by warlordism. My tutors, however, used all this to prove to me that people were longing for the old order.

At the end of the era of Hsu Shih-chang one often met monarchy-struck people. There was a merchant named Wang Chiu-cheng who had made a fortune out of supplying uniforms for the armies of the Chihli clique. His ambition was to be granted the old imperial honour of being allowed to wear a yellow riding-jacket and had

---

[1] "Marquis" in Chinese is pronounced the same as the word for "monkey".

spent a considerable amount of time and money to this end. The eunuchs gave him the nickname of "the spendthrift". I do not know how he fixed it, but every New Year he would come along with the old-timers to kotow and offer tribute to me, and when he did this he always brought thick wads of banknotes which he scattered liberally wherever he went. The eunuchs were always very pleased to see him come as anyone who showed him the way, announced him, pulled aside the door-curtains, poured his tea or even spoke a few words to him would be sure to be the richer by a roll of bank-notes. And this is not even to mention the money he spent in more formal ways. In the end he achieved his ambition and was granted the "honour" of being allowed to wear a yellow jacket.

Men came to the Forbidden City every day or submitted memorials from distant places for the sake of a yellow riding-jacket, the right to say in their family registers that they held a Ching office, or a posthumous title for somebody. There was even one Liang Chu-chuan, known as Lunatic Liang, who threw himself into a pond to win with his dead body and a sodden "posthumous memorial" the title of "True and Upright". Later there were so many requests for posthumous titles that it was decided that they would only be given to people above a certain rank: otherwise the little court would have made itself look cheap. Even tighter restrictions were put on the granting of the privileges of riding a horse or being car-ried in a chair in the palace and on the distribution of scrolls in my writing. The result was that not only the Manchu nobility but even military commanders of the Republic regarded obtaining one of these as a "signal honour".

Some of the so-called new writers of the time, such as Hu Shih, had the same ideas. I had been told about this Doctor Hu Shih, the champion of writing in the vernacular language, by my tutor Johnston when I was fifteen. Johnston jeered at his line "Picnic by the river", written half in English and half in Chinese, but also said that there would be no harm in my looking at some of his writings as a part of my education. Having done so I got the idea that I would like to have a look at this modern personality. One day my curiosity prompted me to telephone him, and to my surprise he came to the palace when I invited him. I shall have more to say about this meeting later; meanwhile I would like to quote a letter that this foreignized doctor wrote to Johnston afterwards in which he revealed that his feelings were not unlike those of an old official of the Ching. One part of it read:

> I must confess that I was deeply touched by this little event. Here I was, standing and sitting in front of the last of the emperors of my country, the last representative of a long line of great monarchs.

What was rather more important was the encouragement the palace received from foreigners' opinions. Johnston used to give me quite a lot of information on this subject: according to him many foreigners thought that a restoration was the wish of the ordinary Chinese. He would read me passages from foreign newspapers, including the following one that he later quoted in his book *Twilight in the Forbidden City*. It was a part of an article from an English paper, the Tientsin *North China Daily Mail*, of September 9, 1919 entitled "Is Another Restoration Near at Hand?":

> The record of the republic has been anything but a happy one, and to-day we find North and South at daggers drawn. The only conclusion to be drawn from this is that republicanism in China has been tried and found wanting. The mercantile classes and the gentry, the back-bone of the land, are weary of all this internecine strife and we firmly believe that they would give their whole-hearted support to any form of government which would ensure peace to the eighteen provinces.
>
> It must not be forgotten that there exists a very strong phalanx of pro-monarchical people who have never become reconciled to the republican form of government, but they have kept quiet for the last few years for obvious reasons. That they are in sympathy with the present militaristic movement goes without saying and the comings and goings of some of the better known of them to various places where officials are known to congregate are not devoid of significance.
>
> The contention of those who secretly favour and hope for a successful restoration of the ex-emperor is that the republicans are destroying the country, and that means, however drastic, must be taken to bring it back to its former prosperous and peaceful condition.
>
> A reversion to a monarchy is not by any means likely to be well received in all quarters. On the contrary, it will probably meet with

considerable diplomatic opposition in more than one Legation, but even opposition of that kind is bound to evaporate if a successful *coup d'état* is brought off, as we all know that nothing succeeds like success.

Despite all the encouraging things that the foreign papers were saying, it was of course the men with guns in their hands who directly controlled the fate of the little court. As the *North China Daily Mail* pointed out, "the comings and goings . . . to places where [military] officials are known to congregate are not devoid of significance." I remember how in the second half of 1919 the little court had close relations with warlords other than those of the old Peiyang group. The first of these was High Inspecting Commissioner Chang Tso-lin, the head of the Fengtien clique.

The palace's dealings with Chang Tso-lin had started when my father received a sum of money sent from Fengtien (modern Liaoning in northeast China where Chang Tso-lin's power was centred) as payment for some estates there that had been the property of the emperor. My father wrote a letter of thanks and the Household Department despatched a high-ranking official with some antiques from the palace collection — a picture by Tung Yuan of the Southern Tang Dynasty (937-975) and a pair of porcelain vases with an inscription by the emperor Chien Lung — as a present to Chang Tso-lin from my father. Chang sent his sworn brother Chang Ching-hui, then the second in command of the Fengtien army and later the premier of "Manchukuo", to accompany our envoy back to Peking and convey his gratitude to my father. This marked a strengthening of the relationship between the Mansion of Prince Chun acting on behalf of the court and the Fengtien army.

Three senior officers of the Fengtien army had come to Peking in 1917 to participate in Chang Hsun's restoration and two others were now given the right to ride a horse in the Forbidden City. When the father of divisional commander Chang Tsung-chang, one of the two, celebrated his eightieth birthday in Peking my father went along to congratulate him. In 1920 the Fengtien clique aligned itself with the Chihli clique to defeat the Anhwei clique and when the Chihli chief Tsao Kun (the successor to the dead Feng Kuo-chang) and

Chang Tso-lin entered Peking the little court sent Shao Ying, an official of the Household Department, to welcome them. The Mansion of Prince Chun became more active than ever. A rumour that Chang Tso-lin was going to come to the palace for an audience caused a special meeting of the senior officials of the Household Department in my father's house to discuss what presents he should be given; it was decided that he should receive an ancient sword in addition to everything else that had been prepared. Chang Tso-lin, however, went back to Fengtien without visiting the palace. Two months later a young Manchu noble, a relation of my father, was appointed as an adviser to Chang and he went to Fengtien for a while. During the period of Fengtien-Chihli co-operation following the defeat of the Anhwei clique the Fengtien Club in Peking became the meeting-place for Fengtien commanders and was frequently visited by a number of princes and nobles. Even the chief steward of the Mansion of Prince Chun was a frequent visitor and became the sworn brother of the leading Fengtien figure Chang Ching-hui there.

These two years were much like the time leading up to Chang Hsun's restoration: the air was full of rumours of a new attempt to put me back on the throne. Two months after my father had sent the presents to Fengtien and Chang Ching-hui had come to the capital, the English-language newspaper *Peking Leader* of December 27, 1919 carried the following item from Fengtien:

During the course of the last few days, the rumour of the coming resuscitation of the Manchu monarchy in Peking in place of the existing so-called republican government of China has been in circulation among all classes of the natives especially among the militarists under general Chang Tso-lin. According to current allegations, the monarchy will this time be started by general Chang Tso-lin with the co-operation of certain monarchical and military leaders of northwest China, and ex-general Chang Tsun . . . will play a very important part in it . . . even president Hsu and ex-president Feng, in view of the existing unsettled political situation of the country and external dangers, are inclined to accept the resuscitation of monarchy without strong opposition or dissatisfaction. With regard to Tsao Kun, Li Shun and other lesser military leaders, it is said that these men can be satisfied by making them princes, dukes or marquises in addition to permitting them to hold their present posts in the various provinces. . . .

When Johnston told me of this some time later I remember that he also told me some other rumours about Chang Tso-lin's restoration activities. News of this sort circulated until Chang returned to the Northeast a defeated man in 1922. Such news made a deep impression on me and made me feel very happy. It also enabled me to understand why the commanders of the Fengtien army were so enthusiastic about the Forbidden City, why Chang Ching-hui went with the princes and Ching officials to kotow to the high consort Tuan Kang on her birthday, why the Fengtien Club was said to be so busy, and why some of the princes were in such a state of excitement. But before my joy had lasted very long it was swept away by the open split between the Chihli and Fengtien cliques and the consequent defeat of the Fengtien army which withdrew to the Northeast.

Disturbing reports arrived in quick succession. Hsu Shih-chang had suddenly resigned. The Chihli army controlled Peking. Li Yuan-hung, who had been forced out of office during Chang Hsun's restoration, had become president again. A new panic swept the Forbidden City; the princes and officials begged Johnston to take me to the British Legation for safety. Johnston arranged with the British Minister Sir Beilby Alston that the British Legation would let him have some rooms in which he could keep me as his private guest if necessary. He also arranged with the Portuguese and Netherlands Legations that other members of the royal family would be allowed to take refuge in the Legation Quarter. I did not agree with this idea: I thought it would be better to go abroad straight away. I proposed to Johnston that he should take me abroad at once. The suddenness with which I sent for him and asked this stunned him. He had no time to think out his answer: "That would be very awkward. Your Majesty should think it over calmly: President Hsu has only just left Peking and if Your Majesty were to disappear from the Forbidden City immediately afterwards it would lead to suggestions that there had been some kind of conspiracy between the palace and Hsu Shih-chang. Moreover Britain would not be able to receive Your Majesty in the present circumstances."

In those days I neither had the sense to work out for myself nor did anyone else tell me that there had been some kind of secret links between Chang Tso-lin and Hsu Shih-chang or between Chang, Hsu and the little court; I was even less aware of any connection between the Legation Quarter and the outbreak of war between the Chihli and Fengtien factions. So when I heard that my request was impossible I let it go at that. When the situation became more stable the matter of taking refuge in the legations was no longer raised, let alone that of going abroad.

A year later, in 1923, the head of the Chihli clique, Tsao Kun, bought the votes of the members of parliament at 5,000 dollars apiece and had himself elected president. The little court had only just stopped being frightened of him when another rising Chihli commander, Wu Pei-fu, attracted their attention. Cheng Hsiao-hsu, later a close adviser of mine, told me that Wu was a soldier with a very bright future who wished to preserve the Great Ching and who could very probably be persuaded to support us. That same year I sent Cheng Hsiao-hsu to Wu Pei-fu's headquarters at Lo-yang with lavish presents to congratulate him on his fiftieth birthday. Kang Yu-wei, the reformer of 1898 who was now a monarchist, also went to try and win him over but did not get any definite reply. As it turned out, Wu Pei-fu's success was short-lived as the year after this birthday celebration his subordinate Feng Yu-hsiang changed sides in the fighting between the Chihli and Fengtien cliques. This led to Wu's total defeat and I was driven out of the Forbidden City by the National Army of Feng Yu-hsiang.

Reginald Johnston

The first time I saw foreigners was at the last reception that the empress dowager Lung Yu held for the wives of the foreign ambassadors. I thought that their strange clothes and their hair and eyes of so many colours were both ugly and frightening. At that time I had never seen foreign men, but I had got a rough idea of what they looked like from illustrated magazines: they wore moustaches on their upper lips; there was always a straight line down the legs of their trousers; and they invariably carried sticks. The eunuchs said that foreigners' moustaches were so stiff that one could hang lanterns from the ends of them and that their legs were rigid. Believing this one senior official had suggested to the empress dowager Tzu Hsi in 1900 that when fighting foreigners it was only necessary to knock them over with bamboo poles for them to be incapable of getting up again. The eunuchs said that the sticks in their hands were "civilization sticks" for hitting people with. My tutor Chen Pao-shen had been in Southeast Asia where he had seen foreigners, and what he told me about the outside world gradually replaced the impressions of my childhood and the stories of the eunuchs. All the same, I was very surprised and disconcerted when I was told that I was to have a foreigner as a tutor.

It was on March 4, 1919 that my father and my Chinese tutors introduced me to Mr. Reginald Fleming Johnston in the Yu Ching Palace. First of all he bowed to me as I sat on a throne according to the protocol for receiving foreign officials and then I got up and shook hands with him. He bowed once more and withdrew. Then he came in again and I bowed to him: this was the way in which I acknowledged him as my teacher. Once these ceremonies were over he started to teach me in the company of my tutor Chu Yi-fan.

I found that Johnston was not so frightening after all. His Chinese was very fluent and much easier to understand than Chen Pao-shen's Fukienese or Chu Yi-fan's Kiangsi dialect. He must have been at least forty at the time and was clearly older than my father, but his movements were still deft and skilful. His back was so straight that I wondered whether he wore an iron frame under his clothes. Although he had no handlebar moustache or "civilization stick" and his legs did bend, he always gave me an impression of stiffness. It was his blue eyes and greying fair hair in particular that made me feel uneasy.

During one lesson about a month after he first came he suddenly turned round and glared furiously at the eunuch who was standing by the wall. His face red with anger, he protested to me in Chinese spoken with an English accent:

"The Household Department is treating me very discourteously. Why do I alone have to have a eunuch standing here when the other tutors don't? I don't like it. I don't like it and I'm going to bring the matter up with President Hsu as it was he who invited me to take this post."

He did not have to go and see President Hsu. At least half of the reason why the Ching house had invited him was to get his protection, and so they did not dare offend him. He only had to go red in the face for my father and the high officials to give way and withdraw the eunuch. I found him very intimidating and studied English with him like a good boy, not daring to talk about other things when I got bored or ordering a holiday as I did with my Chinese tutors.

After two or three months I realized that he was getting more and more like my Chinese tutors. He used the same reverential form of address to me as they did and would push the textbook aside and chat with me when I got tired of reading, telling me stories about things old and new and places near and far. On his suggestion a fellow-student was provided for my English lessons. His way of doing things was the same as that of my Chinese tutors.

This old Englishman was an M.A. of Oxford University who had been formally invited by the Ching house after discussions between the British Legation and President Hsu Shih-chang. He had been a colonial official in Hongkong and was Commissioner of the British-leased territory of Weihaiwei before coming to the palace. As he said himself, he had already been in Asia for over twenty years, had visited every province of China, had seen her famous mountains, rivers and antiquities. He was well versed in Chinese history, familiar with all parts of the country, expert in Confucianism, Mohism, Buddhism and Taoism, and a connoisseur of ancient Chinese poetry. I do not know how many classical Chinese books he had read and

I used to see him wagging his head as he chanted Tang poems just like a Chinese teacher, his voice rising, falling and pausing.

He was as honoured to receive presents from me as the other tutors. After I had awarded him the mandarin hat button of the highest grade he had a full set of Ching court clothes specially made. He posed for a photograph in these clothes standing under a tablet in my handwriting in front of his country house in Cherry Valley in the Western Hills, and distributed prints of it to his family and friends. The Household Department rented an old-style Peking house for him and he furnished it just as a veteran of the Ching would have done: as soon as one entered the front gate one could see red tablets on which were written in black letters "Companion of the Yu Ching Palace", "Entitled to Be Carried in a Chair with Two Porters in the Palace", "Awarded the First Grade Hat Button", and "Entitled to Wear a Sable Jacket". Every time he received a major award he would write a memorial thanking me for my benevolence.

He coined himself a literary name from the saying in the *Analects* of Confucius that "a scholar sets his mind on truth". He was a lover of Chinese tea and peonies and was fond of talking with the Ching veterans. When he retired and went back to England he set aside a room in his house in which to display the things I had given him and his Ching court robes and hat button. He even flew the flag of "Manchukuo" from an island he had bought to show his loyalty to the emperor. But what brought about the closeness between teacher and pupil was his patience. Looking back on it now, I realize that it can have been no easy matter for that testy Scot to adopt the attitude he did to a pupil like myself. One day he brought me some foreign magazines full of pictures of the First World War, mostly showing the aircraft, tanks and artillery of the allied armies. I was intrigued by these funny things. Seeing that I was interested he explained the things in the pictures to me and told me what tanks were for, which country's aircraft were best, and how brave the soldiers of the allies were. I was fascinated at first but as usual I got bored after a while, emptied the contents of a snuff-bottle on the table and started to doodle in it. Without a word Johnston tidied up the magazines and waited there till the end of the lesson while I played.

Another time he brought me some foreign sweets and I was delighted by the tin box, the silver wrapping-paper and their different fruit flavours. He started to tell me how the fruity tastes were produced by chemical techniques and how the neat shape of the sweets was made by machines. I could not understand any of this and did not even want to, and when I had eaten two of the sweets I thought of my ants on their cypress tree and wanted to let them try the flavour of chemistry and machinery. I rushed into the courtyard and old Johnston waited with the sweet tin until the lesson was over.

As I gradually realized how diligently Johnston was teaching me I was very pleased and willing to be more obedient. He did not only teach me English; or rather teaching me the English language was not so important in his eyes as training me to be like the English gentlemen he talked about. When I was fourteen I decided to dress like he did and sent some eunuchs out to buy me a large amount of Western clothing. I put on an outfit that did not fit me at all, and I must have looked a strange sight with my tie hanging outside my collar like a length of rope. When I went to the schoolroom Johnston quivered with anger at the sight of me and told me to go back and take those clothes off at once. The next day he brought a tailor along to measure me and make me clothes that would have done for an English gentleman. Later he explained to me, "It is better to wear your Manchu robes than ill-fitting Western dress. If you wear clothes from a second-hand shop you won't be a gentleman, you'll be. . . ." But what I would be he did not go on to say.

"If Your Majesty ever appears in London you are bound to be invited to tea very often. Tea parties are informal but important occasions that usually take place on Wednesdays. At them one can meet peers, scholars, celebrities and all sorts of people Your Majesty will need to meet. There is no need to be too dressed up but manners are most important. It is very bad to drink tea as if it were water, to eat cakes as if they were a real meal, or make too much noise with your fork or teaspoon. In England tea and cakes are *refreshment* (he used the English word) and not a meal. . . ."

I forgot much of Johnston's careful instruction and threw the caution with which I ate the first cake to the winds by the time I came to the second, but all the same the Western civilization represented by guns and aircraft in the magazines, the sweets made by chemistry and the etiquette of tea parties made a deep impression on my mind. The magazines about the First World War gave me a taste for foreign publications. First of all I was struck by the advertisements and I immediately told the eunuchs to buy dogs and diamonds for me from abroad like the ones shown in them. I made the Household Department buy me foreign furniture and had the red sandalwood table with brass fittings on the *kang* changed for one painted with foreign paint and fitted with white porcelain handles. I also had a wooden floor laid down so that the room was a complete hotch-potch, being neither properly Chinese nor completely Western. Imitating Johnston I bought all sorts of trinkets to hang about myself: Watches and chains, rings, tiepins, cuff-links, neckties and so on. I asked him to give foreign names to myself, my brothers and sisters, my "empress" and my "consort": I was called Henry and my empress Elizabeth. I even imitated his way of talking in a mixture of Chinese and English when I was with my fellow-students:

"*William* (Pu Chieh), sharpen this *pencil* (I used the English word) for me . . . good, put it on the *desk*."

"*Arthur* (Pu Chia), tell *Lily* (my third sister) and the others to come round this *afternoon* to *hear* some foreign military music."

I felt very pleased when talking like this, but when Chen Pao-shen heard me he screwed his face up as if he were suffering from toothache.

I thought that everything about Johnston was first-rate and even went so far as to regard the smell of mothballs about his clothes as fragrant. He made me feel that Westerners were the most intelligent and civilized people and that he was the most learned of Westerners. I do not think that even he realized how deep an influence he was exercising on me: the woollen cloth that he wore made me doubt the value of all the silks and satins of China and the fountain pen in his pocket actually made me ashamed of the writing brushes and hand-made paper that Chinese used to write with. After he had brought a military band from the British barracks to play in the palace I felt that Chinese music was not worth listening to and even found the ancient ceremonial music far less majestic.

A mere remark by Johnston that Chinese queues were pigtails was enough for me to cut mine off. Ever since 1913 the Home Ministry of the Republic had been writing to the Household Department asking that the Forbidden City should co-operate with them in persuading the Manchu bannermen to cut off their queues; they also hoped that the queues in the palace would go. The tone of these letters was very polite and they did not refer to the queues hanging from my head and the heads of the senior officials. The Household Department used all kinds of excuses to put off the Home Ministry, even going so far as to say that queues were a useful way of distinguishing who should be allowed in and out of the palace. Several years after the matter was first brought up the Forbidden City was still a world of queues. But now Johnston's one piece of propaganda was enough to make me have mine off. Within a few days at least a thousand disappeared and only my three Chinese tutors and a few of the senior officials of the Household Department kept theirs.

The High Consorts wept several times at the loss of my plait and my tutors went round with long faces for days. Later Pu Chieh and Yu Chung used the pretext of "obeying an imperial decree" to cut off theirs at home. That day Chen Pao-shen shook with fury at his bald-headed students and finally remarked to Yu Chung with a bitter smile, "If you sold your queue to a foreign woman you could get a good price for it."

The people who most hated Johnston were the staff of the Household Department. In those days expenditure in the palace was still enormous although the payments under the Articles of Favourable Treatment were in arrears every year. In order to meet running expenses the Household Department had to sell or pawn antiques, pictures, calligraphy, gold, silver and porcelain every year.

I gradually learnt from what Johnston said that there was something fishy about this. Once when the Household Department wanted to sell a golden pagoda as tall as a man I thought of Johnston's remarks that by selling gold and silver objects for the value of the metal in them instead of as works of art the Household Department was losing a lot of money. According to Johnston only a fool would act like this. I therefore sent for the officials of the Department and asked them how they intended selling it. When they said they would sell it according to its weight I burst into a fury:

"Only fools would do that. Haven't you got an ounce of sense between you?"

The Household Department reckoned that Johnston was ruining their racket and so they thought out a way of dealing with him: they sent the pagoda to Johnston's house and claimed that the emperor had asked him to sell it for him. Johnston saw through their trick at once, exploded with anger and said, "If you don't take it away I shall report this to His Majesty immediately." The result was that the Household Department officials carried the pagoda away again without making any more trouble.

By my last year of studying in the Yu Ching Palace Johnston had become the major part of my soul. Our discussions of extracurricular topics occupied more and more of our lesson-time and ever widened in scope. He told me about the life of the English royal family, the politics of different countries, the strength of the powers after the Great War, places and customs all over the world, the "great British Empire on which the sun never sets", China's civil wars and her "vernacular writing movement" (as he called the May 4th Movement of 1919) and its links with Western culture. He also talked about the possibility of a restoration and the unreliable attitude of the warlords.

"One can see clearly from all the papers," he said once, "that the Chinese people are thinking of the Great Ching and that everybody is tired of the Republic. I do not think that there is any need for Your Majesty to worry about those military men; nor need Your Imperial Majesty waste so much time trying to find out their attitudes from the papers; nor is there anything to be gained from discussing what difference of ultimate motives they have in supporting a restoration or defending the Republic. Tutor Chen is quite right in saying that the most important thing is for Your Majesty daily to renew your sage virtue. But this must not only be done in the Forbidden City. Your Majesty can acquire much essential knowledge and widen your horizons in Europe, particularly at Oxford University in the land of His Majesty the King of England where the Prince of Wales studied. . . ."

Before I got the idea of studying in England he had already done quite a lot to widen my "vision". He introduced English admirals and the British governor of Hongkong who were all polite and respectful, addressing me as "Your Imperial Majesty".

My intoxication with a European way of life and the way I tended more and more to ape him was not too pleasing to Johnston. On the subject of clothes, for example, our opinions differed as he had a special interest in me. On my wedding day I appeared at the reception given for foreign guests and drank a toast with them; but when I got back to the Mind Nurture Palace I changed my dragon robes for an ordinary gown worn over Western trousers and a peaked cap. Just then Johnston came along with some friends of his. A sharp-sighted old foreign lady saw me standing by the verandah and asked him, "Who is that young man?"

When Johnston spotted me and saw the clothes I was wearing his face went quite red. This gave me a fright, and the disappointed expressions of the foreigners mystified me. Johnston was still in a temper after they had gone and he said to me furiously:

"What do you mean by it, Your Majesty? For the Emperor of China to wear a hunting-cap! Good lord!"

My Wedding

If I was at all interested when the princes told me on the orders of the High Consorts that I was old enough for my "Grand Nuptials" it was because marriage would mark my coming of age and would mean that others could no longer control me as if I were still a child.

The people who felt most concern over the matter were the old ladies. Early in 1921, when I was just fifteen, the High Consorts summoned my father for a number of consultations on the subject and then called a meeting of about ten of the princes to discuss it. Almost two years later the wedding took place. There were a number of reasons why the delay was so long. One was that it would have been wrong for me to marry too soon after the deaths first of the high consort Chuang Ho and then of my own mother. The more important reason was that the political situation was unsettled and there were complicated quarrels over the choice of my bride. This was why my tutors counselled postponing it.

The quarrels occurred because the high consorts Tuan Kang and Ching Yi each wanted to choose a future "empress" who would be friendly to herself. Each put forward her own candidate and would not give way, and each was supported by one of my uncles. The situation was deadlocked.

In the last resort the choice had to be made by the "emperor". The way that this had been done in the time of Tung Chih and Kuang Hsu was for the girls who were candidates to stand in a line and the future bridegroom to select one of them. I have heard two versions of how he indicated his choice. One was that he handed a jade symbol to the girl who took his fancy; the other was that he hung a pouch on the girl's buckle. When it came to my time the princes felt that lining up a row of maidens would no longer be suitable and decided that I should choose from photographs instead. I was to pencil a mark on the picture of the one I liked best.

Four photos were sent to the Mind Nurture Palace. To me the girls seemed much the same and their bodies looked as shapeless as tubes in their dresses. Their faces were very small in the pictures so that I could not see whether they were beauties or not. The only comparison I could make was between the styles of their clothes. It did not occur to me at the time that this was one of the great events of my life, and I had no standards to guide me. I casually drew a circle on a pretty picture.

She was the daughter of Tuan Kung of the Manchu Ordet clan. She was called Wen Hsiu (her other name was Hui Hsin) and she was three years younger than me, so that she would have been twelve when I saw her picture. As she was the girl favoured by the high consort Ching Yi her rival Tuan Kang was most displeased and, overruling Ching Yi's protests, she insisted on summoning the princes to persuade me to choose her candidate. She said that Wen Hsiu came of an impoverished family and was ugly, whereas the girl she supported, Wan Jung (also called Mu Hung), was of a rich family, beautiful and the same age as me. I followed the advice of the princes, wondering why they had not explained things at the beginning, instead of letting me think that there was nothing to this business of making a pencil mark and drew a circle on the photo of Wan Jung.

This met with the disapproval of the high consorts Ching Yi and Jung Hui. After a series of arguments among the High Consorts and princes the high consort Jung Hui came out with this suggestion: "As His Majesty has marked Wen Hsiu's picture it wouldn't do for her to be married to one of his subjects, so he had better take her as a consort." I did not feel that I had much need for one wife, let alone two, and was not at all keen on this proposal; but when the princes and high officials pointed out to me that according to the customs of my ancestors "the emperor has to have an empress and a consort" this was an argument I could not resist. As I had to have all the prerogatives of an emperor I agreed to their suggestion.

I have rather simplified the process of choosing the empress and consort, which in fact took a whole year. After the selection had been made the Chihli-Fengtien war meant that the wedding had to be put off until the winter of 1922. Although this was after the fall of Hsu Shih-chang the large-scale preparations for the ceremony were too far under way to be stopped, so the wedding had to go ahead. The princes did not feel as much confidence in Li

Yuan-hung (now president for the second time) as they had felt for Hsu Shih-chang and were afraid that he might interfere with the pomp of the occasion. As it turned out, however, the help that Li gave far exceeded their expectations and was no less than they would have hoped for from Hsu Shih-chang. The Republic's Ministry of Finance wrote a letter in somewhat humble terms to the Household Department which said that as they were having difficulties at the moment in meeting their expenditure they were unable to pay in full the annual subsidies stipulated in the Articles of Favourable Treatment; they would, however, make a special payment from tax revenue of 100,000 dollars to help with the Grand Nuptials, of which 20,000 dollars was to be regarded as a present from the Republic. At the same time the military, gendarme and police authorities of the Republic presented plans for their men to provide protection for the double wedding, plans involving the participation of many hundreds of men.

From the entry into the palace of the trousseau of the consort to the ceremony at which I received congratulations in the Cloudless Heaven Palace the wedding lasted five days. The celebrations included three days of theatricals and the granting of new titles.

What caused the most public indignation was that after the attempted restoration in 1917 the little court was flaunting its pomp outside the Forbidden City. The ceremonial emblems of the Ching court were paraded with great majesty round the streets of Peking under the respectful protection of large numbers of Republican soldiers and police. On the day of the wedding ceremony proper two princes dressed in Ching court robes with staffs of office in their hands rode on horseback behind two Republican military bands. They were followed by more army bands and cavalry, mounted police, and mounted security police. After them came seventy-two dragon-and-phoenix parasols and flags, four "yellow pavilions" (containing the imperial patent for the new empress and her clothing), and thirty pairs of palace lanterns. This imposing procession set out for the "Residence of the Empress". At the brightly illuminated gate of the "residence" another host of police and soldiers were guarding Wan Jung's father and brothers as they knelt there to greet the "imperial decree" brought by the two envoys.

The rich presents given by leading figures of the Republic also attracted considerable attention. President Li Yuan-hung wrote "Offering of President Li Yuan-hung of the Republic of China to the Hsuan Tung Emperor" on a red card and gave the following presents: four vessels in cloisonné, two kinds of silk and satin, one curtain and a pair of scrolls wishing me longevity, prosperity and good fortune. Ex-President Hsu Shih-chang sent 20,000 dollars and many other valuable presents including twenty-eight pieces of porcelain and a sumptuous Chinese carpet with a dragon and phoenix design. Chang Tso-lin, Wu Pei-fu, Chang Hsun, Tsao Kun and other warlords and politicians also sent cash and many other kinds of presents.

The representative of the Republic at the ceremony, Yin Chang, was a chief aide-de-camp in the Office of the President, and he congratulated me formally as he would have done a foreign sovereign. When he had finished bowing to me he announced, "That was on behalf of the Republic. Your slave will now greet Your Majesty in his private capacity." With this he knelt on the floor and kotowed to me.

At the time many papers severely criticized these strange occurrences but this did nothing to dampen the enthusiasm of the princes and high officials, nor did it prevent veterans of the Ching from emerging all over the country like insects waking up after the winter and converging on Peking in swarms. They brought presents that included money and antiques from themselves and others. The valuables were not as important, however, as the power that the court now seemed to enjoy, which went beyond even their own expectations and made them feel that our prospects were very hopeful.

What caused the High Consorts, princes, high officials and veterans of the Ching the most excitement was the presence of guests from the Legation Quarter. This was the first time that foreign officials had appeared in the Forbidden City since the Revolution of 1911, and although they came in their personal capacities they were still, after all, foreign officials.

On the suggestion of Johnston a reception was given to show our gratitude to the foreigners for attending the ceremony and I read a short speech in English.

While all this hustle and bustle went on around me one question kept running through my mind: "I have an empress and a consort; I'm married. But how are things any different from before?" The answer that I gave myself was, "I've come of age. If there had not been a revolution I would start ruling without regents."

I hardly thought about marriage and my family. It was only when the empress came into my field of vision with a crimson satin cloth embroidered with a dragon and a phoenix over her head that I felt at all curious about what she looked like.

According to tradition the emperor and the empress spent their wedding night in a bridal chamber some ten metres square in the Palace of Earthly Peace (Kun Ning Kung). This was a rather peculiar room: it was unfurnished except for the bed-platform which filled a quarter of it, and everything about it except the floor was red. When we had drunk the nuptial cup and eaten sons-and-grandsons cakes and entered this dark red room I felt stifled. The bride sat on the bed, her head bent down. I looked around me and saw that everything was red: red bed-curtains, red pillows, a red dress, a red skirt, red flowers, and a red face . . . it all looked like a melted red wax candle. I did not know whether to stand or sit, decided that I preferred the Mind Nurture Palace, and went back there.

When I got back to the Mind Nurture Palace I looked at the list of the senior officials of the country during the Hsuan Tung reign that was pasted on the wall and wondered again, "I have an empress and a consort and I'm grown up, but how are things any different from before?"

How did Wan Jung feel, abandoned in the bridal chamber? What was Wen Hsiu, a girl not yet fourteen, thinking? These questions never even occurred to me as my thoughts were preoccupied. "If there had been no revolution I would now be starting to rule with full powers. I must recover my ancestral heritage."

Internal Clashes

From the time when Johnston entered the palace onwards I became a more and more difficult emperor for the princes and palace officials to deal with. About the time of my marriage my actions must have seemed stranger and stranger to them and made them more and more uneasy. One day I would order the Household Department to buy me a diamond costing 30,000 dollars and the day after I would castigate them for failing to make ends meet and accuse them of corruption and waste. In the morning I might summon the high officials and tell them to inspect the collections of antiques, calligraphy and paintings and report the same day, and in the afternoon I might want a car for a trip to Fragrance Hill outside Peking. I was bored with traditional ceremonies and did not even like to ride in the gold-canopied yellow chair. To make cycling easier I had all the thresholds in the gates of the palace, which had caused no inconvenience to my ancestors over the centuries, sawn off. I would accuse the eunuchs of disloyalty to me for trifling reasons and have them sent to the Administrative Bureau to be flogged or discharged. What made the princes and high officials most uncomfortable, however, was the way in which at one moment I would be preparing myself for a reform of the palace and a financial clean-up and the next I would be announcing that I wanted to leave the Forbidden City and go and study abroad. They were in fear and trembling all day and their queues almost went white from worry.

Some of the princes and officials had thought about my going to study abroad before it occurred to me, and this was one of the reasons why they had invited Johnston to be my tutor; and after my wedding I received a number of memorials and suggestions from Ching veterans proposing this. But when I raised the question myself almost everybody opposed it, and the most common reason given was: "If Your Majesty leaves the Forbidden City it will amount to abrogating the Articles of Favourable Treatment. Why should you want to abolish them yourself when the Republic has not done so?"

None of them, whether they sympathized with my wish to go abroad or whether they opposed it, whether they had already despaired of "restoring the ancestral heritage" or whether they still had hopes of it, none of them could do without the Articles of Favourable Treatment. Although the clause which referred to a subsidy of 4,000,000 dollars a year had been shown to be an empty promise, the clause stating that the emperor's "title of dignity is to be retained and not abolished" still held good. It was not only those who still hoped for a restoration who regarded it as important that I should stay in the Forbidden City and keep up the little court; and even those who had lost hope still saw it as the way to safeguard their ricebowls and their positions. Apart from the titles they would be given after their deaths, they could consecrate the ancestral tablets of others and write epitaphs while they were alive.

My ideas differed from theirs. In the first place I did not think that the Articles of Favourable Treatment would be observed for ever and I was more conscious than anyone else of the precariousness of my position. The new outbreak of civil war, the retreat of Chang Tso-lin to the Northeast, the fall of Hsu Shih-chang and Li Yuan-hung's return to power all made me feel that danger had suddenly become imminent. My only concern was whether or not the new authorities would kill me. There no longer seemed to be any possibility of favourable treatment. On top of all this came the report that some members of parliament were proposing the abolition of the Articles of Favourable Treatment. Even if the *status quo* could be maintained, who could tell in the political and military confusion which warlord might be in power tomorrow or which politician might be organizing a cabinet the day after. I knew from many sources, particularly Johnston, that foreign powers were behind all these changes, so would it not be better to contact the foreigners directly rather than depend upon favourable treatment from the latest Republican authorities? Might it not be too late if I waited until someone implacably hostile to me came to power before thinking of some way out? I was only too well acquainted with the way that the last emperors of dynasties had met unpleasant deaths throughout the history of China.

Of course, I did not remind the princes and high officials of these woeful tales. The argument I used with them was:

"I don't want any 'favourable treatment'. I want to let the common people and the world know that I have no hope that the Republic will treat me favourably. To do this is much better than waiting for them to abrogate the articles first."

"But the articles are stored in the state archives and internationally recognized. If the Republic were to abrogate them the foreign powers would certainly help us," was their reply.

"If the foreigners would help us then why don't you let me go abroad? Surely they would be even more helpful when they saw me in person?"

However good my reasons, they would never have agreed. All my arguments with my father, my tutors and the princes had only one result: they speeded up their preparations for my "Grand Nuptials".

There was another reason why I was so anxious to go abroad apart from those I mentioned to the princes and officials: I had been growing tired of my whole environment, themselves included, long before I got the idea of foreign travel. Since Johnston had come to the palace and filled me with knowledge about Western civilization, this and my youthful curiosity had made me dissatisfied with my surroundings and the restrictions that hemmed me in. I agreed with Johnston's diagnosis that the root of the trouble lay in the conservatism of the princes and high officials.

In their eyes everything new was terrifying. When I was fifteen Johnston noticed that I might be short-sighted and advised asking a foreign ophthalmologist to come and examine my eyes. If his guess was correct I should have spectacles. To his surprise this suggestion created as much of an uproar as if he had tipped some water into a pan of boiling oil and the Forbidden City all but exploded. What an idea! That the eyes of His Imperial Majesty should be looked at by a foreigner! His Majesty was still in the vigour of youth. How could he wear "specs" like an old man?

Nobody from the High Consorts down would consent. It was through repeated entreaties by Johnston and determination on my part that it was finally done.

I was particularly annoyed when the princes and high officials would oppose my having things that they had themselves. An example of this was a telephone.

When I was fifteen an explanation from Johnston of the uses of the telephone aroused my curiosity, and when I heard from my brother Pu Chieh that my father's house had one of these toys I told the Household Department to have one installed in the Mind Nurture Palace. On receiving this order the head of the Household Department, Shao Ying, turned pale with horror. · He did not utter a word of protest, however, and withdrew with a "yes, sire". But the next day all my tutors came to offer advice.

"There is no precedent for such a thing in the ancestral code. If a telephone is installed anyone might talk to Your Majesty, a thing that never happened in the times of your ancestors. . . . The ancestors never used these foreign contraptions. . . ."

I had arguments with which to retaliate: "The chiming clocks, pianos and electric lights in the palace are all foreign things that have no place in the ancestral system, but did not my ancestors use them?"

"If outsiders can make phone calls whenever they like will they not offend the Celestial Countenance? Will this not damage the imperial dignity?"

"I have been offended by outsiders often enough in the press. What difference is there between reading insults and hearing them?"

Perhaps even my tutors did not understand at the time why the Household Department asked them to dissuade me. What really frightened the Household Department was not that the "Celestial Countenance" might be offended but that the telephone might enable me to have more contact with the outside world. It was already enough for them that I should have a talkative Johnston by my side and take over twenty different newspapers. In the Peking newspapers of the day one would find statements from the Household Department every month at least either denying that the Ching house was in contact with the authorities of this or that province or some important personality, or else refuting rumours that the palace had recently been pawning or selling some antiques. The great majority of the rumours that were denied were in fact true, and at least half of them were things that the Household Department did not want me to know about. The combination of the newspapers and Johnston kept them quite busy enough: a third link with the outside in the form of a telephone would put them in an impossible position. So naturally they did all in their power to prevent it, and when they saw that the tutors had failed to dissuade me they brought my father in.

My father had by then become a convinced believer in maintaining the existing state of affairs. Provided I made no trouble and stayed quietly in the Forbidden City, he would go on receiving his annual grant of 42,480 taels of silver and be quite contented with his lot; this made him very amenable to the direction of the Household Department. But his tongue was not as glib as the Household Department had hoped. He could produce no argument to dissuade me that my tutors had not already tried and was unable to find an answer to one question I asked him: "Hasn't there been a telephone in Your Highness's home for a long time?"

"That . . . that. . . . But it is quite different from Your Majesty having one. Let's talk the matter over again in a couple of days. . . ."

I was reminded that he had cut his queue off before me, had a telephone before me, and would not let me buy a car although he had already purchased one himself, and so I was not feeling at all pleased.

"Why should it be different for the emperor? Am I not to have even this tiny amount of freedom? No, I insist on a telephone." I turned to a eunuch. "Tell the Household Department I want a telephone installed today."

"Very well," my father nodded his head, "very well, have one then."

With the telephone installed there was more trouble.

The telephone company sent a directory along with the apparatus. In a state of high excitement I leafed through its pages thinking that

I would have some fun with the phone. I rang up a Peking opera actor and an acrobat and hung up before saying who I was, then called up a restaurant and ordered a meal to be sent round to a false address. After amusing myself like this for a while it would be fun to hear what the Dr. Hu Shih, the author of the line "Picnic by the river" whom Johnston had recently mentioned, sounded like and so I called his number. By a piece of luck he answered the phone himself.

"Is that Dr. Hu?" I asked. "Excellent, guess who I am."

"Who are you? I have no idea."

"Ha ha, no need to guess, I'll tell you. I'm Hsuan Tung."

"Hsuan Tung? Is that Your Majesty?"

"Right, I'm the emperor. I've heard your voice now, but I haven't seen you. Come round to the palace when you have time so that I can have a look at you."

This casual joke brought him along. Johnston told me that Hu Shih had come to see him especially to confirm the telephone call as he had not expected "His Majesty" to phone. He anxiously asked Johnston about palace etiquette and decided to come when he found out that he would not have to kotow to me and that I was a reasonably good-tempered emperor. I had forgotten all about our conversation and had not told the eunuchs to inform the guards, so that when Dr. Hu Shih arrived at the palace gate no amount of talking would get him in. Not knowing whether to believe him or not the guards referred the matter to me, and only let him in when I gave the word.

This meeting born of the whim of a moment lasted about twenty minutes. I asked him about the uses of vernacular writing, about his travels abroad and so on. Fishing for compliments, I ended by saying that I did not mind whether I got favourable treatment or not so long as I could study and be a "promising young man" of the sort one read about in the papers. He covered me with the expected flattery: "Your Majesty is most enlightened. If Your Majesty studies conscientiously, there is a bright future ahead of you." I did not know what he meant by this future. He went away and I thought no more of the affair, but to my surprise the princes and senior officials, particularly my tutors, were thrown into an uproar at the news that I had met this "new figure" in a private audience.

As I grew up they saw that I was becoming more and more dissatisfied; and I found them increasingly tiresome. At this time I had already made several trips outside the Forbidden City, a small freedom I had won in the face of much protest on the pretext of going to make offerings to my mother after her death. This taste of freedom had whetted my appetite and I was thoroughly sick of all these timorous and doltish officials. My accumulated impatience at all the incidents mentioned above made me more determined than ever to go abroad, and my conflict with the princes and high officials reached a climax in the summer of 1922 when I formally raised my wish to study in England.

They were not prepared to give way on this as they had done over the installation of a telephone. Even my uncle Tsai Tao, who sympathized with me most strongly, would only give permission for a house to be got ready in the English concession in Tientsin in which I could take refuge in an emergency. As it was impossible for me to leave the Forbidden City openly I asked Johnston to help me. I related in the preceding section that he thought that the time was not ripe and would not agree to my going at the moment. While I forced myself to wait for my chance I made secret preparations for an escape with the assistance of a loyal and willing helper — my brother Pu Chieh.

Pu Chieh and myself were a well-matched pair of brothers, and our feelings and ambitions were even more similar than our faces. His one thought was to escape from his cooped-up life at home, to fly high, and to find a way out; he believed that all his dreams would be realized once he went abroad. The only difference between his environment and mine was the same as that between our two bodies: his was one size smaller. Between the ages of four and seventeen he was dressed every morning by his old nurse. He could do nothing for himself, not even wash his feet or trim his nails. If he picked up a pair of scissors the nurse would shout and scream, terrified that he might cut himself. She would take him everywhere, and did not let him run, climb, or go out of the front gate. He was not allowed to eat fish for fear he might choke. He studied in a family school under a tutor who used to curse the Republic. Our mother urged Pu Chieh to help me faithfully and never to forget that he was a descendant of the Aisin-Gioro clan.

Although Pu Chieh was a year younger than me he knew more about the outside world. This was mainly because he only had to give his family the excuse of going to the palace to be able to move outside freely. The first stage of our escape plan was to provide for our expenses. The way we did this was to move the most valuable pictures, calligraphy and antiques in the imperial collections out of the palace by pretending that I was giving them to Pu Chieh and then store them in the house in Tientsin. Pu Chieh used to take a large bundle home after school every day for over six months, and the things we took were the very finest treasures in the collections. As it happened the heads of the Household Department and my tutors were checking through the pictures and calligraphy at the time, so all we had to do was to take the items they selected as being of the very highest grade. In addition to paintings and calligraphy we also took many valuable ancient editions of books. We must have removed over a thousand handscrolls, more than two hundred hanging scrolls and pages from albums, and about two hundred rare Sung Dynasty printed books. All these were taken to Tientsin and later some dozens of them were sold. The rest were taken up to the Northeast by the Kwantung Army adviser Yoshioka after the foundation of "Manchukuo" and disappeared after the Japanese surrender.

The second stage of our plan was to make a secret escape from the Forbidden City. We had learnt a most important lesson from the history of the first years of the Republic: once I was out of the palace and into the Legation Quarter the Republican authorities and the palace officials would be powerless to touch me. Johnston had thought out the details of how to do it. First I had to get in touch with the doyen of the diplomatic corps, the Dutch Minister W. J. Oudendijk, and let him make appropriate preparations. He had suggested this to me back in February 1923. Nine months previously he had opposed my going abroad on the grounds that the time was not ripe. I did not have the least idea why he thought that the time had now come, or whether he had made any further arrangements with the foreign envoys. This indication from Johnston gave me great confidence and satisfied me completely. First I asked him to go to the legations and inform them, then I spoke to Oudendijk over the phone myself. To make things even more definite I also sent Pu Chieh to visit the Dutch Legation. The results were completely satisfactory. Oudendijk agreed to my requests over the telephone, and arranged with Pu Chieh that although he could not send a car into the Forbidden City for me he would have one waiting outside the Gate of Divine Valour; once I slipped out of this gate there would be no more problems. He would take complete responsibility for everything from my first night's food and lodging right up to my entry into an English university. We fixed the day and the hour for my departure from the palace.

On February 25 the only remaining problem was how to get through the Gate of Divine Valour. I had to reckon with the eunuchs of my own entourage, the eunuchs at each of the palace gates, the sentries of the palace guard outside the palace walls and the Republican patrols outside the Gate of Divine Valour. I reckoned that once the eunuchs in my suite and at the gates were dealt with there would be no other great problem. My ideas were a little too simple, and I thought that all I had to do to win them over was to give them some money. They thanked me profusely for it and I thought that everything was now ready; but an hour before the set time one of the eunuchs who had taken my bribes informed the Household Department. Before I had even left the Mind Nurture Palace I heard that my father had given an order that nobody was to be allowed through any of the palace gates and that the whole of the Forbidden City had been put into a state of siege. Pu Chieh and I sat in the Mind Nurture Palace stupefied at the news.

Before long my father arrived in a very nervous state.

"I — I — I hear that Your — Your Majesty wa — wa — wants to go away. . . ."

He looked so ill at ease that one might have thought that he was the wrong-doer, and I could not help laughing.

"Of course I don't," I replied, suppressing my laughter.

"It's not good of you.   What should we do about it?"

"But I don't want to."

My father glared suspiciously at Pu Chieh, who was frightened into bowing his head.

"I don't want to," I repeated.   My father muttered a few more words before going off, taking my "accomplice" with him.   When he had gone I called the eunuchs of the presence to question them about who had betrayed the plan.   I intended to have the culprit flogged to within an inch of his life.   I could not get the information out of them and I could not have the matter investigated by the Administrative Bureau either; I could only nurse my anger by myself.

From then onwards I hated the sight of the high palace wall.

"Prison, prison, prison," I muttered to myself as I stood on an artificial hill in the palace looking at the wall.   "That the Republic should not be on good terms with me is understandable, but it is quite unreasonable for the princes and palace officials to be so hostile. It is only for the sake of my ancestral heritage of mountains and rivers that I want to go away.   What are your motives in keeping me here? The worst of you are the ones in the Household Department: it must have been them who dragged my father into this."

When I saw Johnston the next day I poured my complaints out to him.   After some words of consolation he advised me to put the matter out of my mind for the time being: it would be more practical to start by reorganizing the Forbidden City.   He recommended me to follow the suggestions of the newly arrived Cheng Hsiao-hsu on the subject of reform.

A new hope was kindled in my mind.   Even if I could not recover my ancestral heritage outside the palace walls, at least I could reform my property within the Forbidden City.   I was very pleased with Johnston's suggestion.   I never dreamed at the time that when he later described my attempted escape in his book he would actually claim to have had nothing to do with it and even say he had opposed it.

The Dispersal of the Eunuchs

Despite its superficial calm the Forbidden City was in complete disorder. From my earliest years I was always hearing about theft, arson and murder, to say nothing of gambling and opium smoking. At the time of my wedding robbery had got to such a state that as soon as the ceremony was over all the pearls and jade in the empress's crown were stolen and replaced by fakes.

I had been told by my tutors that the treasures of the Ching palace were world-famous and that the antiques, calligraphy and paintings alone were amazing both for their quantity and value. Apart from what had been looted by foreign troops in 1860 and 1900, nearly all of the collections that had been amassed by the Ming and Ching Dynasties were still in the palace. Most of these objects were uncatalogued and even those that were catalogued had not been checked so that nobody knew what or how much had been lost. This made things very easy for thieves.

Looking back on it today it all seems to have been an orgy of looting. The looters included everyone from the highest to the humblest; anybody who had the chance to steal did so without the least anxiety. The techniques varied: some people forced locks and stole secretly, while others used legal methods and stole in broad daylight. The former method was the one favoured by most of the eunuchs, while the officials used the latter: they mortgaged pieces, sold them openly, borrowed them "for appraisal" and asked for them as presents. The most advanced technique was the one used by Pu Chieh and myself. Of course, I did not think about it in these terms at the time, and it seemed to me then that everyone else was stealing my property.

One day when I was seventeen my curiosity prompted me to have the eunuchs open up a storeroom by the Palace of Established Happiness (Chien Fu Kung). The doors of the store were thickly plastered with strips of sealing-paper and had clearly not been opened for decades, and inside were a number of large chests. It turned out that the very valuable collection of antiques and scrolls they contained were Emperor Chien Lung's favourite pieces and that they had been put away after his death. The discovery of all this treasure made me wonder how much wealth I really had. I had taken away what I had seen, but how much more was there that I had not seen? What should I do about these enormous stores of treasure? How much of it had been stolen? How could I prevent further thefts?

Johnston told me that many new antique shops had been opened in Ti An Men Street where he lived. Some of these shops were said to be run by eunuchs and others by officials of the Household Department or relations of theirs. Later my other tutors also felt that some measures should be taken to prevent further thefts, and I agreed to a proposal of theirs that an inventory should be made. This decision, however, led to even more trouble.

First of all the number of thefts increased. The lock to the store of the Yu Ching Palace was smashed and one of the windows at the back of the Cloudless Heaven Palace forced open. The situation was getting so badly out of hand that even the big diamond I had recently bought disappeared. In an attempt to investigate the robberies the High Consorts ordered the head of the Administrative Bureau to question the eunuchs responsible for these stores, using torture if necessary; but neither torture nor the offer of rich rewards had any effect. This was not all. On the night of June 27, 1923, soon after the checking of the contents of the store of the Palace of Established Happiness had begun, a fire broke out there and everything, whether checked or not yet checked, was burnt to ashes.

The fire was apparently discovered by the fire brigade of the Italian Legation, and when their fire engine reached the palace gates the guards did not realize why they had come. The conflagration, which was fought all night by fire brigades of all sorts, reduced the whole area round the Palace of Established Happiness to ashes.

These were the places where most of the treasures of the Ching house were stored, and what was lost in the fire is still a mystery. The Household Department published a very rough account which estimated that the losses included 2,665 gold statues of the Buddha, 1,157 pieces of painting and calligraphy, 435 antiques, and tens of thousands of ancient books; but heaven only knows what they based these figures on.

When the fire was being fought the place was full of foreigners and Chinese, residents of the palace and outsiders, all coming and going hither and thither. It can be easily imagined that they were not only concerned with extinguishing the fire, but the Forbidden City expressed its gratitude to all of them. One foreign lady who came to watch the excitement started quarrelling with a Chinese fireman and actually hit her opponent on the nose with her fan. Later she showed me her bloodstained fan as evidence of her courage and I wrote a poem on it as a mark of my gratitude.

One can get an indication of the extent of the losses caused by the fire from the way the pile of cinders left over after the fire and the "salvaging" was dealt with. At the time I wanted to find a stretch of empty land for a tennis court where Johnston could teach me tennis, a game he said that all the English aristocrats played. The ruined site was just right for the purpose and so I told the Household Department to clear it up as quickly as possible. There were no traces of paintings, calligraphy or ancient porcelain in the rubble but there was a great deal of gold, silver, copper and tin. The gold merchants of Peking were invited by the Household Department to submit tenders and one of them bought the right to dispose of the ashes for 500,000 dollars; he picked out over 17,000 taels of gold from them. When he had taken what he wanted the Department packed the rest into sacks and distributed them to its personnel. One Department official later told me that four gold altars one foot in height and diameter that his uncle gave to the Yung Ho Kung Temple and the Cypress Grove Temple in Peking were all made of gold extracted from some of these sacks of ashes.

The cause of the fire is as impenetrable a mystery as the amount of damage it did. My suspicion is that it was deliberately started by thieves to cover their traces. Only a few days later another fire was started above one of the windows of the No Idleness Study in the eastern inner court of the Mind Nurture Palace. Fortunately it was detected early, and a wad of kerosene-soaked cotton wool was extinguished soon after it had been lit. My suspicions grew instantly stronger and I believed that somebody had started this fire not only to cover his traces, but also to murder me.

That there had been thefts and that the fire had been started deliberately to conceal them were facts that even my tutors did not attempt to conceal from me; but perhaps my fears of an attempt on my life were due to excessive nervousness. My suspicious nature was already quite obvious. According to the code of the Ching house the emperor had to read a page of the "instructions" of his ancestors, which were always set out for him in his bedroom, and at that time I particularly admired the "Vermilion Rescripts, Edicts and Decrees" of Emperor Yung Cheng (1723-35) for their cautious cynicism. He and Kang Hsi (1662-1722) warned against putting too much trust in anybody, particularly eunuchs. The message of these remarks was driven home by the fires.

I decided to follow the advice of Yung Cheng to "make things clear through careful investigation." I thought of two methods. One was to question the junior eunuchs of my entourage and the other was to eavesdrop on the eunuchs' conversations. I discovered at the window of one of their lodging places that they were discussing me behind my back, saying that my temper was getting worse and worse. This strengthened my suspicions. On the evening of the fire in the No Idleness Study I eavesdropped again under their windows and found that they had gone even further in their remarks about me and were saying that I had started the fire myself. I now felt that they were completely unreliable and that if I did not strike first there would be no end of trouble.

It was just then that an attempted murder was discovered. One of the eunuchs had been reported for making some mistake and had been beaten by a chief eunuch. Nursing his resentment he had gone into the room where the informer slept carrying some lime and a knife; he had thrown the lime into the man's face to blind him and then stabbed him. The attacker was still at large.

This made me think of all the eunuchs who had been beaten on my orders and I wondered whether they might not make some such attack on me. The thought was so frightening that I was too scared to sleep. There were eunuchs sleeping on mats on the floor from the room next to my bedroom all the way to the outbuildings of the Mind Nurture Palace, and if any of them was ill-disposed towards me and could stand me no longer it would be only too easy for him to finish me off. I wanted to find a reliable person to keep watch for me, and I could think of nobody but my empress. From then on I made Wan Jung sit up all night keeping watch; she was to wake me if she heard any movement, and I kept a club beside my bed ready for use. But after Wan Jung had spent several sleepless nights in a row I realized that this method was no good. Finally I decided to deal with the problem once and for all by expelling all the eunuchs from the palace.

I knew that I was bound to have some trouble doing this and that if I did not cope with my father it would be impossible. I decided to go and see him myself. Suddenly faced with this problem and having no way to discuss it with the head of the Household Department or my tutors he found it harder than ever to get his words out. With a tremendous effort he managed to produce a hotch-potch of objections: my ancestors had always had eunuchs; after all their years of service they could not plan any treachery; and so on. Finally he tried to persuade me to think it over for a few days. I replied that if he did not agree I would never return to the palace.

He was so worked up that he did not know whether to sit or to stand. Scratching his head and his cheek, and walking round in circles he knocked a bottle of lemonade to the floor with his sleeve and smashed it. I could not help giggling, and casually opened a book on the desk as if I had no intention of leaving.

Finally my father gave in and all the eunuchs, except a few from whom the High Consorts could not be parted, were driven out of the palace.

Reorganizing the Household Department

My expulsion of the eunuchs was very well received by public opinion, and under the direction of Johnston I made the Household Department the next object of my determination to govern well. The Household Department had a long tradition of corruption and graft. A friend of mine who was a former official of the Department has described how the Manchus who ran it abhorred scholarship and learning and regarded graft and corruption as practices in which they had imperial authority to indulge.

It will suffice to cite two examples of the Department's embezzlement. One is its astronomical annual expenditure, which could not have been covered by the 4,000,000 dollars annuity due under the Articles of Favourable Treatment even if it had been paid in full. It was revealed in 1924, after I left the palace, that the Department had received 5,000,000 dollars in that year from pawning gold, silver and antiques, and all of this money had been spent. Another example is the way in which the Household Department pawned a large batch of palace gold and jewellery through my father-in-law Jung Yuan at a fraction of its true value.

Although I did not have such evidence of the Department's corruption while I was still living in the palace as I did later, I knew one thing from the annual expenditure figures: they were higher than they had even been in the time of the empress dowager Tzu Hsi. In obedience to an edict of mine ordering that the finances be put in order the Household Department prepared "A Comparison Between the Expenditures of the Seventh Year of Hsuan Tung (1915) and the Past Three Years". According to their figures the Department's expenditure (excluding the set payments to the princes and high officials) was 2,640,000 taels in 1915; 2,380,000 taels in 1919; 1,890,000 taels in 1920; and 1,710,000 taels in 1921. At the beginning of the rule of Tzu Hsi annual expenditure had only been about 300,000 taels, and even in the year in which her seventieth birthday was celebrated it had only gone up to 700,000 taels. The difference would have been surprising to a worse mathematician than myself. At the same time I noticed stories in the gossip columns of the press about how noble and official families had been reduced to destitution or were going steadily downhill; I read about scions of such families being found dead in the gateways of the city wall and about princesses and noble ladies becoming prostitutes. Meanwhile officials of the Household Department were opening antique shops, banks, pawnshops, building firms and so on. Although my tutors sided with the Household Department to oppose my buying a car and installing a telephone, none of them had a good word to say for such behaviour by Department officials. My Manchu tutor Yi Ko Tan said to me not long before his death in 1921 that Chen Pao-shen was guilty of "deceiving his sovereign" because he would not tell me about the corruption of the Household Department and therefore did not deserve the title of "Grand Tutor". Johnston of course regarded the Department as a bloodsucking monster, and this view of his strengthened my resolution to clean it up.

"The Household Department in the palace and the stewards of the princes are all exceedingly rich," he remarked one day. "Their masters know nothing about their own finances and are completely dependent on them: without them they cannot lay their hands on a copper cash. Never mind restoring the old order, if they don't put their stewards in their proper place they won't even keep their remaining wealth for long."

"The Household Department has a motto," he said on another occasion. "It is 'preserve the present order'. Everything from a trifling reform to a major ideal runs into this obstacle and has to stop." He emphasized the last word by putting it into English.

The first use I made of my new authority after my wedding was to choose some of those I regarded as the most loyal and capable of the Ching veterans who had come to the ceremony to be my assistants in this undertaking. They in turn recommended their friends, and in this way another twelve or thirteen pigtails came into the palace. The most important of them were Cheng Hsiao-hsu, Lo Chen-yu,

138

Wang Kuo-wei and Shang Yen-ying. I distributed the titles "Companion of the Southern Study" (the emperor's study) and "Companion of the Great Diligence Hall" (referring to the office that looked after the emperor's stationery). I also put two bannermen in charge of the Household Department: my father-in-law Jung Yuan and the Mongol Chin Liang, the former tutor of Chang Hsueh-liang (the "Young Marshal").

They offered me very full advice on what I should do. In a document dated "First Month of the Sixteenth Year of Hsuan Tung" (1924), which would have been about two months before his appointment to the Household Department, Chin Liang wrote:

"In your subject's opinion the most important thing today is secretly to plan a restoration. To carry out this great enterprise of changing the world there are many things to do. The first priority is to consolidate the base by protecting the court; the next most important task is to put the imperial property into order so as to secure our finances. For it is necessary to have the wherewithal to support and protect ourselves; only then can we plan a restoration." He went on to suggest in more detail how these principles could be carried out, and one of his proposals with which I thoroughly agreed was that we should begin by reforming the Household Department.

Even the majority of the more apathetic Ching survivals supported the domestic reform plans. One group of them, however, led by Chen Pao-shen shook their heads at all talk of cleaning up the Household Department, reckoning that the situation had gone too far to be remedied; attempts to do so had been made in earlier reigns but without success. They thought that reorganization would only lead to trouble. But even they had not a good word to say for the Department.

At the urging of Johnston I had tried unsuccessfully to put my property in order shortly before my wedding, but I attributed the failure of this attempt to my minority and to choosing the wrong man for the job rather than to the machinations of the Department. Now that I had come of age and had all these new assistants I felt that I was in a much stronger position and entrusted Cheng Hsiao-hsu with the responsibility for the reform.

Cheng Hsiao-hsu was a fellow-provincial of Chen Pao-shen's who had served the Ching as a consul in Japan and later as a border commissioner in Kwangsi. Chen Pao-shen and Johnston both recommended him to me, particularly Johnston, who said that he was the man he had most admired in his twenty-odd years in China, and that his character, learning and ability were unmatched in the country. I also knew that he had refused to serve the Republic and had heard that he made his living from selling his calligraphy. I thought that he must be an exceptionally loyal subject.

After Cheng Hsiao-hsu became a "Companion of the Great Diligence Hall" he came to see me several times to explain to me how necessary it was to clean up the Household Department in order to "accomplish the great enterprise", and he told me about his plans for doing so. He thought that four sections would be quite enough to do the work of the Department; great numbers of its staff should be dismissed and enormous economies made. In this way the drain on resources could be stopped and the material position strengthened. If his plan were carried out the financial basis of a restoration could be assured. I was so struck by him that I broke precedent and appointed him Comptroller of the Household Department and "Keeper of the Keys and Seals" although he was a Han and not a Manchu. He thus became the leading official of the Household.

But to imagine that the vulgar and unlettered Household Department could be worsted by Cheng Hsiao-hsu was to underestimate this office which had over two hundred years of running the palace behind it. For all his eloquence and all the support and trust I gave him Cheng Hsiao-hsu only lasted three months.

I never found out who in the Department got rid of him. Did Shao Ying make trouble for him? This would seem unlikely as Shao Ying was famed for his cautious timidity. Was it Chi Ling? He was an outsider where the business of the Department was concerned and took little interest in it. As for the third of the high officials, Pao Hsi, he was a new arrival and unlikely to have been able to operate as effectively as that. Yet it was not likely that their subordinates would have dared to act against Cheng on their own initiative.

The first thing that Cheng Hsiao-hsu encountered on taking office was a backlog of files dating back to the Revolution of 1911. His response was to make a display of his authority by dismissing the holder of a key job and giving it to his friend Tung Chi-hsu. The Household's response was to behave as if it had been paralysed. If he wanted money, there was no money and accounts in black and white proved it; if he wanted some object nobody knew where it was stored, and this too was clearly stated in the records.

In order to win over his subordinates Cheng made a great show of humility and of listening to what they had to say. He held a discussion every week at which they were invited to offer suggestions for reform. One proposal made was that the expenditure on fruit and cakes used in offerings at the various shrines in the palace was too high and that as these offerings were only symbolic it would be just as dignified to use wooden or clay replicas. This suggestion met with Cheng Hsiao-hsu's strong approval and orders were given that it was to be put into effect; the proposer was promoted one grade. But the eunuchs who regarded the offerings as their legitimate income (there were about a hundred eunuchs left after the expulsion) all hated Cheng bitterly for it. Within a few days of taking office Cheng had become the most unpopular man in the Forbidden City.

When he would not abandon his position he received threatening letters saying that he was depriving people of their livelihood and that he had better be careful if he wanted to keep his head on his shoulders. Johnston received similar communications, and neither he nor Cheng paid any attention to them.

I was the person who finished off the reform episode. Soon after I had appointed Cheng Hsiao-hsu to the Household Department I heard some most unwelcome news: a group of members of the Republic's Parliament were reintroducing a bill to abolish the Articles of Favourable Treatment and make the Forbidden City over to the Republic. A bill like this had been presented two years previously on the grounds that the palace had staged a restoration in 1917 and that by granting peerages and posthumous titles to Republican officials it was putting itself above the Republic and clearly still plotting a restoration. Now that the bill was being reintroduced they were saying that I had given a posthumous title to Chang Hsun, the criminal instigator of the 1917 restoration, and had acted illegally in making a Han, Cheng Hsiao-hsu, Comptroller of the Household Department and giving him the right to ride a horse in the Forbidden City.

The appearance of this news in the papers was the signal for a series of attacks on the actions of the Household Department; various forms of corruption that had gone unremarked before now came in for public criticism. The inventory of paintings and calligraphy that was being made by Lo Chen-yu and others of my new batch of pigtailed advisers also came under fire: they were selling rubbings of bronzes and prints of pictures, and the originals themselves became fewer and fewer as the process went on. Then the Republic announced a "Bill for the Protection of Old Books, Antiques and Ancient Relics" that was clearly intended to prevent the palace from selling its art treasures.

My father came to see me and suggested in a roundabout and fawning way that I should carefully reconsider Cheng Hsiao-hsu's methods and think what trouble there might be with the Republican authorities disapproving of them.

One day Shao Ying, the former Household Comptroller, appeared before me looking very timid and said that the commander of the army of the Republic was deeply dissatisfied with Cheng Hsiao-hsu's actions; if Cheng made any more trouble and the Republic took action he would be able to do nothing to help me. I was terrified by this news, and then Cheng memorialized asking to be relieved of his duties. The result of it all was that Cheng reverted to being a "Companion of the Great Diligence Hall" and Shao Ying resumed control of the Household Department.

The Last Days in the Forbidden City

Although my attempt to reform the Household Department had ended in failure I did not abandon my efforts to improve my situation.

Apart from the men in the palace planning for my restoration there were others working for me all over the country. Kang Yu-wei, for example, was operating in China and abroad under the sign of his "Imperial Chinese Constitutional Monarchist Party". Through Johnston I received extravagant and fanciful reports of the support the party was supposed to be gaining, and although nearly all this support was imaginary I believed in it at the time.

I also gave money to charity. I can no longer remember which of my tutors suggested the idea, but the motive behind it was clear enough to me as I knew the value of public opinion. At that time the social pages of the Peking papers would carry items almost every day about gifts to the poor by the "Hsuan Tung Emperor". My "benefactions" generally fell into two types. Sometimes I would send money to a newspaper office to distribute when the paper carried some news about poor people and at other times I would send emissaries with money direct to destitute families. Whichever method I used, the newspapers would carry an item within the next day or two about it. I was able to get good publicity for the price of a few dollars and the papers were glad to help me for the publicity they could gain for themselves.

My biggest donation was made after the Japanese earthquake of 1923. Japan's losses from this disaster had shocked the world, and I thought I would take the chance to display the "benevolence" of the "Hsuan Tung Emperor". My tutor Chen Pao-shen showed more foresight than I did, and after praising "the magnificence of the imperial bounty and the humanity of the celestial mind" he told me that "this action will make its influence felt in the future". As I was short of ready cash I sent antiques, paintings and calligraphy that were valued at about US $300,000. The Japanese minister Yoshizawa came with a delegation from the Japanese Diet to thank me, and the excitement in the palace was like that created by the presence of foreign envoys at my wedding.

In these last days in the Forbidden City I became more absurd and inconsistent than ever. While I upbraided the Household Department for overspending there was no limit to my own extravagance. I told the Household Department to buy me foreign dogs like the ones I saw in Western magazines and even had their food imported from abroad. If the dogs fell ill I would spend more on getting them cured than I would for sick humans. There was a veterinary surgeon at the Peking Police School who must have understood my character and ingratiated himself with me by writing many memorials on the keeping of dogs; he received ten presents, including a green jade wristlet, a gold ring and a snuff bottle for his pains. Sometimes my interest would be drawn by an item in the papers about, say, a four-year-old who could read the ancient classic *Mencius* or somebody who had discovered a new sort of spider, and I would invite them to the palace and give them some money. At one time I had a passion for pebbles and gave huge rewards to people who bought them for me.

When I told the Household Department to reduce its staff they brought their numbers down from seven hundred to three hundred and cut the cooks from about two hundred down to thirty-seven. Yet at the same time I added a Western-style kitchen and the monthly cost of the materials used in the Western and Chinese kitchens was over 1,300 dollars.

My annual expenditure was 870,597 taels according to the reduced figures that the Household Department prepared for me in 1921, figures that did not cover my clothing, my food, or the outlay of the various bureaus and offices of the Household Department and only included my expenses and payments of "charity in obedience to the imperial edict".

This life went on until November 5, 1924, when the National Army of Feng Yu-hsiang drove me out of the Forbidden City.

The battle of Chaoyang in September of that year was the beginning of the second Chihli-Fengtien war. At first Wu Pei-fu's Chihli army was on top, but when Wu Pei-fu was attacking the forces of the Fengtien commander Chang Tso-lin at Shanhaikuan in October his subordinate Feng Yu-hsiang deserted him, marched his troops back to Peking and issued a peace telegram. Under the combined pressure of Feng Yu-hsiang and Chang Tso-lin, Wu Pei-fu's troops on the Shanhaikuan front collapsed and Wu himself fled. (Two years later he made a comeback by allying himself with Sun Chuan-fang, another warlord.) Even before the news of Wu's defeat at Shanhaikuan came through, Feng Yu-hsiang's National Army, now occupying Peking, had put Tsao Kun (the president of the Republic who had bought the votes for his election) under house arrest and dissolved the "piglet parliament". Huang Fu, a reactionary and opportunistic politician, organized a provisional cabinet with the backing of the National Army.

When the news of the *coup d'état* reached the palace I felt at once that the situation was dangerous. The palace guard was disarmed by Feng's National Army and moved out of the city. Feng's troops also took over their barracks and their posts at the Gate of Divine Valour. I looked at Coal Hill through a telescope from the Imperial Garden and saw that it was swarming with soldiers whose uniforms were different from those of the palace guard. The Household Department sent them tea and food which they accepted, and although there was nothing alarming about their behaviour everyone in the Forbidden City was worried. We all remembered that Feng Yu-hsiang had joined the "Army to Punish the Rebels" at the time of Chang Hsun's restoration and that if he had not been moved out of Peking in time he would undoubtedly have marched into the palace then. After Tuan Chi-jui had come to power Feng Yu-hsiang and some other generals had published telegrams demanding that the little court be expelled from the Forbidden City. This made us think that the *coup d'état* and the replacement of the palace guard boded ill for the future. Then we heard that all the political prisoners had been let out of jail and that "agitators" were active. The teachings of Chen Pao-shen and Johnston on the subject of "agitators" and "terrorists" had their effect on me, particularly the story that they wanted to kill every single nobleman. I sent for Johnston and asked him to go and find out the latest news from the foreign legations and arrange somewhere for me to take refuge.

All the princes were terrified. Some of them had already booked into the Wagons-Lits Hotel in the Legation Quarter, but when they heard that I wanted to leave the palace they said that it was not yet necessary: the foreign powers all recognized the Articles of Favourable Treatment and nothing serious could happen.

The inevitable at last occurred.

At about nine o'clock on the morning of November 5 I was sitting in the Palace of Accumulated Elegance (Chu Hsiu Kung) eating fruit with Wan Jung when the senior officials of the Household Department came rushing in. Shao Ying held a document in his hand and panted:

"Your Majesty, Your Majesty ... Feng Yu-hsiang has sent soldiers with an envoy saying that the Republic is going to annul the Articles of Favourable Treatment. They want your signature to this."

I jumped up, dropped my half-eaten apple to the floor, and grabbed the paper he was holding. On it was written:

By order of the President
Lu Chung-lin and Chang Pi have been sent to arrange with the Ching house for the revision of the Articles of Favourable Treatment.
November 5, 13th Year of the Republic of China
Acting Premier Huang Fu

The Revision of the Articles of Favourable Treatment

Whereas the emperor of the Great Ching Dynasty wishes to enter thoroughly into the spirit of the Republic of the Five Races and is unwilling to continue any system which is incompatible with the Republic, the Articles of Favourable Treatment of the Ching house are revised as follows:

1. The imperial title of the Hsuan Tung Emperor of the Great Ching is this day abolished in perpetuity, and he shall henceforward enjoy the same legal rights as all citizens of the Republic of China.

2. From the time of the revision of the Articles the Government of the Republic will grant the Ching house an annual subsidy of 500,000 dollars and will make a special payment of 2,000,000 dollars for the founding of a factory for the poor of Peking in which impoverished bannermen will have the first priority for admission.

3. In accordance with the third clause of the former Articles of Favourable Treatment the Ching house will leave the palace this day. They will be free to choose their own place of residence, and the Government of the Republic will continue to be responsible for their protection.

4. The sacrifices at the ancestral temples and the mausolea of the Ching house will be continued for ever, and the Republic will provide guards for their protection.

5. The Ching house will retain its private property, which will enjoy the special protection of the Government of the Republic. All public property will belong to the Republic.

November . . . , 13th Year of
the Republic of China

Frankly speaking, these revised articles were not nearly as bad as I had expected. What startled me was a remark of Shao Ying's: "They say that we must move out within three hours."

"But is that possible? What about all our property? What about the High Consorts?" I was pacing around in circles in my distress. "Telephone Johnston."

"The telephone has been cut," replied Jung Yuan.

"Send someone to fetch His Highness.[1] I always said there would be trouble, but you wouldn't let me go away. Get His Highness. Get His Highness."

"We can't get out," said someone else. "They've posted men outside and they won't let anyone out."

"Go and negotiate for me."

"Yes, sire."

As Tuan Kang had died a few days previously there were only two High Consorts left in the palace, and they absolutely refused to move out. Using this as an excuse Shao Ying went to negotiate with Lu Chung-lin, the Republic's envoy, and succeeded in getting an extension of the time limit until 3 p.m. After midday it was arranged that my father should be allowed into the palace and when he came my tutors Chu Yi-fan and Chen Pao-shen had also been let in, only Johnston being kept out.

---

[1] My father.

When I learnt that my father had come I went out to meet him, and as soon as I caught sight of him coming through the gate I shouted to him, "Your Highness, what are we going to do?"

At the sound of my shout he stood stock-still as if a spell had been cast on him. He neither came any closer to me nor did he answer my question; his lips quivered for a while and then he got out a completely useless sentence:

"I, I obey the edict, I obey the edict. . . ."

Now angry as well as worried I swung round and went back into my room. Later I heard from a eunuch that when my father heard that I had put my signature to the revised articles he pulled his hat with a peacock feather off and threw it on the floor, muttering, "It's all over, it's all over. I won't need this again."

Before long Shao Ying came back to my room, his face an even more dreadful sight than it had been earlier. He was shaking as he said, "Their envoy Lu Chung-lin is pushing us. He says we can only have another twenty minutes, and that if we aren't out by then . . . they'll open fire with artillery from Coal Hill."

Although the Republic's envoy had only brought twenty soldiers armed with pistols his threat was most effective. My father-in-law was so frightened that he rushed to the Imperial Garden to find somewhere to shelter from the artillery fire and refused to come out again. Seeing the terror of the princes I decided to accept Lu Chung-lin's demands at once and go to my father's house.

The National Army had laid on five cars for us. Lu Chung-lin rode in the front one, I followed in the second, and Wan Jung, Wen Hsiu, Shao Ying and others came behind.

When I got out of the car at the main gate of the Northern Mansion (my father's house), Lu Chung-lin came up and shook hands with me.

"Mr. Pu Yi, do you intend to be emperor in future, or will you be an ordinary citizen?" asked Lu.

"From today onwards I want to be an ordinary citizen."

"Good," said the envoy with a smile, "then we shall protect you." He went on to say that as China was a republic it was not right to have someone calling himself an emperor, and that I should now do my best for the country as a citizen.

"As a citizen," added another republican official, "you will have the right to vote and to stand for election. You could even be elected president one day."

The word "president" made me feel uneasy. As I understood that now I should retire from public life and wait for my opportunity I said:

"I have felt for a long time that I did not need the Articles of Favourable Treatment and I am pleased to see them annulled, so I fully agree with what you say. I had no freedom as an emperor, and now I have found my freedom."

When I finished this little oration the soldiers of the National Army who were standing nearby applauded.

My last sentence was not entirely untrue. I was sick of the restrictions with which the princes and high officials surrounded me. I wanted "freedom", freedom to realize the ambition of regaining my lost throne.

In the Northern Mansion

After speaking these fine words I hurried past the National Army guard and through the main gate of the Northern Mansion. As I sat in my father's study I thought that this was more like the tiger's mouth than a princely mansion. The first thing I had to do was to find out how dangerous my situation was. Before leaving the Forbidden City I had sent messages to my most loyal ministers outside the palace asking them to think up as quickly as possible some way of rescuing me from the clutches of the National Army. Up till now I had not heard any news of their activities nor had I received any other information about what was happening outside. I desperately wanted someone to talk things over with, even if it was only to hear a few words of consolation. In this situation my father was a big disappointment to me.

He was even more flustered than I was. From the time I entered the Northern Mansion he never stood still for a moment. When he was not walking up and down muttering to himself he was rushing in and out in a panic, making the atmosphere very tense. When I could not bear it any longer I said to him:

"Your Highness, sit down and talk it over. We must decide what to do, and before we do that we must get some news from outside."

"Decide what to do? Very well." He sat down, but before two minutes were up he leapt to his feet, exclaimed irrelevantly, "Tsai Hsun has not appeared either," and started pacing up and down again.

"We must get some news."

"Get some news? Very well." He went out and came back again a moment later. "They wo . . . won't let us out. There are soldiers at the main gate."

"Use the telephone then."

"Telephone? Yes, yes." But before he had gone many steps he came back to ask, "Who shall I telephone?"

I saw that the only thing to do was to have the eunuchs fetch the senior officials of the Household Department. But it turned out that Jung Yuan had entered the foreign hospital with nervous disorders, Chi Ling was moving out my clothing and other effects and dealing with the eunuchs and palace maids, and Pao Hsi was looking after the two High Consorts who were still in the palace; only Shao Ying was left with me, and he was in much the same state as my father and incapable of making a single phone call. Fortunately other princes and officials came later, as did my tutors; otherwise I do not know how bad the confusion in the Northern Mansion would have become. The best news was that brought by Johnston in the evening: through his speedy efforts the Dutch minister Oudendijk, the doyen of the diplomatic corps, the British minister Macleay, and the Japanese minister Yoshizawa, had already "protested" to the new foreign minister Wang Cheng-ting (Dr. C. T. Wang) and Wang had guaranteed the safety of my life and possessions to them. This news calmed everyone in the Northern Mansion except my father, for whom the dose was not strong enough. Johnston described the scene in *Twilight in the Forbidden City*:

> He received me in a large reception room which was nearly full of Manchu notables and of officers of the imperial household. . . . My first duty was to announce the result of the visit of the three ministers to the Foreign Office. They had already heard from Tsai Tao of the consultation in the Netherlands Legation that morning and were naturally eager to know what happened at the interview with Dr. Wang. They listened attentively to what I had to say, all but prince Chun, who while I was speaking moved nervously round the room for no apparent purpose. Several times he suddenly quickened his pace and ran up to me uttering a few half incoherent words. The slight impediment in his speech seemed to be more marked than when he was in a normal state. The purport of his words was the same each time he spoke: "Ask *huang-shang* (his majesty) not to be frightened" — a totally unnecessary remark from one who was himself obviously in a state of much greater alarm than the emperor. When he had run up to me four or five times with this inane observation I became slightly irritated and said, "His majesty is here, standing beside me. Why not address him direct?" But he was too much upset to notice the rudeness of my remark and resumed his aimless circumambulations.

Another action of my father's that evening made me particularly cross with him. Soon after Johnston's arrival Cheng Hsiao-hsu came with two Japanese. (Ever since the donation for the relief of the Tokyo earthquake my ministers had been in touch with the Japanese Legation, and when Lo Chen-yu and Cheng Hsiao-hsu came to the palace they also had contacts with the Japanese barracks.) Cheng had made a plan with Colonel Takemoto, the Japanese commander in Peking, by which a subordinate of Takemoto's would come in civilian clothes with a doctor and escort me to the Japanese barracks while pretending to take me to hospital. When Cheng arrived with the Japanese officer and doctor and explained his scheme it met with the unanimous opposition of the princes, officials and tutors. They thought that it would be very difficult to smuggle me past the soldiers guarding the main gate, and that even if I succeeded in evading them there were National Army patrols in the streets. If I were discovered by one of them things would be even worse. My father took the strongest line, and explained his reasons thus: "Even if His Majesty reaches the Legation Quarter, Feng Yu-hsiang will come and ask me about him, and then what will I do?" In the end Cheng Hsiao-hsu and his Japanese were sent away.

The restrictions at the gates of the Northern Mansion were tightened up the next day and people were allowed to enter but not to leave. Later they were relaxed a little, but still only my tutors Chen Pao-shen and Chu Yi-fan and the senior officials of the Household Department were allowed in and out; foreigners were absolutely barred. This really alarmed the Northern Mansion: if the National Army had no respect for foreigners there was no guarantee for the future at all. Later the two tutors went into this question and decided that there had never been any authorities that were not afraid of foreigners and that as the foreign minister of the provisional cabinet had given an undertaking to the three diplomats it was unlikely that he would differ from his predecessors. Although everyone else thought that their analysis was correct I was still worried: who knew how the soldiers at the gates felt? There was a saying in those days:

> Even when right a scholar never can
> Win an argument with a military man.

What difference did the word of the provisional government make to the soldiers who were only a few yards away? If they made trouble no guarantee would make the slightest difference. The more I thought about it the more frightened I got. I wished I had gone away with the Japanese that Cheng Hsiao-hsu had brought and cursed my father for only thinking of his own interests at the expense of my security.

Just then Lo Chen-yu came back from Tientsin where he had gone by the international train[1] to get help when Feng Yu-hsiang was taking over the palace guard. At the headquarters of the Jap-

---

[1] During the civil wars trains were often detained by warlords, so that the service between Peking and Tientsin was very irregular. This international train was organized at the wishes of the foreign legations, and neither side dared to interfere with it.

anese garrison in Tientsin he had been told by a staff officer about the capture of the Forbidden City and asked on behalf of the garrison commander to go and see Tuan Chi-jui. Tuan Chi-jui had also received a telegram asking for help from Cheng Hsiao-hsu that had been sent on by Colonel Takemoto in Peking. Tuan Chi-jui issued a circular telegram opposing Feng Yu-hsiang's "oppressive" measures against the palace. When he saw the draft of the telegram Lo Chen-yu realized that as Tuan Chi-jui was going to come back into public life the situation was not so serious. To be on the safe side, he asked the Japanese command in Tientsin to declare itself openly as my "protector". He was told that Colonel Takemoto in Peking would look after me. Acting on the Tientsin commander's instructions Lo Chen-yu returned to Peking and went to see Takemoto. Takemoto asked him to tell me that Japanese cavalry were patrolling near the Northern Mansion and that if the National Army were to start anything the Japanese barracks would take "decisive action". Chen Pao-shen also told me that the Japanese barracks wanted to send some military carrier pigeons to the Northern Mansion that could be used to give the alarm, and although we did not accept them for fear that the National Army might hear of it I felt more grateful than ever to the Japanese. After this Lo Chen-yu won a position in my affections equal to that of Cheng Hsiao-hsu, and I felt even more alienated from my father.

When I saw Tuan Chi-jui's telegram opposing Feng Yu-hsiang's measures against the palace and heard the news that Feng's troops were going to clash with the Fengtien army of Chang Tso-lin I gained new confidence. At the same time Chen Pao-shen brought me a secret telegram from Tuan Chi-jui, sent via the Japanese barracks in Peking, which included this sentence: "I will support the imperial house with all my strength and protect all its property." After this the control on the gates was relaxed a little more and everyone from princes to Dr. Hu Shih was allowed in, only Johnston being excluded.

Soon afterwards there was a new development in the relationship between Chang Tso-lin and Feng Yu-hsiang in which the Northern Mansion was so interested, when it was reported that Feng Yu-hsiang had been detained in Tientsin by Chang Tso-lin's Fengtien army. Although this story later proved to have been only a rumour, it was rapidly followed by some news that was even more exciting to the Northern Mansion: the provisional cabinet of Huang Fu that was supported by Feng Yu-hsiang's National Army met with refusals when it invited the foreign diplomats to a banquet. The Northern Mansion optimistically reckoned that the days of the provisional government with which I could not coexist were numbered and that it would be replaced by Tuan Chi-jui, who was far more to the liking of the Legation Quarter, particularly the Japanese Legation. The next day's news confirmed Lo Chen-yu's report: Feng Yu-hsiang had to accept Chang Tso-lin's proposal and allow Tuan Chi-jui to return to public life. Within a few days both Chang Tso-lin and Tuan Chi-jui were in Peking.

The news of the alliance between Tuan Chi-jui and Chang Tso-lin changed the atmosphere in the Northern Mansion. The first thing the princes did was to write a secret letter to Chang asking for his protection. After he and Tuan had entered the capital the princes sent their representatives along with Cheng Hsiao-hsu to welcome them, and later they divided their efforts. They sent Cheng Hsiao-hsu to see Tuan Chi-jui and the chief steward of the Northern Mansion, who was Chang Tso-lin's sworn brother, to see Chang. What most delighted the Northern Mansion was the invitation that Chang sent Johnston asking him to come and see him. Chang's aim in inviting Johnston was to sound him on the attitude of the Legation Quarter towards himself, while the Household Department hoped to find out Chang's attitude to me through Johnston. I gave Johnston a signed photograph of myself and a ring set with a large diamond to take with him. Chang Tso-lin accepted the photograph, refused the ring, and expressed his sympathy. At the same time Tuan Chi-jui indicated to Cheng Hsiao-hsu that he might consider restoring the Articles of Favourable Treatment. With the "sympathy" of the Legation Quarter and the support of these two men the Northern Mansion dared to "counter-attack" although Feng Yu-hsiang's troops were still in Peking.

On November 28, the day after the National Army soldiers were withdrawn from the front gate of the Mansion and Feng Yu-hsiang issued his telegram of resignation, the Northern Mansion sent an official communication to the Home Ministry in the name of the Household Department:

> . . . According to the provisions of the principles of jurisprudence as applied to criminal law, all those who use violence to compel others to do things may be held guilty of assault; and according to the principles of civil law anything that is extorted through violence or terror has no legal validity. We wish to make it known through this letter that the Ching house is unable to recognize the legal validity of the five revised articles imposed by the provisional cabinet. . . .

Letters appealing for the support of foreign ministers were published at the same time as this. The Northern Mansion also ceased to recognize the "Committee for the Readjustment of the Affairs of the Ching House" although the Ching house sent representatives to participate in its first few meetings.

That day I was interviewed by a reporter from the Japanese-run paper *Shuntien Times* (a paper supported by the Japanese Legation which openly backed me and printed absurd atrocity stories about the expulsion from the palace), and what I said to him was the exact opposite of what I had said on the day I had been forced to leave the palace:

"I certainly did not gladly assent when I was forcibly compelled to sign the document by the soldiers of the National Army pretending to act in the name of the people."

Decision at the Crossroads

Although the people in the Northern Mansion shared the same excitement their views on what we should do differed. One of them, Chin Liang, later wrote in his *Journal of the Coup*:

After Tuan Chi-jui and Chang Tso-lin entered the capital they appeared to be very friendly to us but their friendship extended only to words, not to deeds. Everyone was deceived into believing that a return to the palace was imminent; when it did not take place people were of various opinions. Some said that we should not allow a word of the original Articles to be altered; some that the emperor should return to the palace with his title restored; some that he should change his title to Retired Emperor; some that annual expenditure could be cut, but foreign guarantees should be obtained; some that he should move to the Summer Palace; and some that a house should be bought in the eastern part of the city. But as real power was in the hands of others all these plans were dreams: I do not know what cause they had to think as they did.

The storm of November 5, 1924 blew me out of the Forbidden City and dropped me at the crossroads. Three roads stretched out before me. One was to do what the revised Articles suggested: to abandon the imperial title and my old ambitions and become an enormously wealthy and landed "common citizen". Another was to try and get the help of my "sympathizers" to cancel the new Articles and restore the old Articles in their entirety, to regain my title and return to the palace to continue to live my old life. The third possible course was the most tortuous: first to go abroad and then to come back to the Forbidden City, the Forbidden City as it had been before 1911. In the words of the time, this course was "using foreign power to plan a restoration".

As I faced this decision I was surrounded by men who argued endlessly over the merits of the different choices. They regarded the first possibility as not worthy of serious consideration, but fought stubbornly over the other two; and even the advocates of the same course would differ in their specific proposals.

The argument centred on whether I should stay in the Northern Mansion or take refuge in the Legation Quarter, and the party led by my father which advocated my staying put was successful at first. But their victories were insecure as their attempts to keep me in the Mansion made me more and more determined to get out. Although I had no definite ideas about my future one thing was clear in my mind from the moment I entered the portals of the

Northern Mansion: come what might I was going to leave. I had not left a big Forbidden City just to stay in a miniature one, particularly when I was in such danger there.

At this stage a new advocate of my going abroad appeared: my old friend Dr. Hu Shih.

Not long before I had seen in the papers an open letter of his to the foreign minister of the provisional cabinet in which he had roundly abused the National Army and expressed his "indignation" at the revision of the Articles of Favourable Treatment through "military intimidation". Although my tutor Chen Pao-shen still regarded him as a reptile Cheng Hsiao-hsu had made friends with him, and some of the former Ching officials thought that he was better at any rate than the revolutionaries and the National Army. Nobody tried to keep him out of the Northern Mansion. I welcomed him and praised his open letter. He inveighed against the National Army once more and said, "In the eyes of Europe and America this is all oriental barbarism."

This visit of Hu Shih's was not just a courtesy call: it sprang from his "concern" for me. He asked me what plans I had for the future. I replied that the princes and high officials were working for a restoration of the old order but that I was not in the least interested as I wanted to lead an independent life and acquire some learning.

"Your Majesty has high ideals," he said with a nod of approval. "After my last visit to the palace I told my friends that Your Majesty had high ideals."

"I want to go and study abroad but there are so many difficulties."

"Of course there are difficulties, but they can't be too serious. If you go to England Mr. Johnston can look after everything, and you will have no trouble in finding people to help you if you go to America."

"The princes and high officials won't let me go, particularly His Highness."

"That was what Your Majesty said at my last audience in the palace. I think that you will have to take some decisive action."

"I am not sure whether the Republican authorities would let me go."

"That will be no problem. The important thing is for Your Majesty to make a firm decision."

Although I felt instinctive reservations about this "modern personality" his remarks encouraged me. He made me realize that my plan of going abroad would have the sympathy of quite a lot of people. He also made me feel more tired than ever of the princes and officials who were opposed to the idea.

I felt that those who wanted to go back to the old life in the palace only wanted to do so for the sake of their titles. What enabled them to feed their families was not the emperor but the Articles. Only under the old order could they continue to occupy their lucrative sinecures or draw their pensions.

Johnston came back to me after my meeting with Hu Shih and conveyed Chang Tso-lin's concern to me. I thought that Hu Shih was right in saying that the authorities would not prevent me from going abroad. While Johnston and I were discussing how to arrange this, Chang Tso-lin indicated that I would be welcome to go and stay in the Northeast. I thought that it might be a good idea to spend some time in the Northeast first as once I was there I would be able to go abroad whenever I liked, but just when I had come to this decision a new problem arose.

The atmosphere had become much more relaxed after the withdrawal of the National Army guard from the gate and I had been very bold in cursing the National Army to the journalist as I mentioned above. Then Cheng Hsiao-hsu suddenly appeared and asked me if I had seen the papers or not.

"I've seen them, but there isn't much in them."

"Your Majesty, look at the *Shuntien Times*." He showed me a headline reading "Reds Advocate People's Self-rule". This news item said that since the entry of Feng Yu-hsiang's troops into the capital "reds" had started activities; recently tens of thousands of leaflets had appeared advocating "self-rule, not government; freedom, not laws" and so on. I had often been told by Cheng Hsiao-hsu, Chen Pao-shen, Johnston and others and read in the *Shuntien Times* that Communists were reds and radicals and that communism meant "raging floods and wild beasts", common property and common wives. I had also heard that Feng Yu-hsiang's army had contacts with the "reds" and "radicals" and various other stories. Now Cheng Hsiao-hsu explained to me that the country was on the brink of violent upheavals and that there was no question but that the "reds" would murder me.

My alarm became even worse when Lo Chen-yu came in with a grim expression on his face. I had always attached great importance to the news that Lo obtained from Japanese sources, and this time he reported that the Japanese had heard from their intelligence that Feng Yu-hsiang and the "reds" were planning action against me. "Feng's troops are now occupying the Summer Palace," he said, "and something may happen in the next day or two. Your Majesty must leave here as soon as possible and take refuge in the Legation Quarter."

Johnston then turned up with the news from the foreign press that Feng Yu-hsiang was going to make a new move against Peking. I was no longer able to restrain my anxiety and even Chen Pao-shen was so alarmed that he agreed to the suggestion that I should take shelter in the Legation Quarter while Feng Yu-hsiang's troops were not at the Northern Mansion. He suggested that I first enter the German Hospital as a doctor there was an acquaintance of mine. Chen Pao-shen, Johnston and myself discussed these plans secretly as they had to be kept not only from the Republican authorities but also from my father.

We acted according to the secret plans and carried out the first stage: I went with my tutor Chen Pao-shen to visit the two High Consorts, who had moved out of the palace a few days after me and were now living in Chilinpei Lane, and then came back to the Northern Mansion. This was to make the Northern Mansion feel that I was trustworthy. We decided to carry out stage two the following day. I was to say that I was going to inspect a house that we were intending to hire in Piaopei Lane and then slip into the Legation Quarter and enter the German Hospital. The third stage would be to go to a legation. Once I was in the Legation Quarter the third stage and the fourth one of bringing Wan Jung and Wen Hsiu to rejoin me would be quite easy. But when we had got into the cars and were about to start on stage two my father sent his chief steward to come with us. I rode in the first car with Johnston and the steward sat behind Chen Pao-shen in another.

"That's a bit awkward," said Johnston in English with a frown when he had got into the car.

"Never mind him." I was furious. I told the driver to start and we drove out of the Northern Mansion. I never wanted to enter those gates again in my life.

Johnston thought that we could not ignore the steward and would have to think of some way of shaking him off. As we drove along he decided that we should stop at a shop to buy something and send him back.

There was a foreign-run shop selling watches, clocks and cameras situated at the entrance to the Legation Quarter. When we reached the shop I went in with Johnston. After looking around I chose a French pocket-watch, but although I dillied and dallied for a long time the steward waited outside and obviously had no intention of going. Johnston had to fall back on his last resort and tell the steward that I did not feel well and was going to visit the German Hospital. He was suspicious and he followed us there, but once we arrived we pushed him aside. Johnston told Dr. Dipper why I had come and showed me into an empty ward to rest. The steward, seeing that something was wrong, disappeared at once. We knew that he would be bound to go back to the Northern Mansion to report to my father, so Johnston lost no time in going to negotiate with the British Legation. As time passed and I had no news from him I became extremely anxious, fearing that the steward would fetch my father. Just then Chen Pao-shen arrived followed by Cheng Hsiao-hsu. This is how Cheng Hsiao-hsu described the events that followed in his journal:

> I recommended to His Majesty that he go to the Japanese Legation and he ordered me to go and tell the Japanese. I thereupon visited Colonel Takemoto, and told him of the emperor's arrival, and he informed Mr. Yoshizawa. Takemoto then asked me to invite the emperor to come to the legation forthwith. A strong wind was blowing at the time and the sky was filled with yellow sand so that one

could only see for a distance of a few paces. When I returned to the hospital I was worried that the chauffeur might disobey orders and so advised His Majesty to travel in my carriage. I was also concerned about the crowd of people outside the front entrance of the hospital, so I took the carriage round to the back door. A German doctor with the keys and a nurse led the way and the emperor got into the carriage with myself and a servant. The distance between the German Hospital and the Japanese Legation is about one *li* (half a kilometre), and there are two routes, one going from east to west through the Quarter and turning north, and the other along Changan Street[1] and turning south. I told the coachman to go back to the Japanese Legation. As the second route was slightly shorter he drove into Changan Street. His Majesty exclaimed in alarm, "Why did we come this way? There are Chinese policemen in the street." As the carriage was going at a good speed I said, "We will be there in a moment. Nobody could know that this carriage contains an emperor. Please do not be alarmed, Your Majesty."

When we turned south along the bank of the stream I was able to report that we were in the Legation Quarter again, and then we arrived at the Japanese Legation. Takemoto met the emperor and took him to the barracks, where Chen Pao-shen joined us.

Cheng Hsiao-hsu was very pleased with the role he had played in my flight and wrote two poems and painted a symbolic picture to commemorate the occasion. His main cause for satisfaction was that he had beaten his secret rival Lo Chen-yu in this struggle for mastery. Lo had been unable to rise to the occasion and had even allowed his valuable connections with Colonel Takemoto to be delicately filched by Cheng. The rivalry between the two men had at first been concealed behind their common struggle against the princes, but from now on the battle was on.

In *Twilight in the Forbidden City* Johnston corrected a mistake in Cheng's account of the flight to the Legation Quarter. Cheng thought that Colonel Takemoto had gained the consent of the Japanese minister before he received me in the barracks. Such was the relationship between the military and civil officials in the Japanese Legation, however, that Takemoto did not in fact report his con-

---

[1] Changan Street was outside the Legation Quarter and thus not under foreign control.

versation with Cheng to the minister as he did not want his guest to be taken away from him.

But taken away from Takemoto I was. As soon as the minister heard that I had arrived at the barracks he invited me to move over to the legation proper and I accepted the invitation.

From Legation Quarter to Concession

In those days the Legation Quarter and the foreign concessions were definitely "hospitable" places. Seven years previously President Li Yuan-hung had been driven to take shelter in a legation by Chang Hsun when I became emperor for the second time, and Chang Hsun himself had become a "guest" of the Dutch Legation a few days later. Whenever a legation was going to receive such guests the hotels and hospitals in the Legation Quarter would always be very busy. Many nervous people whose status was too low to get into a legation would pack these places so full that some of them were willing to pay even for a place under the stairs.

My reception was the first and probably the last of its kind. When I sent for my wives from the Northern Mansion the Republican police there would not let them out, so the Japanese Legation sent a secretary to arrange the matter. When his efforts were unavailing the minister went to see Chief Executive Tuan Chi-jui himself, and as a result Wan Jung and Wen Hsiu with their eunuchs and ladies-in-waiting rejoined me.

Seeing the size of my entourage the minister realized that three rooms were clearly inadequate to accommodate us, and he cleared a whole building for us to live in. There was room for everyone, from Companions of the Southern Study and senior officials of the Household Department to dozens of attendants, eunuchs, ladies-in-waiting, maids and scullions. The essential administrative offices of the Great Ching Emperor functioned once more in the Japanese Legation.

What was more important was that Yoshizawa persuaded the Provisional Government to take an understanding attitude to me. Apart from explaining its views to Yoshizawa the Provisional Government sent an envoy to visit Colonel Takemoto and repeat: "The Provisional Government has every intention of respecting the Retired Emperor's wish for freedom and will do all within the bounds of possibility to protect the security of his life, his property and his dependants."

A group of princes led by my father came to try and persuade me to return to the Northern Mansion. They said that it was now safe as the presence of Tuan Chi-jui and Chang Tso-lin in the capital kept the National Army under restraint; in addition, Tuan and Chang had offered guarantees of my safety. But I believed Lo Chen-yu and the others who said that these guarantees had only been offered because I had entered the legation, and that if I were to return to the Northern Mansion with the National Army still in Peking no guarantee would have any force. I refused to go back. The princes were in fact finding themselves places to stay in the Legation Quarter themselves at the time.

The enthusiasm with which the Japanese Legation looked after me stirred many Ching veterans who were previously unknown to me into action. They sent telegrams from all over the country asking Chief Executive Tuan Chi-jui to restore the original favourable treatment; they sent me money to cover my expenses; and some of them even came to Peking to pay their respects and offer me grand strategies. The Mongol princes acted as if they had taken some stimulant, publishing circular telegrams and sending petitions to the Provisional Government demanding to know what was going to happen about their own favourable treatment. The Provisional Government replied that it would continue unchanged. The Ching princes and high officials took a harder line and refused to take part in the meetings of the "Committee for the Readjustment of the Affairs of the Ching House". This committee, which had been formed not long previously, was to make an inventory of the property of the Ching house and divide it into private and public. Shao Ying and the other Ching members of the committee followed up their refusal to attend by announcing publicly to the authorities that they did not recognize it.

More and more former Ching officials came to the Japanese Legation every day to show their integrity, pay their respects, offer money, and secretly explain their "grand strategies for a revival". On Chinese New Year's Day my small drawing room was full of pigtails; I sat facing south in imperial style on a Western-style chair that substituted for a throne and received congratulations.

Many of the old-timers were full of gratitude for my Japanese hosts. They saw grounds for hope in the reception I received from the legation and drew at least a modicum of satisfaction from it. One of them, Wang Kuo-wei, wrote in a memorial: "The Japanese minister . . . does not only take Your Majesty's past glory into account, he sees you as the future ruler of China: how can your subjects and officials fail to be gratified?"

Thirteen days after the Chinese New Year came my twentieth birthday (by Chinese reckoning).[1] As I was in a stranger's house I had not intended to celebrate it, but my host was determined to please me and offered me the main hall of the legation in which to receive congratulations. The hall was furnished for the occasion with magnificent carpets, and behind the arm-chair with a yellow cushion that served as a throne stood a glass screen covered with yellow paper. All the pages wore large Ching hats with red tassels. Over a hundred former Ching officials came from several large cities for the birthday celebrations, which were also attended by members of the Diplomatic Corps as well as princes, high officials, and local Ching veterans, making a total of over 500 people.

I wore a blue patterned silk gown and a black satin jacket, and all the princes, court officials and Ching veterans wore the same. Apart from this the ceremonial usages were much the same as they had been in the palace. Imperial yellow, queues and ninefold kotows combined to give me feelings of anguish and heartbreaking melancholy. After the ceremony I made an impromptu speech. A version of it was printed in the Shanghai press, which, while not entirely accurate, contained the following fairly authentic passage:

---

[1] By Western reckoning my nineteenth birthday.

As I am only a young man of twenty it is not right that I should be celebrating "long life", and I am particularly unenthusiastic about doing so in the present difficulties as a guest under a stranger's roof. But as you have come a great distance I wish to take this opportunity to meet you and talk to you. I am fully aware that in the modern world emperors can exist no longer and I am resolved not to run the risks involved in being one. My life deep in the Great Within was that of a prisoner, and I took no delight in my lack of freedom. I have long nourished the ambition of going abroad and have studied English assiduously to that end, but I was under too many restrictions to be able to realize my hopes.

The continuation or abolition of the Articles of Favourable Treatment seems to me a matter of no importance. Had I ended them voluntarily that would have been acceptable, but it is intolerable for others to do so through compulsion. The Articles were a bilateral agreement and can no more be altered by the decree of one of the parties than an international treaty. The sending of troops to the palace by Feng Yu-hsiang was a violent act devoid of ordinary human feelings when the matter could easily have been settled by negotiation. I have long had a sincere wish not to use that empty title, but being compelled to drop it by armed force has made me feel most unhappy. From the point of view of the Republic such barbarous actions do great damage to the country's name and its reputation for good faith.

Of the motives for my expulsion from the palace I will not speak, and they are probably already known to you. As I was completely powerless it was no martial feat on Feng Yu-hsiang's part to act against me as he did, and it is hard to describe the humiliating intimidation to which I was subjected after leaving the palace. Even if he had been justified in driving me out, why did he impound all the clothes, vessels, calligraphy and books left by my ancestors? Why did he not allow us to take away the rice bowls, tea cups and kitchen utensils that were in daily use? Was this a case of "preserving antiques"? Were they worth anything? I do not think that he would have acted so harshly even in dealing with bandits.

When he says that the restoration of 1917 invalidated the Articles of Favourable Treatment he should remember that I was only a child of twelve[1] at the time and incapable of organizing a restoration myself. But leaving that matter aside, has the so-called "annual subsidy" ever been paid on time since the Articles were signed? Have the grants to

---

[1] Eleven by Western reckoning.

the princes and nobles ever been paid as stipulated in various agreements? Have the living expenses of bannermen ever been met as they should have been according to the articles providing for their favourable treatment? The responsibility for ending the Articles lies with the Republic: to ignore this and give the restoration of 1917 as a pretext is exceedingly biassed.

I do not wish to complain, but I cannot miss this opportunity to reveal the sorrows that lie in my heart, so that if the parliament of the Republic hears of them it will, if it has a whit of human feeling left, feel that this matter must be settled equitably. I would accept such a settlement without demur.

I have another important announcement to make. I will never agree to any proposal that I should seek foreign intervention on my behalf: I could never use foreign power to intervene in domestic Chinese politics.

About the time of my birthday celebration the press was full of attacks on my group, attacks that reflected the indignation of the great majority of people. There were public outcries when the "Committee for the Readjustment of the Affairs of the Ching House" published such things as the postscript to the Articles of Favourable Treatment that Yuan Shih-kai wrote when he was emperor and documentary proof of the way the Household Department had been mortgaging, selling, and removing palace treasures. What caused the most wrath, however, were the connections between the little court and the Japanese and the attempts by Ching fogeys to restore the Articles. A "League Against the Favourable Treatment of the Ching House" appeared in Peking and started to take vigorous action against the little court. Public disapproval expressed itself in the papers in various ways: small satirical items, direct accusations, well-meaning advice and warnings to the Japanese Legation and the Republican authorities. When I look at them today I realize how different my life would have been if I had accepted any of these criticisms. Some of the articles exposed the plots of the Japanese, and I reproduce a part of one of them here. It was carried in the *Peking Daily*, and its account of the plans that the Japanese had for me was so close to what happened later it startles me to read it today:

The darkest part of the plot is to keep him until there is an incident in a particular province, when a certain country will send him there with armed protection and revive the rank and title of his distant ancestors. The province will be separated from the Republic and will receive that country's protection. The second step will be to deal with it in the same way as another country that has already been annexed was dealt with. . . .

Pu Yi's terror and flight were the result of deliberate intimidation by certain people. He has fallen into their trap, which was a part of a prearranged long-term plan. . . . In their present treatment of him they are willing to go to any expense to provide him with everything. The country in question has bought the friendship of each of his followers, who have come under its control without realizing it and will be its tools in future.

These true words seemed to me at the time to be slander and treachery, and I thought that they were intended to trick me into going back to the Northern Mansion and to persecution.

When I was living in the Japanese Legation I went for several bicycle rides at night out of curiosity, taking one or two servants with me; later the main gate of the legation was closed and I was not allowed to go out. On one of these trips I rode as far as the moat outside the Forbidden City and as I looked at the turrets and battlements I thought of the Mind Nurture Palace and the Cloudless Heaven Palace that I had left so recently, and of my throne and of imperial yellow. A desire for revenge and restoration welled up in my heart. My eyes filled with tears as I resolved that I would return here in the future as a conquering king just as the first of my line had done. Muttering an ambiguous goodbye I remounted my bicycle and rode away at a high speed. . . .

Every day of the three months I spent in the legation I received the diligent attentions of my Japanese hosts, oaths of loyalty from old-timers and protests from the public. Under these three influences my ambition and hatred grew unceasingly. I thought that it would not do for me to carry on living there as I ought to be making some preparations for my future. My wish to go abroad and study in Japan came back to me, and one of the legation secretaries was very enthusiastic about the idea.

The struggle between Lo Chen-yu and Cheng Hsiao-hsu with me as the object continued while I was in the legation. This round ended with a victory for Lo when Cheng asked to be relieved of his duties and went back to Shanghai.

Not long after my birthday Lo Chen-yu informed me that he had arranged with one of the legation officials that I should make preparations for going abroad in Tientsin as it was not at all convenient for me to go on staying in the legation. It would be best for me to find a house in the Japanese concession as the one I had already bought was unsuitably situated in the British concession. This all seemed sensible enough to me, particularly as I wanted to see the big city of Tientsin, so I agreed at once. I sent a "Companion of the Southern Study" to find me a house in the Japanese concession in Tientsin, and I finally settled on the Chang Garden. A few days later Lo Chen-yu told me that the house was ready and the National Army was changing its garrisons, so we should take this good opportunity and move at once. I talked it over with Yoshizawa and he agreed to my departure. He also had Tuan Chi-jui informed, and in addition to giving his consent Tuan offered to provide me with a military escort. Yoshizawa had already decided to bring the police chief of the Japanese consulate-general in Tientsin to Peking together with some plainclothes policemen; first I was to go under their protection and then my wives were to follow. All was now settled.

At 7 p.m. on February 23, 1925 I took my leave of the Japanese minister and his wife. We posed for photographs, I thanked them, and they wished me a safe journey. I then left by the back gate of the legation with a Japanese official and some plainclothes policemen and walked to the Chienmen railway station. Here I met Lo Chen-yu and his son. At every station where the train stopped several Japanese policemen and special agents in black civilian clothes would get on, and by the time we reached Tientsin the carriage was almost full of them. As I got out of the train I was met by the Japanese consul-general in Tientsin, Yoshida Shigera, and several dozen officers and men of the Japanese garrison.

Three days later the *Shuntien Times* printed a statement issued by the Japanese Legation stating that my intention of leaving Peking had long been known to the Provisional Government, and that it had never wished to interfere with the plan. My sudden departure had been the result of the unstable situation in Peking.

CHAPTER FOUR

▣▣▣

TIENTSIN

P'u Yi's six years in Tientsin, the most Westernized of northern Chinese cities, were spent in the Japanese concession, a tiny colonial enclave outside the control of the Chinese government. Throughout this period Japan was holding him ready for future use in its plans for China, though the army and foreign office were treating each other as dangerous enemies; hence the differences between policies of the Japanese consulate-general and garrison.

For the court in exile these were years of learning to accept that the Republic was not on the point of abolishing itself and that the various war-lords and other adventurers (including the former tsarist general-turned-bandit Semionov), in whom they placed their hopes at one time or another, could not bring about a restoration. While P'u Yi enjoyed the semi-foreign life he could lead in Tientsin, away from the restrictive traditions of the Forbidden City, the Republic seemed more and more of a threat during and after the revolutionary upheavals of 1924–8 that swept away the familiar war-lord governments in Peking and replaced them with Chiang Kai-shek's Kuomintang regime in Nanking.

These were also years in which Japan replaced Britain as the dominant power in China. While China held only a small part of the global interests of Britain or the United States, it was the main field for the imperial ambitions and appetites of Japan. In Northeast China, Japan had the South Manchuria Railway, the ports of Talien and Lüshun, much industrial and other investment, and the Kwantung Army. Tientsin was its main military base for north China.

Gradually the Ch'ing house and its advisers, despite their rivalries, came to see that Japan was their only hope. Though P'u Yi preferred the English language and things British, only Japan had any real need of him.

The Efforts of Lo Chen-yu

When I reached Tientsin I found that Lo Chen-yu had not told the truth when he told me that my house was ready, and I spent my first day in the Yamato Hotel. The next day Wan Jung, Wen Hsiu and all the others who had been in the Japanese Legation with me arrived, and we all moved into the hastily furnished Chang Garden.

The Chang Garden covered over three acres and included a large house. It belonged to a former Ching general who would not take any rent for it from me, and at first he swept the yard for me himself as a sign of his loyalty. We stayed there for five years, and moved from there to the Quiet Garden after his death when his son asked us for rent.

My aim in coming to Tientsin had been to go abroad, but I ended up by spending seven years there, seven years in which I wavered between different factions and different ideas. The princes, my father included, had far less power over me, and Johnston ceased to be my tutor, although he did visit me in 1926 and canvassed unsuccessfully for support for me from the warlord Wu Pei-fu and others. He later returned to England.

One could divide the people who struggled to win my favour in those seven years into various groups. There were the old ministers" led by Chen Pao-shen who at first hoped for the restoration of the Articles of Favourable Treatment and later just wanted to maintain the status quo. They could be called the "back to the palace faction". Another group round Lo Chen-yu put their hopes in my going abroad and in getting help from foreign countries, principally Japan; they could be considered as the "ally with Japan" or "going abroad" faction, and they included Ching veterans, as well as one or two of the Manchu princes, such as Pu Wei. A third party, in which I was the leading figure, thought that the best method was to contact and buy over warlords. Our "employing military men" group was rather heterogeneous, including Ching veterans and Republican politicians.

When Cheng Hsiao-hsu came back to my service he attached himself to no clique. He seemed both to praise and to attack the proposals that the others put forward; then he would suggest ideas that none of them had brought up, such as the use of foreign advisers and the "open door" (co-operating with any country that was willing to help in a restoration), and his suggestions were opposed by all the other factions. When he later settled on a policy of relying on Japan he overcame all his opponents including his old rival Lo Chen-yu, the leader of the pro-Japanese clique.

Leaving these later developments aside, let us first take a look at Lo Chen-yu. When he came to the Forbidden City he was about fifty. A man of medium height, he wore gold-rimmed spectacles (which he took off when in my presence), and had a yellow-white goatee and a white queue. He spoke slowly in the accent of the part of Chekiang Province from which he came. I first met him after my marriage when he was appointed a "Companion of the Southern Study" and given the job of authenticating the palace's ancient bronzes. In addition to having got himself a reputation as a scholar, he had also caught my attention as a monarchist.

Lo, who had been an official under the Ching, had lived either in Japan or in Japanese concessions in China for nearly all the time since the Revolution of 1911. He had built himself up as an "authority" on antiques through various underhand means, and was a forger of ancient books and seals, willing to "authenticate" fake paintings and pieces of calligraphy for a fee. He ruthlessly plagiarized the scholarship of his associate Wang Kuo-wei. When Wang Kuo-wei committed suicide, possibly because he could tolerate Lo Chen-yu's cruelty no longer, Lo made the most of the occasion. He forged a suicide note from Wang which he used to propagate a myth that Wang had killed himself because of his loyalty to the Ching. Thus Lo improved his standing with me through exploiting the death of his own colleague.

The first thing over which Lo Chen-yu and Cheng Hsiao-hsu quarrelled was the question of whether or not I should go abroad. After I fled from the Japanese Legation to the Japanese concession in Tientsin public opposition to me reached a new peak. An "Anti-Ching League" appeared in Tientsin for the sole purpose of attacking me. Lo Chen-yu and his associates took this opportunity to impress on me that for the sake both of my safety and of my restoration I had no alternative but to go abroad. Their opinion had a considerable amount of support for a time among former Ching officials.

Chen Pao-shen and his clique regarded such ideas as rash. They did not think that I was in any great danger and feared that I might not be welcome in Japan. If it was going to be impossible for me to stay in Japan or China, there was no point in thinking that Tuan Chi-jui, Chang Tso-lin and their like would allow me to return to the Forbidden City and live as I had done before. Although I was not attracted by Chen Pao-shen's advice, the warnings that he gave me made me doubtful about Lo Chen-yu's suggestions.

In 1926 the political situation developed as Chen Pao-shen and his group had hoped. Chang Tso-lin switched to co-operation with Wu Pei-fu and clashed with his former associate Feng Yu-hsiang. Feng Yu-hsiang's National Army was attacked by Chang Tso-lin's Fengtien army, and Feng had to withdraw his men from Tientsin; his units in Peking, meanwhile, were surrounded. When Feng Yu-hsiang uncovered the connections between Tuan Chi-jui and Chang Tso-lin, Tuan escaped from his clutches. After this Feng Yu-hsiang's position in Peking was untenable, and he withdrew from the city. In July the two "Marshals" Chang Tso-lin and Wu Pei-fu met in Peking, an occasion that aroused unbounded optimism among the group that wanted to return to the palace and prompted them to great activity. Chen Pao-shen went up to Peking to see some of his acquaintances and the new prime minister, while Kang Yu-wei, the reformer of 1898, sent telegrams to Chang Tso-lin, Wu Pei-fu, Chang Tsung-chang and others calling on them to restore the Articles of Favourable Treatment. He also wrote Wu Pei-fu a long letter in which he enumerated the "achievements and virtues" of the Ching Dynasty and begged Wu to restore it.

But these were in fact the last days of the Peiyang warlords. Although all the northern warlords suddenly started to co-operate and Chang Tso-lin made himself the commander of the "Army of Pacification", the Northern Expedition, born of the co-operation between the Kuomintang and the Communist Party, began in 1926 to defeat the forces of the northern warlords. With their fronts disintegrating the northern generals had no inclination to worry about articles of favourable treatment. Chen Pao-shen's activities achieved nothing and Wu Pei-fu replied curtly and hypocritically to Kang Yu-wei's letter: "Your loyalty is as unchanging as stone and metal, but if the tune is pitched too high nobody can join in the song." A year after this Kang Yu-wei died of disappointment in Tsingtao.

With all hopes of returning to the palace gone, Chen Pao-shen and his group despaired and Lo Chen-yu became more active. In March 1926, a time when the approach of the Northern Expedition had made me very anxious, the Manchu noble Pu Wei sent a messenger from the Japanese-held city of Lushun with a memorial for me and a letter to Lo Chen-yu. In these he said that he was on the best of terms with the Japanese officials and that he hoped I would move to Lushun, where I would "first be free of danger and then be able to make far-reaching plans. . . . Before travelling abroad one must have a settled residence". I had heard rather too much gossip about Lo Chen-yu to be able to trust him implicitly, but I had a very good impression of Pu Wei. Soon after my arrival in Tientsin he had come down from Lushun to see me and had moved me deeply with one remark: "As long as I am alive the Great Ching shall not perish." So I was naturally stirred by his letter advising me to go to Lushun, and my suspicion of Lo Chen-yu was weakened because Pu Wei chose him as his spokesman.

When the armies of the Northern Expedition captured Wuchang in 1926 and the whole front of the Northern warlords was tottering, Lo Chen-yu told me that the revolutionary armies were "raging floods and wild beasts" and "murderers and arsonists": if I fell into their hands there would be no hope for my life. I resolved to go with him to the Japanese-occupied port of Talien, but then I changed my mind on the advice of Chen Pao-shen. Chen had heard from the Japanese Legation that the situation was not as bad as it looked, a diagnosis that was borne out soon afterwards when the news came through of the Kuomintang purges. Chiang Kai-shek was slaughtering wholesale the Communists who were allegedly "raging floods and wild beasts". About this time we also received reports of British naval vessels bombarding Nanking and of Japanese troop movements in Shantung to block the northward advance of the southern troops. All this news gave me more confidence in the steady attitude of Chen Pao-shen and his group and made me sure that the situation was not as threatening as Lo Chen-yu and the others made out. Chiang Kai-shek was, after all, as frightened of the foreigners as Yuan Shih-kai, Tuan Chi-jui, Chang Tso-lin and their like. I lived in a foreign concession and was as safe as I had been before.

Of course, the advocates of a return to the palace and the advocates of my going abroad did not differ in their ultimate hope of restoration. After seeing their dreams of returning to the palace smashed, Chen Pao-shen and his party reverted to their old theme of advising me to live in obscurity and wait for my chance. On the question of allying with Japan, however, they were not really opposed to Lo Chen-yu's clique. Chen Pao-shen himself conceded that if there was no alternative to my going abroad, the only problem was that of choosing the right people to go with me.

The Ching veterans who stubbornly opposed the idea of my going abroad were, as I remember, very few. There was one of them who said that "Japan is only interested in profit and is incapable of being devoted to the cause of aiding the restoration". Such men as he believed that a restoration could only be achieved by Ching veterans, and they wanted to expel Lo from their ranks.

The quarrel between the two factions was not so much a struggle over proposals and methods as a fight between individuals. Apart from the open memoranda and discussions there was far more bitter secret fighting to win me over. Although the techniques he used were more varied, Lo Chen-yu lost this contest.

Lo came to see me one day in my small audience chamber carrying a long and thin bundle wrapped in cloth.

"Your subject deserves to die ten thousand deaths for disturbing the celestial heart like this; yet if I were to conceal a man's faults because of personal friendship I would be lacking in loyalty and righteousness."

"What are you talking about?" I looked at him in perplexity and watched him open the bundle as slowly and deliberately as an old eunuch washing his face and combing his hair. The bundle contained a pair of scrolls which he unhurriedly unrolled. Before he had finished I recognized them as a couplet that I had written especially for Chen Pao-shen.

"Your subject found these products of the imperial brush in the market. By a great good fortune I have been able to bring them back."

I did not know at the time that Lo Chen-yu and his friends all engaged in such underhand practices as buying over the servants of their rivals, and so I really believed that Chen Pao-shen had been so lacking in respect for the "gracious gift" of the emperor as to allow some of my calligraphy to be sold on a market stall. I was so angry that I did not know what to say. I waved Lo away at once.

Chen Pao-shen was in Peking at the time, and when his friend Hu Sze-yuan heard of the affair he insisted that Chen Pao-shen could not have been guilty of such a fault. Nor did he believe that a servant of Chen's would have dared to steal the scrolls for sale in the market. It was much more likely that he would have stolen them to sell privately to someone. If he did not sell them in the market who could he have sold them to? How did they get into Lo Chen-yu's hands? These were questions that Hu Sze-yuan would not answer. When I pressed him he only told me a story about a minister of one of my imperial ancestors who was unwilling to speak too openly to the emperor about the dangers of making a journey at a time when the emperor was ill and his high officials unreliable. The minister only advised the emperor not to go and did not give his reasons. His advice was shown to have been good when the emperor died on the trip.

I asked, "What do you mean by this story? What has it got to do with Chen Pao-shen?"

"It is Chen Pao-shen to whom your subject refers. He has something to say but he will not say it in so many words."

I lost patience and told him to come to the point, but he would only say that Chen was a loyal subject and that I was of course intelligent enough to get the point of his story myself. Although I did not fathom it I was relieved to hear Hu Sze-yuan speak well of Chen Pao-shen, and the unpleasant impression that had been made by the two scrolls was now removed. After a further series of defeats Lo Chen-yu finally moved to Lushun at the end of 1928 to pursue a different career.

But let us change the subject from the quarrels between the Ching veterans to another reason why I stayed in Tientsin and did not go abroad: the hopes I placed in the warlords.

My Relations with the Commanders of the Fengtien Clique

I was able to associate with as many warlords as I liked during my seven years in Tientsin, and they all gave me illusions of some sort or other. Wu Pei-fu called himself my subject in a letter, Chang Tso-lin kotowed to me, and Tuan Chi-jui asked for an audience with me on his own initiative. The ones in whom I had the fondest hopes were the Fengtien warlords, and it was with them that I associated most closely and for the longest time. This began when Chang Tso-lin kotowed to me.

My father-in-law Jung Yuan came to tell me in great excitement one day in June 1925 that Chang Tso-lin had sent a trusted envoy to give me 100,000 dollars and the message that Chang hoped that he would be able to meet me in the house where he was staying. Chen Pao-shen objected to this as soon as he heard of it; he said that it would be quite impossible for the emperor to go to visit a Republican general, particularly as the place suggested was outside the concessions. I agreed that it would be too humiliating and dangerous and therefore refused. To my surprise Jung Yuan brought Chang Tso-lin's envoy in again the following night, saying that Chang was waiting for me in his quarters and that I would be in no danger in Chinese territory; it was not convenient for him to enter the concession, which was why he was repeating his invitation to me to go to see him. Jung Yuan repeatedly stressed Chang Tso-lin's loyalty, and I remembered the concern he had recently shown for me and what I had been told when I lived in the palace: that Chang Tso-lin's pro-Ching sympathies were second only to those of Chang Hsun. Without telling anyone else I got into a car and set off.

This early summer evening was the first time I had ventured out of the Japanese concession. When I arrived at the Tsao Family Garden where Chang Tso-lin was staying I saw a strange guard of honour, tall soldiers dressed in grey and holding ancient halberds and modern rifles who were lined up by the main gate. The car passed between them and into the garden.

When I got out of the car I was led into a brightly-lit hall, where I saw a short man with a moustache wearing civilian clothes coming towards me. I recognized him at once as Chang Tso-lin. I did not know how I should greet him as this was the first time I had gone out to visit an important Republican figure and Jung Yuan had given me no directions. But to my astonishment he knelt on the floor before me without a moment's hesitation and kotowed, asking, "How is Your Majesty?"

"How are you, Marshal?" I hastened to help him to his feet and we walked into the reception room together. I was in very good spirits and grateful for what he had just done to end my uneasy feeling that I had lowered my dignity by coming to see him. What made me even more pleased, of course, was to discover that this very important man had not forgotten the past.

The room was furnished grandly but inconsistently with Chinese hardwood tables and chairs, a Western-style couch and a glass screen. We sat down at a round table and Chang Tso-lin started talking as he smoked one cigarette after another. No sooner had he opened his mouth than he started to curse Feng Yu-hsiang for forcing me out of the Forbidden City in order to get at the palace treasures. He himself, on the other hand, attached the greatest importance to the preservation of China's ancient culture and riches, had looked after the Ching palace in Fengtien very well, and was planning to get hold of a set of the famous collection *The Complete Books of the Four Libraries*[1] from Peking to preserve in its entirety. He said in a reproachful tone of voice that I should not have fled to the Japanese Legation at a time when he had plenty of troops in Peking with which to ensure my safety. He asked me about my life since my departure and said that I had only to tell him if I wanted anything.

I said that I was well aware of how thoughtful he had been on my behalf, but as Feng Yu-hsiang's men were still in Peking at the time I had been forced to flee to the Japanese Legation. I went on to observe that I had long known how well the imperial palaces and mausolea in Fengtien had been looked after and that I understood his feelings.

"If Your Majesty would like to come up to Fengtien and live in the palace there, it would be quite possible for me to arrange it."

"Marshal Chang, you are too kind."

But Marshal Chang changed the subject to my daily life. "If you need anything in future just write to me."

The only thing I lacked was a throne, but I could scarcely say so in as many words.

During our conversation we were alone in the room except for some flies. It occurred to me that there were never flies in the middle of the night in the concession.

A junior officer came in after a while and said, "The chief of staff wants to see you, sir." Chang Tso-lin waved his hand and said,

---

[1] A huge collection of books made at the orders of the emperor Chien Lung.

181

"There is no hurry, tell him to wait for a moment." I got up at once and said that I would be going as he must be very busy. He replied at once, "No hurry, no hurry." I caught a glimpse of a woman's face behind the screen (later I heard that this was his fifth concubine) and I felt that he must really be in a hurry. I took my leave of him again and this time he did not try to keep me.

Every time I went out I was accompanied by one of the plain-clothes Japanese policemen who were stationed at the Chang Garden, and this evening was no exception. I did not realize that Chang Tso-lin had not noticed him standing beside my car, and as he was seeing me off he said in a loud voice:

"If those Japanese put the finger on you let me know and I'll sort them out."

The car drove out of the grounds past the strange guard of honour and back to the concession. The next day the Japanese consul-general came to give me a warning:

"If Your Majesty makes another secret trip to Chinese territory the Japanese government will no longer be able to guarantee your safety."

Despite Chang Tso-lin's claim that he knew how to deal with the Japanese and the protest of the consul it was common knowledge at the time that there were links between the Japanese and Chang Tso-lin, and that without the munitions supplied by Japan Chang would have been unable to maintain so large an army as he did. So the hopes this meeting had given me were not damped by this protest or by the objections of Chen Pao-shen and his group.

When the Tanaka cabinet came to power in Japan in 1927 my hopes of restoration grew even stronger. The prime minister of this government was Tanaka Giichi who became notorious for the memorial in which he outlined the plans for Japanese expansion in East Asia and elsewhere. His cabinet made it quite clear that they had a special interest in the Northeast of China, which they regarded as being quite different from other parts of the country and where they were prepared to intervene militarily to protect Japan's interests.

After Chang Tso-lin gained the support of the Tanaka cabinet he became the leader of all the warlords of north China and the commander of the Army of Pacification. When the troops under Chiang Kai-shek advanced northwards the Japanese soldiers who were "protecting" Japan's "legitimate interests" in the Northeast and Inner Mongolia came as far south as Tsinan, hundreds of miles from either, where they perpetrated the Tsinan massacre. The Japanese commander Okamura issued a warning to Chiang Kai-shek (and the chief staff officer of the Japanese garrison in Tientsin sent me a copy of it as a token of the concern he felt for me). Eager to win favour with imperialism, Chiang Kai-shek, whose hands were still dripping with the blood of the Communists, workers and students he had been slaughtering since his betrayal of the revolution on April 12, 1927, respectfully withdrew from Tsinan on receiving this warning and banned all anti-Japanese activities by the people.

At this time my relations with the Fengtien warlords were growing closer than ever, and they became open after my meeting with Chang Tso-lin. My father's chief steward, who had many sworn brothers among the Fengtien commanders, was one of the people who introduced Fengtien generals to me. When they came to the Chang Garden the etiquette observed was no longer that of the Forbidden City. they did not kotow to me and I did not confer upon them the right to ride a horse or be carried in a litter at court. They would bow to me or shake hands, and from then on we would behave as equals; and I did not affect the style of an emperor when writing to them. The closeness of the relationship between me and any Fengtien general would be decided by his attitude to my restoration.

One of the Fengtien generals in whom I had the highest hopes was Chang Tsung-chang. When I saw him in Tientsin he was a hefty fellow of over forty, and his bloated face was tinged with the livid hue induced by opium smoking. He had drifted to Yingkow at the age of fifteen or sixteen and had worked in a gambling shack where he spent his time with local crooks, vagabonds and gamblers. After a spell as a petty bandit chief in the Northeast he went to the Russian port of Vladivostok and became the chief private detective of the Chinese chamber of commerce. As he threw his money around generously and was good at building up his connections he became a leading figure in the Vladivostok underworld by co-operating closely with the tsarist civil and military police. He ran brothels, gaming houses and opium dens. After the Wuchang Rising of 1911 the southern revolutionaries sent emissaries to the Sino-Russian frontier who managed to persuade a local bandit chief called Bullet Liu to join their side with his men, whom they turned into a cavalry regiment under Liu's command. As Chang Tsung-chang had been the middleman he accompanied them to Shanghai where, by some piece of cunning, he became a regimental commander in the revolutionary army with Bullet Liu under him as one of his battalion commanders. With the outbreak of the "Second Revolution" (the attempt to overthrow Yuan Shih-kai in 1913) he switched to the side of the counter-revolution and won the admiration of the Peiyang warlord Feng Kuo-chang for his achievements in slaughtering revolutionaries. He was put at the head of Feng Kuo-chang's guard battalion, and later rose through various means to the command of the 11th Division.

After being defeated in Kiangsu and Anhwei he fled to the Northeast where he sided with Chang Tso-lin and was given a brigade. As the fortunes of the Fengtien army prospered he rose to head first a division and then an army, and to be Commissioner for Military Affairs in Shantung and Head of Bandit Extermination for Kiangsu, Anhwei and Shantung. He went on to become Commander of the Combined Armies of Chihli and Shantung, a position in which he was virtually a local emperor. Because of his disreputable origins the southern press gave him the nickname of "the Dog-meat General". Later he was rechristened "the Long-legged General" because he always ran away the moment he lost a battle.

In April 1928 he fled to Japan after his army collapsed under a pincer attack on the Luan River in Hopei Province by Chiang Kai-shek and Chang Tso-lin's son Chang Hsueh-liang. He returned to Shantung in 1932 on the pretext of sweeping his family tombs and secretly persuaded a local officer to rebel in the hope that he would be able to use his troops to restore his rule in Shantung. In September his murder was arranged by the provincial chairman of Shantung, and such was the odium in which he was held that his body was left to lie in the open: the head of his secretariat could find nobody willing to move it away at any price, and the local undertakers refused to provide the wood for his coffin. Finally his corpse had to be removed by the very provincial authorities who had organized his killing.

This universally detested monster was a welcome visitor to the Chang Garden and a man in whom I placed the greatest hopes. When I lived in the Northern Mansion in Peking Chang Tsung-chang had come in disguise to visit me and show his concern for me. After I moved to Tientsin he would come and see me whenever he was in the city. His visits were always in the middle of the night as he slept by day and smoked opium in the evening, after which he was in very good spirits and would talk for hours about anything.

In 1926 Chang Tso-lin and Wu Pei-fu joined forces to attack Feng Yu-hsiang and challenged him to battle at Nankou to the northwest of Peking. The first units to occupy Nankou after Feng Yu-hsiang's retreat were those of Chang Tsung-chang. On hearing of Chang Tsung-chang's success I sent him a letter-cum-edict of congratulation on his victory against the "reds" and salvation of China from "communism".

I did not have to wait for the newspaper reports to hear of Chang Tsung-chang's victory as I had my own intelligence service. There were people who gathered information for me and others who translated foreign papers. When I learnt from the Chinese and foreign press and from my own intelligence reports of Chang Tsung-chang's victory and his increasing influence I went almost wild with joy. I hoped that Chang Tsung-chang's victory would be complete and that he would thus lay the foundations for my restoration. During his giddy rise the "Dog-meat General" would not commit himself definitely on this, and it was only after he became the "Long-legged General" that he seemed to think about it.

In 1928 Chiang Kai-shek, Feng Yu-hsiang, Yen Hsi-shan (the warlord ruler of Shansi Province) and others announced their co-operation and made a co-ordinated attack in north China. Skirting round the Japanese troops who were helping Chang Tsung-chang along the Tientsin-Pukow Railway they swallowed up Chang Tsung-chang's Shantung base and forced him to flee towards the Northeast. Chang Tso-lin had been killed by the Japanese in an explosion and his son and successor, the "Young Marshal" Chang Hsueh-liang, refused to allow Chang Tsung-chang through the passes leading to the Northeast.

Chang Tsung-chang's troops were in a desperate position on the Lutai-Luanchou sector as they were under attack from two directions, and disaster was imminent. Just at this moment a staff officer of Chang's came to see me with a letter in which he boasted how many troops and how much artillery he had left and claimed that he would have no difficulty in recovering Peking and Tientsin. He went on to say that he was in the process of training new armies which cost 2,500,000 dollars a month to maintain. "I humbly beg that in your wisdom you will grant me something and thus enable your humble soldier to know that he has something on which he can rely." The officer who had brought this message repeatedly stressed that Chang Tsung-chang was in sight of victory and that all he needed was some support from me.

When Chen Pao-shen and Hu Sze-yuan heard that I was thinking of throwing away some more money they came and talked me out of it, and I ended up by sending Chang nothing more substantial than a hortatory edict. Soon after this came Chang Tsung-chang's complete collapse and his flight to Japan. The further he got from me the more people there were who carried messages and letters between us. Chang Tsung-chang's letters, which became fuller and fuller of expressions of loyalty to the Ching house, all asked me for money. I heeded the pleas of Chen Pao-shen and stopped giving him money or writing to him. All the same, I still felt grateful to the Fengtien clique, although Chang Tso-lin was already dead.

It is common knowledge that Chang Tso-lin was murdered by the Japanese. I later heard that the reason why they killed him was because he was becoming less and less obedient; this was because he was under the influence of his son the "Young Marshal" Chang Hsueh-liang who wanted to break with Japan and make friends with

America. Because of this the Japanese said that he was "ungrateful and unfriendly".

I later heard an account of Chang's murder from the Japanese war criminal Colonel Kawamoto who participated in the plot. He said that he directed the personnel of the Japanese Kwantung Army staff who first arranged that the place where Chang would meet his end would be Huangkutun Railway Station at the junction of the Peking-Fengtien and the South Manchuria lines. "We buried thirty sacks of high explosive at the junction, and installed electric equipment in a watch-tower some 500 metres away to set off the explosion. We placed a derailing device north of the junction and had a platoon of shock troops hidden nearby. At 5.30 on June 4, 1928 Chang Tso-lin's blue armoured train arrived. The button was pressed and Chang and the train were destroyed together." To cover up the truth the Kwantung Army sent soldiers and workmen to repair the damaged track, and killed two Chinese whose bodies they placed at the scene of the murder. They stuffed their pockets with forged letters and documents from the Kuomintang's Northern Expedition and also arrested ten innocent local inhabitants, saying that the whole business had been planned by the Northern Expedition. "We had all the pro-Japanese warlords under very tight control," said Kawamoto. "When they could be useful to us we helped them; and when we had no use for them we found ways to eliminate them."

Although Chang Tso-lin's murder startled me and some of the former Ching officials tried to make me see a warning in it, I ignored their advice as I regarded myself as not in the same class as Chang Tso-lin. He, after all, was only a military chief and they could find others to replace him; I was the emperor, and the Japanese could not find another one in the whole of China. The members of my entourage advanced the argument that "the people of the Northeast loathe the Japanese from the bottom of their hearts and the Japanese try to prohibit Chang Hsueh-liang from co-operating with the Kuomintang. The Japanese are strong enough to take the Northeast by force, but if they did so it would not be capable of running itself; without Your Majesty on the throne they will find it very difficult to achieve anything". I was completely convinced that Japan recognized this, and built my policy on this assumption. If I wanted to rely on the strength of Japan I had first to win the hearts of the people of the Northeast. I therefore looked for former military chieftains of Chang Tso-lin whom I could use in my restoration activities. The man who acted on my behalf among the commanders of the Fengtien clique was Shang Yen-ying, a Ching veteran who came from a Manchu family that had been stationed in Kwangtung and was a former Hanlin academician; he was now a member of the Red Swastika Society of the Northeast. As Chang Hsueh-liang had made it quite clear that he wanted to co-operate with Chiang Kai-shek, Shang Yen-ying had to operate in the greatest secrecy. To put it briefly, his activities achieved nothing.

Semionov and the "Second Chukeh Liang"

I cannot remember how much money I spent or how much jade, pearls and jewellery I gave away in trying to win the friendship of military men and buy them over, but I do know that the one who got the most was the White Russian Semionov.

Semionov was a tsarist general who led the remnants of his troops into the Chinese frontier regions of the Northeast and Inner Mongolia after his defeat by the Soviet Red Army. There they looted, raped and burnt and engaged in every other kind of evil-doing. They once tried to invade the Mongolian People's Republic, and after being put to rout they tried to establish a base on the Sino-Mongolian frontier, where they were driven away by the local Chinese forces. By 1927 they had been reduced to being a small bandit group. At this time Semionov was very active in Peking, Tientsin, Shanghai, Lushun, Hongkong, Japan and other places looking for a backer among Chinese warlords and foreign politicians. When he found that there was no market for what he was trying to sell he became a swindler pure and simple. He was captured by Soviet troops after the Second World War and while I was a prisoner in the

Soviet Union I heard that he was hanged. Throughout my seven years in Tientsin I was constantly in contact with this murderer of the Chinese, Soviet and Mongol peoples. He received huge sums of money from me, and in him I placed unbounded hopes.

Semionov was first recommended to me by the Mongol noble Sheng Yun and Lo Chen-yu, but when Chen Pao-shen objected I refused to see him. Later Cheng Hsiao-hsu met Semionov through an introduction from Lo Chen-yu and thought that he had the makings of a most useful foreign official. He sang Semionov's praises to me and recommended that we should first get him and Chang Tsung-chang (the "Dog-meat General") to co-operate. As I happened at the time to be very hopeful about Chang Tsung-chang I agreed to Cheng's suggestion. Cheng Hsiao-hsu's activities enabled Chang Tsung-chang to receive foreign mercenaries from Semionov and also brought about an increase in the numbers of the White Russian troops. Chang and Semionov later signed a "Sino-Russian Anti-Bolshevik Military Convention".

After much encouragement from Cheng Hsiao-hsu I met Semionov at the Chang Garden in October 1925. I was very pleased with the interview and thought that he was bound to "accomplish great deeds in the face of difficulties, overthrow communism and restore the dynasty". I gave him 50,000 dollars on the spot to help him in his activities. Later Cheng Hsiao-hsu, Semionov, Liu Feng-chih and others had their photograph taken together and became sworn brothers, showing their great loyalty to the Ching house.

At that time a new wave of anti-Soviet and anti-communist activities was sweeping the world after the defeat of the fourteen-nation intervention against the Soviet Union. I remember Cheng Hsiao-hsu and Semionov telling me that Britain, America and Japan had decided that his men were to be the anti-Soviet shock troops and that he was to be supported with munitions and money. The "Russian imperial family" was also supposed to have the highest hopes in him. Tsarist representatives were in contact with Cheng Hsiao-hsu but I cannot remember the details. What I do recall is that Semionov had a plan which involved me very closely: he was going to use his supporters and troops in the Northeast and Inner

Mongolia to set up an "anti-communist" base there with me as ruler. I opened a bank account for Semionov to help him meet his operating expenses; this account was managed by Cheng Hsiao-hsu and provided Semionov with money whenever he wanted it. I think that the first deposit in it was 10,000 dollars.

Semionov once explained to me that he did not really need this money from me as he was going to raise contributions of 180,000,000 roubles from White Russian émigrés (later he pushed the figure up to 300,000,000); later he would receive financial support from the finance ministries of America, Britain and Japan. It was only because the money was not yet in his hands that he needed a little from me for the moment.

After this he often asked Cheng Hsiao-hsu to provide him with more funds, always on the grounds that the astronomical sums of money were not yet to hand, and he never failed to outline some astounding project in which they would be used. He once said that the Japanese military commander in Tientsin had arranged with Chang Tso-lin that he should go forthwith to Fengtien to discuss the "great plan"; but unfortunately he had no way of meeting his travel expenses. Another time he said that the Soviet consul in Shanghai had seen him on instructions from his superiors in order to come to an agreement with him by which the Soviet government would grant him a certain part of the Far East in which to set up a self-governing region. He asked for money to pay for a trip to Tokyo to investigate the matter. I have no way of calculating how much money he had from me, but I do recall that in the three months before the "September 18th Incident"[1] alone he relieved me of 800 dollars.

One of the numerous intermediaries between Semionov and myself was a Wang Shih, who claimed that he enjoyed the implicit confidence of Semionov and also had the closest connections with important Japanese and with Chinese warlords. I was always hearing from him such phrases as: "This is the most critical stage"; "this is

---

[1] On September 18, 1931 the Japanese imperialists launched a large-scale invasion of China's Northeast.

the last chance"; "now is the decisive moment when the course of the next thousand years will be settled: this chance must not be missed"; "do not lose this opportunity — it will never come again"; and so on. He had the knack of talking me into a state of high excitement.

He was also capable of writing memorials filled with such heady statements as a claim that the Japanese had decided to enlist 8,000 Koreans to serve under Semionov and provide all the pay and supplies, and were also going to muster another 10,000 White Russians on the same terms. The British were going to break off relations with Soviet Russia and give him the 80,000,000 dollars that were deposited in the Hongkong and Shanghai Banking Corporation. "They are only waiting to confirm the truth of the report before handing the money over. . . . France and Italy also sympathize and both want to contribute; America wants to offer a preliminary grant of 5,000,000 dollars and will give further assistance for the organization of an international anti-communist army of volunteers in Manchuria and Mongolia with him [Semionov] as its leader, an army that will co-operate in the destruction of Soviet Russia."

As Cheng Hsiao-hsu was not at the Chang Garden at the time Wang Shih's request for a personal interview with me to discuss this wild scheme of his was blocked by Chen Pao-shen and Hu Sze-yuan and he never got through the main gate.

Hu Sze-yuan was in charge of my office in Tientsin and was the person who sieved out the people and memorials I would see from those I would not. I had given him this job as I thought that he was honest. He pointed out to me that the memorials of Wang Shih were a tissue of lies. I accepted his advice and that of Chen Pao-shen and decided to have nothing to do with this Wang Shih or any other representatives of Semionov.

But as soon as Cheng Hsiao-hsu came back to Tientsin he talked me into paying out more money for his "foreign officials", including an Austrian and an Englishman. The Austrian was a former nobleman who had held office in the department of works of the Austrian concession in Tientsin. He said that he was a very important man in Europe, where he could build up support for my restoration. I appointed him as an adviser and sent him to Europe to act on my behalf, giving him 1,800 dollars as six months' salary. The Englishman was a journalist called Ross who said that it was essential to have a newspaper to achieve a restoration and asked me for 20,000 dollars with which to run one. I gave him 3,000, but the paper folded after a few days.

In spite of Hu Sze-yuan's attempts to keep them out, many people managed to get into the Chang Garden on the strength of having links with military men or supporting the restoration. From 1926 onwards batch upon batch of defeated generals and failed politicians flocked to the concessions, and the number of my protégés increased faster than ever.

Liu Feng-chih, the "second Chukeh Liang",[1] was the one of the more noteworthy of these. He was recommended by a former subordinate of Chang Hsun's as "a modern Chukeh Liang. He is a first-rate strategist, and with him on your side the great enterprise of the restoration is almost bound to succeed." Liu Feng-chih was then about forty, and when I met him he first boasted that he was a man of fantastic ability, and then went straight on to suggest that I give him some antiques, paintings and calligraphy with which he could make contact with the men in power.

"Scrolls in Your Majesty's handwriting get nowhere with people like that." This was the first time I had heard such a thing said, and although it made me feel uncomfortable I admired him for his frankness. I felt that as he dared to say things that others would not, his words were bound to be true. I was most liberal with him, allowing him to take large quantities of some of the most valuable objects in my possession. Later he specified precisely what he wanted. For one of Chang Tso-lin's subordinates he requested jewellery to the value of ten thousand dollars. To win over three other Fengtien generals he indicated that they should each be given ten court pearls, and for someone else he demanded the pearl that

---

[1] The name of Chukeh Liang (181-234), a statesman of the Three Kingdoms period, was a byword for political and military skill.

was on the top of the imperial hat. Letters containing such requests would arrive from him every three to five days. They would be full of such statements as: "To win a true genius one must spend a lot of money. Meanness will make people think little of one; in great undertakings one must not be small-minded."

If one were to believe his reports, then nearly all the officers of the Fengtien clique who were of the rank of brigade commander or above (and some regimental commanders also) as well as Red Spear Society[1] chiefs with 400,000 men under their control and bandit kings of the forests, had all received pearls, ancient porcelain and diamonds, and were all greatly moved by my lack of small-mindedness and were only waiting for my command to rise. But, although there was no end to the number of treasures that Liu Feng-chih took away, there was no sign of action from these forces. Under Chen Pao-shen's persuasion I began to have my doubts and was less willing to hand out money. In his conversations with me and in his letters the "second Chukeh Liang" frequently used such arguments as: "I have already spent such-and-such an amount, and this does not include my travelling and entertainment expenses;" "having used up my family fortune I am finding great difficulty in advancing any more money for you;" and, "the situation is urgent and this is the decisive moment: whatever happens I must receive 20,000 dollars."

I realized that something was wrong and so I did not send him any more money. Later he came and told me about his poverty with tears in his eyes; this time he only asked for ten dollars. I believe that he was finally shot by the Fengtien army for making trouble in the Northeast.

It was nearly the time of the September 18th Incident when I saw the last of this tribe of "advisers", a little after the northern warlords had all acknowledged the authority of the Kuomintang government. By now I no longer had any illusions about them and had placed my hopes elsewhere.

---

[1] A primitive secret society of the common people.

The Affair of the Eastern Mausolea

1928 was for me a year of excitement and shocks.

In that year the Japanese Tanaka cabinet issued a statement that Chinese troops would not be permitted to enter "Manchuria or Mongolia" and sent Japanese soldiers to Tsinan to block the northward advance of the Kuomintang forces. The armies of Chang Tso-lin, Wu Pei-fu, and Chang Tsung-chang, the warlords with whom I had connections, crumbled away in a series of defeats. While my agents were sending me sensationally good news about the way they were gaining the support of warlords, I would often read in the papers that one or other of these military men who were apparently so loyal to me had gone into exile or been shot.

I heard that the governments of both north and south in China had broken off relations with the Soviet Union, as had Britain, and that the Kuomintang was carrying out a major purge of the party. It seemed that the threat to me from the "raging floods and wild beasts" that Cheng Hsiao-hsu, Chen Pao-shen and the Japanese told me about had diminished. But these very people told me that I was in imminent danger and that my enemies were operating everywhere. I read in the papers that there had been an uprising in Kwangtung, and meanwhile Feng Yu-hsiang, whom I had always regarded as an "extremist" and a "red", had allied with Chiang Kai-shek and had launched an attack against the Northern warlords along the Peking-Hankow Railway. In the second half of 1928 depressing news came thick and fast: Chang Tso-lin was dead, the American minister had arranged an alliance between his son Chang Hsueh-liang and Chiang Kai-shek, and so on. But the event that gave me the biggest shock was the robbery of the Eastern Mausolea.

The mausolea are in Malan Valley, which is in Tsunhua County of Hopei Province, and are the tombs of the emperor Chien Lung and the empress dowager Tzu Hsi. In 1928 Sun Tien-ying, an exgambler, opium pedlar and former subordinate of Chang Tsung-chang's who was now an army commander under Chiang Kai-shek, brought his troops to this area and began to carry out systematic tomb robbery.

First he posted notices announcing that he was going to carry out military manoeuvres and cut all communications. Then he set his troops to digging, and after three days and nights they cleared out all the treasure that had been buried with Chien Lung and Tzu Hsi.

Chien Lung and Tzu Hsi were the most extravagant of the rulers of the Ching. I have read a description of the tombs, though it may not be too accurate.

> The tunnel to the tomb was lined with white marble and led through four marble gates. The vault was octagonal with a domed ceiling on which were carved nine gleaming golden dragons. It was about the same size as the Palace of Central Harmony in the former palace. Chien Lung's inner and outer coffins were made of hard wood that had been seasoned by long burial and were placed on top of an eight-sided well. Apart from ingots and funerary vessels of gold and silver everything in the tombs was made of rare jewels. The funerary objects of Tzu Hsi mostly comprised pearls, gems, emeralds and diamonds, and her phoenix crown was made of enormous pearls and gold wire. On her coverlet was a peony consisting entirely of jewels, and on her arm was a bracelet of dazzling brilliance in the form of a large chrysanthemum and six small plum blossoms all set with diamonds of various sizes. In her hand was a demon-quelling wand over three inches long made of emerald, and on her feet she wore a pair of pearl shoes. Apart from all this the coffin contained seventeen strings of pearls and gems strung together as prayer beads and several pairs of emerald bracelets. The things buried with Chien Lung were calligraphy, paintings, books, swords, ornaments fashioned from jade, ivory and coral, golden statues of the Buddha and so on; of these the articles made of silk had already perished and could not be distinguished.

The report of Sun Tien-ying's grave-robbery from the official responsible for the protection of the Eastern Mausolea gave me a shock worse than the one I had received when I was expelled from the palace. The royal clan and the former Ching officials were all roused by it. Men of every faction, whether they had been lying low or not, all flocked to my house and expressed their hatred for the troops of Chiang Kai-shek, and Ching veterans from all over the country sent funds pouring in for the restoration of the mausolea.

They had spirit tablets for Chien Lung and Tzu Hsi set up in the Chang Garden with tables for incense and mats for people to kneel on. The veterans came in an unending stream to bow, kotow and weep as if it were a funeral. The Ching house and the veterans published telegrams to Chiang Kai-shek and to Yen Hsi-shan, the commander of the garrison of the Peking-Tientsin region, demanding the punishment of Sun Tien-ying and insisting that the authorities repair the tombs. It was decided that the funeral services at the Chang Garden would continue until the job of reconstruction was completed.

The initial reaction of the Chiang Kai-shek government was satisfactory. Yen Hsi-shan was ordered to carry out an investigation and a divisional commander whom Sun Tien-ying had sent to Peking was arrested by Yen. But it was not long before the news came through that the officer had been released, and Chiang Kai-shek decided not to follow the matter up. It was said that Sun Tien-ying sent some of the booty to Chiang Kai-shek's new bride Soong Mei-ling: the pearls from Tzu Hsi's phoenix crown became decorations for Madame Chiang Kai-shek's shoes. My heart smouldered with a hatred I had never known before, and standing before the dark and gloomy funerary hall I made an oath before my weeping clansmen:

"If I do not avenge this wrong I am not an Aisin-Gioro."

I remembered what Pu Wei had said to me the first time he saw me in Tientsin.

"As long as I am alive the Great Ching shall not perish," I announced.

My longing for restoration and revenge reached a new intensity.

In those days Cheng Hsiao-hsu and Lo Chen-yu were the people closest to me, and every historical anecdote or piece of news they told me served to move me to indignation and strengthen my determination to achieve restoration and revenge. To fight the National Government of the Kuomintang to the end and continue the funeral until the mausolea were repaired were both ideas they suggested to me.

The situation grew more and more unfavourable for us. The investigation into the grave-robbery was dropped and the new authorities in the Peking-Tientsin area included no old friends like Tuan Chi-jui. My father moved his whole family from Peking to Tientsin as he was afraid to live there any longer. My mood changed from indignation to depression. The inmates of the Chang Garden understood that the wedding between Soong Mei-ling, the daughter of a family of compradors in the service of Britain and the U.S.A., and Chiang Kai-shek, a stockbroker who was also connected with the underworld, showed that Chiang Kai-shek had more powerful backing than Tuan Chi-jui, Chang Tso-lin, Sun Chuan-fang or Wu Pei-fu had ever had. By the end of the year Chiang Kai-shek's National Government in Nanking had been recognized by all countries including Japan, and his power was greater than that of any previous warlord. I felt that my prospects were very gloomy and thought that under the rule of so ambitious a man there was no question of a restoration; even maintaining my foothold in his sphere of influence would be a big problem. I used to resort to divination to try and find out what the fate of the Chiang Kai-shek government and myself would be.

Nobody burning with ambition and longing for revenge as I was could have left everything to the will of heaven and not tried to do something himself. My experience of the past few years and the story of Chiang's rise to power combined to make me believe that if one wanted to achieve anything it was necessary to have military power, for the foreigners would support the man with an army as a matter of course. If a full-blooded "Great Ching Emperor" like myself had troops the foreigners would be bound to take me more seriously than some marshal who had started as nothing more than a bandit chief or a gangster. I decided to send some of the most trusted members of my family to military school in Japan, and regarded this as more important than going abroad myself.

I chose my brother Pu Chieh and my brother-in-law Jun Chi and asked the Japanese consul in Tientsin to recommend a private tutor to teach them Japanese. The man he selected, Toyama Takeo, turned out to be a member of the Japanese Black Dragon Society who knew quite a few Japanese politicians. He later went to Japan to work for my dream of restoration, but after I went to the Northeast he was squeezed out as he did not belong to the army clique. When he had taught Pu Chieh and Jun Chi Japanese for some time he went back to Japan to try and make arrangements for them to study there. He reported that although they would not be able to enter the Japanese Army Cadet School for the moment, they could first go to a special school for the sons of the Japanese nobility. My two future generals left for Japan with Toyama in March 1929, seven months after the affair of the Eastern Mausolea.

Consulate, Garrison and Black Dragon Society

By 1928 most of my advisers thought that the only hope of a restoration lay with Japan, to whom I could be very useful in the Northeast. They consequently advised discreet negotiations with the Japanese, and I found myself more and more in agreement with them.

I have already told how I began to trust the Japanese after being an object of their "concern" from the time I entered the Northern Mansion. After staying in the Japanese Legation and moving to Tientsin I grew increasingly confident that Japan would be the main source of foreign support for my future restoration.

The Japanese consul-general had invited me to visit a primary school for Japanese children during my first year in Tientsin. The Japanese children lined the road with paper flags in their hands and welcomed me with shouts of "banzai" ("ten thousand years"). This scene made my eyes fill with tears and my chest heave with sighs. When the fighting in one civil war between warlords was approaching Tientsin all the foreign garrisons in the city were organized into an allied army, and when they announced that they would deal with the National Army if it came too close to the concessions the Japanese garrison commander paid a visit to the Chang Garden especially to say to me: "Please do not worry, Your Majesty. We are determined not to allow the Chinese soldiers to put one foot inside the concessions." I was very gratified to hear this.

At New Year and my birthday the Japanese consul and the senior officers of the garrison used to come to congratulate me. They would also invite me to watch the military parade on the Japanese emperor's birthday. I remember that the Japanese commander invited a number of high-ranking refugees to one of these reviews. When I arrived at the parade ground the commander rode over especially to salute me, and when the review was over all we Chinese guests joined the Japanese in shouting "Tenno banzai" ("Long live the Japanese Emperor").

Colonels on the staff of the Japanese garrison used to come and tell me about current affairs, and they did this job most conscientiously for many years: sometimes they brought along diagrams and tables that they had specially prepared. One of these was Yoshioka, who was later "Attaché to the Imperial Household". He was with me for ten years during the "Manchukuo" period, and I shall have more to say about him in Chapter Six.

The main subjects of these talks by the Japanese staff officers were the civil wars, and they would often put forward their analysis as "The root cause of China's disorders is that she lacks a leader and has no emperor." They would go on to discuss the superiority of the Japanese imperial system and say that the hearts of the people of China could be won only by the "Hsuan Tung Emperor". The feebleness and degeneracy of the Chinese armed forces was a favourite topic of theirs: they compared them, of course, with the Imperial Japanese Army. The combination of these talks and the military reviews gave me a strong belief in the might of the Japanese armed forces and great confidence in the support it was giving me.

Once when I was taking a stroll beside the Pai River I saw a Japanese naval vessel moored in the river. I do not know how the captain realized who I was, but he suddenly appeared on the riverbank and respectfully invited me to come on board his boat for a visit. When I went aboard the boat, the *Fuji*, I was saluted by the Japanese naval officers. As this was an impromptu occasion there were no interpreters on either side and we had to converse in writing.[1] The captain later paid me a return visit with a number of officers. I gave him a signed photograph when he asked me for one, and he indicated that he regarded this as a very great honour. This incident made me feel that the Japanese respected me from the depths of their hearts. After the total failure of my efforts to win over warlords and buy up politicians and foreign advisers the Japanese occupied an even more important place in my thoughts.

At first I considered the Japanese as a single entity, which did not, of course, include the common people, and consisted of the Japanese of the Peking Legation and the Tientsin consulate and garrison, as well as the *ronin* friends of Lo Chen-yu and Sheng Yun who held neither military nor civil office. The reason why I had this view of them was that they all "protected" me and treated me as an "emperor", all shared the same contempt for the Republic, all praised the Great Ching, and all expressed their willingness to help me when I first brought up the question of my going to Japan.

I had decided that I wanted to go to Japan under the persuasion of Lo Chen-yu when I was frightened by the approach of the Northern Expedition in 1927. After discussions with the consul-general the matter was referred to Japan. The Tanaka cabinet had indicated that it would welcome me and decided that I would be received in the manner appropriate to a foreign sovereign. Lo Chen-yu told me that the Japanese military authorities had made preparations to give me a military escort for my journey. But after the crisis cooled down Chen Pao-shen and Cheng Hsiao-hsu persuaded me not to go. When "Down with imperialism" and "Abolish the unequal treaties" ceased to be official slogans after the founding of the National Government in Nanking I began to realize that while the Japanese were as "respectful" as ever and they still "protected" me, they were divided in their attitudes as to whether I should go abroad. This split aroused my strongest indignation, and this was how I found out about it.

---

[1] Chinese and Japanese can communicate to a certain extent by writing the Chinese characters that are used in the scripts of both languages.

Lo Chen-yu said to me one day in the latter part of 1927: "Although the Japanese concession is fairly safe there are all sorts of people around here. According to the Japanese command a number of plainclothes agents (he referred to men doing underground work who, in the understanding of the Chang Garden, carried weapons) of the revolutionary party (a term used in the Chang Garden to refer to both the Communist Party and the Kuomintang) have slipped in and Your Majesty's safety is consequently a matter of concern. In your subject's opinion it would be advisable to stay in Japan for the time being; there would be no objection to going to Lushun first. Prince Kung (Pu Wei) has arranged everything there and the Japanese military authorities are willing to help and be responsible for Your Majesty's protection." I was already nervous of the "plainclothes agents of the revolutionary party", and after hearing these suggestions from Lo Chen-yu and receiving a letter from Pu Wei I resolved once more to go abroad. Ignoring Chen Pao-shen and Cheng Hsiao-hsu's protests I ordered Cheng to go to the Japanese consul-general Kato at once and ask him to see me personally.

Cheng Hsiao-hsu hesitated for a moment and then asked, "If Your Majesty invites Kato to come and see you, who will interpret? Hsieh Chieh-shih?"

I saw what he meant. Hsieh Chieh-shih was very close to Lo Chen-yu, and Cheng Hsiao-hsu was clearly displeased at having one of Lo's men interpret for me, and I was aware that Lo would not be pleased at having Cheng's son or Chen Pao-shen's nephew do the job either. I thought it over and announced my decision: "I'll have an English interpreter. Kato knows English."

Kato arrived with the two assistant consuls. After listening to my request Kato replied:

"I cannot give an immediate reply to Your Majesty's question, which I must refer to Tokyo."

I wondered why it was necessary to refer the matter to Tokyo when the military headquarters had told Lo Chen-yu that there would be no problem about it. Some of the wealthy refugees in Tientsin used to go to Lushun to avoid the heat of summer without even having to inform the consulate-general, so why was there so much fuss about me? Before I had finished saying all this Kato asked an awkward question: "May I ask whether this was Your Majesty's own idea?"

"Yes, it was," I answered irritably. I also said that recently I had heard that I would be in danger if I stayed in Tientsin. According to the Japanese garrison the revolutionaries had sent in a number of secret agents recently: surely the consulate was aware of this.

"Those are all rumours. Your Majesty need not believe them." Kato was visibly distressed. I found it most odd that he should dismiss military intelligence reports as rumours. On the basis of those reports I had previously asked him to increase the strength of my guards, and he had complied with my request. Did he believe the reports or not?

"How could the military intelligence reports be rumours?"

Kato was silent for a long time while his two assistants fidgeted uncomfortably on the sofa.

"Your Majesty can be quite confident that there is no danger whatever," Kato said at last. "Naturally I shall refer the question of going to Lushun that Your Majesty raised to my government."

This conversation gave me my first intimation of the discord between the consulate and the garrison, and I regarded it as both strange and annoying. I sent for Lo Chen-yu and Hsieh Chieh-shih and questioned them about it, and they told me that what they heard from Japanese in or associated with the garrison all confirmed that things were so. They also said:

"The military intelligence reports are thoroughly reliable. They have always given a very clear picture of every move of the revolutionaries. Anyhow, even if the reports of a planned assassination are only a rumour we must still take precautions."

A few days later my father-in-law Jung Yuan told me that some friends of his who lived outside had told him that assassins in the service of Feng Yu-hsiang had been arriving in the British and French concessions recently, so that the situation was very alarming. A member of the household told me that he had noticed suspicious people near the main gate peering into the grounds. I hastily summoned the head of my general affairs office and the commander of my guard and told them to ask the Japanese police to tighten the precautions at the gate. I also gave instructions that the guards keep a careful watch on strangers outside the gate and allow nobody in or out at night.

I was woken up one night by a gunshot outside the window which was soon followed by another one. I jumped up from my bed and ordered the guard to muster, convinced that Feng Yu-hsiang's plain-clothes agents were here at last. The whole household got up and guards were posted everywhere. The policemen on the main gate were put on the alert and the Japanese detectives stationed in the house went out to investigate. When they captured the man who had fired the shots he turned out, to my astonishment, to be a Japanese.

Tung Chi-hsu, the head of my general affairs office, told me the next day that he was a member of the Black Dragon Society called Kishida and that when he was taken to the Japanese police head-quarters the Japanese military authorities had removed him at once. I now had a good idea of how things really stood.

I had had some previous contact with members of the Black Dragon Society. In 1925 I had met Tsukuda Nobuo, an important figure in the society, as the result of Lo Chen-yu's urgings. Lo had told me that many powerful people in Japan, including some in the army, were planning to help me achieve my restoration, and had sent their representative Tsukuda to have a private talk with me. He said that as this was a chance that should not be missed I should send for the man at once. I had never heard of this Tsukuda before, but some of the Household Department officials who knew him said that he had been a frequent visitor at the various princely mansions since the 1911 Revolution and was on quite good terms with a number of the princes of the royal clan. Although I was stirred by what Lo Chen-yu told me I felt that as the Japanese consul-general was the formal representative of his country and my pro-tector he should be invited to be present at the conversation. I therefore sent someone to inform him and invite him to be present at the occasion. As soon as Tsukuda saw the consul he turned and fled, to the astonishment of Chen Pao-shen, Cheng Hsiao-hsu and everyone else present. As I look at it today it is clear that this move of Lo Chen-yu's and the attempt by Kishida to frighten me with gunshots in the night were all connected with Tsukuda's activities, which were in turn undoubtedly backed by the Japanese garrison.

I sent for Chen Pao-shen and Cheng Hsiao-hsu to ask them their views on the affair of the gunshots. "It looks," said Cheng, "as though both the Japanese army and government want to have Your Majesty living under their protection in areas under their control. Although they are not co-operating with each other this does us no harm. But Lo Chen-yu's way of doing things is too reckless and can only lead to disaster; he must on no account be given important work to do."

"Both the Japanese garrison and the Black Dragon Society act completely irresponsibly," was Chen Pao-shen's opinion. "You should ignore everyone except the Japanese minister and consul-general." After thinking the matter over I felt that they were right and decided not to ask the consul-general to be allowed to leave Tientsin. I lost interest in Lo Chen-yu and the next year he sold his house in Tientsin and went to Talien.

Strange to relate, as soon as Lo Chen-yu had gone there were fewer rumours, and Jung Yuan and Chi Chi-chung brought no more alarming intelligence reports. It was only a long time later that I began to understand why.

It was my English interpreter who explained things to me. Because he was related by marriage to my father-in-law Jung Yuan, and because he had been in contact with the Japanese garrison in the course of his work he knew something of what had been going on behind the scenes, and later he told me about it. The Japanese garrison had set up a special secret organization to deal with the Chang Garden, and Lo Chen-yu, Jung Yuan and Hsieh Chieh-shih at least were connected with it. This network had a base in a house known to the public as the Mino Residence.

After translating for my interview with Kato my interpreter had been kept by Lo, Jung and Hsieh who wanted to hear about the conversation. They had started shouting when they heard that Kato had not been at all keen to let me go abroad, and the interpreter gathered from their discussion that a member of the military staff had said to Lo that they wanted to take me to Lushun. Lo and the others took the interpreter to the Mino Residence to find the staff officer, and although they did not find him the interpreter discovered the secret establishment. He later heard from Jung Yuan and others that they got opium, girls and money there.

Mino Tomoyoshi who owned the place was a staff major who often came to the Chang Garden with the Japanese commanding officer. I never dreamed at the time that this man had established secret links with members of my household, that he knew everything that went on there, and that he had used Jung Yuan and others to pass the rumours on to me which had made me want to flee to Lushun. When I heard something of the truth about the Mino Residence I realized that the reason why the Japanese army was going to such lengths to win control over Jung Yuan and his like was because they were struggling with the consulate-general over me. This quarrel, as Cheng Hsiao-hsu had pointed out, could only benefit me.

Later on Cheng Hsiao-hsu told me something about the Black Dragon Society. This society, the biggest of the *ronin* organizations, had previously been called the "Black Ocean Association". It had been founded by the *ronin* Hiraoka Kotaro after the Sino-French War (1883-85) and was the first organization of agents to carry out espionage activities in China. It started out with bases in Foochow, Yentai (Chefoo) and Shanghai and operated under such covers as consulates, schools and photographers. The name of the Black Dragon Society implied "beyond the Amur River" (the Chinese name for the Amur is Black Dragon River) and was first used in 1901. The society played an important role in the Russo-Japanese War of 1904-05 and its membership was said to have reached several hundred thousand with correspondingly huge funds. Toyama Mitsuru was the most famous of its leaders and under his direction its members had penetrated every stratum of Chinese society. They operated everywhere: at the side of Ching nobles and high officials and among pedlars and servants, including the attendants in the Chang Garden. Many Japanese personalities (such as Doihara, Hirota Koki, Hiranuma Kiichiro, Arita Hachiro and Kazuki Seiji) were disciples of Toyama's. Cheng Hsiao-hsu said that Toyama was a Buddhist with a long silver-grey beard and a "kindly" face who was passionately fond of roses and hated to leave his garden. Yet he was the man who planned such appalling conspiracies and murders.

Lo Chen-yu should be given the credit for Cheng Hsiao-hsu's recognition of the power of the Black Dragon Society and the Japanese army. Cheng, Lo and Chen Pao-shen originally represented three different schools of thought. Lo regarded anything that military men or Black Dragon figures said as completely reliable, and the main reason why he trusted Semionov was because of his connections with the society. Chen Pao-shen on the other hand thought that no Japanese were trustworthy except those in the consulate-general who represented the Japanese government. Cheng Hsiao-hsu sided openly with Chen Pao-shen at first, but later Lo's boastings and the infamous conduct of the Black Dragon Society enabled him to see the way some forces in Tokyo were heading and to divine the real intentions of the Japanese authorities. He saw that Japan was a force on which he could rely and finally decided to modify his plan of working for the joint administration of China by all the foreign powers. He went to Japan to see the Black Dragon Society and the Japanese general staff.

Cheng Hsiao-hsu had begun to hope for increased intervention by Japan in Chinese politics when he despaired of getting international support for the White Russian brigand Semionov. When he changed his line he took a much longer view than Lo Chen-yu and had no time for the Mino Residence or the garrison in Tientsin: his objective was Tokyo. At the time, however, he did not regard Japan as our only potential foreign helper; he thought of her rather as our first.

He went to Japan with my permission and the consent of the Japanese minister Yoshizawa. In Japan he made contact with the army and the Black Dragon Society, and he reported with great satisfaction to me on his return that the majority of influential people expressed "concern" and "sympathy" for me and my restoration and showed an interest in my plans for the future. He said that we only had to wait for the moment to come in order to ask for assistance.

While in Japan he met all kinds of people who were interested in my restoration. They included military and civil officials who had been connected with me in Peking and Tientsin, the important Black Dragon figure Tsukuda who had fled at the sight of the consul-general, and Kishida, the member of the society who had fired the shots in the night. He also met some important men who had previously stayed in the background and who would later be prime ministers or war ministers or hold other important posts.[1] Cheng Hsiao-hsu was probably too excited by the way they reacted to his "policy of opening up the whole country". When the first batch of Japanese "guests" came rushing through the open door after the foundation of "Manchukuo" he was still clinging to his dream of joint administration and proclaiming to the outside world the "open door and equal opportunity". He was like a servant who helped a gang of robbers and opened the gate of his master's house to let them in and then wanted to send invitations to all the other gangs. The first gang naturally kicked him aside in a fury.

Life in the Temporary Palace

After I had been living in the Chang Garden for a while I felt that this would be the best place for me to stay until the time was ripe for my restoration or I was forced to leave. This was one of the reasons why my enthusiasm for going abroad faded.

It seemed to me that the Chang Garden (and later the Quiet Garden) was free of all the things I disliked about the Forbidden City while preserving all the essentials. The things I most loathed in the Forbidden City were the rules which did not even allow me to ride in a car or go for a walk in the streets, and what came next

---

[1] They included Konoe Fumimaro, Ugaki Kazushige, Yonai Mitsumasa, Hiranuma Kiichiro, Suzuki Kantaro, Minami Jiro and Yoshida Shigeru.

on my hate list was the infuriating Household Department. I now had the freedom to do as I liked, and while others could remonstrate they could not interfere.

The one essential element of my life in the Forbidden City, my authority, was preserved. Although I now wore an ordinary Chinese jacket and gown or, more often, Western clothes instead of the cumbersome imperial robes, people still kotowed and bowed to me. The place where I now lived had been built as an amusement park and had no glazed tiles or carved and painted beams, but it was still called a "temporary palace". I found a foreign-style house with flush lavatories and central heating far more comfortable than the Mind Nurture Palace, and nobles would come from Peking in rotation to stand in attendance. What had been the ticket office in the days when it was a pleasure ground was now a substitute "Guard Office of the Cloudless Heaven Gate". Although there was no longer a Southern Study, a Great Diligence Hall or a Household Department, people saw the "Office in Charge of the Affairs of the Ching House During Its Stay in Tientsin" as their combined reincarnation. I was still addressed in exactly the same way as before and dates were still given in terms of the reign period of Hsuan Tung. All this seemed to me both natural and essential.

The only former senior official of the Household Department still with me was Jung Yuan. The others were either looking after my property in Peking or had retired on grounds of old age. The first batch of edicts I issued after my arrival in Tientsin included the following two. One was, "Cheng Hsiao-hsu, Hu Sze-yuan, Yang Chung-hsi, Wen Su, Ching Fang-chang, Hsiao Ping-yen, Chen Tseng-shou, Wan Sheng-shih and Liu Hsiang-yeh shall be advisers in Tientsin". The other read, "An Administrative Office shall be established under Cheng Hsiao-hsu and Hu Sze-yuan and a General Affairs Office shall be set up under Tung Chi-hsu. The Finance Office shall be headed by Ching Fang-chang and the Office for External Relations shall be headed by Liu Hsiang-yeh". Chen Pao-shen, Lo Chen-yu and Cheng Hsiao-hsu were the "privy ministers" whom I saw daily. They and the other advisers had to come every morning and wait in a row of single-storeyed buildings to the west of the main building to be "summoned to audience". People who had asked for an "audience" would wait to be called in a small lodge by the main gate, and their numbers included soldiers, politicians, former Ching officials, all kinds of "modern" figures, poets, writers, doctors, soothsayers, astrologers, physiognomists, the head of the reactionary Youth Party, a tennis star, journalists and a member of the Control Commission of the Kuomintang. The Japanese police stationed at the Chang Garden lived in a house opposite and used to note down all the comings and goings. Whenever I went out a Japanese plainclothes policeman would follow me.

The economics of the Chang Garden were naturally on a far smaller scale than those of the Forbidden City, but I still had a considerable fortune. Of the large quantities of valuables I had brought with me from the Forbidden City, some had been converted into money which was now earning interest in foreign banks and some had been turned into real estate to bring in rent. I still owned a lot of land in the Northeast and north China. The Ching house and the Republican authorities set up a special office to deal with the renting and sale of these lands which were the "private property of the emperor". The two sides split the loot, and our share from the sale of some of this property was one of our sources of income. In addition we still had the great quantities of art treasures that Pu Chieh and I had moved out of the palace over a period of six months, as I described in Chapter Three.

After I moved to Tientsin there were many places to which money had to be sent every month and a number of offices were set up for this purpose: the "Peking Office", the "Office of Mausolea and Temples", the "Liaoning Office", the "Imperial Clan Bureau" and the "Office for the Administration of (the Emperor's) Private Property" (this was the joint Ching-Republican office mentioned in the previous paragraph). There were also officials appointed to look after the imperial tombs of the Ching house. According to a document I have found, the monthly expenditure for Peking and the mausolea alone was 15,837 dollars 84 cents; and the Tientsin figure must have been over ten thousand. The biggest item on the budget was the money spent on trying to buy over or influence warlords, and this was not included in the sum mentioned. Purchases, excluding such items as cars or diamonds, probably accounted for two-thirds of an average month's expenses. I spent far more money on buying things when in Tientsin than I had done in Peking, and the amount increased every month. I never tired of buying pianos, watches, clocks, radios, Western clothes, leather shoes and spectacles.

Wan Jung had been a young lady of Tientsin, and so she knew even more ways of wasting money on useless objects than I did. Whatever she bought for herself Wen Hsiu would want too, and, when I bought it for Wen Hsiu, Wang Jung would want more, as if a failure to do so would have detracted from her status as empress. This in turn would make Wen Hsiu complain and ask for more. This competitive buying eventually compelled me to set a limit to their monthly expenditure; Wan Jung's allowance was naturally somewhat higher and was at first a thousand dollars with Wen Hsiu's about eight hundred. When we ran into financial difficulties the allowances were cut to three hundred and two hundred respectively. There was of course no limit to my personal spending.

As a result of our astounding extravagance the Chang Garden was reduced to desperate financial straits just as the Forbidden City had been, and sometimes we were unable to pay our bills, our rent, and even the salaries of the "privy ministers" and the "advisers".

While spending incalculable sums of money on buying enormous quantities of useless objects I became far more convinced than I ever had been in the days when Johnston was with me that everything foreign was good and everything Chinese, except the imperial system, was bad.

A stick of Spearmint chewing-gum or a Bayer aspirin would be enough to make me sigh at the utter doltishness of the Chinese, though I did not include myself as I saw myself as superior to all my subjects, and even thought that the brilliant foreigners shared my own estimate of myself.

The treatment I received in the foreign concessions was quite unlike that accorded to any other Chinese. In addition to the Japanese, the consuls and senior military officers of America, Britain, France and Italy and the heads of foreign firms were all extremely respectful to me and addressed me as "Your Imperial Majesty". On their national days they would invite me to review their troops, visit their barracks and see their newly-arrived aircraft and warships; and they would all come to congratulate me at New Year and on my birthday.

Before Johnston left me, which was not long after my arrival in Tientsin, he introduced me to the British consul and the commander of the British garrison. They introduced me to their successors, who in turn introduced me to theirs, so that my social contacts with the British military commanders continued unbroken. When the Duke of Gloucester, the third son of King George V of England, came to Tientsin he visited me and accepted a photograph of me to take to his father, and George V later wrote a letter thanking me for it, and also sent his own photograph for the British consul-general to present to me. I also exchanged photos with the king of Italy through the Italian consul-general.

I visited a number of barracks and watched many parades of foreign troops. When these soldiers — whose presence in China had been conceded by my ancestress Tzu Hsi in 1901 — marched before me in their martial splendour I was very pleased as I felt that the way the foreigners were treating me proved that they still regarded me as emperor.

There was a "Country Club" in Tientsin run by the English, a very grand establishment where only the foreign bosses were allowed to set foot, Chinese being absolutely forbidden to pass the main entrance. I was the only exception to this rule.[1] I was allowed to enter freely and even to take members of my household, and we all enjoyed the delights of being "special Chinese".

I made the most of the clothes and diamonds of the foreign stores such as Whiteway, Laidlaw & Co. to dress myself up like a foreign gentleman from the pages of *Esquire*. Whenever I went out I used to wear the very latest in Western clothes tailored from English cloth. I would have a diamond pin in my tie, diamond cuff-links

---

[1] In its last days a few Chinese of the comprador-capitalist type were allowed in if accompanied by foreign members. This place was taken over after liberation and turned into a people's club.

in my sleeves, diamond rings on my fingers, a "civilization stick" in my hand, and German Zeiss spectacles on my nose. My body would be fragrant with the combined odours of Max Factor lotions, eau-de-Cologne and mothballs, and I would be accompanied by two or three Alsatian dogs and a strangely dressed wife and concubine.

This way of living drew many criticisms from Chen Pao-shen and Hu Sze-yuan. They never opposed my spending habits or my relations with foreigners, but when I went to the Chung Yuan Company for a haircut, or happened to go to the theatre or the cinema wearing Western clothes they would always come to remonstrate about the loss of imperial dignity. When repeated protests had no effect Hu Sze-yuan submitted a memorial in which he took the blame on himself and asked my permission to retire.

He had previously asked leave to retire when he had reckoned that I had lost something of my imperial dignity by going to the theatre with my wife Wan Jung to see the famous Peking opera actor Mei Lan-fang. When I repeatedly begged him to stay, rewarded him with two fox-fur coat linings, and stressed my determination to accept his criticisms his sorrow had turned to joy. He had praised me as an "illustrious ruler" because I accepted the remonstration, and both sides were happy. I dealt with his new resignation over my visit to the barber's shop in much the same way.

Wan Jung's twentieth[1] birthday occurred in our first year in Tientsin and her father arranged for a foreign orchestra to come and play for the occasion. As soon as one old former Ching official heard this news he hastened to remonstrate with me, protesting that "foreign music has a mournful sound" and could not possibly be played on the birthday of an empress. The old fellow was given two hundred dollars and the foreign orchestra cancelled. This must have been the time when I started to give rewards to ministers who criticized me.

From then until my imprisonment I never went out to a theatre or a barber's saloon again. The reason why I followed Hu's advice was not because I was worried that he might go on complaining but

---

[1] Nineteenth by Western reckoning.

because I thought he was right in saying that it was undignified for me to go to a theatre. I can give an example to show the "progress" I made. When a Swedish prince visited Tientsin and wanted to meet me I refused because I had seen a picture of him with the actor Mei Lan-fang in the papers and thought that I should show my disapproval of his degrading behaviour.

Hu Sze-yuan and other members of Chen Pao-shen's party differed from Cheng Hsiao-hsu, Lo Chen-yu and their associates in that they seemed to have despaired of a restoration and were opposed to trying out anything dangerous. They attached more importance than Cheng and the others to my royal dignity, which was another reason why I obediently did as they told me. Although I found many of their suggestions bigoted I always accepted ones in which they showed their loyalty. Although I was living a strange life in a foreign settlement I never forgot my position and remembered that an "emperor" had to abide by precedent.

When my consort Wen Hsiu suddenly asked for and obtained a divorce in 1931 the old-timers did not neglect to ask me to issue an edict demoting her from the rank of consort to that of commoner, and I naturally complied.

Wen Hsiu's divorce reminds me of my irregular relationship with her. The reason she left me was not so much a matter of emotions as of the emptiness of our life in the Chang Garden. Even if I had only had one wife she would not have found life with me at all pleasant as my only interest in life was in restoration. Frankly speaking, I did not know what love was, and where husband and wife were equal in other marriages, to me wife and concubine were both the slaves and tools of their master.

Wen Hsiu had been brought up from her earliest years to accept the inferior role of a woman in feudal society and she began the life of a "palace consort" before she reached the age of fourteen, so that the ideas of her duty to her sovereign and her husband were very deeply embedded in her. That she dared to ask for a divorce in spite of this was a sign of great courage. She overcame all kinds of obstacles to obtain it, and was badly treated afterwards. It has been said that she was egged on to ask for it by her family for the sake of a considerable alimony, but in fact the difficulties her family created for her caused her great distress. She had very little of the 50,000 dollars alimony left after she had paid her lawyers and the middlemen and when her family had taken what they wanted; and her psychological losses were even worse. A brother of hers actually published an open letter to her in a Tientsin paper in which he attacked her and accused her of ingratitude to the Ching house.

It appeared on the surface that Wen Hsiu was forced out by the "empress" Wan Jung, and while this was not the whole truth it was certainly one of the reasons for Wen Hsiu's departure.

I do not know much about what happened to Wen Hsiu after her divorce except that she became a primary-school teacher and died in 1950. She did not remarry.

CHAPTER FIVE

□□

TO THE NORTHEAST

In 1931 the Japanese army was ready to start using P'u Yi in Northeast China. This vast area, which used to be known as Manchuria in English, had been central to Japan's ambitions since the late nineteenth century. Japan had seized many positions there in wars against China in 1894–5 and against Russia ten years later. As the effective control of China's central government weakened under the Republic, Japan's military, economic, and political domination of the region was strengthened, a process that went even further with the collapse of tsarist power. For many years Japanese interests were best served by supporting local war-lords, the so-called Fengt'ien clique headed by Marshal Chang Tso-lin. But by 1928 Chang was proving less amenable. The Japanese Kwantung Army, which had the free run of the Japanese-leased territory the Kwantung Peninsula and the Japanese-owned South Manchuria Railway that criss-crossed the region, killed him on 4 June 1928 by the characteristically and unnecessarily flamboyant method of blowing up his train.

Chang Tso-lin's son and successor Chang Hsüeh-liang defied Japanese warnings by pledging allegiance to the Kuomintang government at Nanking in December of that year. This posed the threat that Chiang Kai-shek might be able to establish effective central government control in the Northeast, an area that Japan wanted to keep separate and manageable. There were, however, differences between the civilian cabinet in Tokyo and the Kwantung Army's buccaneers over timing and methods. The military acted on their own initiative and launched a series of actions on 18 September 1931 aimed at bringing the whole of the Northeast under direct Japanese control. Civilian politicians in Tokyo may have been slightly embarrassed, but they did not curb the colonels.

By agreeing to be smuggled out of Tientsin in November to go to the Northeast, P'u Yi was committing himself still further to being a client of Japan, and more specifically of the military. This meant siding with those of his advisers, notably Cheng Hsiao-hsu, who saw the Kwantung Army as the faction to depend on. Because of the divisions among the Japanese and the storms of protest stirred up by the aggression of 18 September, P'u Yi had to be kept in the Northeast, out of sight but under Japanese control, till the spring of 1932. His return to the region where his Manchu ancestors had formed the military machine that overran China in the seventeenth century could hardly have been less glorious; and before long he found that Japan had no intentions of restoring him as emperor of the Ch'ing dynasty ruling the whole of China. All that they had to offer him was the nominal headship of a bogus state: Manchukuo.

The Unquiet Quiet Garden

In July 1929 I moved from the Chang Garden to the Quiet Garden. This house had previously had a different name, and the change to "Quiet Garden" was not without significance.

After the Northern Expedition the power of the Kuomintang extended to the north of China. The warlords with whom I was on good terms were collapsing, and the Northeast, in which I had placed such high hopes, had proclaimed its allegiance to the National Government in Nanking. Everyone in the Chang Garden had despaired. Some of the Ching veterans in my entourage had scattered, and of the ministers who stayed with me, only Cheng Hsiao-hsu, Lo Chen-yu and a few others still talked about restoration. The only question that the others considered was how the new dynasty of Chiang Kai-shek was going to treat me. I too was very worried about this.

Our anxiety did not, however, last long. We soon saw that under the Nanking Kuomintang government civil wars continued just as they had under the Peking warlord regime. The unification achieved by Chiang Kai-shek became more and more illusory, and hopes revived in the Chang Garden when all had seemed lost. It seemed to us that the great enterprise of unification could be accomplished only by me, a view that was expressed not only by the Ching veterans in my service but also by the Japanese staff officers who came to give me my talk about current developments every week. The name I chose for my new house — Quiet Garden — did not mean that I wanted peace and quiet: it implied that I intended to wait quietly for my opportunity.

After two years of waiting in the Quiet Garden we got some news in the summer of 1931.

Two months before the "September 18th Incident" my younger brother Pu Chieh, who was studying in Tokyo, was about to come back to China on holiday when he received an invitation from a battalion commander named Yoshioka Yasunori to stay with him for a few days before going back to China. Yoshioka had previously been a staff officer with the Japanese forces in Tientsin and had frequently come to the Chang Garden to give me weekly summaries of current events. Pu Chieh was treated with great hospitality by Major Yoshioka and his wife. When he was saying goodbye to them Yoshioka took him aside and said gravely, "When you get to Tientsin you can tell your elder brother that Chang Hsueh-liang has been behaving disgracefully recently and that something may be happening soon in Manchuria. Please ask Emperor Hsuan Tung to look after himself: his situation is by no means hopeless." Pu Chieh told me about this when he arrived in Tientsin on July 10. On July 29 the Japanese viscount Mizuno Katsukuni came to visit me and I received him in the presence of Cheng Hsiao-hsu and Pu Chieh. In the course of this ordinary meeting my visitor gave me an extraordinary present: a Japanese fan on which was written a couplet, "Heaven will not let Kou Chien fail. The age does not lack a Fan Li".[1]

Viscount Mizuno had gone to see Pu Chieh before his return to China and had explained to him the significance of the couplet. Pu Chieh wrote to me to tell me about it. It referred to a story of the civil war in Japan between the northern and southern dynasties. The emperor Godaigo, who was under the control of the Kamakura shogunate, brought about his own fall, was captured by the shogunate, and was exiled to Oki. During his exile a warrior carved this couplet on the trunk of a cherry tree as a hint to him. Later this Japanese "Kou Chien" overthrew the shogunate with a crowd of "Fan Li's" and returned to Kyoto. This was the beginning of the "Kemmu Restoration". What Viscount Mizuno omitted to mention

---

[1] Kou Chien was a king of the state of Yueh in the Spring and Autumn Period who had been badly defeated by the neighbouring state of Wu. Fan Li was an able minister who enabled King Kou Chien to avenge his defeat and destroy the state of Wu.

was that less than three years after his return to Kyoto Emperor Godaigo was driven out by a new military leader, Ashikaga Takauji. But I was interested not in the history but in receiving this hint from a Japanese. The crisis in the Northeast was building up, and I had been dreaming of reascending the throne for several nights running. This hint seemed to me to be a call to action, irrespective of whether it sprang from the concern of an individual or was the result of prompting from some official quarter.

The attack launched by Japanese troops in Shenyang on September 18 and the retreat of the Chinese troops galvanized the Quiet Garden. As soon as I heard the news I longed to go to the Northeast, but I knew that this was impossible without the consent of the Japanese. Cheng Hsiao-hsu told me that the situation in Shenyang was still confused and advised me not to be too impatient: sooner or later the Japanese were bound to invite me to go and the best thing at the moment was to get in touch with as many people as possible. I therefore decided to send Liu Hsiang-yeh to see the senior Japanese officers in the Northeast, including Uchida Yasuda (the head of the South Manchuria Railway) and Honjo Shigeru (the commander of the Kwantung Army). I also sent my chief steward Tung Chi-hsu to the Northeast to see the Ching veterans there. Another member of my entourage, Shang Yen-ying, thought of going to visit the Northeastern military commanders with whom he was acquainted. Soon after these three had gone Cheng Hsiao-hsu's prediction was fulfilled and an emissary of the Japanese Kwantung Army came to see me.

On the afternoon of September 30 an interpreter named Yoshida from the Japanese Tientsin garrison came to the Quiet Garden to tell me that the Japanese commander, Lieutenant-General Kashii Kohei, wanted me to come alone and see him about an important matter. I went to the Japanese barracks full of happy anticipation, and when I arrived General Kashii was waiting for me outside the front door of his house. In the drawing room two people were standing respectfully: Lo Chen-yu wearing a Chinese jacket and gown and a stranger in Western clothes. From his bow I guessed that the stranger was a Japanese, and then General Kashii introduced him to me. His name was Kaeisumi Toshiichi and he had been sent by Colonel Itagaki of the Kwantung Army staff. After introducing him General Kashii left.

There were only three of us in the room. Lo Chen-yu greeted me and produced a large envelope containing a letter from a distant relation of mine, Hsi Hsia, who was chief of staff to Chang Tso-hsiang, the deputy head of public security in the Northeast. Hsi Hsia had taken advantage of the absence of Chang Tso-hsiang, who was also chairman of Kirin Province, to order that the gates of Kirin city be opened to welcome the Japanese troops, who were thus able to take Kirin without firing a shot. He said in his letter that the chance for which he waited for twenty years (since the 1911 Revolution) had at last arrived. He begged me not to miss this opportunity and to come at once to the "land where our ancestors arose" to take charge of the plan. He also said that I could win the Northeast with Japanese support and then go on to think about the rest of the country. As soon as I reached Shenyang, Kirin would proclaim my restoration.

After I had finished reading the letter Lo Chen-yu repeated its main theme and told me at length about his activities and "the unselfish assistance" of the Kwantung Army. According to him, "restoration" could be expected throughout the Northeast in a matter of days, my "subjects" were longing for my return, and the Kwantung Army had agreed to my restoration and sent Kaeisumi to contact me. Everything was settled: I only had to set out and a Japanese naval vessel would take me to Talien. He was so excited as he spoke that his face went red, his whole body quivered, and his eyes all but popped out of their sockets.

I looked at Lo Chen-yu and Kaeisumi feeling unsettled. It was clear that this meeting with Lo was unlike any previous one. We were now talking in the Japanese garrison and he had with him a representative of the Kwantung Army. In the second place he had the letter from Hsi Hsia. Moreover, I had read in the Talien press the previous day that "all walks of life in Shenyang are ready to greet the former Ching emperor", and the Tientsin papers were full of reports of the retreats of the Chinese troops in the Northeast and of the way that Britain was covering up for Japan at the League of Nations.

I told Lo and Kaeisumi that I would give them an answer when I had thought the matter over. General Kashii then reappeared and said that I would be in danger if I stayed in Tientsin and that he hoped I would take the advice of Colonel Itagaki and go to the Northeast. These words of his seemed truer and truer as I drove home in my car. My suspicions had been swept away, but my excitement was doused with cold water when I got back to the Quiet Garden.

The first to come out against the idea was Chen Pao-shen, followed by Hu Sze-yuan and Wan Jung's tutor, Chen Tseng-shou. Their reaction was that Lo Chen-yu was being reckless as usual and that one should not put one's trust too lightly in the representative of a mere colonel. They said that the situation in the Northeast, the real attitude of the powers and the state of public opinion were not yet clear. I should at least wait until Liu Hsiang-yeh returned from his mission of investigation before taking any decisions. I shook my head impatiently at this disappointing advice.

"Hsi Hsia's letter cannot be nonsense."

The eighty-four-year-old Chen Pao-shen was visibly embarrassed, and he hesitated for a while before saying very sadly: "It has always been the hope of your humble subject that the old order would be restored, as it is only natural that heaven will comply with the wishes of the people. But to act rashly in the present confusion might lead us into inextricable difficulties."

Seeing that these old fellows could not be convinced I had Cheng Hsiao-hsu sent for at once. I imagined that Cheng, who was full of vigour for all his seventy-one years, would be delighted by the invitation from the Kwantung Army and Hsi Hsia's letter. His reactions, however, were not what I had hoped for.

"After the ups and downs of the past a new dawn is breaking. The restoration will undoubtedly begin in Manchuria, and could not be prevented even if the Japanese did not welcome Your Majesty." After a moment's thought he added, "It would be safer, however, to wait until Tung Chi-hsu returns before Your Majesty moves."

Differences Among the Japanese

With the factions in the Quiet Garden still at odds the Japanese deputy consul in Tientsin came to see me the following day. The consulate knew all about my visit to the Japanese garrison. They understood my feelings and my circumstances, but felt that I would do best to act with caution and stay in Tientsin for the moment. As they were responsible for my protection they were obliged to give me this warning.

From that day onwards the deputy consul advised restraint either in person or through Chen Pao-shen and his nephew or Cheng Hsiao-hsu and his son. At the same time Yoshida, the interpreter attached to the Japanese garrison, was constantly telling me that the Japanese military were determined to help me reascend the throne as he tried to persuade me to go to the Northeast at once.

My new view of the Japanese army and government differed from that of Chen Pao-shen. He believed that according to the natural order civilians should rule, and stoutly maintained that I should not do what I was told by military men in the absence of any indication from Tokyo. My view was different. I thought that my fate was in the hands of soldiers, not politicians. I saw that while the Japanese were announcing to the world that they were ready to adopt peaceful methods to solve the "Sino-Japanese differences", the Kwantung Army was continuing to advance and attack the retreating Chinese troops. Although I did not understand that the shouts of protest of Chiang Kai-shek and Wang Ching-wei as they yielded national territory to the enemy were nothing but deceptions, I could see that the decisive element in the situation were the Japanese soldiers. Where Chen Pao-shen felt that the lukewarm attitude of the foreign powers was worrying, I thought that Britain at least supported me. Soon after my visit to the Japanese barracks, Brigadier F. H. Burnell-Nugent, the commander of the British troops in Tientsin, had come to see me, and had offered his personal congratulations on the opportunity that the "September 18th Incident" had created for me and even said that he would be proud to serve as a soldier under my dragon flag if I came to the throne in Manchuria. Soon after this I met Johnston again. He was in China on British Foreign Office business and he took the opportunity to come and see me. He was excited about my prospects, and he asked me to write a preface for his book *Twilight in the Forbidden City*. He said that he was going to add an epilogue called "The Dragon Goes Home".

The news that Liu Hsiang-yeh and Tung Chi-hsu brought back with them when they returned from the Northeast was fairly encouraging. Tung Chi-hsu came back first and said that the opinion of the Ching veterans he had met in Shenyang was that the time was ripe and I should not delay. When Liu Hsiang-yeh returned his news was that although he had been unable to see Uchida or Honjo he had met the Kwantung staff officer Colonel Itagaki and the Ching veteran Chin Liang and was able to confirm that what I had been told by Lo Chen-yu and Kaeisumi was quite true. Chin Liang had been extremely optimistic: "Everything in Fengtien is ready and we are only waiting for the arrival of Your Majesty." He had also been to Kirin and found out that it was true that the Japanese army controlled the whole of the province, and that Hsi Hsia and others were ready to support a restoration at any time.

In addition to this there were rumours circulating at the time that made me impatient to move. Tientsin journalists were very fast news gatherers, and my visit to the Japanese barracks was soon common knowledge. Some papers were even saying that I had already gone to the Northeast by boat. At the same time rumours were being spread from an unknown source that the Chinese were planning to take some action against me. I was more convinced than ever that I could not stay in Tientsin any longer.

I sent Cheng Hsiao-hsu's son Cheng Chui to say to the Japanese consul-general that even if the time had not yet come for me to go to Shenyang there could surely be no harm in my going to stay in Lushun first, where I would be safer. The consul replied at once that there was no need for me to go to Lushun, and he asked Cheng Chui to tell me that Uchida Yasuda could not agree to my moving at present. As Uchida was a veteran politician greatly respected by the army it would be best to act cautiously; as for my safety, he was prepared to take full responsibility for it. The consul ended up by saying that he intended to have an exchange of views with the garrison commander, General Kashii. The next day his deputy came to tell Cheng Chui that he and the general had agreed that neither of them was in favour of my leaving Tientsin at once.

This information left me feeling confused, and I invited the garrison interpreter to come and see me to clarify the situation. To my surprise he told me that the meeting between the consul-general and the garrison commander had never taken place and that General Kashii wanted me to leave with Kaeisumi at once. He suggested to me that I write a letter to the garrison command stating clearly that I wanted to go. I wrote the letter. Somehow the consul-general heard of it and hurried over to see Chen Pao-shen and Cheng Hsiao-hsu to find out whether I had really written it or whether it was a forgery.

I was very annoyed about the friction between the Japanese civil and military authorities, but I did not know what to do about it. Then a letter came from Liu Hsiang-yeh who had gone to the North-east again in which he said that he had found out the real feelings of Honjo, the commander of the Kwantung Army: as the three provinces of the Northeast were not yet entirely under control, it would be better to wait until they were unified and stable. As this was the opinion of the supreme arbiter of my destiny I had no choice but to obey him and wait. I now realized that in addition to the difference of opinion between the consulate-general in Tientsin and the garrison there was even discord within the Kwantung Army.

Having told Lo Chen-yu and Kaeisumi that I would not be leaving for the time being I waited for news as the days dragged past like years. I issued numbers of "imperial edicts" and sent my two nephews Hsien Yuan and Hsien Chi to the Northeast to win over some Mongol princes and give jade to Chang Hai-peng and Kuei Fu who had been among the first to submit to the Japanese occupation forces. At the request of a Japanese officer I wrote letters to the resistance fighter Ma Chan-shan and some patriotic Mongol princes advising them to surrender. I distributed a large batch of appointments and prepared a plentiful reserve of edicts of appointment to official posts with blank spaces for the names.

I should mention that at this time I acted on a suggestion from Cheng Hsiao-hsu, who was becoming less cautious now, and sent my brother's Japanese teacher to Japan to make contact with the new Army Minister, Minami Jiro, and the Black Dragon Society leader Toyama Mitsuru. I wrote each of them a letter (copied from drafts by Cheng Hsiao-hsu) whose authenticity I later denied at the International Military Tribunal for the Far East. Three weeks later I met the Kwantung Army staff officer Doihara and it was decided that I would go to the Northeast.

Meeting Doihara

Of the twenty-five war criminals tried by the International Military Tribunal for the Far East the two found guilty of the most offences were Doihara and Itagaki. The charges against them were roughly similar and covered seven "crimes against peace" as well as the most important of the "conventional war crimes and crimes against humanity", namely "ordering and permitting the violation of treaties". They were hanged in 1948.

Doihara was a Japanese soldier who built his career out of aggression against China. He first came to China in 1913 and was adjutant to a Kwantung Army adviser to the Northeastern warlords for over ten years. He was closely associated with Chang Tso-lin, but when the Kwantung Army decided to eliminate Chang in 1928 Doihara took part in the plot to blow him up. Soon after this he was promoted to the rank of colonel and was in charge of a secret service organization in Shenyang. From 1931 to 1935 he was involved in many Japanese plots against China, planning riots, setting up local puppet authorities, and engineering outbreaks of fighting.

After a short spell as a brigade commander Doihara was put in command of the secret service network of the Kwantung Army.

After the "July 7th Incident" of 1937 Doihara reverted from under-cover work to an open military role as a divisional commander, later rising to command Japanese armies in China and Southeast Asia.

Because of the mysterious stories that were told about him the Western press described him as the "Lawrence of the East" and the Chinese papers said that he usually wore Chinese clothes and was fluent in several Chinese dialects. But it seems to me that if all his activities were like persuading me to go to the Northeast he would have had no need for the cunning and ingenuity of a Lawrence: the gambler's ability to keep a straight face while lying would have been enough. When I met him he wore not Chinese clothes but Japanese-style Western ones, and his spoken Chinese was nothing marvellous, as he had to use the services of the Tientsin garrison interpreter Yoshida to be sure that there would be no misunder-standings.

He was forty-eight, and the flesh round his eyes was going flabby. He had a little moustache on his upper lip, and throughout our interview his face wore a kindly and respectful smile. This smile was enough to make one feel that every word he spoke was com-pletely reliable.

After politely inquiring about my health he got down to business. First he explained the Japanese action to me. He said it was aimed solely at dealing with the "Young Marshal" Chang Hsueh-liang, under whose rule "the people of Manchuria were reduced to destitu-tion and the Japanese had no guarantees for their rights and safety, so that Japan had no alternative but to take military action". He claimed that the Kwantung Army had no territorial ambitions in Manchuria and "sincerely wants to help the Manchurian people to set up their own independent state". He hoped that I would not miss this opportunity and would soon return to the land from which my ancestors had arisen to undertake the leadership of the new state. Japan would sign a treaty of mutual defence with this country and its sovereignty and territorial integrity would be protected by Japan with all the might at her disposal. As head of this state I would be able to take charge of everything.

His sincere tone, his respectful smile, his reputation and his position all prevented me from taking the same attitude to him as I had to Lo Chen-yu and Kaeisumi. Chen Pao-shen's fears that Kaeisumi did not represent the Kwantung Army and that the Kwantung Army did not represent the Japanese government now seemed unfounded. Doihara was an important figure in the Kwantung Army and he had stated unambiguously that "His Majesty the Emperor (of Japan) trusts the Kwantung Army".

There was still one big problem that worried me. I asked what form the new state would take.

"As I have already said, it will be independent and autonomous, and it will be entirely under Your Majesty's control."

"That is not what I asked. I want to know whether it will be a republic or a monarchy."

"This problem will be solved after you come to Shenyang."

"No," I insisted. "I will only go if there is to be a restoration."

He smiled slightly and without changing the tone of his voice replied: "Of course it will be a monarchy; there's no question of that."

"Very well. If it is to be a monarchy I will go."

"In that case I must ask Your Majesty to leave as soon as possible, and to be in Manchuria by the sixteenth without fail. We can discuss the details in Shenyang. Yoshida can arrange your journey."

He wished me a safe voyage and bowed to me as politely as before. Our interview was over. After he had gone I met Chin Liang, who had come with him. He brought me news from some of the Ching veterans in the Northeast and said that they could obtain the submission of the former Northeastern army. I now felt that there were no more obstacles in my way.

After Doihara's departure the army interpreter Yoshida told me that I should not tell the consulate-general about the interview and that he would arrange my journey to Talien. I decided that I would discuss the matter with nobody but Cheng Hsiao-hsu, but as the news of my interview with Doihara was in the press the next day I had to answer advice and criticism from many quarters. Chen Pao-shen was horrified about it, as were several others of my close advisers.

Three days or so after Doihara's visit I agreed to see an emissary from the Chiang Kai-shek government in Nanking, which was offering to revive the Articles of Favourable Treatment and pay me either a yearly grant or else a single lump sum provided that I lived anywhere except in Japan or the Northeast. But I remembered the desecration of the Eastern Mausolea by Kuomintang troops and distrusted Chiang, suspecting that he was only interested in getting me away from the Japanese to save his face, and that once he had me in his power I would be helpless. Besides, what was the imperial title he was offering me worth compared with the imperial throne that Doihara had promised, and how could a sum of money be a greater attraction than the whole Northeast? I gave the emissary a noncommittal answer, and by the time he came to see me again I had left Tientsin.

In addition to the many visitors who tried to see me in those crowded days I also had a heavy mail. In some letters the writers offered me advice and warnings. There was one from a member of my own Aisin-Gioro clan who begged me not to "acknowledge a bandit as my father" and advised me to value my reputation in Chinese eyes. But I was too far carried away by my dream of restoration to heed any warnings. Naturally, I did not make my true feelings public. In an interview with a Tientsin journalist I vigorously denied that I had any intention of going to the Northeast; but by the time this was printed in his paper I was already on the boat.

There was another incident that took place two days before my departure from Tientsin that I should mention. A personal assistant called Chi Chi-chung came running into the room shouting, "Bombs, two bombs".

I was sitting in an armchair, and this news gave me such a fright that I was incapable of standing up. In the ensuing confusion I found out a stranger had delivered a present with the card of a former adviser to the pacification headquarters of the Northeast. The stranger had deposited the parcel and disappeared. When it was inspected two bombs were found inside a basket of fruit.

Before the excitement had died down Japanese police and army officers arrived and took the bombs away. The next day the interpreter Yoshida told me that investigation had proved that the two bombs had been produced in the arsenal of Chang Hsueh-liang. "Your Majesty must receive no more strangers, and the sooner you leave the better."

"Very well. Please make the arrangements as quickly as possible."

"Yes, sire. I hope that Your Majesty will not talk about this to anybody who is not directly concerned."

"I won't. I'll only take Cheng Hsiao-hsu and his son and a couple of assistants."

In those two days I received a number of threatening letters and a phone call that was taken by my personal assistant Chi Chi-chung. According to Chi, the call had come from a waiter in the Victoria Café who warned me that I should not go and eat there for the time being as some "suspicious people" had been making inquiries about me. This considerate waiter had apparently gone on to say that these suspicious characters looked as if they had weapons concealed in their clothing. More surprisingly still, he had been able to see that they had been sent by Chang Hsueh-liang.

I do not know who that waiter was, if he ever existed, but the servant Chi Chi-chung, who was also the man who reported the delivery of the bombs, had accompanied me to Tientsin from Peking as a trusted page. He was a favourite of mine, one of the three personal assistants who accompanied me to the Northeast, and he undoubtedly helped Cheng Hsiao-hsu and the Japanese to get remarkably accurate information about my actions and moods. I sent him to a military academy in Japan, and he became a major-general in the puppet army of North China before being suppressed after liberation for counter-revolutionary activities.

After the bombs, the threatening letters and the telephone call came the "Tientsin Incident". This was one of Doihara's masterpieces. The Japanese arranged for a crowd of Chinese agents of theirs to make trouble in the Chinese-administered part of the city. A state of emergency was then announced in the Japanese concession and communications with the Chinese city cut. Armoured cars drove up to "protect" the Quiet Garden, which was now isolated from the outside. The only people allowed in and out were Cheng Hsiao-hsu and his son Cheng Chui.

As I look back now I think that the reason why Doihara was in such a hurry to get me to the Northeast may have been because the young officers in the Kwantung Army were impatient to force the hands of a rival faction.

If it was simply because he was frightened that I would change my mind, he overestimated the influence that the people around me had on me. I had decided to go, and even some of my advisers who were supporters of Chen Pao-shen were starting to advocate active co-operation with Japan, though they still did not have much trust in the Japanese army and thought that it would be better to deal with the government. All the same, they did not want to miss this chance any more than I did; but they were worried that serving Japan might bring only dishonour without any compensating rewards. The condition on which they suggested I should collaborate with Japan was that I should have the right of making appointments. They were concerned that they might not be able to become high officials, and were fully prepared to trade the honour and the economic interests of the nation in exchange for positions for themselves.

The Secret Crossing of the Pai River

I was to leave for the Northeast on November 10, 1931. According to the plan I was to slip out of the main gate of the Quiet Garden that evening without anyone noticing. This gave me a lot of worry. My first idea was not to go out of the main gate but to tell my driver at the last moment to leave by the garage gate. When I sent my most trusted personal assistant, Big Li, to go and see whether the garage door could be opened he reported that it had not been used for so long that the outside was pasted over with advertisements. The method I finally used was one suggested by Chi Chi-chung. I hid in the luggage compartment of a convertible while one of my servants acted as a driver with Chi Chi-chung sitting beside him, and thus we left the Quiet Garden.

Not far from the main gate the interpreter Yoshida was waiting for us in a car, and when he saw our car come out of the gate he followed us at a discreet distance.

This was the third day of the Tientsin disturbances and there was a state of martial law in the Japanese concession and the neighbouring Chinese-administered district. Whether the disturbances and the martial law were deliberately arranged or simply a coincidence I cannot say for sure, but they created most suitable circumstances for my flight. When my convertible was stopped by Japanese troops at a roadblock, past which no other Chinese vehicles were allowed to go, a wave of the hand from the interpreter was enough to let us through. Although my substitute driver was terrible (the first thing he did after coming out of the Quiet Garden was to hit a telegraph post and make me bump my head badly) we managed to reach our destination, a Japanese restaurant.

After the car stopped Chi Chi-chung sent the driver away and the interpreter opened the compartment in the back of the vehicle, helped me out, and went into the restaurant with me. Here another Japanese officer was waiting and he produced a Japanese army greatcoat and cap which he put on me. He then accompanied me and the interpreter in a Japanese military car which drove straight to a dock on the bank of the Pai River without obstruction. They helped me out of the car, and when I saw that we were no longer in the Japanese concession I was alarmed. The interpreter Yoshida told me in a low voice that it did not matter as we were in the British concession.

I hurried along the concrete wharf supported on both sides by the two officers until a tiny and unlit motor launch appeared before us. In the cabin I saw Cheng Hsiao-hsu and his son Cheng Chui and was relieved to see that they were there as had been arranged. There were also three other Japanese, of whom one was the Kaeisumi I had met at the garrison headquarters and another was a *ronin* called Kudo Tetsusaburo who had previously worked for the Mongol noble Sheng Yun. The captain of the vessel told me that there were ten soldiers on board to protect it. The boat belonged to the transport section of the garrison, and it had been specially fitted with sandbags and armour plating for this "transport" mission. About twenty years later I read some reminiscences by Kudo in the Japanese magazine *Bungei Shunju* in which he recalled that there was a large drum of petrol hidden in the boat, and that if we had been discovered by Chinese troops and been unable to escape, the Japanese soldiers would have set light to it and destroyed the boat and us along with it. While I sat only a few feet from this petrol drum I thought that I was getting closer and closer to "happiness".

The interpreter and the other officer who had brought me to the dock went ashore and the boat left the wharf. I gazed at the shore as our lights came on and was overcome with emotion as I gazed at the river. I had been to the Pai River before in daytime and had even begun to dream about it as my future route to the other side of the ocean and to restoration. Now that I was actually sailing down it I was overcome with emotion and searched for words with which to express my excitement.

My happiness was a little premature, as I discovered when Cheng Chui told me that once we were outside the foreign concessions we would be within the power of the Chinese and might encounter Chinese troops there.

My heart jumped into my mouth. The faces of everyone I could see were set and nobody spoke. After two hours of total silence there suddenly came a shout from the riverbank: "Halt!"

I lay on the floor paralysed as if all my nerves had been cut. The Japanese soldiers in the cabin went up on deck, and from the deck I heard orders given in low voices and footsteps.

I saw through the window that there were soldiers behind each of the sandbags ready to fire. The boat seemed to be slowing down and heading for the bank. The lights went out and there was a sound of rifle-fire from the shore. Almost at once the motor roared into life and the boat leapt forward and away from the bank. The shots and shouting on the shore sounded fainter and fainter. The

Japanese plan had succeeded. First they had gone towards the bank as if they were obeying instructions and then they had bounded away, taking the soldiers on the bank by surprise.

A moment later our lights came on again and the atmosphere in the cabin became lively. In the middle of the night we reached the mouth of the river at Taku, and while we waited for the merchant-man *Awaji Maru* to meet us outside the river the Japanese troops produced *miso* soup, pickled cabbage and Japanese *sake*. Cheng Hsiao-hsu grew very lively and started talking about the racial and cultural links between China and Japan, reciting impromptu poems and describing the episode as a part of a "heroic enterprise".

Cheng Hsiao-hsu had another reason that he did not mention for being happy that evening. He had realized before any other of my advisers that underneath the friction between the Japanese govern-ment and army there lay unity. He wrote in his diary on the day after I was visited by Doihara that his son Cheng Chui had been told by the Japanese consul-general that the purpose of Doihara's visit was to invite me to go to Shenyang and that the consulate would pretend to know nothing about it.

Isolated

Aboard the *Awaji Maru* Cheng Hsiao-hsu talked all day about his ambition to govern the country, and on the morning of the 13th we put in at the South Manchuria Railway dock at Yingkow in Liaoning Province.

I never thought about why it was necessary to land at Yingkow in order to go to Shenyang, as all that I had wondered about was how the people of the Northeast would greet me at the harbour. I had imagined that there would be a crowd to give me the sort of welcome I had received when I went to the Japanese primary school in Tientsin — people waving flags and cheering. But the nearer the boat drew to the dock the less sign there was of such a welcome.

There were no crowds, no flags. When I went ashore I found out that the handful of people there to meet me were all Japanese.

When I was introduced to them I learnt that they had all been sent by Colonel Itagaki and that they were led by one Amakasu Masahiko. This fellow had not got much of a name in China but was notorious in Japan. At the time of the great earthquake of 1923 he had killed the progressive Osugi Sakae, his wife and nephew on behalf of the army which wished to take advantage of the confusion caused by the disaster to put pressure on the Left. Public opinion forced the army to make him a scapegoat and sentence him to life imprisonment through a court martial, but he was soon released and sent to study in France. The subjects Amakasu chose were art and music, and a few years later he returned to Japan and was posted to work in an undercover organization of the Kwantung Army. According to a book published in Japan after the Second World War the explosion on the railway line at Liutiaokou that was the signal for the "September 18th Incident" of 1931 was Amakasu's work. But when I met him on the Yingkow wharf I never would have dreamed that this polite bespectacled man had such an unusual past, or that without his handiwork I might never have gone to the Northeast.

Amakasu showed Cheng Hsiao-hsu, Cheng Chui and myself into a waiting carriage and took us to the station. After about an hour in a train we changed into another carriage. Without having been given a word of explanation on the journey I arrived at the warm springs sanatorium district of Tangkangtzu, and full of suspicion I entered the Tuitsuike Hotel.

This hotel was run by the Japanese South Manchuria Railway Company and was a luxuriously furnished Western building in the Japanese manner. It was reserved for Japanese army officers, high officials of the South Manchuria Railway and Chinese bureaucrats. I was taken to a grand drawing room on the first floor where Lo Chen-yu, Shang Yen-ying and Tung Chi-hsu were waiting. After greeting me Lo Chen-yu told me that he was in the middle of discussing my restoration and the founding of the new state with the Kwantung Army and explained that it would not do for the news of my arrival to leak out before the conclusion of the discussions;

234

it would also be wrong if any of us but him were to be seen outside. I did not understand the real significance of this and simply thought that I had now found out why nobody had come to welcome me. I thought that the talks with the Kwantung Army would present no problem and that soon the secrecy would be over and it would be announced that I, the Great Ching Emperor, had returned to the throne in the palace of my ancestors in Shenyang. The thought made me so excited that I paid no attention to the worried expressions of Cheng Hsiao-hsu and Cheng Chui. I happily ate an exotic Japanese supper and gazed out of the window at the beautiful sunset then went to bed, at peace with the world.

The next morning I discovered that my joy had been too early. After washing I called for my assistant Chi Chi-chung and said that I wanted to go out for a stroll to look at the scenery.

"It's not possible. They won't let anyone out," said Chi Chi-chung with a worried expression on his face.

"Why not?" I asked in surprise. "Who said so? Go downstairs and ask."

"They won't even let us downstairs."

I found out that I was isolated in the Tuitsuike Hotel: that strangers were forbidden to come near the hotel and that the people staying downstairs could not come up to the first floor, which was only being used by my little party. What most perplexed me was why we were not allowed downstairs. I sent for Lo Chen-yu but nobody knew where he had gone. Cheng Hsiao-hsu and his son were both furious and wanted me to demand an explanation from the Japanese. The senior of the Japanese who were staying with us were Kaeisumi and Amakasu, and when Chi Chi-chung brought the former to see me his face was covered with smiles.

"This is a safety precaution, a safety precaution for Your Majesty," he said in Chinese with a Japanese accent.

"How long are we going to stay here?" asked Cheng Hsiao-hsu.

"That depends on Colonel Itagaki."

"What about Hsi Hsia and the others? Didn't Lo Chen-yu say that Hsi Hsia was going to take me to Fengtien?"

"That too depends on Colonel Itagaki."

"What about Lo Chen-yu?" asked Cheng Chui.

"He's gone to Fengtien to see Colonel Itagaki. They are still discussing the new state, and when they have reached agreement Lo will come to take His Majesty to Fengtien."

"This is terrible." Cheng Chui walked away with an angry gesture. I was taken aback by this breach of court etiquette, but what really caught my attention was Kaeisumi's remark that the nature of the "new state" was still under discussion. This was very odd. Had not Doihara and Hsi Hsia both said that there were no problems and that all that was necessary was for me to come and ascend the throne? What did Kaeisumi mean when he said that it was still under discussion? When I asked this question Kaeisumi's reply was vague:

"To carry out so great an undertaking is easier said than done. Be patient, Your Majesty. When the time is ripe you will be invited to go."

"To go where?" cut in Cheng Chui. "To Fengtien?"

"That will be decided by Colonel Itagaki."

I left them in a bad temper and called Tung Chi-hsu to come and see me in another room. I asked him why he had sent me a telegram from Shenyang saying "everything ready". Tung replied that he had been told to send it by Yuan Chin-kai and did not know anything about it. I asked Shang Yen-ying what he thought of the matter, but he was incapable of a sensible reply; he wished he had his planchette, and then he would have been able to seek an explanation from the gods.

I did not know at the time that the Japanese were in a state of desperate confusion. Japan was internationally isolated, and within the country there were still differences of opinion over what form their rule over this new colony should take, so that the Kwantung Army could not yet allow me to take the stage. My only reaction was that the Japanese were not being as respectful towards me as they had been in Tientsin and that Kaeisumi was behaving quite differently from the way he had when I had met him there. After a week of uneasy waiting I received a telephone call from Itagaki asking me to move to Lushun.

Why was I not going to Shenyang? Kaeisumi explained with a smile that this would be settled after I talked to Itagaki. Why go to Lushun? Kaeisumi answered that in Tangkangtzu I was in great danger from "bandits" and that I would be much better off in Lushun as it was a big city and far more convenient. This sounded reasonable to me and so I caught a train which arrived in Lushun the following morning.

In Lushun I stayed in the Japanese Yamato Hotel. Here, as before, the whole of the upper part of the building was reserved for the use of my little party. I was told that I was not to go downstairs, and the people downstairs were not allowed up. Kaeisumi and Amakasu also told me that talks about the new state were continuing and that there was no need for me to be impatient as someone would come and invite me to Shenyang in due course. After a few days here Cheng Hsiao-hsu and his son were given the same treatment as Lo Chen-yu and allowed out freely; they were even able to go to Talien. The gloomy expression disappeared from Cheng Hsiao-hsu's face and he started to talk in the same way as Lo Chen-yu: "It would injure Your Majesty's celestial dignity were you to show your face. If you wait until your ministers have arranged everything then Your Majesty can ascend the throne at the appropriate time and receive homage with decorum and propriety." He also said that I should not meet anybody as it would not be right to publicize my presence before everything was settled. The Kwantung Army were my hosts for the time being, and until I ascended the throne I should regard myself as their guest. Meanwhile it was only right that I should do as my hosts thought fit. So although I was still feeling impatient I had no choice but to force myself to wait.

But these people who were always addressing me as "Your Majesty" and serving me with such apparent diligence thought of me not as a real monarch but as a king in a pack of cards. The Japanese, who were under pressure from the Western powers and domestic opinion, had me up their sleeves, and they wanted to keep me secret until the time came to play me. Cheng, Lo and the others also each wanted to have me to himself in order to beat their opponents and be the only one to get rewards from the Japanese. This was why I was isolated. When I was in Tangkangtzu Lo Chen-yu took advantage of restrictions imposed by the Japanese to prevent me from making any contacts, cutting Cheng Hsiao-hsu and myself off from the Kwantung Army. Once we reached Lushun Cheng Hsiao-hsu was able to establish his own links with the Japanese in competition with Lo. Then the two of them combined to keep out any third rival while they fought for favour with the Japanese.

I did not understand all this at the time. All I could see was that Lo and the two Chengs were hand in glove with the Japanese and isolating me from everyone else. They were not worried by Tung Chi-hsu or by Shang Yen-ying, who only knew how to consult the oracles and beg for help from the gods, but they took the strictest measures against people who came from Tientsin to see me and were even rude to my wife Wan Jung.

Before my departure from Tientsin I had left an edict with a servant to be given to Hu Sze-yuan. In it I had told him to follow me to the Northeast and had instructed Chen Tseng-shou (Chen Pao-shen's nephew) to bring Wan Jung. When they heard that I was in Lushun they went to nearby Talien. Lo Chen-yu told them that the Kwantung Army had given orders that they were not to be allowed to go to Lushun. Wan Jung was suspicious of this order and thought that something must have happened to me, so she started to weep and shout. In this way she managed to get permission to come to Lushun to see me just once. After about a month the Kwantung Army moved me to the house of the son of the former Prince Su, and only then were Wan Jung and my second and third sisters allowed to live in the same place as me.

I had wanted Chen Tseng-shou and Hu Sze-yuan to move in with me, but Cheng Hsiao-hsu told me that the Kwantung Army had laid it down that nobody was to see me except himself, his son, Lo Chen-yu and Wan Sheng-shih. I asked him to try and arrange something with Amakasu and Kaeisumi; the only result was that Hu Sze-yuan was allowed to see me once, on condition that he returned to Talien the same day.

As soon as he saw me Hu Sze-yuan started to cry and say that he would never have thought that after so many years in my service he would be prevented even from seeing me. Although this frightened me, I tried to console him by telling him that when I was free to do so I would send an edict calling him and Chen Tseng-shou to my side. Hu stopped crying and told me in detail how Cheng Hsiao-hsu and Lo Chen-yu were making difficulties for them and accusing them of nourishing private ambitions and trying to squeeze out "good and loyal people".

Hu and his friends never succeeded in defeating Lo Chen-yu and Cheng Hsiao-hsu. Chen Pao-shen came to Lushun when I had been there for about two months, but Cheng Hsiao-hsu, who had all but defeated Lo Chen-yu in the battle for the favour of the Kwantung Army and did not want another rival on the scene, managed to get Chen Pao-shen sent away after only two days.

During my first few weeks in the Northeast Lo Chen-yu and Cheng Hsiao-hsu fought out their last battle. Lo Chen-yu held the initiative at first, but was foolish enough to insist on a Ching restoration in his negotiations with the Japanese although it would have been politically embarrassing for them. When Cheng Hsiao-hsu and I moved to Lushun Lo found to his surprise that the Kwantung Army had invited Cheng to join the talks. He did not know about Cheng's links with the Japanese military in Tokyo or with Kaeisumi in Tientsin. Just as he had previously taken over Lo Chen-yu's connections with Colonel Takemoto in the year I left the Forbidden City, Cheng had now made Lo's Kaeisumi into his own friend. Amakasu realized after a few conversations with Cheng Hsiao-hsu and his son Cheng Chui that they were far more "flexible" than Lo Chen-yu, who craved for all the ritual and ceremony of the old Ching empire. Although Cheng Hsiao-hsu was shocked when he first heard that the Kwantung Army wanted me to be "President of the Republic of Manchuria and Mongolia" he soon adapted himself to the idea that the Japanese did not want an emperor and made it clear that provided he was premier of the new regime he would persuade me to agree to become head of state.

After the foundation of "Manchukuo" Lo Chen-yu was not satisfied with the post he was offered and went back to his antique
business, while Cheng Hsiao-hsu became puppet premier.

Disappointment

I felt very frightened while I was in Lushun. The reason for this
was not my isolation but being told by Kaeisumi and other Japanese
that the Kwantung Army had not yet settled the form of the new
state. This was even more vexing than having nobody to greet me
at the harbour had been; then I had believed that "preparations were
incomplete" or my arrival had "not yet been announced". But
what did they mean when they said that the form of the state had
not been settled? Why had Doihara asked me to come to the Northeast if it had not been decided?

Cheng Hsiao-hsu and Kaeisumi told me that Doihara had not
been lying and that it was quite true that the Kwantung Army supported my restoration. But as this was a Manchurian affair it had
to be discussed with the Manchurians, and naturally the matter was
"undecided" until the consultations were over.

On February 19, 1932 came the news that the "Administrative
Committee for the Northeast" had passed a resolution to set up a
republic in the Northeast. This committee was composed of a
number of high officials who had submitted to the Japanese and
was chaired by Chang Ching-hui. This body also issued a "declaration of independence" on the same day. Everyone in my entourage
except Cheng Hsiao-hsu and his son was terrified and indignant.

I was seething with hatred of Doihara and Itagaki as I paced up
and down like a madman, breaking cigarettes in half. I threw a
book of divination that I had been using to the floor. I remembered my Quiet Garden and thought that if I could not be a real
emperor I would be much better off leading a comfortable life as
an exile. I could sell some of my treasures and have a good time

The empress dowager Tzu Hsi (*centre*)

Myself at the age of two

Myself at the time of my first
wedding

Wan Jung

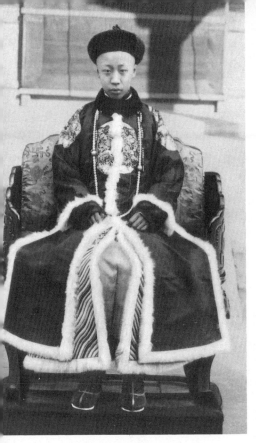

Myself in 1917

Johnston in Ching robes

Tientsin life

Above: With my brothers and sisters

Left: Golf

Birthday greetings at the Chang Garden from the Ching veterans

Above: A group photograph including my "supreme emperor", the Kwantung Army commander Hishikari Takashi (*fifth from left*), taken after my enthronement as puppet emperor

Setting out to sacrifice to heaven before the ceremony of my "accession" to the "Manchukuo" throne: March 1, 1934

Learning from scratch

Receiving my special pardon on December 4, 1959

Working at the Peking
Botanical Gardens

abroad. I decided to let the Kwantung Army know that if they would not agree to my demands I was going back to Tientsin. Neither Lo Chen-yu nor Cheng Hsiao-hsu opposed this idea when I told them about it. I agreed to a suggestion of Lo's that I should send a present to Itagaki, and I gave Lo some of the valuables I had brought with me to take to him. Just then Itagaki telephoned asking Lo and Cheng to go for talks with him. I asked Chen Tseng-shou to write out for me the reasons why the "right system" (the restoration of the Ching monarchy) was necessary and gave the document to Cheng and Lo to hand to Itagaki, instructing them to stand firm and make my views clear to him.

There were twelve reasons, of which the last four were added by Chen Tseng-shou:

1. The right system is essential if we are to follow the moral code of East Asia that dates back five millennia.

2. The right system is essential to the carrying out of the Kingly Way[1] and moral principles.

3. To rule the state one must have the trust and respect of the people, and for this the right system is essential.

4. China and Japan are fraternal countries, and for their joint survival and welfare they must respect the time-honoured morality and ensure that both peoples have an identical spirit. For this the right system is essential.

5. China has suffered from the disasters of democracy for over two decades, and, apart from a selfish minority, the great majority of the people loathe the Republic and long for the Ching Dynasty. For this reason the right system is essential.

6. The Manchu and Mongol peoples have always preserved their ancient customs, and the right system is essential if we are to win their allegiance.

7. The Republican system is very widespread while the numbers of the unemployed daily increase. This constitutes a

---

[1] A political philosophy of the Confucianists of ancient China. They wanted the feudal rulers to rule the country with "benevolence" and "righteousness", and they called this the "Kingly Way".

most serious threat to the Japanese Empire, but if the imperial order is revived in China this will do a great deal to preserve the intellectual and spiritual qualities of the peoples of our two countries. For this reason the right system is essential.

8. The Great Ching has a history of over two hundred years in China and of over a century in Manchuria before that. To observe the way of life of the people, calm their minds, maintain the peace of all parts of the country, preserve the oriental spirit, carry out the revival of Kingly government and consolidate the imperial order in our two countries, it is essential to have the right system.

9. The rise of Japan dates from the Kingly rule of Emperor Meiji. His edicts to his ministers all propagate morality and give instruction in loyalty and righteousness. While science was learnt from Europe and America, morality was based on Confucius and Mencius. As the ancient spirit of the Orient was preserved and the people were saved from the contagion of disgusting European practices, they love and esteem their elders, and protect their country as readily as one's hand protects one's head. That is why I respect him. The right system is essential if we are to follow in the steps of the great Emperor Meiji.

10. The Mongol princes continue to use their old titles, and if they are abolished under a republic they will be disappointed and disaffected, and there will be no way of ruling them. For this reason the right system is essential.

11. Japan deserves our deepest admiration for the way in which she has assisted the Three Eastern Provinces (the Northeast) and taken thought for the welfare of their thirty million people. My wish is that we should not restrict ourselves to thirty million people but should take the Three Eastern Provinces as a base from which to arouse the whole nation and save the people from the disasters that have befallen them. This would lead to the common survival and prosperity of East Asia, a matter which closely involves all of the ninety

million people of Japan. There should therefore be no divergence between the political systems of our two countries. To bring about the prosperity of both countries the right system is indispensable.

12.   Since I retired from office in 1911, I have lived among the people for twenty years. I have had no thought for my personal glory and have been guided only by a wish to save the people. If someone else would undertake the responsibility for the country and bring disasters to an end with the True Way, I would be happy to remain a commoner. If I am forced to assume this burden, it is my personal opinion that without the correct title and real power to appoint officials and administer the country, I will be unable to bring twenty years of misgovernment to an end. If I am ruler only in name and am hedged in by restrictions I will be of no help to the people and will only make their plight worse. This would not be my original intention, and would increase my guilt, and I absolutely refuse to bear the responsibility for this. If I were only concerned about my personal glory, I would be only too pleased to be given the land and the people after two decades of living in obscurity. What would I care whether I become president or monarch? It is purely for the sake of the people, of the state, of our two countries of China and Japan, and of East Asia as a whole, and not because of the slightest self-interest, that I maintain that the right system is indispensable.

But although Cheng Hsiao-hsu agreed to present my demands for a restoration of the Ching Dynasty to Itagaki he never did so. Instead he agreed to the Japanese proposal that the new state be a republic, and he undertook to persuade me to become its "chief executive". I was told much later that he said to Itagaki, "His Majesty is like a blank sheet of paper on which your army can paint whatever it likes." While I did not know at the time that he had said this, I was furious with him and the others for having allowed themselves to be tricked by the Japanese. Cheng Hsiao-hsu tried to pacify me by citing historical precedents and telling me that my hopes of restoration would be finished if I did not go along with the Japanese now. When this did not work he said that as Itagaki wanted to see me that afternoon I could talk to him then.

"Let him come," I angrily replied.

Meeting Itagaki

I met Itagaki Seishiro[1] on the afternoon of February 23, 1932, in the presence of an interpreter from the Kwantung Army. Itagaki was a short man with a shaven head and the pallor of his clean-shaven face was in contrast to the blackness of his eyebrows and his small moustache. He was the most neatly-dressed Japanese officer I had ever seen: his shirt cuffs were of dazzling whiteness and the creases in his trousers razor-sharp. This elegance and his habit of gently rubbing his hands made one feel that he was cultured and debonair.

First he thanked me for the presents I had sent him and then he went on to say that he had come on the orders of General Honjo, the commander of the Kwantung Army, to report to me on the "foundation of the new state of Manchukuo". Starting with "the failure of the tyrannical government of the Chang family to gain the people's allegiance and the total absence of guarantees for Japan's interests in the Northeast" he went on to elaborate slowly and at length on the "justice" of the actions of the Japanese army and its "sincerity in helping the Manchurian people to establish a paradise of the Kingly Way". As he spoke I nodded in approval and hoped that he would hurry up and answer the question in which I was really interested. At last he came to the point:

---

[1] Itagaki Seishiro had been on the staff of the Kwantung Army since 1929 and was one of the chief plotters behind the September 18th Incident and the consequent setting up of a Japanese puppet state in the Northeast. He later played a leading and disreputable role in other events, such as the Japanese invasion of the rest of China, the setting up of other Chinese puppet regimes, and the attack on the Soviet Union at the Khasan Lake.

"The new state will be called Manchukuo ('Manchuland'). Its capital will be Changchun, which will be renamed Hsinking ('New Capital'), and it will be composed of five races: Manchus, Hans, Mongols, Japanese and Koreans. In view of their efforts in Manchuria over many decades the legal and political position of the Japanese will naturally be the same as that of the other nationalities: they will, for example, have the same right as the others to hold office in the new state."

Without waiting for the interpreter to finish translating he produced the "Declaration of Independence of the Manchu and Mongol People" and the five-coloured "Manchukuo flag" from his briefcase and put them on the table in front of us. I was almost bursting with indignation. Pushing these objects aside with a trembling hand I asked:

"What sort of state is this? It certainly isn't the Great Ching Empire!"

"Of course, this will not be a restoration of the Great Ching Empire," answered Itagaki, unflustered as always. "This will be a new state. The Administrative Committee for the Northeast has passed a unanimous resolution acclaiming Your Excellency head of state. You will be the 'Chief Executive'."

"Your Excellency" sent the blood rushing up to my face. Never before had I been thus addressed by the Japanese, and I was not prepared to tolerate the abolition of my imperial title, not even in exchange for the two million square *li* and thirty million people of the Northeast. I was so worked up I could scarcely sit still.

"If names are not right then speech will not be in order, and if speech is not in order then nothing will be accomplished. The people of Manchuria are longing not for me as an individual but for the Great Ching Emperor. If you abolish the title their loyalty will be lost. I must ask the Kwantung Army to reconsider this."

Itagaki gently rubbed his hands and said, his face wreathed in smiles:

"The Manchurian people have expressed their wishes by acclaiming Your Excellency as the head of the new state, and the Kwantung Army is in full agreement with them."

"Japan has an imperial system, so how can the Kwantung Army agree to the founding of a republic?"

"If Your Excellency does not like the word 'republic', then we will not use it. This will be a state built on the chief executive system."

"I am very grateful for all the enthusiastic help your country has given, but I cannot accept a 'chief executive system'. The imperial title has been handed down to me by my ancestors, and were I to abandon it I would be lacking in loyalty and filial piety."

Itagaki seemed to be most understanding. "The office of chief executive will only be temporary. It is perfectly well known that Your Majesty is the twelfth emperor of the Great Ching Dynasty, and I am sure that after the formation of a national assembly a constitution will be adopted restoring the imperial system."

The words "national assembly" enraged me once more, and shaking my head for emphasis I said, "There are no good national assemblies, and the first Great Ching Emperor was never given his title by any assembly."

The argument continued for over three hours without our reaching agreement. Finally Itagaki, who had smiled throughout the discussion, picked up his case as a sign that he did not want to go on any longer. The smile vanished from his face, which was now paler than ever, and when he addressed me he reverted from "Your Majesty" to "Your Excellency": "Your Excellency should think it over carefully. We will continue our discussions tomorrow." With that frosty remark he left me.

That evening I gave a banquet for Itagaki as Cheng Hsiao-hsu had warned me that it would be dangerous to get on bad terms with the Japanese, reminding me of the fate of Chang Tso-lin. The occasion passed off smoothly, and the subject of the day's talks was carefully avoided.

The next morning Itagaki summoned Cheng Hsiao-hsu, Lo Chen-yu and other advisers of mine to the Yamato Hotel and asked them to give me his final decision:

"The demands of the Army cannot be altered in the least. We will regard their rejection as evidence of a hostile attitude and act accordingly. This is our last word."

This reply stunned me. My legs turned to jelly and I collapsed speechless into an armchair.

While Lo Chen-yu and the others were silent Cheng Chui urged me to accept the Japanese proposals. His father backed him up, speaking in an excited voice:

"The Japanese always do what they say they will, and we must not walk straight into trouble. Besides, they are well-disposed towards you and will allow Your Majesty to be head of state, which is the same as being emperor. Is today's opportunity not the reason why I have been serving Your Majesty all these years? If Your Majesty insists on refusing, I am afraid that I must pack my belongings and return home." This threat made me feel desperate.

"If Your Majesty agrees to the Japanese army's demands," added Cheng Chui, "you will be able to strengthen your position in the future and we will be able to do things the way we want to."

"Although one may regret the present situation there is nothing we can do about it," was Lo Chen-yu's dejected view. "Our only course is to set a time limit of one year, and if the imperial system is not restored by then Your Majesty can resign. Let us see how Itagaki reacts to that." Seeing no other way out I sighed and sent Cheng Hsiao-hsu to see if Itagaki would agree.

Cheng soon returned, his face beaming, to say that Itagaki had agreed and was going to give "a little banquet for the future Chief Executive" that evening.

Thus it was that both trembling with fear and dreaming of my future restoration I shamelessly became a leading traitor, and the cover for a sanguinary regime which turned a large part of my country into a colony and inflicted great sufferings on thirty million of my compatriots. I also laid the foundations for the rise of Honjo, Itagaki and the rest of them; as Cheng Hsiao-hsu observed in his diary, all of their careers would have been finished had I refused to co-operate.

CHAPTER SIX

□□

FOURTEEN YEARS OF "MANCHUKUO"

The Japanese decision to set up the puppet state that called itself Manchukuo marked an irrevocable break with the principle of respecting the formal unity of China even when in reality carving up the country. The status of the Northeast was and is a sensitive issue in China. The People's Republic, like the Republic before it, claims to be the heir to the multinational Ch'ing empire and its territories. The Northeast included the ancestral lands of the Manchus, who after their conquest of the rest of China reserved nearly all of this vast area for themselves and other small ethnic groups living mostly by hunting, herding, or fishing. By the 1890s Russian threats to this thinly populated region forced the Ch'ing authorities to throw it open to Han Chinese settlement. This continued under the Republic, and by 1931 the overwhelming majority of the inhabitants of the Northeast were Han Chinese.

This did not prevent the Japanese from claiming that the region had a special and separate Manchurian identity and using this to justify the setting up of the puppet state of Manchukuo ('Manchu State') in the spring of 1932 with P'u Yi as nominal chief executive. Their claim was that the local people wanted the new state, which was to be a bulwark against the Red (both Russian and Chinese) peril, but few independent observers were convinced, not even the League of Nations commission of inquiry that visited the area in 1932. Though Manchukuo was independent of Chinese control it was far from being independent of Japan, which held all real power, military, political, and economic.

The empire of Manchukuo, on the throne of which P'u Yi was placed in 1934, was transparently fraudulent from the outset. It involved inventing a nation, where none really existed, that was distinct from China and in which a small minority of Japanese officials, soldiers, business people, and colonists had a dominant part. Even if the Ch'ing dynasty had some appeal to the Manchu race, not many of its members were left in the Northeast by then, and the centre of Ch'ing loyalism remained Peking. There is little to suggest that the Han majority of inhabitants of the Northeast were in any way won over to the Japanese-sponsored regime by the fact that its nominal head was the former Ch'ing emperor.

It was impossible for P'u Yi to collaborate with Japan in separating the Northeast from the rest of China without making himself a traitor in the eyes of nearly all Chinese. It was not just that he had broken with the Republic. That, after all, was only a government, and one that other patriotic Chinese, among them the Communists (who had set up their own Chinese Soviet Republic in 1931), had broken away from with a good conscience. P'u Yi's much more fundamental offence against Chinese national sentiment was to participate in formally detaching a part of China. Throughout the history of the Republic some local war-lords had exercised de facto independent control of their territories, but they had always respected the forms of national unity. Foreign powers had likewise stopped short of ending nominal Chinese sovereignty over their spheres of influence in China. While P'u Yi was later to be pardoned for his part in the Manchukuo business, it is unlikely that Chinese national sentiment will ever forgive him. That he had in his childhood been Ch'ing emperor was something beyond his control, a mere accident of history. His voluntary collaboration with a foreign occupier in adult life was a different matter altogether. This reason alone is sufficient to make it very hard for Chinese people to see him in the romantic light that some foreigners detect around a former occupant of the dragon throne. The boy emperor in the Forbidden City may arouse an indulgent smile; but the adult quisling will long remain the object of contempt.

His decision also involved compromising the pretensions of the Ch'ing house to rule all of China, for when the scope of Japanese aggression extended during the 1930s first to Inner Mongolia and North China and then to the whole of China, his patrons did not extend his notional *authority beyond the borders of Manchukuo. Because of the extremely factional and divided nature of the Japanese effort in China, separate client regimes were set up in Peking (Peip'ing) and Nanking. Japanese arguments about the separateness of the Northeast and its Manchu identity would have made it hard to explain the region's reintegration into a revived Ch'ing empire. Besides, Japan had enough difficulty legitimizing its conquests in China without the additional burden of having to impose a discredited monarchy on even more unwilling subjects.*

The Northeast was an important economic and military base for Japan in China, and Japan seems to have kept a firmer grip there than in most other occupied areas of China. Northeastern industry, mines, and farms contributed much to Japan's war effort in China and, from December 1941, the Pacific. The end of P'u Yi's third spell as an emperor came when the Soviet Union, which till then had stayed neutral in the war in the east, fulfilled its pledge given at the Teheran Conference in 1943 to join the fight against Japan after the defeat of Germany. When the Red Army swept into Manchukuo three days after Hiroshima, the Japanese collapse was rapid. P'u Yi was captured, and his new masters were Soviet.

P'u Yi probably enjoyed being emperor of Manchukuo rather more than he admits in these pages, though it is clear from this and other accounts that his authority was very limited: he was not even given a free hand in his own palace. His empress Wan Jung was becoming increasingly unstable and dependent on opium. Given the life she had to lead this is hardly surprising. P'u Yi preferred child brides to keep him company. His first consort, Wen Hsiu, had left him in his Tientsin days. In 1937 he took a schoolgirl of sixteen, T'an Yü-ling, as a minor consort; and when she died in 1942 he resisted strong pressures to marry a Japanese as replacement. Instead he chose a fifteen-year-old Chinese girl from a local Japanese-run school, Li Yü-ch'in, who was taken into the palace in 1943. From her account of the marriage it appears that her role, as far as he was concerned, was to be a cheerful, sweet, and comforting companion when he chose to call, while also being absolutely and unquestioningly obedient. She, like the wretched Wan Jung, was left behind when P'u Yi was taken to the Soviet Union.

The Puppet Play Begins

My feelings were confused and contradictory at the private banquet Colonel Itagaki gave for me on the evening of February 24, 1932 to celebrate my consenting to become "Chief Executive" of the new Japanese puppet state of "Manchukuo". Itagaki had provided Japanese prostitutes for the guests, and he fondled and embraced them without bothering about the conventions of polite behaviour. As he drank freely and roared with laughter he made no attempt to conceal his pleasure at his success in forcing me to accept his terms. While he still had some control over himself he toasted me most respectfully, wishing me a successful future and the fulfilment of my ambitions, and I was very pleased to hear this. But as the evening wore on and he drank more and more his face became increasingly livid and things started to go wrong. One Japanese prostitute asked me in forced Chinese, "Are you in trade?" When Itagaki heard he burst into a strange laugh, and I realized that I had little to be pleased about.

On February 28 the "All-Manchurian Assembly" in Shenyang passed a resolution at the bidding of the Kwantung Army proclaiming the independence of the Northeast and appointing me "Chief Executive of the new state". Kaeisumi and Cheng Hsiao-hsu told me that as delegates from this "assembly" were going to come to Lushun to invite me to accept the office, we would need to prepare a reply in advance, or rather two replies. The first would be a refusal and the second an acceptance, to be produced when the delegates pressed me a second time. On March 1 the nine-man delegation arrived in Lushun, and Cheng Hsiao-hsu, who met them on my behalf, handed them the first reply. Afterwards I met them myself, and both sides made the set speeches they had been told to make; they "earnestly beseeched" me, I "modestly refused", and before twenty minutes had passed the meeting finished. On March 5 the "delegation" was increased to twenty-nine members at the bidding of the Fourth Section[1] of the Kwantung Army and came once more to "plead earnestly" with me. This time they accomplished their mission, and my final answer ran as follows:

> As you entrust me with this great responsibility, how could I venture to refuse for the sake of idleness and leisure? But, after careful reflection, I feel that I should disappoint the hopes of the masses. . . . I shall exert my feeble abilities to the utmost and act as a temporary Chief Executive for one year; and if my shortcomings are too many I shall respectfully retire after that year. If within the year a constitution is created and the form of the state settled in accordance with my original intention I shall then carefully reconsider my virtue and my strength and decide what to do.

This interlude over, I left for Changchun the following day with Wan Jung, Cheng Hsiao-hsu, Chang Ching-hui and others. As my train pulled into Changchun station at 3 p.m. on March 8, I heard the sound of military bands and cheering crowds. When I stepped on the platform surrounded by Chang Ching-hui, Hsi Hsia, Amakasu, Kaeisumi and others I saw Japanese gendarmes and rows of people wearing all sorts of clothes; some were in Chinese jackets and gowns, some in Western suits and some in traditional Japanese clothes, and they were all holding small flags in their hands. I was thrilled, and I reflected that I was now seeing the scene I had missed at the harbour. As I walked past them Hsi Hsia pointed out a line of dragon flags between Japanese ones and said that the men holding them were all Manchu bannermen who had been waiting for me to come for twenty years. These words brought tears to my eyes, and I was more strongly convinced than ever that my future was very hopeful.

When I climbed into my car my thoughts were on my Forbidden City, my expulsion from it, the robbery of the Eastern Mausolea,

---

[1] This section dealt with political and military affairs in the Northeast.

and the oath I swore as a result. I was too preoccupied with my hopes and hates to notice the streets I was driving through, or to observe the cold welcome that the citizens of Changchun, silent from terror and hatred, were giving me. After a short journey the car drove into the courtyard of an old building. This was to be the "Residence of the Chief Executive", although it was far from being the grandest house in the city.

I took office ceremonially the next day in a large reception room that had been put hurriedly in order. Uchida, the director of the Japanese South Manchuria Railway, Honjo, the commander of the Kwantung Army, Miyake, its chief of staff, and the staff officer Itagaki were among those present. Many of my "old ministers" attended: in addition to Cheng Hsiao-hsu, Lo Chen-yu, Hu Sze-yuan and Chen Tseng-shou they included other former Ching officials and a number of Mongol princes. There were also former members of the Fengtien clique, such as Chang Ching-hui, Tsang Shih-yi, Hsi Hsia and Chang Hai-peng; and there was a former staff officer of the Dog-meat General Chang Tsung-chang.

I wore Western evening dress. Under the gaze of the Japanese dignitaries the "founders of the nation" bowed to me three times and I bowed once to them. Then Tsang Shih-yi and Chang Ching-hui, acting on behalf of "the people of Manchuria", presented me with the "seal of the Chief Executive" wrapped in yellow silk. After this Cheng Hsiao-hsu read out the "Proclamation of the Chief Executive" on my behalf.

Mankind should respect morality, but as racial discrimination exists people oppress others to exalt themselves, thus weakening morality. Mankind should respect benevolence, but because of international strife some try to injure others for their own advantage, thus weakening benevolence. Morality and benevolence are the principles on which our country is founded, and with the removal of racial discrimination and international strife it will inevitably become a paradise of the Kingly Way. I hope that all my people will endeavour to achieve this.

When I met the foreign guests after the ceremony the director of the South Manchuria Railway made a congratulatory address and Lo Chen-yu read out my reply. Then we went into the courtyard for the raising of the new flag and for photographs. The proceedings ended with a banquet.

That afternoon Cheng Hsiao-hsu came with some "official business" to the "Office of the Chief Executive".

"General Honjo has recommended that your servant become prime minister and organize a cabinet." He bowed as he spoke, his voice smooth and his bald pate glistening. "This is a list of special appointments and of ministers.[1] Will Your Majesty please sign it."

As the Japanese agent Amakasu had already discussed this with me in Lushun I took my brush and signed. I had transacted my first item of "Manchukuo" state business.

---

[1] Here is a list of the chief traitors who held office in the "Manchukuo" regime.
Prime Minister and Minister of Education: Cheng Hsiao-hsu
Minister of Civil Affairs and Governor of Fengtien Province: Tsang Shih-yi
Foreign Minister: Hsieh Chieh-shih
Minister of Defence and President of the Privy Council: Chang Ching-hui
Minister of Finance and Governor of Kirin Province: Hsi Hsia
Minister of Industry: Chang Yen-ching
Minister of Communications: Ting Chien-hsiu
Minister of Justice: Feng Han-ching
Governor of Heilungkiang Province: Cheng Chih-yuan
President of the Legislative Council: Chao Hsin-po
President of the Supervisory Council: Yu Chung-han
President of the Supreme Court: Lin Chi
President of the Supreme Procurator's Office: Li Pan
Deputy President of the Privy Council: Tang Yu-lin
Privy Councillors: Chang Hai-peng, Yuan Chin-kai, Lo Chen-yu, Kuei Fu
Chief Secretary of the Office of the Chief Executive: Hu Sze-yuan
Members of the Secretariat of the Office of the Chief Executive: Wan Sheng-shih, Shang Yen-ying, Lo Fu-pao, Hsu Pao-heng, Lin Ting-shen
Head of the Bureau of Internal Affairs: Pao Hsi
Special Officials of the Bureau of Internal Affairs: Chang Yen-ching, Chin Pi-tung, Wang Chi-lieh, Tung Chi-hsu, Wang Ta-chung, Shang Yen-ying
Head of the Security Bureau: Tung Chi-hsu
Commander of the Guard: Chang Hai-peng
Secretaries to the State Council: Cheng Chui, Cheng Yu

I had been deeply impressed by the bands and the dragon flags on Changchun station, the ceremony of taking office and the speech of praise made when I met the foreign guests, and as a result I was feeling light-headed. But by taking office openly I had put myself into a position from which there was no retreat. Moreover, if I got along with the Japanese they might even help me to recover my imperial title. When I looked on the bright side, being "Chief Executive" seemed to be not a humiliation but a step towards the imperial throne. The problem to which I now gave my attention was how best to use this position. After thinking it over for several days I announced my conclusions to Chen Tseng-shou and Hu Sze-yuan, who were both now in my secretariat:

"I have made two vows and a wish, and I want to tell you about them. First, I am going to overcome all my old faults, and I vow that I will never again be lazy or frivolous as Chen Pao-shen said I was ten years ago. Secondly, I vow that I shall not rest until I have overcome all obstacles and restored my ancestral heritage. Thirdly, I beg that heaven will send me an heir to continue the line of the Great Ching. If these three things are accomplished I can die happy."

About a month after I took office the "Residence of the Chief Executive" was changed to a redecorated building that had previously been the Kirin-Heilungkiang Salt Tax Office. At first I rose early every morning and went straight to my office, not going back to my living quarters until evening. Hoping to carry out my vows and return to the throne, I followed the instructions of the Kwantung Army while working long hours under the illusion that I would be able to use my power as head of state. But this diligence did not last long as there was no state business to transact and I soon found out that the powers of the "Chief Executive" existed on paper only.

Majesty Without Power

The thirteen clauses of the first section of the "Organizational Law of Manchukuo" laid down my powers in black and white. The first clause stated that "the Chief Executive rules Manchukuo", and the second to the fourth stipulated that I had legislative, executive and judiciary power. Other clauses laid it down that my proclamations would be as binding as laws; that I determined the official structure and made official appointments; that I was the supreme commander of the army, navy and air force; that I had the power to issue pardons and amnesties, to lighten punishments and to restore rights to men who had been deprived of them; and so on.

In fact I did not even have the power to decide when I would go out of my own front gates. One day I thought of going for a stroll and took my wife Wan Jung and two of my sisters for a walk in the "Tatung Park". Before I had been in the park for many minutes Japanese gendarmes and men of the "Security Bureau of the Residence of the Chief Executive" drove up and asked me to go back. Apparently my absence from my residence had been reported to the Japanese gendarmerie, and large numbers of troops and police had been mobilized to search for me, causing a great commotion throughout the city. After the affair my adviser Kaeisumi told me that for the sake of my dignity and my security I should not go out again by myself. From then on I never went out of the front gate except on expeditions arranged by the Kwantung Army.

At first I believed the explanation about why I should not go out by myself, but after a few days of working on "state business" in my office I began to have doubts. Although I seemed to be very busy and had many visitors, mostly government ministers and high-ranking advisers, they only expressed their loyalty to me and gave me presents, never discussing official business. If I asked them about such subjects their reply was either, "The vice-minister is looking after that", or, "I must ask the vice-minister about it". The vice-ministers were Japanese, and they never came to see me.

Hsu Sze-yuan was the first to lose patience. He pointed out to Cheng Hsiao-hsu, now premier of the puppet regime, that the ministers should have control of their ministries and that important decisions should first be made by the Chief Executive and then carried out by the ministries. It was quite wrong that the vice-ministers should settle everything. "We are carrying out responsible cabinet government," was Cheng's reply, "and affairs of state must first be decided at the meetings of the State Council. The cabinet is responsible to the Chief Executive, and every week the premier refers the proposals it has adopted at its meetings to the Chief Executive for decision. This is the way it is done in Japan." Cheng agreed that the minister should control his own ministry and said that he was going to bring up this point with the commander of the Kwantung Army. He had, in fact, met the same problem in his relationship with the Japanese head of the General Affairs Office of the State Council.

I do not know how Cheng Hsiao-hsu's conversation with the Kwantung Army commander on this subject went, but I learnt what was really meant by "responsible cabinet government" and the relationship between ministers and vice-ministers from the account Hu Sze-yuan gave me of a meeting of the State Council.

The subject under discussion was official salaries. As usual, the draft bill was prepared by the General Affairs Office of the State Council and a printed copy was handed to each of the ministers. They had agreed quickly enough to previous bills, which had been on such subjects as the take-over of the property of the previous Northeastern government, the provision of grain and fodder to the Japanese army and the confiscation of four major Northeastern banks. But they were not so casual now that their own interests were directly involved. They went into the bill thoroughly, and when they found that the pay scales for Japanese officials were about 40 per cent higher than those for "Manchurian" ones, they made their dissatisfaction clear in the angry discussion that followed. Hsi Hsia, the Minister of Finance, protested that the higher salaries for Japanese were incompatible with the racial equality and friendship on which the state was supposed to be founded. Seeing the awkward turn the meeting was taking, the head of the General

Affairs Office of the State Council, Komai Tokuzo, stopped the discussion and sent for the drafter of the bill, the Japanese head of the personnel department, to answer their questions. The personnel department head calmly explained that before one could consider equality one had first to see whether people were equal in ability. As the Japanese were very able it was only natural that they should be paid more; they were also used to a higher standard of living, and were accustomed to eating rice, not *kaoliang* like the "Manchurians". As for friendship, would not that call for higher salaries for Japanese? This speech, however, failed to appease the ministers, and Komai had to adjourn the meeting until the next day.

The following day Komai reopened the meeting by saying that he had gone into the matter with the vice-ministers, and the Kwantung Army had agreed that the salaries of ministers would be raised to the same level as those of vice-ministers. "But as the Japanese officials will be living far from home," he added, "and are going to build a paradise of the Kingly Way for the Manchurians we should be grateful to them. We are therefore going to give them special supplementary payments. This decision is final and there can be no further discussion on it." Most of the ministers felt that they had got their money and that making more trouble would get them nowhere, but Hsi Hsia, who thought that he was on especially good terms with the commander of the Kwantung Army, was not going to be put off by Komai. "I'm not going to argue over a few cents," he put in, "but I would like to ask where the Japanese are going to establish this paradise of the Kingly Way if not in Manchuria. Could they establish it without the Manchurians?"

Komai was incensed, and he thumped the table. "Do you know the history of Manchuria?" he bellowed. "Don't you realize that the Japanese paid for it with their blood and sweat when they took it from the Russians?"

"Will you let me talk?" retorted Hsi Hsia, his face white. "General Honjo has never shouted at me."

"I'm telling you," roared Komai. "This has been decided by the Army." There was nothing more that Hsi Hsia could say, and the whole room was silent.

From then onwards "responsible cabinet government" and "the meetings of the State Council" fooled no one. The real prime minister was not Cheng Hsiao-hsu but Komai, the head of the General Affairs Office of the State Council. Even the Japanese did not conceal this, and the Japanese magazine *Reform* openly referred to him as the "premier of Manchukuo". And the real premier regarded the commander of the Kwantung Army as his superior, not the nominal chief executive. Similarly, the bills discussed at the meetings of the State Council had already been decided at the weekly discussions of the vice-ministers who formed the real cabinet of "Manchukuo", responsible to "His Imperial Majesty" the commander of the Kwantung Army. The Fourth Section of the Kwantung Army always participated in these discussions, and many of the bills were drafted to meet its requirements.

All this soon became obvious to anybody and should have shattered my illusions, but that was not in my character. The talkative Hu Sze-yuan was always reminding me of my unique position, and I recalled a view that I had held in my Tientsin days: "Without me, the true emperor, the Japanese will be in a very difficult position." The outwardly respectful way in which the Japanese behaved towards me misled me into believing that I was entirely different from Hsi Hsia and that the Japanese were obliged to treat me with respect. This was what I thought at the time of the foundation of the "Concordia Association".

One day about a month after I had taken office, Cheng Hsiao-hsu told me in the course of one of his regular reports that the Kwantung Army wanted to form a political party and call it the "Concordia Party". The purpose of the party was to "organize the masses to co-operate in building the nation" and to cultivate a spirit of "respect for the rites and glad acceptance of the heavenly commands". The word "party" always terrified me, and hearing this news made me even more alarmed than I had been when I was told about Komai thumping the table. I cut Cheng's remarks short and waved my hand in disapproval. "What do they want a party for? What good can a party do? Wasn't the fall of the dynasty the work of a party? Have you forgotten that Confucius said that a gentleman should have nothing to do with parties?" Cheng Hsiao-hsu's face fell. "Your Majesty is quite right, but the Army has already made up its mind." He had hoped that this would silence me, but to his surprise I regarded this as a matter of life and death and refused to agree to it. I was sick of hearing that everything had been decided by the Army. "Either go and inform the Japanese," I said angrily, "or tell them to come and see me."

Two days later Itagaki and two other officers from the Fourth Section of the Kwantung Army came to offer me explanations, but they all failed to convince me, so that the matter dragged on unresolved.

In July, three months later, I thought that I had won. The Kwantung Army decided to form not a "Concordia Party" but a "Concordia Association". Its function would be to support the government, and the association and its affiliated organizations were meant to include the whole population of "Manchukuo" above the age of ten.

The real reason why the Kwantung Army changed it from a "party" to an "association" was nothing to do with me. They thought that the latter would be more effective than a political party for propagandizing, spying on and enslaving the people. I, of course, did not realize this and thought that they were complying with my wishes. As I was under this illusion it was not surprising that I got nowhere after the signing of the secret treaty between "Manchukuo" and Japan.

The Signing of the Secret Treaty and After

Cheng Hsiao-hsu had settled with Honjo the conditions on which I would take office as Chief Executive and he would become premier back at the time when we were staying in Lushun. Cheng told me about this on the eve of Honjo's resignation.

On August 18, 1932 Cheng Hsiao-hsu came to my office with a pile of documents. "This is an agreement your subject has made with General Honjo," he said. "Will Your Majesty please approve it."

I looked at the agreement. "Who told you to sign this?" I was furious.

"These are all the conditions that Itagaki laid down in Lushun," he replied with icy calm. "Itagaki told Your Majesty about them a long time ago."

"Nonsense. He never told me, and even if he had done so you still have no right to sign before consulting me."

"I did it on Itagaki's instructions. He said that he was afraid that it would only cause trouble if Hu Sze-yuan and the others saw it beforehand as they don't understand the situation."

"Who is in charge here? You or I?"

"Your subject would not dare to presume. This agreement is a temporary measure. How can Your Majesty refuse to sign it if you want the help of the Japanese? All that is conceded in it is what the Japanese already have in fact, and we can sign another agreement in future stating that after a few years you will resume these powers."

He was right in saying that the Japanese already had the powers that were conceded in the agreement. The essence of the agreement was that Japan would have complete control over the "defence and security" of "Manchukuo"; that Japan would administer the railways, harbours, waterways, and airways of "Manchukuo" and could carry out further construction; that the supplies and equipment needed by the Japanese troops would be provided by "Manchukuo"; that the Japanese would have the right to open mines and exploit natural resources; that the Japanese would be allowed to hold office in "Manchukuo"; that Japan would have the right to move immigrants into "Manchukuo"; and many other items. The agreement ended by stating that it would be the basis for a formal treaty between the two countries. Cheng Hsiao-hsu was right in saying that we would have to pay a price for the "support" of Japan. But all the same, I could not help feeling angry. I felt that Cheng Hsiao-hsu had gone too far on his own initiative in selling "my" country to the Japanese. I was also angry with Japan for deceiving me. Although it had refused to give me an imperial throne, it still wanted to take so much from me.

Although I was furious, there was nothing I could do as the matter was already settled. I signed the secret agreement and Cheng took it away with him. Hu Sze-yuan came in, and was indignant when I told him what had happened.

"Cheng Hsiao-hsu is disgraceful. Chen Pao-shen said a long time ago that he is generous with other people's property, and now he has dared to take it on himself to do this."

"It's too late to do anything about it now," I said dejectedly.

"It may not be. We must see what news we get from Tokyo."

Some time previously we had learnt that Honjo, the commander of the Kwantung Army, was going to be replaced and that Japan was going to recognize "Manchukuo". Hu Sze-yuan attached great importance to this news as he thought that the change of command probably indicated a slight difference in Tokyo's attitude, and reckoned that we should send somebody to Japan to make the most of this opportunity. In his view it was impossible to avoid giving Japan some privileges, such as the control of the country's mining, railways, natural resources and defence, but it was essential that I keep the appointment of officials in my hands. On Hu's recommendation I sent two emissaries to Tokyo to see some senior military men, and they put my demands to the chief of the Japanese army staff, to Kashii, the former Japanese commander in Tientsin, and to Muto Nobuyoshi, the incoming Kwantung Army commander. On Hu Sze-yuan's advice I overstated my demands to allow room for concession without giving way on the vital point of control of official appointments. These additional demands were that the ministers have real control of their ministries, that the system of Japanese-run general affairs offices be abolished, that new troops be trained, that the Legislative Council settle the form of the state, and that I be allowed to reorganize the cabinet.

Two days later an excited Hu Sze-yuan told me that a letter had come from my emissaries in Tokyo in which they said that some Japanese elder statesmen and military men who sympathized with me and disapproved of Honjo's attitude towards me were willing to support all my demands. Hu went on to say that this showed that things would change with the arrival of the new Kwantung Army commander, and that I would be able to choose my own officials and rule my own country. But to rule it successfully I would need an obedient prime minister. I agreed, and decided to dismiss Cheng Hsiao-hsu and replace him with Tsang Shih-yi, who would feel grateful to me and obey my directions. I sent for Tsang Shih-yi, but instead Cheng Chui came to see me and protest at the reports that I wanted to reorganize the cabinet. A little later Tsang Shih-yi refused to become prime minister. He knew that he would only be asking for trouble if he accepted without the permission of the Kwantung Army.

When Cheng Hsiao-hsu heard that Tsang Shih-yi had refused he decided to adopt the tactic of asking for leave on grounds of ill health. I had been emboldened by the encouraging news from Tokyo and to his surprise I seized this chance to be rid of him. "It is time you retired," I said, not making the least effort to persuade him to stay on. "I shan't keep you. Please nominate a successor."

The shine disappeared from his bald pate. "Your servant only wanted a few days' sick leave."

"Very well."

As soon as Cheng Hsiao-hsu had gone I sent for Tsang Shih-yi and asked him to be acting prime minister, thinking that I could find a way of getting rid of Cheng Hsiao-hsu later. But before Tsang Shih-yi had committed himself one way or the other Cheng was back at his post.

I decided that when the new Kwantung Army commander arrived I would raise my demands in person. Hu Sze-yuan backed me on this and reminded me to insist on the removal of Cheng Hsiao-hsu.

All this happened at the beginning of September. In the middle of the month Muto Nobuyoshi, the new commander of the Kwantung Army and the first Japanese "Ambassador to Manchukuo", arrived in Changchun. On the 15th Muto and Cheng Hsiao-hsu signed the "Japan-Manchukuo Protocol". This was the public treaty envisaged by the secret agreement.

When the ceremony was over and we had drunk champagne I was most impatient to have a private talk with Muto. I was confident about its outcome as my emissaries in Tokyo had reported that Muto sympathized with my demands and was even willing to consider restoring my imperial title. Muto had commanded the Japanese forces that occupied Siberia during the First World War. He came to the Northeast this time in three concurrent capacities — commander of the Kwantung Army, governor of the "Kwantung Leased Territory", and "Ambassador to Manchukuo". He was the real ruler of the Northeast, the true emperor of "Manchukuo". The Japanese press called him the "guardian deity of Manchuria", and in my eyes this white-haired old fellow of sixty-five really was as powerful as a god. When he bowed to me for the first time, with the greatest politeness, I was overwhelmed with a feeling of being specially favoured by heaven. Having heard me out he replied courteously, "I shall go into Your Excellency's suggestions most carefully."

He took away the list of demands that Hu Sze-yuan had written out for me, but days passed without my hearing the results of his deliberation. As I normally saw the commander of the Kwantung Army three times a month I met him again ten days later. I asked him what his conclusions were, and he replied that he was still considering the demands.

Every time I saw him he was unfailingly courteous, bowing deeply, smiling, always saying "Your Excellency", and talking of each of my ancestors with the greatest respect; but he never once referred to my demands. If I tried to steer the conversation that way he would change the subject. Having been deflected like this a couple of times I did not have the nerve to ask him about them again. Right up to the time of Muto's death in July 1933 we only talked about Buddhism, Confucianism and "friendship". While there was no growth in my power his authority seemed to me to increase every day.

The Report of the League of Nations Commission of Enquiry

In May 1932 the Commission of Enquiry of the League of Nations arrived in the Northeast. Cheng Hsiao-hsu and Cheng Chui had placed high hopes in the Commission, and when its report was published in October of that year they were sure that their dream of international administration was going to be realized within the foreseeable future. I did not share their passion, but I learnt quite a lot about international affairs from their discussions. Unlike them, I only got an even stronger belief in the might of Japan from the Commission.

The Chengs often spoke about the attitude of the Western powers to the "Manchurian question", and what they said was usually something like this: "Don't pay any attention to the noisy meetings (of the League of Nations) in Geneva and Paris. None of those countries is in fact prepared for a head-on clash with Japan; and America, the one really powerful country since the World War, does not want to take a tough line with Japan either." Cheng Chui, who was highly proficient in English and Japanese, often told me what the foreign press was saying. He reported that quite a few American papers were pro-Japanese, and he once revealed to me that there was a secret agreement between the United States and Japan, one of the terms of which was that America would be understanding about Japan's actions in the Northeast. He also told me in great detail that even before the events of September 18, 1931 an important American personage had advised Chiang Kai-shek to sell Manchuria to Japan and thus bring Japan into direct conflict with the Soviet Union.

"The Commission of Enquiry has come," said Cheng Hsiao-hsu, "at the invitation of the Kuomintang. The Kuomintang hopes that the Commission will help them to deal with Japan, but they are going to be disappointed, as the Commission is interested in the open door, equality of opportunity, and resisting Soviet Russia.

That was what they discussed with Uchida[1] in Tokyo. There is no need to worry; when the time comes you will only have to say a few words to them. In your subject's view the Kuomintang knows that the Commission is not going to achieve anything, and may well see the advantages of international administration of Manchuria." Later events showed that the Chengs were not far wrong.

After the outbreak of fighting in the Northeast on September 18, 1931 Chiang Kai-shek had repeatedly instructed Chang Hsueh-liang to order his troops in the Northeast "not to resist under any circumstances, in order to avoid the spreading of the incident". Four days later, on September 22, Chiang Kai-shek proclaimed at a Kuomintang rally in Nanking that China should "meet might with right, meet savagery with peace, bear her humiliation, restrain her wrath, and temporarily accept the unacceptable until international justice gives its verdict". Yet at the same time he was pursuing the civil war with the utmost barbarity at home, casting "peace" and "right" to the winds.

On September 30 the Kuomintang asked the League of Nations to send a neutral investigating commission to the Northeast. After protracted discussions, Japan agreed to this on December 10, and the motion calling for the setting up of a Commission of Enquiry was passed. It was made up of the nationals of five countries — Lord Lytton of Britain (chairman), Major-General Frank Ross McCoy of the U.S.A., Lieutenant-General Henri Claudel of France, Count Aldrovani of Italy and Dr. Heinrich Schnee of Germany. The group set out on February 3, 1932, and after visiting other parts of China and Tokyo they arrived in the Northeast in May. During this time the Japanese had been expanding the scope of their aggression while the Nanking government made further concessions.

On May 3 I had a meeting with the Commission of Enquiry that lasted about a quarter of an hour. They asked me two questions: how had I come to the Northeast and how had "Manchukuo" been founded?

---

[1] The former director of the South Manchuria Railway who was now Japan's Foreign Minister.

Before I answered them a thought flashed through my brain. I remembered that in the past Johnston had told me that the gates of London were open to me, and wondered whether they would agree to take me to London if I told them that I had only become the "Chief Executive of Manchukuo" as a result of the trickery of Doihara and the threats of Itagaki. But then I remembered that Itagaki and the Kwantung Army chief of staff Hashimoto Toranosuke were sitting beside me. With a glance at the pallid face of Itagaki I obediently started to say what I had been told to say beforehand: "I came to Manchuria after being chosen by the Manchurian masses. My country is completely independent. . . ."

The members of the Commission of Enquiry all nodded and smiled, and they asked no more questions. Then we were photographed together and drank toasts to each other in champagne. After the commission left Itagaki's cold, white face was wreathed in smiles as he praised my performance. "Your Excellency's manner was perfect; you spoke beautifully." Cheng Hsiao-hsu also congratulated me.

I was shown a translation of an article by Komai that was published by the Japanese magazine *Chuokoron* in October, and soon after that the Report of the Commission of Enquiry also came into my hands. Both these documents confirmed the view of the Chengs that the questions that really interested the Commission were "equality of opportunity" and the "open door".

The title of Komai's article was "Manchukuo Speaks to the World", and it contained an account of his conversations with Lord Lytton and others. Komai said that the first question Lytton asked him was, "Was not the founding of Manchukuo a little premature?" His answer had been some nonsense about its foundation being not too early but too late. The talks continued as follows:

General McCoy then asked me, "Is Manchukuo's proclamation of the principle of the open door being carried out?" I replied at once that the open door and equality of opportunity were two of the corner-stones of the country. "Of all the countries that formerly had dealings with China, America was the guiding spirit in initiating this policy. But while this principle is now universally accepted, China has

269

closed her doors. Where in China can open doors now be found? Now we have opened the doors of Manchukuo with a very powerful key, and for this we deserve the thanks and not the protests of you gentlemen. . . . I must add, however, that there is no open door when it comes to national defence, any more than there is in any other country in the world."

Lytton then asked, "Is Manchukuo putting equality of opportunity into practice?"

"Equality of opportunity," I replied without hesitation, "is a subject on which your country has set a precedent. At the end of the former Ching Dynasty, a time when China's political decay had brought her to the brink of partition, Robert Hart warned the Ching court that if China continued the way she was going, she would cease to play any role in international affairs. She would do better to rely on Westerners, and a customs administration was absolutely essential. Thereupon the Ching government appointed Hart as Inspector-General of the Imperial Maritime Customs, and the Imperial Maritime Customs was established. As the customs employed many Englishmen, Frenchmen and Japanese it was known as the most reliable government organization in China, and because of it the powers made loans to China that afforded her great financial assistance. The British regarded the customs as affording equality of opportunity, but if we Japanese wanted to work for the customs we had to pass an almost impossibly stiff test in English.

". . . Manchukuo is a state founded through the co-operation of Manchukuoans and Japanese, which is why all documents of the new state are published in Manchukuoan and Japanese. We will warmly welcome any person of any nationality who is fluent in the Manchukuoan and Japanese languages and would be satisfied with the terms that Manchukuo has to offer. This is what we mean by equality of opportunity."

I asked them if they had any other questions, and they all replied, "There is no need to ask anything else as we fully understand the position of Manchukuo. We are completely satisfied."

When I was seeing the members of the League of Nations Commission of Enquiry off from Hsinking (Changchun) station, Lytton shook me firmly by the hand and said quietly, "I wish the new state of Manchukuo a healthy development."

This conversation made Cheng Hsiao-hsu and his son most excited, and Cheng Chui even reckoned that the League might pass a resolution bringing about the international administration of Manchuria. They were even surer that this was going to happen when the Report of the Commission of Enquiry was published. This document stated openly that China should accept international control. It described Japan's wish for "stable government" as not "unreasonable", but added that "it is only in an atmosphere of external confidence and internal peace . . . that the capital which is necessary for the rapid economic development of Manchuria will be forthcoming". It looked as though the Chengs had been right in expecting that the Commission would advocate international management with pickings for all the foreign powers.

Cheng Hsiao-hsu's forecast of anti-Sovietism was also borne out. The Commission expressed sympathy with Japan regarding Manchuria as her "lifeline". It acknowledged "the interest of Japan in preventing Manchuria from serving as a base of operations directed against her own territory, and even her wish to be able to take all appropriate measures if in certain circumstances the frontiers of Manchuria should be crossed by a foreign power". But, the Commission went on to say, "it may be questioned whether the military occupation of Manchuria for an indefinite period, involving, as it must, a heavy financial burden, is really the most effective way of ensuring against this external danger; and whether . . . the Japanese troops would not be seriously embarrassed if they were surrounded by a restive or rebellious population backed by a hostile China." Japan "might even find it possible, with the sympathy and goodwill of the rest of the world and at no cost to herself, to obtain better security than she will obtain by the costly method she is at present adopting" if she thought of some solution "analogous to arrangements concluded by other Great Powers in various parts of the world".

The Commission opposed the restoration of the *status quo ante* and suggested that "a satisfactory regime for the future might be evolved out of the present one [i.e. the "Manchukuo" regime] without any violent change". It could be given a high degree of autonomy and have foreigners from all countries serving as advisers. As the interests of Japan in the Northeast were much the greatest there would be a high proportion of Japanese, but there would also be set quotas for the nationals of other countries. To put this new form of government into effect the Commission suggested as the first step the setting up of an Advisory Conference composed of the representatives of the Chinese and Japanese Governments and "neutral observers". This conference would refer to the Council of the League of Nations if it failed to agree. The Commission was of the opinion that the method of "international co-operation" was suitable for the rest of China as well as for "Manchuria". The reason they gave for this was the one that the Chengs were constantly giving: China only had labour power, and if she did not draw her capital, technology and talent from abroad she would be unable to build herself up.

In the first few days after seeing the Commission's report, Cheng Hsiao-hsu told me with great glee that things were "very hopeful". He said that Hu Shih had published an article in which he proclaimed the report as the "world's verdict".

But the Chengs were cast into deep depression by the Japanese reaction. Although the Commission had repeatedly stressed that it respected Japan's rights and interests in the Northeast and even described the "September 18th Incident" as an act of self-defence by Japan, the Japanese Foreign Ministry spokesman had only agreed with them on one point: "The proposals on Manchuria of the Commission of Enquiry could probably be applied with profit to the relations between China and the powers, as for example the plan for international control." But Japan was not in the least interested in the plans for international administration of the Northeast. As I have mentioned above, Cheng Hsiao-hsu's enthusiasm for the "open door" and "equality of opportunity" was the reason why he later lost favour with the Japanese and was finally discarded by them.

Before the publication of the Commission's report I had imagined that if the Northeast was put under international control, as the Chengs hoped, I might be much better off than with only the Japanese. But I also had two worries. One was that the Nanking government of Chiang Kai-shek might take part in the "international control", which would put me in a very difficult position; and the other was that even if Nanking left me alone, the international control committee would not want me as emperor if the "autonomous government" were not a monarchy. More important than these worries, however, was the deep impression I had of the savagery of Japan, which had not been restrained in the least by any international action. When I remembered the thought that had flashed through my mind at the time I met the Commission I reflected that it was lucky that I had done nothing foolish, as otherwise my fate would have been sealed. The most important thing now was not to provoke the Japanese, as I would be unable to reascend the throne without their help.

"Emperor" for the Third Time

It had been agreed that if the Kwantung Army did not institute a monarchy after I had been Chief Executive for a year I could resign. I did not do so, however, as I had not got the necessary courage, and even if the Kwantung Army had allowed it I would have had nowhere to go.

A few days after the anniversary of my taking office, the Kwantung Army commander Muto raised the question, to my great surprise, during one of our regular meetings. He said that Japan was considering the form of the state of "Manchukuo", and that when the time was ripe this problem would be solved.

Soon afterwards, on March 27, 1933, Japan left the League of Nations to increase her freedom of movement. At the same time she stepped up her military attacks on China, pushing south of the Great Wall and encircling Peking and Tientsin. At the end of May the Nanking government, preoccupied with the civil war against the Communists, made further concessions to Japan in signing the "Tangku Agreement". Under this agreement Chinese troops were withdrawn from a large area south of the Great Wall and Japan's control over north China was strengthened. These events were a strong stimulus to the advocates of my restoration, who became active again in the Northeast and north China. In July, Komai, the head of the General Affairs Office of the "State Council of Manchukuo", resigned his post to go and work secretly for the "independence" of north China. He told Cheng Hsiao-hsu that he was going to work for the restoration of my rule throughout the country. All these reports made me and my associates most excited.

My dreams of empire became more vivid. I followed the news with the closest attention, and placed even higher hopes on the Japanese soldiers who were slaughtering my compatriots. After the Japanese occupation of Jehol[1] in 1933 I gave a banquet to congratulate Muto and other officers who had taken part in the fighting, and to wish them ever greater victories. When a Japanese column halted after occupying Miyun, only about fifty kilometres from Peking, I was deeply disappointed. Cheng Hsiao-hsu told me that the Japanese military occupation of north China and even of south China was only a matter of time, and the urgent question of the moment was to settle the form of the "Manchukuo" state. He said that this would be decided not by the Kwantung Army but by Tokyo; he had heard that many of the elder Japanese statesmen were in favour of my return to the throne. I therefore felt that I had to have someone to lobby for me in Tokyo, or at least let me know the latest news.

The man I chose for this job was my guard Kudo Tetsusaburo, a Japanese who had accompanied me from Tientsin to the Northeast. He had given me the impression of being dissatisfied with the attitude of the Kwantung Army, and was the only Japanese who addressed me as "Your Imperial Majesty" after I became Chief Executive. He once demonstrated his loyalty to me by tasting a cup of tea that I suspected of containing poison. I gave him the Chinese name of Chung ("Loyal") and treated him as a member of

---

[1] This province was abolished in 1955 and its territory divided between Hopei, Inner Mongolia and Liaoning.

my own household. When he returned from his short stay in Japan he told me that he had seen Minami Jiro and some leading figures in the Black Dragon Society. He had heard that the military authorities were in favour of a monarchy. This news made me believe that my chance was just about to come.

Kudo's reports were confirmed in October 1933. Hishikari Takashi, the new commander of the Kwantung Army, informed me officially that the Japanese Government was about to recognize me as the "Emperor of Manchukuo".

I went wild with joy, and my first thought was that I would have to get a set of imperial dragon robes.

These were brought from Peking, where they had been in the keeping of one of the High Consorts, but I was unable to wear them as the Kwantung Army pointed out to me that Japan recognized me not as the Great Ching Emperor but as the "Emperor of Manchukuo". Instead I had to wear the "dress uniform of the Generalissimo of the Land, Sea and Air Forces of Manchukuo".

"This won't do at all," I said to Cheng Hsiao-hsu. "I am the descendant of the Aisin-Gioro, so I have to continue the imperial system. Besides, what will the members of the Aisin-Gioro clan think if they see me ascend the throne in foreign-style uniform?"

"Your Majesty is quite right," said Cheng Hsiao-hsu, nodding as he looked at my dragon robes laid out on the table. "Your Majesty is quite right, but what will the Kwantung Army say?"

"Go and see them for me."

After he had gone I gazed with emotion at the dragon robes that the High Consort Jung Hui had preserved for twenty-two years. They were real imperial dragon robes that had been worn by the emperor Kuang Hsu, the robes I had been dreaming of for twenty-two years. I would wear them to reascend the throne, and that would mark the restoration of the Ching Dynasty.

Cheng Hsiao-hsu came back before I had calmed down and told me that the Kwantung Army insisted that I wear military uniform for the enthronement. I was not satisfied, so I sent Cheng to negotiate with them again. They later agreed to allow me to wear the dragon robes to perform the ceremony of "announcing the accession to heaven" and this satisfied me.

On March 1, 1934 I performed the ancient ritual of announcing my accession on an earthen "Altar of Heaven" that had been erected in the eastern suburbs of Changchun, and after this I returned to my residence to change from the dragon robes into the "generalissimo" uniform to enact the enthronement ceremony. The "Office of the Chief Executive" was renamed the "Palace Office" and the place where I lived was now called the "Emperor's Palace". (The term "Imperial Palace" could not be used as that was the name of the palace of the Japanese emperor.) Apart from one new building, the palace was just the "Residence of the Chief Executive" redecorated and given a new name, and it was in one of its halls that the enthronement was held.

The floor was covered with a crimson carpet. A part of the north wall was hung with silk curtains in front of which was a high-backed chair carved with the "imperial emblem" of orchids. I stood before this, flanked on both sides by palace officials. The civil and military officials, headed by "Premier" Cheng Hsiao-hsu, stood in line before me and bowed low three times. I bowed in reply, then Hishikari, the commander of the Kwantung Army, presented me with his credentials as Japanese "Ambassador" and congratulated me. The ceremony over, the members of the Aisin-Gioro clan, who had come from Peking in all but full strength, and some former members of the Household Department performed the ninefold kotow to me as I sat on the chair.

Congratulatory memorials were sent by Ching veterans from China south of the Great Wall, and the Shanghai underworld boss Chang Yu-ching was among those who proclaimed themselves my subjects.

On June 6 Prince Chichibu (Chichibu-no-Miya Yasuhito) came to congratulate me on behalf of his brother the emperor of Japan and give the Japanese Grand Cordon of the Chrysanthemum to me and the Order of the Crown to Wan Jung.

I had not yet got the rights that Hu Sze-yuan repeatedly reminded me to ask for, but I was oblivious to that. The way I received my father at Changchun station when he came up from Peking with my brothers and sisters a month later is a good illustration of how deeply intoxicated with myself I was.

I sent a group of palace officials and a guard to line up on the platform to receive him, while I and Wan Jung waited outside the palace gate. She wore court dress, while I was in military uniform, my chest covered in Japanese and "Manchukuoan" decorations, as well as ones of the "Great Ching Empire" that I had sent for from south of the Great Wall. As I did not dare to wear these Ching decorations in front of the Kwantung Army I was glad of this chance to show them off.

When my father's car arrived at the palace I saluted and Wan Jung knelt, then I accompanied him into a drawing-room where nobody else was present. I knelt to him and greeted him in the old style.

A great banquet was held that evening. The cuisine and the etiquette were Western. Wan Jung and I sat at the head of the table as host and hostess. I had arranged that an orchestra would play from the moment we entered the banqueting hall; I cannot remember what they played, and I probably had not chosen any particular pieces as I liked anything with trumpets in it.

When we reached the stage of drinking champagne my brother Pu Chieh raised a glass, as I had arranged beforehand, and shouted, "Long live His Majesty the Emperor". My family all joined in the call, and the sound of it made me reel with self-satisfaction.

The next day the senior palace official, Pao Hsi, told me that the Kwantung Army Headquarters had sent someone along to protest in the name of the Japanese Ambassador that in sending an armed guard along to the station I had infringed an agreement between the former Northeastern authorities and Japan that "Manchukuo" had undertaken to observe. Under this agreement a strip of land on either side of the railway lines was to be the territory of the South Manchuria Railway, and no armed men were to be allowed into it except those of the Japanese Army. The Kwantung Army Headquarters — no, the Japanese Ambassador — wanted an assurance that no such incident would recur.

This should have been enough to bring me to my senses, but the Japanese still allowed me plenty of face. They did not make any public protest, and they said no more about the incident after I had sent someone to apologize and promise that it would not happen again. What was more important was that they arranged that I should have plenty of pomp and circumstance to satisfy my vanity and blind me to reality.

What I found most intoxicating were "imperial" visits and "progresses".

The Kwantung Army arranged that I should make one or two trips outside Changchun every year, and they called these "imperial progresses". I also had to take part in four ceremonies every year in Changchun. Of these one was the sacrifice at the "Pagoda of the Loyal Souls" to the Japanese killed in the aggressive war; another was the sacrifice to the dead soldiers of the "Manchukuo" puppet army at the "Temple of the Loyal Souls Who Founded the Country"; another was the visit to the Kwantung Army Headquarters to offer congratulations on the birthday of the Japanese emperor; and the fourth was the annual meeting of the "Concordia Association". A description of my visit to the "Concordia Association" meeting can illustrate the absurd fuss that accompanied these occasions.

I drove there in a motorcade worthy of an emperor. First went gendarmerie cars, and these were followed at a distance by an open red car in which was seated the Chief of Police. Behind this came my car, also red, with two motor-cyclists on each side. At the end of the procession came the cars of my attendants and of more police.

The day before I went out the Changchun police and gendarmes would arrest "suspicious characters" and unsightly "vagabonds", and on the day itself gendarmes would be posted along my route to stop people from moving along it. Nobody was allowed to enter or leave the shops or houses beside the road or even to put their heads out of the window, and sand was spread on the drive of the "Concordia Association". Before my car left the palace the radio station would broadcast to the whole city in Chinese and Japanese that "the carriage of His Majesty the Emperor is leaving the palace". At this announcement the officials of the "Concordia Association" all had to go out to meet me, and when my car arrived they bowed low to the strains of the "national anthem". After a short rest I met my "ministers". This interlude over, I went into the main hall and climbed on to the platform while a band played and the whole assembly bowed low. The Kwantung Army commander bowed slightly to greet me and I nodded to him in reply. I then read an address to the assembly, who all stood there with their heads lowered and were not allowed to look up, then they all bowed low once more as I left the hall. When I started my journey back to the palace there was another announcement on loudspeakers throughout the city, and a third one was broadcast on my return.

It was said that all this was borrowed from Japan. The words printed on my photograph were also taken from Japanese. Originally it was called "Imperial Countenance", but when the Japanese-style Chinese that the Japanese tended to use was being promoted under the name of "Concordese" the photographs were renamed "True Imperial Images". These pictures had to be displayed in offices, schools, army units and all public organizations. For example, a kind of shrine had to be set up in the conference rooms of offices and the head teacher's study in schools; on the outside was a curtain, and behind this hung my picture and a copy of my "Imperial Rescripts". Anyone who entered the room first had to bow towards the curtain. Although there was no law saying that ordinary citizens had to have a "True Imperial Image" in their houses, the "Concordia Association" often forced people to buy photos of myself and Wan Jung to hang in their main rooms.

The focal points from which this idolatry was spread were the schools and the armed forces. A meeting was held in all schools and military units every morning at which the participants had to bow low, first in the direction of the imperial palace in Tokyo and then towards my palace in Changchun; and whenever the anniversary of the issue of one of my "rescripts" came round, it would be read aloud. I shall have more to say about these "rescripts" later.

I will not go into the "imperial progresses" with which the Japanese built up my majesty. They did it all most conscientiously, and in my experience this was not only to make the Chinese accustomed to blind obedience and feudal, superstitious beliefs, but also to have the same effect on Japanese people. I remember that on a visit to a coal-mine a Japanese foreman was so moved by the "signal honour" of a few words from me that he wept. This, of course, made me feel that I was really somebody.

The time when I was under the gravest misconceptions and thought that I had reached the very pinnacle of authority was after my visit to Japan in April 1935.

All the arrangements for this visit were made by the Kwantung Army. They said that it would be necessary both as a sign of my gratitude to the Japanese emperor for sending Prince Chichibu to congratulate me on my accession and in order that I might give a personal demonstration of "Japan-Manchukuo friendship".

The Japanese government organized a reception committee of fourteen headed by Baron Hayashi Gonsuke, a Privy Councillor. The battleship *Hie Maru* was sent to take me, and other warships provided an escort. When I set sail from Talien I inspected the destroyers *Tamama* No. 12 and No. 15, and there was a fly-past of a hundred aircraft to greet me at Yokohama. I remember that I wrote a toadying poem while I was suffering from seasickness and overwhelmed with the honours that had been paid me on that voyage.

> The sea as flat as a mirror,
> I make a long voyage.
> The two countries hold hands
> To consolidate the East.

On the fourth day of the voyage I watched manoeuvres by seventy warships, and penned some more verses:

> The boats that sail ten thousand *li*
>   cut through the flying waves,
> While heaven and earth
>   commingle in one azure blue.
> This journey is not only
>   to admire mountains and waters,
> But to make our alliance shine
>   like the sun and moon.

Thus even before landing in Japan I had already been deeply struck by her might, and regarded all the honours that had been paid me on the voyage as proof that Japan sincerely respected me and was genuinely helping me. All my misgivings of the past now seemed to have been groundless.

When I arrived in Tokyo the emperor Hirohito himself came to meet me at the station, and then he gave a banquet for me. When I went to visit him, he returned my call. I received Japanese elder statesmen who offered me their congratulations; I inspected a military parade with Hirohito; I went to visit the shrine to the emperor Meiji and a military hospital where there were some soldiers who had been wounded in the invasion of China. I also went to pay my respects to Hirohito's mother. The Japanese press described a walk we took together, saying that the spirit in which I helped the empress dowager of Japan up a slope was the same as that in which I helped my father up steps in the palace in Changchun. In fact I had never once helped my father up a single step, and it was only to ingratiate myself that I supported Hirohito's mother. On the last day of my visit Yasuhito (Prince Chichibu) was at the station to see me off on behalf of his brother the emperor.

"This visit of Your Imperial Majesty to Japan," he said in his farewell speech, "is a great contribution to the close friendship between Japan and Manchukuo. It is my hope that Your Imperial Majesty will return to your country rightly convinced that friendship between our two countries can certainly be achieved."

My reply was as fawning as ever. "I have been most deeply moved by the magnificent reception given me by the Japanese Imperial Family and the warm welcome I have received from the Japanese people. I am determined to do all that is in my power to strive for eternal friendship between Japan and Manchukuo."

When I went on board my ship I was actually in tears as I asked Baron Hayashi to convey my thanks to the emperor and his mother, and this moved him to cry as well. There was nothing Chinese about me at all.

The treatment I had received from the Japanese imperial house really went to my head, and the air seemed to have a different tang to it now that I was emperor. According to my logic I was the equal of the Japanese emperor, and consequently I occupied the same position in "Manchukuo" that he did in Japan; the Japanese should therefore treat me in the same way that they treated their own monarch.

My head full of these illusions, I returned to Changchun and issued the "Admonitory Rescript on the Occasion of the Emperor's Return" that was packed with toadying expressions. I invited the new commander of the Kwantung Army, General Minami Jiro, to come and see me so that I could express my gratitude to him; the next day (April 29) I was an enthusiastic participant in the celebration of Hirohito's birthday. The following day I issued an order that all senior officials in the capital, whether they were Chinese or Japanese, were to come and hear me talk about my visit to Japan. I did not discuss this in advance with the Japanese, nor did I prepare any notes from which to speak. When the time came I gushed away about my visit, describing in detail how the Japanese emperor had met me and elaborating on the respect with which his subjects had treated me. My speech ended:

The friendship between Japan and Manchukuo has led me to hold the firm belief that if any Japanese acts against the interests of Manchukuo he is guilty of disloyalty to His Majesty the Emperor of Japan, and that if any Manchurian acts against the interests of Japan he is being disloyal to the Emperor of Manchukuo. Disloyalty to the Emperor of Manchukuo is the same as disloyalty to the Emperor of Japan, and disloyalty to the Emperor of Japan amounts to disloyalty to the Emperor of Manchukuo.

Within a month of my return to Changchun the Kwantung Army commander Minami told me during one of our regular meetings that "Premier Cheng Hsiao-hsu wishes to retire as he is exhausted by his efforts". He advised me to grant the request and replace Cheng with a new prime minister. I had already heard that Japan was dissatisfied with Cheng and was myself looking for some excuse to get rid of him, so that when Minami raised the matter I agreed at once and suggested Tsang Shih-yi as his successor. I thought that Minami, who had heard my views on Japan-Manchukuo friendship twice in recent days, would be bound to comply with my order; but to my surprise I found that I had run straight into a brick wall. "No," he replied, shaking his head. "The Kwantung Army has already considered the question and chosen a suitable man. There is no need for Your Majesty to worry; all will be well if you choose Chang Ching-hui for the job."

Not long before this Cheng Hsiao-hsu had annoyed his Japanese masters by saying that as "Manchukuo" had now grown up there was no longer any need for them to exercise such tight control; they had therefore kicked him aside. His bank account was frozen, and he was forbidden to move out of Changchun. He lived at home, a disappointed man, under the surveillance of the Japanese gendarmerie until he died a sudden death three years later. His son had also died suddenly, three years before him. It was rumoured that both deaths were the work of the Japanese. Even if this was untrue, Cheng Hsiao-hsu's fall should have been enough to smash my illusions; but it was another year before I began to see what my real position was.

The End of Illusion

From Japan's withdrawal from the League of Nations at the beginning of 1933 onwards she threw herself with less inhibition than ever into expanding her armed forces and preparing for war. She devoted special attention to speeding up her arrangements for the invasion of the whole of China. Even before the Lukouchiao Incident of July 7, 1937, Japan continued to use armed force and to make coups in north China, while the Kuomintang government in Nanking made concession after concession. It signed the "Ho-Umezu Agreement" in 1935, the "Chin-Doihara Agreement" and other secret treaties which gave the Japanese control of north China. It permitted the functioning of the "Autonomous Military Government of Inner Mongolia", the "Anti-Communist Autonomous Government of

Eastern Hopei", and other puppet bodies. It repeatedly assured the Japanese that "not only do we engage in no anti-Japanese activities or thoughts, but we do not even have any cause for being anti-Japanese". It promulgated to the people of China the "Harmony with Our Neighbour Order" and issued many bans on anti-Japanese activities on pain of heavy penalties. All this greatly strengthened Japan's position in north China, and made it clear that it would only be a matter of time before the five provinces of the North were completely lost to China. This was the time when restoration fanatics were active in the Northeast and in north China and I was intoxicated with my third enthronement. But as Japan sunk her claws deeper into north China she tightened her grip on "Manchukuo", and in the end I felt it too.

The process of colonization in the Northeast was very profitable for the Chinese traitors. When the monarchy was introduced, for example, the restorationists gained more than psychological satisfaction. The leading traitors from Cheng Hsiao-hsu downwards were given "rewards for efforts in establishing the country" that ranged from 50,000 to 600,000 dollars each and totalled 8,600,000 dollars; and whenever there was a major act of plunder, such as a "provision of grain" or "patriotic donations", all officials from the prime minister downwards would receive their rewards. Rather than go into the details of all the Japanese measures I will describe how my dreams of restoration gave way to terror.

The Kwantung Army had officially told me at the time they decided to install a monarchy that this was not a restoration of the Ching Dynasty. They had not allowed me to wear the dragon robes for my enthronement and had ignored my opinion in choosing a prime minister. I should have realized how hollow was my majesty, but I was too intoxicated to come to my senses. The first time I knew the taste of disillusion was over the affair of Ling Sheng.

Ling Sheng was the son of Kuei Fu, a former Ching military governor in Mongolia, and had been an adviser in the headquarters of Chang Tso-lin's Peace Preservation Army. He had been one of the members of the delegation that had come to Lushun to invite me to become "Chief Executive", and on the strength of this had been included in the ranks of the "Founders of the Nation". At the time of his sudden arrest in the spring of 1936 by the Kwantung Army he was the governor of the "Manchukuo" province of Hsingan.

The Kwantung Army sent Colonel Yoshioka Yasunori, the "Attaché to the Imperial Household", to tell me that Ling Sheng had been engaged in anti-Manchukuo and anti-Japanese activities. According to information I was given by Tung Chi-hsu, he had voiced his complaints at the last joint meeting of the provincial governors, to the irritation of the Japanese. Apparently Ling Sheng had accused the Japanese of failing to keep their word; Itagaki had originally told him in Lushun that Japan was going to recognize "Manchukuo" as an independent country, but later the Japanese had interfered everywhere. Ling Sheng was powerless in Hsingan as the Japanese controlled everything. After returning from this meeting to Hsingan he was arrested.

I found this news most disquieting as it was only six months back that his son had become engaged to my fourth sister. Just as I was wondering whether I should go and tell the Kwantung Army about this, Ueda Kenkichi, the latest Kwantung Army commander and Japanese "Ambassador", came to see me.

"A few days ago we solved a case in which the criminal was an acquaintance of Your Majesty's — Ling Sheng, the governor of Hsingan province. He had been plotting rebellion and resistance to Japan with the collusion of foreign countries. A military tribunal has found him guilty of crimes against Japan and Manchukuo, and has sentenced him to death."

"Death?" I was shocked.

"Death." He nodded to his interpreter as he repeated the word, wanting to be sure that I understood. "This will be a warning, Your Majesty," he went on to say. "It is essential that he should be killed as a warning to others."

After Ueda's departure Colonel Yoshioka told me that I had better break off the engagement between my sister and Ling Sheng's son at once, and I hurriedly complied.

Ling Sheng's sentence was carried out by decapitation, and several members of his family were killed at the same time. This was the first case of the Japanese killing a high "Manchukuo" official that had come to my knowledge, and the man had only recently wanted to become a relation of mine. I had thought that Ling Sheng must be very loyal to me if he wanted this matrimonial link; but the only criterion by which the Kwantung Army had judged him was his attitude to Japan. Doubtless they used the same criterion with me too. Ueda's statement about killing him as a warning to others now seemed even more ominous.

I remembered that the Kwantung Army had questioned me at the time of some Ching restoration activities at the end of the previous year, and I had decided that I must be more careful in future. How then did the Japanese like people to behave? I thought of a man whose fate had been in direct contrast to that of Ling Sheng's. He was Chang Ching-hui, the "premier", and clearly the Japanese intended me to see two examples in him and Ling Sheng. One can get an idea of the character of this bandit turned "prime minister" and of the appreciation that the Japanese had of him from the way they repeated a saying of his: "Japan and Manchukuo are like two dragonflies tied on a single string." The Japanese used this saying to "educate" the officials of "Manchukuoan" nationality.

When the Japanese were carrying out their policy of settling their own people in the Northeast they wanted to get a bill passed by a "cabinet meeting" to enable them to expropriate agricultural land in the Northeast at a quarter or a fifth of its market price. Some of the "ministers" protested as they were frightened that this might lead to rebellion or that they might lose heavily on their own large landholdings. Chang Ching-hui made this comment: "Manchukuo has masses of land, and the Manchurians are so crude and ignorant. If the Japanese come to open virgin land and teach them modern techniques, both sides will benefit." The bill was passed. "Both sides will benefit" became another favourite Japanese quotation.

Chang Ching-hui uttered a third saying when the Japanese were making so many compulsory grain purchases that the peasants of the Northeast had none left. Some of the "ministers" whose own interests were affected by the low prices protested at a "cabinet meeting" that the peasants were starving, and clamoured for higher prices. This was, of course, something that the Japanese were not prepared to concede. Chang Ching-hui said, "Soldiers of the Imperial Japanese Army are giving their lives, and for us in Manchuria to send some grain to them is nothing in comparison. The people who are hungry will be all right if they tighten their belts." "Tightening belts" became a popular expression with the Japanese, though they did not, of course, apply it to themselves.

The Kwantung Army commander was always praising Chang Ching-hui to me as a good prime minister and "a man who puts Japan-Manchukuo friendship into practice". I had not previously thought what significance all this had for me, but now that I knew the fate of Ling Sheng I understood well enough.

After the Ling Sheng affair I was even more deeply disturbed by a meeting I had with Prince Te.

Prince Te, or Demchukdongrub, was a Mongol prince whom the Japanese had used to set up the "Inner Mongolian Autonomous Military Government". He had sent me money in my Tientsin days, given thoroughbred Mongol horses to Pu Chieh, and shown his loyalty to me in many other ways. He had come to see the Kwantung Army on business and had obtained its permission to come and visit me. He told me about his experiences over the past few years and about the founding of the "autonomous military government". Before long he was grumbling and complaining that the Japanese in Inner Mongolia were too domineering and that the Kwantung Army had not kept a single one of the long string of promises it had made to him before the founding of the Inner Mongolian "government". What made him most angry was his complete lack of power. I found myself echoing his complaints and trying to console him. The next day the Kwantung Army sent Yoshioka, the "Attaché to the Imperial Household", to ask me with a grim expression on his face: "What did Your Majesty discuss with Prince Te yesterday?"

Realizing that something was wrong I said that we had only been chatting.

He pursued his questioning relentlessly: "Did he express dissatisfaction with Japan?"

My heart was pounding. I knew that I could either make a firm denial, or, better, "retreat by advancing". "Prince Te must have been telling a pack of lies."

Although Yoshioka did not go into the matter any further with me I was in a state of terror for several days. My mind seethed with suspicions, and I decided that there were two possibilities. One was that the Japanese had installed some kind of listening device in my room, and the other was that Prince Te had told them everything. I spent a long time trying to solve this mystery, searching the room for a listening device. When I did not find one I suspected that Prince Te had deliberately betrayed me, but I had no proof of that either. I was completely bewildered.

This incident taught me more than the Ling Sheng business. From then on I did not talk frankly to any outsider and behaved cautiously towards all visitors. People who came of their own accord to see me had become fewer and fewer since the speech I made after my return from Japan, and they almost stopped coming altogether after Prince Te's visit. The Kwantung Army thought up a new rule in 1937 and insisted that the "Attaché to the Imperial Household" should be present whenever I saw a stranger.

I felt more and more tense from 1937 onward. The Japanese stepped up their preparations for the full-scale invasion of China during the first six months of that year and carried out whole-scale repression of the anti-Japanese patriots in the Northeast. They issued a penal code in my name, started the *pao-chia* system of mutual surveillance, forced everybody to join the "Concordia Association", repaired roads, built fortifications, and combined villages and hamlets. They used about twenty divisions to try to deal with the 45,000 men of the Anti-Japanese Allied Army that was operating in the Northeast, while at the same time they arrested many members of the Anti-Japanese National Salvation Society and other "unstable" people. These operations were so unsuccessful that they had to be repeated on an even larger scale the following year, when a million Japanese and puppet troops were used. But, according to Tung Chi-hsu, people disappeared all over the Northeast, while the arrests never came to an end.

I never heard any real news from my talks with the Kwantung Army commander or from the reports of the "prime minister". Tung Chi-hsu was the only person who kept me in touch with what was really happening. He told me that the reports of victories in the "punitive" campaigns that the Kwantung Army commander gave me were not reliable, and that it was hard to say who the "bandits" the Japanese wiped out really were. He said that a relation of his had been taken off to do forced labour on some secret project, and that after the job was completed all the labourers had been slaughtered except for him and a few others who had been lucky enough to escape. In his view, one of the gangs of "bandits" whose destruction had been reported with a great fanfare in the press was this group of labourers.

Soon after I heard about this a former English interpreter of mine disappeared. One day my brother Pu Chieh told me that after being arrested because he had been in contact with Americans while attached to our "embassy" in Tokyo he had been killed by the Japanese gendarmerie. Pu Chieh also said that this interpreter had sent him a letter via his warder begging him to ask me to speak for him, but he had not dared to tell me about it at the time. I told Pu Chieh to say not another word about the matter.

Many of the policies and laws to which I gave my assent in those days were connected with Japan's war preparations and the strengthening of her rule over her Northeastern colony. They included the "First Five-Year Plan for Developing Production", the "Property Control Law", the "Reorganization of the Government" to strengthen Japanese rule, and the adoption of Japanese as a "national language"; but none of them made such an impact on me as Pu Chieh's marriage.

After finishing at the school for the children of the Japanese nobility, Pu Chieh had gone on to the Japanese Army Cadet School. He returned to Changchun in the winter of 1935 and was made a lieutenant in the Imperial Guard. From then on his associates in the Kwantung Army were always bringing up the subject of marriage and extolling the virtues of Japanese wives. Yoshioka, the Japanese officer who was always at my side, told me that the Kwantung Army hoped that Pu Chieh would marry a Japanese girl for the sake of friendship between the two countries.

I was very alarmed to hear this and decided to get Pu Chieh a wife from Peking to forestall this Japanese plot. Clearly they intended to bring Pu Chieh completely under their control and, what was more important, to get a child of Japanese descent who could replace me in future. Pu Chieh agreed to my plan, but when Yoshioka put pressure on him by telling him that General Honjo was acting as matchmaker on his behalf in Tokyo, he obeyed the Kwantung Army, and on April 3, 1937 married Saga Hiro, daughter of the marquis Saga. Less than a month later the "State Council", prompted by the Kwantung Army, passed a bill by which Pu Chieh and his son would be the successors to the throne if I had no male offspring.

After Pu Chieh's return from Tokyo I decided that I could no longer speak frankly in front of him or eat food that his wife sent me. If Pu Chieh was eating with me I would make an exception to this latter rule only if he tasted his wife's cooking first. When Pu Chieh was about to become a father I was deeply concerned for my own safety and even for his, as the Kwantung Army seemed quite capable of killing both of us for the sake of getting an emperor of Japanese descent. I breathed a deep sigh of relief when the child turned out to be a girl.

I was even worried about what would happen if I had a son, as the Kwantung Army had made me sign a document saying that I would send any son of mine to Japan when he was five to be brought up by a nominee of theirs.

On June 28, nine days before the July 7 fighting at Lukouchiao, I was frightened once more, this time by the affair of my Palace Guard.

This force was distinct from the "Imperial Guard" that came under the control of the "Ministry of Defence", and I paid for it out of my own pocket. My object in founding it had been not only to protect myself but also to have a skeleton military force under my personal control. All its 300 men were given officer training. Tung Chi-hsu, who was in charge of them, had told me long ago that the Kwantung Army was not happy about their existence, but before now I had been unable to understand Tung's forebodings.

On June 28 some members of my Palace Guard went to amuse themselves in a park and were arguing with some Japanese in civilian clothes about hiring boats when a crowd of Japanese surrounded them and started hitting them. The guards, forced to defend themselves, beat off the Japanese, whereupon the latter set dogs on them. My guards kicked the dogs to death, broke through the encirclement and returned to their barracks. Little did they know that this had caused a disaster. Soon afterwards some Japanese gendarmes appeared outside the palace office demanding that Tung Chi-hsu hand over all the guards who had gone to the park, and the terrified Tung complied. The Japanese gendarmes took them away and tried to force them to admit that they had been engaged in "anti-Manchukuo and anti-Japanese" activities. When the guards refused, the Japanese inflicted a variety of tortures on them, and the guards now realized that the incident had been a deliberate plot by the Kwantung Army. The Japanese in civilian clothes had been sent there by the Kwantung Army, two Kwantung Army staff officers had been injured in the brawl, and the dogs that had been kicked to death were Kwantung Army dogs.

When I heard of their arrest I assumed that they must have started some trouble accidentally, and so I asked Yoshioka to go straight to the Kwantung Army Headquarters and speak for them. He came back with three conditions on which they would be released: Tung Chi-hsu must apologize to the wounded officers; the members of the Palace Guard who had "caused the trouble" must be expelled from the country; and I must guarantee that such an incident would never recur. When I had complied with these conditions I was forced to dismiss Tung Chi-hsu from his post as Commander of the Palace Guard and to appoint a Japanese to succeed him. I also had to cut down the size of the Palace Guard and change their rifles for pistols.

I had previously sent a number of young men to military academies in Japan with the intention of building up my own military power, but when they came back their postings, even that of Pu Chieh, were all made by the "Ministry of Defence", and I had no say in the matter.

So my plans for an army under my own control now turned out to have been nothing but a dream.

When the July 7 fighting broke out and led to the Japanese occupation of Peking, some princes and old-timers in Peking were eager for a revival of the old order, but by now I knew that this was impossible. My only remaining concerns were how to preserve my own safety in the face of the Japanese and how to deal with Yoshioka, the "Attaché to the Imperial Household" and embodiment of the Kwantung Army.

Yoshioka Yasunori

If one compares the Kwantung Army to a source of high-tension electric current and myself to an electric motor, then Yoshioka was a wire of high conductivity.

He was a short man with a small moustache and high cheek-bones, and he never left me during the ten years from the time he first came to the palace in 1935 to the Japanese surrender in 1945, when he was captured by the Soviet Army at the same time as I was. In those years he rose from lieutenant-colonel to lieutenant-general. He had two posts: one was as a senior staff officer in the Kwantung Army and the other was "Attaché to the Manchukuo Imperial Household". This latter was a Japanese term, but it does not make much difference how one translates it as the words did not describe his real function. He was the wire through which the Kwantung Army transmitted its intentions to me. The excursions I made, the visitors I received, the protocol I observed, my admonitions to my subjects, the toasts I proposed, and even my nods and smiles were all under Yoshioka's direction. He decided what meetings I was to attend and wrote out my speeches in his own Japanese-style Chinese.

After the Japanese unleashed their full-scale invasion of China in July 1937 they wanted grain, men and supplies from "Manchukuo". I ordered Chang Ching-hui to read out an exhortation written by

Yoshioka at a meeting of the puppet provincial governors. In this document I urged them to "carry out their duties diligently to support the holy war". The Pacific War faced Japan with a shortage of soldiers, and they wanted "Manchukuo" troops to replace some of the Japanese units engaged in China. I read out another of Yoshioka's scripts, this time at a banquet given for the commanders of the various military zones, in which I expressed my determination to "live or die with Japan, and, united in heart and virtue, smash the power of Britain and America".

Every time Yoshioka reported to me that the Japanese had occupied a major Chinese city he would make me get up with him and bow low in the direction of the battlefield as a mark of mourning for the Japanese soldiers killed in the fighting. After he had made me do this a number of times I needed no prompting to make my bow when he told me of the capture of Wuhan.

As I made more progress he would increase the number of my lessons. After the fall of Wuhan, for example, he suggested to me that I should write a congratulatory letter to the butcher Okamura who had taken the city and send a telegram to the Japanese emperor.

When the "National Foundation Shrine" was built I used to go there every month to pray for the victory of the Japanese troops, and this too was after receiving an impulse along the same electric wire.

The Kwantung Army did not interfere much in my private and domestic affairs before the July 7 Incident, but things changed after that. Before the incident some of my relations would come up from south of the Great Wall every year to see me on my birthday and at other times. But after July 7 the Kwantung Army only allowed a few of them to come to Changchun at specified times. The Japanese army also insisted that, with the exception of my closest relations, they should only bow to me and not talk. All my mail was read by Yoshioka's Japanese underlings in the palace office, and he decided whether or not I was to see it. The Kwantung Army was of course perfectly well aware that I was not anti-"Manchukuo" or anti-Japanese, but they were worried that I might become involved in plans to revive the Ching Dynasty south of the Great Wall, which would have been a nuisance to them.

It would have been completely impossible in those days for me to meet an outsider or receive a letter without the knowledge of Yoshioka. There was a gendarmerie office in the palace staffed by dark-green uniformed Japanese gendarmes; no one could come or go without being seen by them, and they heard everything that went on in the courtyard. All this, and the fact that the Japanese in the Palace Office were Yoshioka's tools, meant that I was under very strict control.

Yoshioka had shown considerable cunning in getting his post in the palace, making friends with Pu Chieh when he was one of his instructors at the Army Cadet School in Japan. Some accounts say that he was also a friend of mine before I went to the Northeast, but in fact he had only given me a few talks on current affairs in Tientsin. All the same, he managed to use his friendship with Pu Chieh to convince the Kwantung Army that he was a personal friend of mine, and it was on the strength of this that he got the twin appointments as "Attaché to the Manchukuo Imperial Household" and as a senior staff officer with the Kwantung Army.

During his time with me he made frequent visits to Japan, and often carried little presents between me and the Japanese empress dowager. Once he persuaded me to record some greetings in Japanese to the Japanese emperor.

When Yoshioka spoke he would often grunt "uh" and "ha" while twitching his eyebrows, a habit that got worse with time and which I found increasingly irritating. As this tic grew more pronounced his attitude to our relationship changed.

After my visit to Japan in 1934 the Japanese empress dowager wrote me some *waka* poems, and what Yoshioka said then was music in my ears:

"Her Majesty the Empress Dowager is the equivalent of Your Majesty's mother, and as I am almost a relation of yours I feel very honoured at this."

At that time he said to Pu Chieh, "You and I are related like hand and foot, and although I cannot claim such a relationship with

His Majesty the Emperor, I can feel that I am to him as a toe to a finger. We are almost kinsmen."

In about 1936 he said to me:

"Japan is the equivalent of Your Majesty's father, uh, and the Kwantung Army represents Japan, uh, so the commander of the Kwantung Army is the equivalent of Your Majesty's father, ha."

As the Japanese army ran into more and more trouble at the front my standing went down in the eyes of the Kwantung Army. Yoshioka finally went so far as to say, "The Kwantung Army is your father, and I am the representative of the Kwantung Army, uh."

Yoshioka used to make frequent visits to the palace throughout the day. Sometimes he would stay for ten minutes then leave, only to return five minutes later. He would give ridiculous reasons for these frequent comings and goings, such as that he had forgotten to say something, or not remembered to ask me if there was anything I wanted him to do for me the following day. I naturally feared that he was using these lightning attacks as a way of spying on me; and I thought that the only way I could avoid suspicion was to agree at once to everything he suggested and never keep him waiting. I would even see him in the middle of a meal if he came while I was eating.

"Imperial Rescripts"

All who studied in "Manchukuo" schools were compelled to learn my "Imperial Rescripts" by heart. On the anniversary of the issue of each rescript all schools, government offices and units of the armed forces would assemble to hear the rescript read out. In schools, for example, all the staff and pupils in their dark-green "Concordia" uniforms would stand solemnly in front of the platform. The school official responsible for ideology and discipline would enter wearing white gloves and holding a yellow cloth bundle above his head. The whole assembly would bow while he carried the bundle up to the platform, put it on the table, and opened it. He would take out the rescript and pass it with both hands to the head of the school who would accept it with gloved hands, unroll it, and then read it aloud. If the date happened to be May 2 he would read out the "Admonitory Rescript on the Occasion of the Emperor's Return":

Ever since we ascended the Throne we have been eager to pay a personal visit to the Imperial House of Japan, in order that by cultivating our friendship and enjoying their company we might show our great admiration for them. By making this voyage to the East we were able to fulfil our long-cherished ambition.

The Japanese Imperial House was most hospitable to us and made magnificent preparations, while their subjects welcomed us and saw us off with sincere enthusiasm, being without exception extremely courteous and respectful. This is engraved on our heart, and we shall never forget it.

We are deeply aware that from the foundation of our State to the present day we have relied throughout on the devotion to righteousness and the great efforts of this Friendly Country in strengthening the Great Foundation; and on this occasion we were fortunate enough to be able to express our heartfelt gratitude. Moreover, we ascertained through careful observation that the government in that country is based on benevolence and love, while the emphasis of education is on loyalty and filial piety; the people respect their Emperor and love their superiors as they do heaven and earth; and every one of them is loyal, brave, public-spirited, and sincerely devoted to his motherland. This is why they are able to enjoy domestic peace, resist foreign powers, and take pity on their neighbours, in order to maintain the Imperial line that shall continue unbroken for ten thousand generations. We have personally come in contact with high and low in that country, and they are united with the greatest sincerity in a common temperament and a shared morality; their mutual reliance is unshakable.

We and His Majesty the Emperor of Japan are of one spirit. All ye our subjects should therefore be mindful of this and be one in heart and virtue with our ally, in order to lay a firm and everlasting foundation for our two countries and display the true meaning of Oriental morality. Then will it be possible for the world to be at peace and mankind to be happy.

Let all our subjects strive to observe this our Rescript for ever and ever.

By the Command of the Emperor.

There were six "Imperial Rescripts" altogether:

The "Accessional Rescript" of March 1, 1934;

The "Admonitory Rescript on the Occasion of the Emperor's Return" of May 2, 1935;

The "Rescript on the Consolidation of the Basis of the Nation" of July 15, 1940;

The "Rescript on the Current Situation" of December 8, 1941;

The "Rescript on the Tenth Anniversary of the Founding of the Nation" of March 1, 1942;

The "Abdication Rescript" of August 15, 1945.

The "Accessional Rescript" was later replaced by the "Rescript on the Tenth Anniversary of the Founding of the Nation"; and the "Abdication Rescript" of August 15, 1945 was never read aloud by anybody. Thus four rescripts were the important ones. Schoolchildren, students and soldiers had to be able to recite them fluently, and anyone who forgot them or repeated them inaccurately would be punished. In addition to being part of the slave propaganda put out by the Japanese in the Northeast, they were also used as the ultimate legal justification for the repression of all forms of resistance. Any Northeasterner who revealed the slightest trace of dissatisfaction with his colonial rulers could be punished for infringing this or that clause of a rescript.

The origin of each of these rescripts illustrates how low a man can sink. As I have already mentioned the way the first two were issued, I will now talk about how the third, the "Rescript on the Consolidation of the Basis of the Nation", came to be published.

One day I was sitting in my room with Yoshioka. Neither of us was talking as he had said what he came to say, but as he had not gone I guessed that he had some other important business on his mind. He stood up and walked over to the part of the room where there was a statue of the Buddha. He stopped there and grunted.

297

"Buddhism came from abroad," he said, turning towards me. "Uh, a foreign religion. As Japan and Manchuria share the same spirit they should have the same beliefs, ha?"

Then he explained to me that the Japanese emperor was the divine descendant of the Heaven Shining Bright Deity,[1] that every emperor was a reincarnation of the great god, and that all Japanese who died for the emperor would become gods themselves. From my experience I knew that the Kwantung Army was transmitting current along the high-tension wire, but after this statement of Yoshioka's the current was cut off. I spent many days thinking about these myths but I reached no conclusion about what they meant.

The Kwantung Army had in fact thought of something it wanted me to do, but its commander, Ueda, was preoccupied with the defeats his troops had suffered in the border fighting they had provoked with the Soviet Union and the Mongolian People's Republic. Before returning to Japan stripped of his office for this failure he indicated that, for the sake of "Manchukuo-Japanese friendship" and their unity in spirit, there should be religious identity between the two countries; he hoped that I would think the matter over.

I had always obediently followed the instructions of my "supreme emperor", but this time I did not know what to do. All my old advisers had either left or been thrown out by the Japanese, and my young brothers-in-law and nephews were too inexperienced to be of any use to me. I had to think this problem out for myself, but before I could reach any conclusion the new Kwantung Army commander and fifth "Ambassador to Manchukuo", Umezu Yoshijiro, arrived. He told me through Yoshioka that Japan's religion was "Manchukuo's" religion, and that I should welcome the "Heaven Shining Bright Deity", the divine ancestor of the Japanese imperial family, and make this cult into the religion of "Manchukuo". He added that as this year was the two thousand six hundredth anniversary of Emperor Jimmu it was a highly suitable time to introduce the

---

[1] The Japanese Sun Goddess Ama-terasu-o-mi-Kami. Her worship forms part of the Japanese Shinto religion.

great goddess into this country. He suggested that I should go to Japan to offer my congratulations and arrange the matter.

I later heard that there had been disagreements over this within the Kwantung Army as some of the officers who knew China better thought that it would arouse fierce opposition among the people of the Northeast and increase Japan's isolation. Later it was decided that with the passage of time the Shinto religion would take root among the young while the older generation would get used to it. The decision to go ahead with this policy was unpopular with most of the Chinese collaborators, to say nothing of ordinary people, and I found it even more difficult to stomach than the robbery of the Eastern Mausolea. I had previously been prevented by Yoshioka from sacrificing publicly at the graves of my imperial ancestors, and now I was being called upon to acknowledge myself as the descendant of a foreign line. This was very hard to bear.

Although my every action since the time I yielded to Itagaki's pressure in Lushun had been an open betrayal of my nation and my ancestors, I had managed to justify my doings to myself. I had represented them as filial deeds done for the sake of reviving the ancestral cause, and pretended that the concessions I made were only for the sake of future gains. I had hoped that the spirits of my ancestors in heaven would understand this and protect me. But now the Japanese were forcing me to exchange my ancestors for a new set. Surely my forbears would never forgive me for this.

But I remembered that I had to agree to this proposal if I wanted to preserve my life and safety. Even in reaching this conclusion I was able to justify myself: I would continue to sacrifice to my own ancestors at home while publicly acknowledging the new ones. My mind made up, I sacrificed to the tablets of my forefathers and set off for Japan.

I made this second trip to Japan in May 1940, and I stayed there for eight days.

When I met Hirohito I read out an address that had been written out for me by Yoshioka. The gist of it was that I hoped that for the sake of the "indivisible unity in heart and virtue" between the two countries I would be allowed to worship the Heaven Shining Bright Deity in "Manchukuo".

The Japanese emperor's reply was very short: "If that is Your Majesty's will, I must comply with your wishes." He then rose to his feet and pointed to three objects lying on a table: a sword, a bronze mirror, and a curved piece of jade, three sacred objects which were supposed to represent the Heaven Shining Bright Deity. As he explained them to me I thought that the antique shops of Liulichang in Peking were full of things like that. Were these a great god? Were these my ancestors?

I burst into tears on the drive back.

On returning to Changchun I built a "National Foundation Shrine" beside my palace and founded a "Bureau of Worship" under the former chief of staff of the Kwantung Army Hashimoto Toranosuke. On the first and fifteenth of every month I would lead the Kwantung Army commander and the puppet officials to go and make offerings at the shrine. Later on such shrines had to be built all over the Northeast, and offerings were made there at set times. Everyone who walked past one of these shrines had to do a ninety-degree bow on pain of being punished for "disrespect". The result of this was that the places where the shrines were built became deserted.

The Kwantung Army tried to induce me to wear the strangest clothes to perform these rituals, but I countered this proposal by saying that as this was wartime it would be best if I wore military uniform with my Japanese decorations to show my determination to support my ally Japan.

I would always kotow to my own ancestors at home before going to the shrine, and when I was bowing to the altar of the Heaven Shining Bright Deity at the shrine I would say to myself, "I am bowing not to that but to the Palace of Earthly Peace (Kun Ning Kung) in Peking."

Despised and cursed by the entire people of the Northeast, I issued the "Rescript on the Consolidation of the Basis of the Nation". This was written not by Cheng Hsiao-hsu (who had been dead for two years) but by a Japanese sinologue called Sato Tomoyasu who had been commissioned by the "General Affairs Office of the State Council". The text was as follows:

Whereas we are respectfully establishing the NATIONAL FOUNDATION SHRINE in order to consolidate the basis of the Nation in perpetuity and spread the principles of the Nation to infinity, we issue this rescript to you, our subjects.

Since the inception of our State the foundation of our Country has grown stronger and its destiny has been glorious. It enjoys sound government that improves with every passing day. When we reflected upon this great achievement and looked to its source, we saw that it was all thanks to the divine blessing of the HEAVEN SHINING BRIGHT DEITY and the protection of His Majesty THE EMPEROR OF JAPAN. Therefore did we visit in person the JAPANESE IMPERIAL HOUSE and in order to express our heartfelt thanks and deep gratitude we issued a Rescript to our subjects instructing you in the duty of being one in virtue and in mind with Japan. Profound was the meaning of this.

The purpose of our recent voyage to the East was to celebrate the two thousand six hundredth anniversary of Emperor Jimmu and to worship the AUGUST DEITY in person. On the occasion of our happy return to our own country we have respectfully established the NATIONAL FOUNDATION SHRINE in which to make offerings to the HEAVEN SHINING BRIGHT DEITY. We shall pray in our own person, and with the deepest reverence, for the prosperity of the Nation; and we shall make this an eternal example that our sons and grandsons for ten thousand generations shall follow without end. Thus may the basis of the Nation be consolidated by venerating the Way of the Gods,[1] and the principles of the Nation be founded in the teaching of Loyalty and Filial Piety. Pacified through Benevolence and Love and civilized through Concord, this land will be pure and illustrious, and will be assured of the divine blessing.

Let all our subjects understand our meaning. Strengthen the basis and extend our principles; strive to carry this out unremittingly, and do not pause in your efforts to make the country strong.

By the Command of the Emperor.

---

[1] The Japanese Shinto religion.

The toadying expressions "the divine blessing of the Heaven Shining Bright Deity" and "the protection of His Majesty the Emperor of Japan" were from then onwards an essential part of all rescripts.

The Kwantung Army went to great efforts to prepare me and the puppet ministers to receive the "Way of the Gods" (Shinto), and provided me with a famous Shinto expert to instruct me. The teaching materials he used were decidedly odd. One was a scroll picture of a tree. He explained that the root of the tree was Shinto, while the branches were all the other religions of the world; in other words, all the other religions had sprung from Shinto. I and the puppet ministers found it hard not to laugh or sleep during these lectures.

When Japan declared war on the U.S.A. and Britain on December 8, 1941, the Kwantung Army made "Manchukuo" issue the "Rescript on the Current Situation" in which I announced my support for the Japanese declaration of war and enjoined my "subjects" to do their utmost to help the Japanese war effort. Previous rescripts had been issued by the "State Council", but this time a special "Imperial Council" meeting was called on the evening of December 8 at which Yoshioka made me read the rescript out myself.

Whenever the Kwantung Army commander came to visit me I would open my mouth and pour out such remarks as "Japan and Manchukuo are one and indivisible, and they live or die together; I am determined to devote the whole strength of this nation to the struggle for victory in the Great East Asian holy war, and for the Greater East Asian Co-Prosperity Sphere headed by Japan."

Tojo Hidemichi, the Japanese premier and former Kwantung Army chief of staff, paid a lightning visit to "Manchukuo" in 1942. When I met him I burst straight into "Your Excellency may rest assured that I shall devote the full resources of Manchukuo to supporting the holy war of our parental country Japan."

At the time of Tojo's visit Japan had been already changed from "ally" into a "Parental Country". This new humiliation had been introduced in the "Rescript on the Tenth Anniversary of the Founding of the Nation". On the eve of this anniversary, which fell in March 1942, Yoshioka had said to me, "There could have been no Manchukuo without Japan, uh, so Japan should be regarded as Manchukuo's father. So, uh, Manchukuo should not call Japan an ally or friend as other countries do; it should refer to Japan as its Parental Country. Meanwhile the Japanese head of the "General Affairs Office of the State Council" was giving a similar talk to the puppet ministers. After this the "Rescript on the Tenth Anniversary of the Founding of the Nation" was issued.

From the publication of this "rescript" on, Japan was always referred to as the "Parental Country".

In 1944, when it was becoming increasingly obvious that Japan was losing the war and even I could see that her armies would soon be finished, Yoshioka came to beg me to make a donation of materials, particularly metal, for the war effort as an example for others. In addition to doing this I spontaneously gave a lot of gold, silver and jewellery to the Kwantung Army. Later I presented them with the carpets from the palace floors and hundreds of items of clothing. All these actions of mine were widely publicized and made the task of looting easier for the Japanese officials, who sent vast quantities of goods, including 300,000 tons of rice, to Japan in the closing months of the war.

Home Life

As I was not allowed to play any part in politics, or to go out as I pleased, or to send for my "ministers" for consultations, I had nothing to do when the Kwantung Army was not transmitting current to me. I developed the habit of getting up at eleven and going to bed after midnight, sometimes as late as 3 a.m. I ate two meals a day: breakfast between noon and one, and supper between nine and eleven at night, or even later. I would take a nap from 4 p.m. to 5 or 6 p.m. Apart from eating and sleeping, my life could be summarized as consisting of floggings, curses, divination, medicine, and fear.

All these elements were interconnected. As the signs of the Japanese collapse became clearer, I became more and more frightened that the Japanese would kill me to stop me talking afterwards. So I was fawning and affable with them, while I flogged and cursed as my temper became increasingly violent at home. I became more and more superstitious, eating vegetarian food, reciting sutras, consulting oracles, and seeking the protection of Buddha and the gods. My health, which had already been ruined, became even poorer as I lived this neurotic and unstable life, so I desperately took medicine and had injections.

My tendency to cruelty and suspicion went back to my years in the Forbidden City, and had been strengthened in Tientsin, where I had made this set of Household Rules for the servants:

1. Irresponsible conversations are prohibited to prevent underhand dealings.
2. You are not allowed to shield each other or cover up for each other.
3. Embezzlement and profiteering are forbidden.
4. When your colleagues do something wrong you must report it at once.
5. Senior staff must beat their juniors immediately they discover that they have done wrong.

The severity of the punishment will be increased by one grade if there is any slackness in the enforcement of these rules.

After the move to the Northeast I made my staff swear, "If I break these rules may heaven punish me and strike me with a thunderbolt."

I became so savage that I would have my staff beaten incessantly and even use instruments of torture on them. There were many different kinds of beatings, and I always got other people to administer them for me. This job would be entrusted to any of the members of my household present. They had to flog very hard, or else I would suspect that they had conspired with each other, and if this happened they would find themselves the victims of the rod.

My victims included almost everyone in my household except my wife, my brothers, and my sisters. In those days a number of my nephews were studying in the palace. They used to keep me company, talk to me and wait on me. I was bringing them up to be my trusted relatives, but that did not save them from scoldings and beatings. The words they most dreaded hearing me say were "Take him downstairs", as this meant that they were to be taken down for a flogging.

These actions of mine go to show how cruel, mad, violent and unstable I was.

I suffered from piles while in Changchun. When a young nephew saw the medicine I used he thoughtlessly remarked that it looked like bullets. This infringed one of my taboos: did he mean that he wanted me to be shot? At my suggestion another cousin belaboured him with the rod.

The most wretched victims of my rule were the pages. There were about a dozen of them, and they came from a Changchun orphanage. Most of their parents had been killed by the Japanese. For fear they would grow up with a longing for revenge the Japanese had made the puppet government bring them up in an orphanage, change their names, teach them to be slaves, and wear them out through heavy labour. Some of them had been very hopeful when they were told that they were being sent to the palace, thinking that life would be much better there than in the orphanage. It turned out to be even worse. They ate *kaoliang* of the lowest grade, dressed in rags, had to work fifteen or sixteen hours a day, and sometimes had to sit up on duty all night as well. In winter they were so tired, cold and hungry that they would sometimes fall asleep leaning on the radiators while they were working and wake up covered with burns. They were always being beaten — for falling asleep on the job, for not sweeping clean enough, or for talking too loud. When my personal assistants were in a bad temper they took it out on the pages, who were in their charge, putting them in a solitary confinement cell. So wretched was their life that at the age of seventeen or eighteen they were as small as ten-year-olds.

One page called Sun Po-yuan died of his sufferings. Finding life in the palace intolerable he had tried to escape. After being recaptured on his first attempt he was given a savage beating. The next time he tried to get out through the tunnel for the central heating, but after crawling round for two days he found no way out. Suffering from hunger and thirst, he came out for a drink of water and was captured. When I was informed of this by my assistants I ordered, "Let him have something to eat and then give him a good lesson." But before he could be given a "good lesson" he was beaten till he was almost dead. The news that he was nearly dead gave me a terrible fright, as I was afraid that he might turn into a ghost and take my life in revenge, so I gave orders that a doctor was to be sent for to save him. It was too late.

I spent several days after this kotowing and reciting scriptures in front of a Buddhist altar, praying for his soul to cross safely to the next world, in the hope that I could thus avoid retribution. I ordered that the assistants who had beaten him were to strike the palms of their own hands with bamboo rods every day for six months as a penance. It was as if these measures would absolve me of all responsibility for the killing. My cruelty to the pages later developed to an extreme because of my neurotic state.

I took the most careful precautions to make sure that I was not swindled of a cent when the kitchen staff bought vegetables, sending spies to tail them when they did their shopping, and questioning my sisters about the prices of pork and chicken. The cooks would be fined if the food was not to my liking or if I found anything dirty in it. Of course, they were sometimes rewarded if I was pleased. While I was powerless outside, I was the absolute ruler in my own house.

At the close of the "Manchukuo" period the coming defeat of Japan became more and more obvious. The news from Allied radio broadcasts and Yoshioka's low spirits strengthened my feeling that this was the end of an era. My temper became worse than ever, and I behaved even more viciously at home than before. One of the elders of my clan who came to greet me on my birthday in early 1944 became the innocent victim of my love of throwing my weight around.

A skating display had been arranged in the palace to celebrate my birthday, and he had politely greeted some Japanese officers in my presence. This apparently harmless act was reported to me by one of my nephews at the banquet after the show, as to pay respects to anyone else in the presence of the "Son of Heaven" was forbidden in the palace, and he had been taught that it was his duty to report such occurrences. As I was in a good temper at the time and the offender was of an older generation I let the matter drop. But the old man was inquisitive enough to ask the nephew what he had whispered in my ear. This second act of "gross disrespect" was too much for me, and I flared into a rage, shouting at him and thumping the table. He went white with terror, and knelt on the floor and kotowed to me. I was not to be pacified, and I left my seat to accuse him of disloyalty not only to myself but to our imperial ancestors as well. The whole assembly was silent. In my vanity I thought that this old fellow was worse than the Japanese, who at least were never rude to me in public.

While in Changchun I read huge quantities of superstitious books, and became addicted to them. When I read that all living things had a Buddha-nature I became afraid that the meat I ate was the reincarnation of some relation of mine. So in addition to the Buddhist scriptures that I read morning and evening I would say a prayer before every meal for the better reincarnation of the soul of the animal whose meat I was going to eat. At first I recited it silently to myself in front of everyone else, but later I made all other people leave the room until I had finished reciting it and only then allowed them back in again. I remember that I once kotowed to an egg three times before eating it in the palace's air-raid shelter. By that time I was eating vegetarian food only.

I did not allow my staff to kill flies, insisting that they drive them away instead. I knew that flies could carry disease, so I never ate food that a fly had touched. If one landed on my lip I would dab the spot with cotton-wool soaked in surgical spirit from a tin I always carried about with me, and if I found a fly's leg in my food I would fine the cook; but despite all this I did not allow anyone to kill a single fly. And when I saw a cat catching a mouse I had the whole staff chase the cat away to save the mouse's life.

The more I read Buddhist books the more I believed them, and this belief was strengthened by dreams of visiting Hell. I once read that if you recited scriptures for many days the Buddha would appear and would want something to eat. So I prepared a room. and after reading scriptures I proclaimed to everyone that "Buddha has come" and crawled into the room on my knees. The room was, of course, empty, but I was trembling with fear as I kotowed to nothing.

Under my influence the whole household started intoning Buddhist chants, while the air echoed with the sound of the wooden drum and brass gong. The palace seemed to have become a temple.

I continued with my old practice of consulting oracles, and I would repeat my divinations until I got a good omen. When I was frightened that the Kwantung Army was going to murder me I used to consult the oracle every time Yoshioka came to see me. Avoiding calamity and bringing on good fortune became the guiding thought behind my every action. I ended up by asking myself what place, what garment, or what food was propitious and what was unlucky. There were no fixed criteria by which to answer these questions. If I was walking along a path and I saw a brick in front of me I would make a ruling: "If I pass it on the left it is lucky, and if I pass it on the right it is unlucky." Then I would pass it to the left. I could cite numerous other examples, like whether to cross a threshold with one's right or one's left foot first, and whether to eat something white before something green or *vice versa*. Wan Jung was as engrossed in this as I was, and she made a rule that whenever she encountered anything unlucky she would blink or spit. This became such a habit with her that she would blink and spit incessantly as if she were suffering from some mental illness. My nephews, young men of about twenty, all turned into ascetics under my guidance. Some of them would meditate every day, some would not go home in the evening although they were newly married, some would hang pictures of skeletons above their beds, and some would intone spells and prayers all day as if they had just seen ghosts.

I used to "meditate" every day. All sounds were forbidden while I did this, even that of heavy breathing. I kept a large crane in the courtyard, and it ignored this rule, calling whenever it happened to feel in high spirits. I made the pages responsible for it, and fined them fifty cents whenever it made a noise. After losing many dollars this way the pages found a way of dealing with the bird: whenever it stretched out its neck they would hit it, and then the crane kept quiet.

Because I was terrified of death I was frightened of illness. I became a medicine addict, giving a lot of trouble to myself as well as to my household. I used to collect the stuff as well as take it: I had a store of Chinese-style medicine and a dispensary for Western drugs, and I spent thousands or even tens of thousands of dollars importing drugs from abroad that I never used. Several of my nephews had to spend the time when they were not studying looking after all this medicine, and they and my personal doctor gave me injections for several hours every day.

When I lived in the Forbidden City I had often suffered from imaginary illnesses, but now I was really sick. I once made a "royal progress" to Antung to inspect a hydro-electric generating station that the Japanese had recently built. When I got there I had to hold myself up stiff and straight in front of the Japanese as I was in military uniform. Before I had walked very far I was fighting for breath, and on my return journey I nearly blacked out. My physical weakness and mental anxiety made me fear that I was on the brink of the grave.

One day I saw "Haven't you had enough humiliation from the Japanese?" written in chalk on a palace wall. I forgot all about the game of tennis that I was going to play and gave orders for it to be erased at once. I went back to my bedroom, my heart pounding, feeling too weak to last much longer. I was terrified that the Japanese would find out about it and hold a full-scale investigation of my household, and I did not know what that might lead to. I was even more frightened by the discovery that there was an "anti-Manchukuo, anti-Japanese element" in my own court. If he dared write that on the wall, what would stop him from killing me?

As I was so confused and terrified all day I had even less interest than ever in my family life. I had married a total of four wives, or, to use the terms employed then, one empress, one consort, and two minor consorts. But in fact they were not real wives, and were only there for show. Although I treated them differently they were all my victims.

The experiences of Wan Jung, who had been neglected for so long, would be incomprehensible to a modern Chinese girl. If her fate was not determined at her birth, her end was inevitable from the moment she married me. I have often thought that if she had divorced me in Tientsin as Wen Hsiu did she might have escaped it. But then she was quite different from Wen Hsiu. To Wen Hsiu an ordinary family life was more important than a high status and feudal morality. Wan Jung, however, attached great significance to her position as "empress", and was prepared to be a wife in name only for the sake of it.

After she had driven out Wen Hsiu I felt a revulsion for her, hardly ever talking to her or paying her any attention. So she never told me of her feelings, her hopes and her sorrows; and all I knew was that she had become addicted to opium and behaved in a way that I could not tolerate. When our ways parted after the Japanese surrender her opium addiction was very serious and she was extremely weak; she died the following year in Kirin.

In 1937 I chose a new victim called Tan Yu-ling as a punishment for Wan Jung and because a second wife was an essential piece of palace furniture. She had been recommended by a relation in Peking, and she became a Minor Consort. She was of the old Tatala Manchu clan, and was a schoolgirl when I married her at the age of sixteen. She too was a wife in name only, and I kept her in the palace as I might have kept a bird until her death in 1942. The cause of her death is still a mystery to me. She was suffering from an attack of typhoid that should not have been fatal according to the Chinese doctor who saw her. Then Yoshioka said that he wanted to "look after" her, and moved into the palace office. Under the supervision of Yoshioka and the ministrations of a Japanese doctor she died suddenly the next day.

What seemed odd to me was that the Japanese doctor was most diligent in his care of her at first, but that after going into another room for a long talk with Yoshioka he lost his enthusiasm and stopped giving her injections and blood transfusions. Yoshioka made the Japanese gendarmes keep ringing up the nurses in the sickroom all that night for information, and the following morning Tan Yu-ling died.

As soon as I had been informed of her death Yoshioka came to express the condolences of the Kwantung Army commander, and immediately produced a wreath. This amazing speed naturally strengthened my suspicions. I remembered that Tan Yu-ling often used to talk to me about the Japanese and knew a lot about the way they had behaved south of the Great Wall from the books she had read in Peking. I had suspected that the Japanese had listened in to my conversation with Prince Te, and Tan Yu-ling's death naturally reminded me of my old fears.

Soon afterwards I suspected more strongly than ever that the Kwantung Army must have been connected with her death when Yoshioka brought me a sheaf of photographs of Japanese girls for me to choose from.

I refused to consider such a matter while Tan Yu-ling's corpse was still warm. He, however, insisted that he wanted to arrange this for me to console me in my grief. I then said that it should not be done in haste, and pointed out that there was, besides, the language barrier.

"You will be able to understand each other, uh. She will be able to speak Manchukuoan."

I hastened to explain that while this was not a question of race, I had to have someone who was suited to me in her tastes and living habits. I dared not refuse in as many words to have a Japanese wife.

The "Attaché to the Imperial Household" really seemed to attach himself to me, and he kept bothering me about this day after day. Finally he realized that I was adamant — or perhaps the Kwantung Army changed its mind — and he produced some pictures of Chinese girls from a Japanese school in Lushun. Although my second sister warned me that they would all have been so indoctrinated as to be virtually Japanese, I felt that I could not put the Kwantung Army off for ever. I chose a girl who was young and not very highly educated, thinking that I would be able to deal with her even if she had been trained by the Japanese.

Thus it was that a fifteen-year-old schoolgirl became my fourth victim as a Minor Consort. Within two years of her arrival "Manchukuo" collapsed and she was sent back to her home.

The Collapse

While I was in the prison for war criminals a former "Manchukuo" brigade commander told me a story. In the winter in which the Pacific War broke out he led a body of puppet troops to attack some anti-Japanese forces on Kwantung Army orders. His men drew a blank in the forests, and could only find one injured anti-Japanese fighter hiding in a dugout. This man's clothes were so ragged and his hair so unkempt that he looked as if he had been in prison for years. At the sight of this captive the officer had jeered at him:

"From the state you're in, it's obvious that your lot can't achieve anything. Don't you know that the Imperial Japanese Army has occupied Hongkong and Singapore?"

The captive burst out laughing. The "Manchukuo" major-general banged the table. "What are you laughing at? Don't you realize that you're on trial?"

"Who is on trial? Your end is near, and it won't be long before you are tried by the people."

All the puppet officers and civilian officials knew that the people of the Northeast loathed them and the Japanese, but they could not understand why the people had such courage and so much self-confidence, or why they were so sure that their powerful rulers were doomed. I had always regarded the might of Japanese imperialism as both matchless and unshakable. I did not think that even the Great Ching Empire or the Republic of China, whether ruled by the Peiyang warlords or the Kuomintang, was a match for Japan; and the common people never entered my calculations.

Although countless facts should have taught me who was really strong and who was weak, I remained completely in the dark until Yoshioka revealed it to me. Even then I only understood vaguely.

One year the annual "imperial progress" arranged for me by the Kwantung Army was to the Yenchi area, which is mainly inhabited by people of the Korean nationality. When my train arrived I saw that I was surrounded by huge numbers of Japanese gendarmes and six battalions of puppet troops. When I asked Yoshioka why they were there, he replied, "To guard against bandits." "Why are so many soldiers needed to guard against bandits?" "These bandits aren't the old sort; they are the Communist army." "How is it that Manchukuo has Communist forces too? Aren't the Communist armies in the Republic of China?" "Yes, there are some here . . . but very few." Yoshioka then changed the subject.

On another occasion when a Kwantung Army staff officer was making one of his regular reports on the military situation he made a special announcement of a victory. In this campaign the anti-Japanese leader General Yang Ching-yu had sacrificed his life. The staff officer told me with great glee that the death of General Yang had eliminated "a great threat to Manchukuo". The words "great threat" prompted me to ask how many bandits there were in "Manchukuo". He gave the same reply as Yoshioka had: "Very few, very few."

In 1942 the Japanese troops launched their big mopping-up campaign in north and central China. In some places they carried out the "Three All" policy of burn all, kill all and loot all, thus totally devastating some areas. Yoshioka once told me how the Japanese Army used all sorts of tactics against the "Communist armies" of north China, such as "iron encirclements" and "using a fine comb". "The fighting history of the Imperial Japanese Army has been immeasurably enriched." Hearing this bombastic account I asked, "The Communist armies are tiny, so why does His Majesty the Emperor of Japan need to use all these new tactics?"

To my surprise he mocked at me. "If Your Imperial Majesty had battle experience you would not say that."

"May I ask why?"

"The Communist army is different from the Kuomintang army. There is no division between soldiers and people, uh. It's like, uh, for example, red beans mixed up with red pebbles." Seeing my incomprehension he used the Chinese saying "fish eyes mixed with pearls" to make me understand. He said that when the Japanese Army was fighting the Eighth Route Army or New Fourth Army[1] it often found itself completely surrounded. Later he explained to me that no matter where the "Communist armies" went the common people were not afraid of them. Moreover once men had been in their ranks for a year they would not desert, something which made their army unprecedented in the history of China. These armies were getting bigger and bigger, and would be quite impossible to cope with in future. "Terrifying, quite terrifying," he sighed and shook his head. The sight of an officer of the "Imperial Japanese Army" rating the "tiny" enemy in these terms made me so uneasy that I did not know what to say. I screwed myself up to remark, "They really are dreadful, the way they burn and kill, and communize property and wives."

"Only an idiot could believe that," he interrupted me rudely. A moment later he looked at me with a mocking expression and said, "This was not an official comment; I must now ask Your Majesty to listen to the report of the chief of staff of the Kwantung Army."

I gradually came to realize that Yoshioka's unofficial comments were closer to reality than the official briefings of the Kwantung Army commander and chief of staff. When the Kwantung Army started the Nomanhan campaign in 1939 its commander Ueda invited me and some other puppet officials to see a demonstration of how much faster the Japanese aircraft were than the Soviet ones. But the Japanese were disastrously defeated in that campaign, losing over 50,000 men, and Ueda was cashiered. Yoshioka's unofficial

---

[1] Both led by the Communist Party.

314

comment was that "the Soviet heavy artillery has a far longer range than ours".

As I listened to the radio I gradually understood more of Yoshioka's hidden anxieties. There were more reports of Japanese military defeats on all fronts, and these were confirmed by reports of "smashed jade" ("heroic sacrifices") in the "Manchukuo" press. Even in my isolation I could see that there was a shortage of material supplies. Old brass and iron, such as door-knockers and spittoons, disappeared from the palace, while court officials were so short of food that they had to ask me to help them out. For fear that I knew how poor the food of the soldiers was, the Kwantung Army invited me to see a special exhibition of military rations; and to counteract the influence of foreign radio broadcasts they sent films propagandizing Japanese victories for me to see. Neither I nor the youngest of my nephews was taken in.

What made the deepest impression on me was the fear that the Japanese revealed. Yamashita Tomoyuki, who had been so proud when he had been transferred to the Kwantung Army after capturing Singapore, was a changed man when he came to take his leave of me on being posted back to Southeast Asia in 1945. Covering his nose and weeping, he said, "This is our final parting. I shall never come back again."

I saw even more tears at a farewell ceremony for "human bullets". Human bullets were soldiers selected from the Japanese Army who had been poisoned with a belief in *Bushido* and loyalty to the Japanese emperor and chosen for the task of stopping aircraft and tanks with their own bodies. Yoshioka always spoke of such deeds with the greatest respect, but they horrified me. This ceremony had been devised by the Kwantung Army for me to encourage the men who had been chosen as human bullets and wish them success. It was a cloudy day, and there was a big dust-storm blowing. The courtyard in the palace was made even more depressing by the sandbags that were piled up as an air-raid precaution. The dozen or so victims were drawn up in a line in front of me; and I read out the speech of good wishes that Yoshioka had written out, then toasted them. Only then did I see the ashen grey of their faces and the tears flowing down their cheeks, and hear that some of them were sobbing.

The ceremony came to a scrappy end in the swirling dust, and as I hurried back to my rooms to wash, my mind was in turmoil. Yoshioka followed close behind, so I knew that he must have something to say to me and waited for him to catch me up. He cleared his throat, hummed and hawed, and said, "Your Majesty spoke very well and moved them deeply, which was why they shed manly Japanese tears."

"You really are frightened," I thought. "You're frightened that I've seen through the human bullets. Well, if you're frightened, I'm even more scared."

The German surrender in May 1945 made Japan's position more desperate than ever, and it was now only a matter of time before the Soviet Army entered the war. Even I realized that Japan's plight was hopeless.

The final collapse came at last. On the morning of August 9, 1945 the last commander of the Kwantung Army, Yamata Otozo, and his chief of staff came to the palace to report to me that the Soviet Union had declared war on Japan.

Yamata was a short, thin old man who was normally grave in manner and slow in speech. But today he was completely different; he gave me a rushed account of how well prepared the Japanese troops were and told me that they were fully confident of victory. Before he could finish speaking an air-raid siren sounded and we all hid in a shelter. Before long we heard bombs exploding nearby, and while I quietly invoked the Buddha he was silent. He did not refer again to his confidence in victory before we parted after the all-clear.

From that night onwards I slept in my clothes, kept a pistol in my pocket, and ordered martial law in the palace.

Yamata and the chief of staff came again the next day to tell me that the Japanese Army was going to withdraw and hold southern Manchuria, so that the "capital" would be moved to Tunghua. I would have to be ready to move the same day. Realizing that it would be impossible to move my large household and all my property so soon, I pleaded for and won a delay of two days.

I now started to undergo new mental torments. These were partly caused by the further change in the attitude of Yoshioka and partly because of my morbid suspicion. I noticed the change in Yoshioka's attitude from a remark he made after Yamata had gone: "If Your Majesty does not go, you will be the first to be murdered by the Soviet troops." He spoke in a very sinister way, and what made me even more frightened was the obvious implication that the Japanese suspected that I did not want to go and was planning to betray them.

"If they think that I might be captured by the allied armies, might they not want to kill me to keep me quiet?" This thought made my hair stand on end.

I remembered a trick I had used over ten years previously to demonstrate my "loyalty and sincerity" in front of Yoshioka. I sent for the "premier" Chang Ching-hui and Takebe Rokuzo, the director of the General Affairs Office of the State Council, and ordered them: "We must support the holy war of our Parental Country with all our strength, and must resist the Soviet Army to the end, to the very end."

I turned to look at Yoshioka's expression, only to find that the "attaché" who normally stayed with me like a shadow had gone. Full of terrible forebodings, I paced up and down the room. I looked out of the window and saw some Japanese soldiers advancing towards the building with their rifles at the ready. My heart almost jumped out of my mouth, and I thought my hour had come. Realizing that I had nowhere to hide, I went to the top of the stairs to meet them. When they saw me the soldiers went away.

I thought that they must have come to test whether I would run away or not. The more I thought about it the more frightened I felt, so I picked up the telephone to ring Yoshioka. I could not get through. It looked as though the Japanese had gone without me, and that terrified me too.

Later I managed to get through to Yoshioka. His voice was very faint, and he said that he was ill. I expressed my concern, said some kind words, heard him say, "Thank you, Your Majesty", and rang off. I heaved a sigh of relief, and realized that I had not eaten all day and was very hungry. I asked my last personal attendant, Big Li, to bring me some food, but he told me that the cooks had all gone. I had to make do with biscuits.

A little after nine in the evening of the 11th Yoshioka arrived. My brother, sisters, brothers-in-law, and nephews were already at the railway station, and of my family only myself and my two wives were left in the palace. Yoshioka addressed me and the servants who were still with me in a peremptory tone:

"Whether we are walking or in cars, the sacred objects carried by Hashimoto Toranosuke will go in front. If anyone passes the sacred vessels they must make a ninety-degree bow."

I realized that we must now be going to set out. I stood respectfully and watched Hashimoto, the President of the Bureau of Worship, carry the bundle containing the sacred Shinto objects and enter the first car. I got into the second, and as we left the palace I looked round and saw flames rising above the "National Foundation Shrine".

The train took three days and two nights to reach Talitzukou. The original plan had been for it to go via Shenyang, but it was re-routed along the Kirin-Meihokuo line to avoid air-raids. Throughout the journey we only ate two proper meals and some biscuits. We saw Japanese military vehicles all along the route, and the men in them looked like a cross between soldiers and refugees. The train stopped at Meihokuo for Yamata, the commander of the Kwantung Army, to come aboard. He reported to me that the Japanese Army was winning and had destroyed numbers of Soviet tanks and aircraft. But his story was belied by what I saw at Kirin station. Crowds of Japanese women and children, screaming and shouting, were pushing towards the train as they wept and begged the gendarmes to let them pass. At one end of the platform Japanese gendarmes and soldiers were brawling.

On August 13 I arrived at Talitzukou, a coal-mine set amid mountains whose beauty I was too terrified to appreciate, and two days later the Japanese surrender was proclaimed.

When Yoshioka said, "His Imperial Majesty has proclaimed our surrender, and the American government has given guarantees about his position and safety", I fell on my knees and kotowed to heaven, intoning, "I thank heaven for protecting His Imperial Majesty." Yoshioka also knelt down and kotowed.

Yoshioka then said with a dejected expression that the Kwantung Army had been in touch with Tokyo. It had been decided to send me to Japan. "But," he added, "His Imperial Majesty cannot assume unconditional responsibility for Your Majesty's safety. This will be in the hands of the Allies."

I felt that death was beckoning to me.

Chang Ching-hui and Takebe Rokuzo came with a group of "ministers" and "privy councillors". As there was one more farce to be played out they had brought with them a new composition of the Japanese sinologue Sato — my "Abdication Rescript". They looked like so many lost dogs as I stood before them and read it out. I have forgotten the wording of this sixth rescript, but I do remember that the indispensable references to the "Divine Blessing of the Heaven Shining Bright Deity and the Protection of His Imperial Majesty the Emperor of Japan" were struck out by Hashimoto with a wry smile. Hashimoto had formerly been a commander of the Japanese Imperial Guard Division, and he had later been made president of the "Manchukuo" Board of Ritual with the responsibility for guarding the Heaven Shining Bright Deity: as such he could be regarded as an expert on the emperor and the goddess.

Had I known at the time that the status I enjoyed was even lower than that of Chang Ching-hui and his group I would have been even more depressed. When the Japanese decided that I was to go to Tokyo they arranged for the secret return of Chang Ching-hui and Takebe to Changchun to make arrangements for the future. When Chang Ching-hui got back to Changchun he made radio contact with Chiang Kai-shek in Chungking and announced the establishment of a "Committee for the Preservation of Public Order" that was preparing to receive the Kuomintang troops. He and his group hoped that they would be able to make a lightning change into representatives of the Republic of China before the Soviet troops arrived, but the Soviet advance was much quicker than they had expected, and the Communist-led Anti-Japanese Allied Armies were sweeping aside the resistance of the Japanese soldiers as they approached the capital. The day after the Soviet Army reached Changchun Chang Ching-hui's dreams were shattered when he and his fellow-ministers were put into an aircraft and flown off to captivity in the U.S.S.R.

On August 16 the Japanese learnt that there had been clashes between the palace guards and the Japanese army in Changchun, so they disarmed the guard company that had come with me. At the same time Yoshioka told me that I was to go to Japan the next day. I nodded rapidly in agreement and pretended to be very pleased.

Yoshioka told me to decide who I would take with me. As we would be flying in a small aircraft I only chose my brother Pu Chieh, two brothers-in-law, three nephews, a doctor and my personal attendant Big Li. My concubine asked me amid sobs what she was to do. "The plane is too small," I replied, "so you will have to go by train."

"Will the train get to Japan?"

"Of course it will," I answered without a moment's thought. "In three days at the most you and the Empress will see me again."

"What will happen if the train doesn't come for me? I haven't got a single relation here."

"We'll meet again in a couple of days. You'll be all right."

I was far too preoccupied with saving my own life to care whether there would be a train for her or not.

We landed at Shenyang, where we were to change to a large aircraft at eleven in the morning, and sat in the airport rest-room waiting for the second aeroplane.

Before we had been waiting for long the airfield reverberated to the sound of aircraft engines as Soviet aircraft landed. Soviet troops holding submachine-guns poured out of the planes and immediately disarmed all the Japanese soldiers on the airfield, which was soon covered with Soviet troops.

The next day I was put on a Soviet aircraft and flown to the U.S.S.R.

▣▣▣▣▣▣▣▣▣▣▣▣▣▣▣▣▣▣▣▣▣▣▣▣▣▣▣▣▣▣▣▣▣▣▣▣▣

CHAPTER SEVEN

IN THE SOVIET UNION

P'u Yi's four-and-a-half years in the Soviet Union were a kind of limbo. He was a prisoner, but he and his entourage—he was even allowed to send back to China for more followers to join him in exile—were extraordinarily privileged captives, especially by contrast with the countless Soviet and foreign citizens who died in Stalin's prison camps during these years.

The very brief account P'u Yi gives of this extended interlude raises a number of questions that it does not answer. The main one is: why did the Soviet Union treat him the way that it did? The Soviet Union did not have a very deep hostility towards Manchukuo, with which it had reached an early accommodation. A border conflict at Nomonhan (Khalkhin Gol) in 1939 had ended with a massive defeat for the Japanese forces and their Manchukuo clients by the Soviet Red Army and its clients, the Mongolian People's Republic, and had been decisive in persuading Japan to give up the option of making an all-out drive against Mongolia and Siberia. Had Japan hit the USSR instead of the United States and Britain in the winter of 1941, when the military and economic resources east of the Urals were critical to stopping Hitler's advance on Moscow, it is doubtful whether the Soviet state would have survived. So while the Soviet forces subjected Northeast China to a very thorough looting they soon withdrew, leaving the Chinese Communists and Kuomintang to settle the future of the Northeast and of the rest of China on the battlefield.

It can hardly have been humanitarian scruples that stopped Moscow from returning P'u Yi to China immediately to face trial and execution as a traitor by the Kuomintang regime. Nor does it seem plausible that P'u Yi was kept at such expense for so long with the sole intention of handing him over to the Chinese Communists when the civil war finally ended. The information he gave cannot have taken that long to be drawn out of him.

Now it is on public record that Stalin reasserted many former tsarist Russian rights in Northeast China in 1945, and there are many indications that he tried hard to keep a special position for the USSR in that region after 1949. Is it entirely inconceivable that before the outcome of the Chinese civil war became clear in 1948 P'u Yi was being held in reserve, just in case he might have proved useful in some Soviet-imposed settlement in the Northeast? There is no evidence to back so wild a hypothesis, but it is not impossible, especially when we remember how useful P'u Yi was later to be to the Chinese Communists. Until the relevant Soviet archives are opened we can only speculate about this, and about what was in P'u Yi's repeated written requests to be allowed to continue enjoying Soviet hospitality.

Fear and Illusion

When we landed in Chita it was all but dark. My party, the first batch of "Manchukuo" war criminals to arrive in the Soviet Union, was driven away from the airfield in a Soviet Army car. As I looked out of the windows it appeared that we were driving across a plain that stretched out black and immense on either side. After a while we went through woods and started climbing. The road became narrow and bending, and the car slowed down considerably. Suddenly it stopped, and a voice shouted in Chinese from the darkness, "Get out if you want a pee".

I was terrified, thinking that the Chinese had come to take me back; but the speaker turned out to be a Soviet officer of Chinese descent. As happened so often in the first part of my life, I had suffered quite unnecessary mental agony because of my morbid suspicion. I was terrified of falling into Chinese hands, as I thought that while in the power of foreigners I had a chance of staying alive, but was bound to be killed by the Chinese. It was, of course, absurd to imagine that I would be sent back to China just after arriving in the Soviet Union.

After we had relieved ourselves we got back into the car, and two hours later we stopped at a large, lighted building in a mountain valley. We got out of our car and looked at this handsome building; someone muttered, "This is a hotel." Everyone's spirits rose.

When we entered the hotel we were greeted by a man in his forties wearing civilian clothes, and behind him was a group of Soviet officers. He announced solemnly that the Soviet Government had ordered that we were to be detained here. This man later turned out to be the major-general in command of the Chita garrison. After making his announcement he told us kindly that we were to wait here calmly until a decision was made on how we were to be dealt with. Then he pointed at a bottle of water on the table and told us that the place was famous for its health-giving mineral springs.

At first I did not like the mineral water, but later I became very fond of it. We spent a privileged detention in this sanatorium. with three large Russian meals a day and afternoon tea as well. There were attendants to wait on us, doctors and nurses to look after our health, radios, books, papers, and facilities for other kinds of recreation. There were even people to take us on frequent walks. I was satisfied with this life from the first.

Before I had been there long I had the wild hope that as Britain and America were allies of the Soviet Union I might be allowed to go and live in one of those two countries as a refugee; I had brought enough jewellery with me to last me for the rest of my life. To achieve this ambition I had first to make sure that I would be allowed to stay in the U.S.S.R., and apart from verbal requests I made three written applications to the Soviet authorities during those five years asking to be allowed to stay permanently in the Soviet Union. All three went unanswered.

The other "Manchukuo" detainees[1] took a completely different attitude. Chang Ching-hui, Tsang Shih-yi, Hsi Hsia and some others arrived at the sanatorium a few days after I did, and the next day they came to see me. I thought that this must be a courtesy call until Chang Ching-hui said:

"We hear that you want to stay in the Soviet Union, but our families are in the Northeast and need us to look after them. Besides, we have some official business to do there. We would like you to ask the Soviet authorities to let us go back soon. Do you think that would be possible?"

What the "official business" might be I did not know or care, and I did not take the slightest interest in their request. But when they pleaded with me I told the Soviet officer in charge of us about it. He gave the same reply as he did to my own requests — "Very well, I shall pass it on." Nothing came of it.

---

[1] The civilian "Manchukuo" officials enjoyed the status of detainees, while the military officers were war criminals.

The reason they wanted to go back was that they understood the Kuomintang better than I did. They knew that the Kuomintang needed them, and believed that they would be able to do well for themselves. Some of them almost went mad in their longing to return.

While we were in the Soviet Union we were told about the news by the Soviet interpreters, and we often saw the Chinese-language paper *Shih Hua Pao* that was published by the Soviet Army in Lushun. The former puppet ministers followed the development of the Chinese civil war closely, and their sympathies were naturally with the American-backed Kuomintang, which they expected to win. When the war ended with the defeat of the Kuomintang, however, they wanted to send a telegram of congratulations on the founding of the People's Republic of China. But I took no interest in the war as I felt that it made no difference to me who won — the Communists and the Kuomintang would both want my life. My only hope was that I would never return to my country.

Still Giving Myself Airs

I never stopped giving myself airs during my five years in the Soviet Union. Although there were no more attendants when we were moved to the reception centre at Khabarovsk, there were still people to wait on me. Members of my family would fold up my quilt, tidy the room, bring me food and wash my clothes. As they did not dare to address me as "Your Majesty", they called me "Above"; and they would come into my room every morning to pay me their respects just as in the old days.

One day soon after my arrival in Khabarovsk I decided to go for a stroll. As I started downstairs I noticed a former minister sitting in a chair at the bottom of the staircase, and when he saw me he ignored my presence completely. I was so angry that I never thought of going downstairs again, and spent most of my time reciting scriptures. Most of the ex-"ministers", however, still behaved respectfully towards me. When we ate *jiaozi*[1] at the Chinese New Year, for example, they would always give me the first bowl.

On top of doing no work myself, I was not pleased if the members of my family worked for anyone else. When my brother and brothers-in-law were laying the table for everyone at one meal, I stopped them. I was not going to have my relations waiting on anyone but myself.

For some time in 1947 and 1948 the members of my household were moved to another reception centre in the same city, and I found this most inconvenient, as I had never been separated from my family before. The Soviet authorities were very kind to me and allowed me to eat by myself, but who was to bring me my food? Fortunately my father-in-law volunteered to do this and my washing into the bargain.

In order to make us parasites do a little light labour we were given a corner of the yard of the reception centre where we could grow vegetables. I and my household members were given a small plot where we grew green peppers, tomatoes, aubergines, beans and other things. I watched with fascination as the green shoots grew day by day, and I greatly enjoyed filling the watering can and watering them. This was a new experience for me. But the main reason why I was interested was because I liked eating peppers and tomatoes; I often thought that it would be far more convenient to buy them from a greengrocer's.

The authorities of the reception centre gave us some books in Chinese for us to study, and there were set times when my brother and brothers-in-law would read out *Problems of Leninism* and the *History of the Communist Party of the Soviet Union (Bolsheviks)* to everyone. But the books did not mean anything to the readers or the audience. I found them depressing and irrelevant. If they were not going to let me stay in the Soviet Union but were sending

---

[1] A traditional north Chinese New Year dish. *Jiaozi* are made by putting finely-chopped meat and vegetable fillings into flour "skins". They are then boiled.

me back to China, what good would it do me even if I learnt the two books by heart?

The word "study" seemed less real to me in those days than peppers and tomatoes. As I sat in my special place I would listen to the "teacher" mumbling away about words like "Menshevik" and "State Duma" that I neither understood nor wanted to understand; meanwhile I would be wondering how long the jewellery I had brought with me could last me in Moscow or London, or asking myself, "If the Russians don't eat aubergines, how am I going to eat the ones we've picked?"

After supper came the time for free activities. At one end of the corridor would be some mah-jong tables, while at the other end people would be looking out at the sky with their hands joined as they invoked Amitabha Buddha and the Bodhisattva Kuanyin. From upstairs, where the Japanese war criminals were kept, drifted the sounds of Japanese opera. The strangest sight was that of men crowded round a divination stand trying to find out when they would be allowed home and what had happened to their families. Some would consult the planchette secretly in their bedrooms, always asking about their return home. For the first few days the sentries would be startled by the shouting and come and peer at these strange men and shake their heads; later they got used to it.

I spent most of my time during this period in my own room, shaking my coin-oracle and reciting the *Diamond Sutra*.

I Refuse to Admit My Guilt

As I did not stop behaving like a superior being and refused to study, there was no fundamental change in my thinking and I naturally did not admit my guilt.

I knew that legally I was guilty of treason, but I thought that this was just a quirk of fate. "Might is right" and "The victor becomes a king and the loser a bandit" was my attitude in those days. I did not think that I bore any responsibility, I did not wonder what kind of ideology it was that caused my crimes, and I had never heard of the necessity of thought reform.

In order to avoid punishment I resorted to my old tricks and tried to curry favour with the Soviet authorities who were now the controllers of my destiny. So I offered my jewellery as a contribution to the Soviet Union's post-war reconstruction.

I did not offer all of it, keeping the best for myself. I gave the jewels I kept to a nephew to hide under the false bottom of a suitcase. Unfortunately he could not conceal them all in this space, so I had to try and put the rest of them in every hiding place I could think of. But when even my soap could hold no more I had to throw away what was left.

One day a Soviet officer came into the main hall with an interpreter. Holding a bright object in his hand he asked everybody, "Whose is this? Who put it in the old radiators in the yard?"

The prisoners in the hall all crowded round and saw that the officer was holding a piece of jewellery. "It's got the hallmark of a Peking silversmith," someone observed. "I wonder who put it there."

I recognized it at once as one of the pieces I had told my nephews to get rid of, but as they were now separated from me I could not have this out with them. I hastily shook my head and said, "Very odd, very odd. I wonder who put it there."

To my surprise the interpreter walked over to me with a wooden comb in his hand. "This was found with it, and I remember that it was yours."

I was desperate. "No, no, it isn't mine."

The two men hesitated for a while, astounded at the naivety of my denial and then went away.

Apart from throwing away jewellery, I burnt some pearls in a stove and told Big Li to hide some remaining ones in the chimney just before we left the Soviet Union.

Because of my hatred for the Japanese I enthusiastically gave the Soviet authorities a lot of information when they questioned me about Japanese crimes in the Northeast. When I was summoned to appear as a witness at the International Military Tribunal for the Far East in August 1946 I denounced Japanese war crimes with the greatest vehemence. But I never spoke of my own crimes, for fear that I would be condemned myself. My testimony lasted eight days, and was the longest one in the trial. It gave first-rate news to those papers throughout the world that deal in sensation.

The reason why I was asked to give evidence was to expose the truth about the Japanese invasion of China, and to demonstrate how Japan had used me as a puppet to help them rule the Northeast. I now feel very ashamed of my testimony, as I withheld some of what I knew to protect myself from being punished by my country. I said nothing about my secret collaboration with the Japanese imperialists over a long period, an association to which my open capitulation after September 18, 1931 was but the conclusion. Instead I spoke only of the way the Japanese had put pressure on me and forced me to do their will.

I made several displays of emotion at the tribunal. When I spoke about introducing the cult of the Heaven Shining Bright Deity into the Northeast a Japanese lawyer asked me whether my attack on the ancestor of the Emperor of Japan conformed with Oriental morality. "I never forced him to adopt my ancestor as his ancestor," I shouted in reply. The whole room burst out laughing, but I was most indignant. When the death of my wife Tan Yu-ling was brought up I spoke as if my suspicions about her death were established facts, and said tragically: "Even she was murdered by the Japanese." I was, of course, worked up emotionally, but I was also deliberately portraying myself as the victim of the Japanese.

The defence counsel tried all sorts of devices against me in the hope of discrediting my evidence, and even suggested that I was not qualified to be a witness. These attempts naturally failed, and even had they been successful it would have made no difference to the fate of the accused. When they deliberately played on my fear of punishment to make me keep quiet, however, they were partially successful. I remember that after I had enumerated a list of Japanese war crimes an American lawyer shouted: "You put all the blame on the Japanese, but sooner or later the Chinese government will condemn you for your crimes." His shot hit the mark. It was precisely because I was afraid of this that I maintained that I had not betrayed my country but had been kidnapped; denied all my collaboration with the Japanese; and even claimed that the letter I had written to Minami Jiro was a fake. I covered up my crimes in order to protect myself. This meant that I did not make a full exposure of the crimes of the Japanese imperialists. Thus I was really doing them a good turn.

CHAPTER EIGHT

▣▣▣▣▣▣▣▣▣▣▣▣▣▣▣▣▣▣▣▣▣▣▣▣▣▣▣▣▣▣▣▣▣▣▣

FROM FEAR TO RECOGNIZING
MY GUILT

The story of P'u Yi's 'remoulding' as told in Chapters Eight and Nine is open to a number of different but not necessarily mutually exclusive readings. First and foremost it is the picture of prison re-education that the Ministry of Public Security wanted to give the world when their publishing house first brought out the Chinese original of the book. Both then and now P'u Yi's story has been officially treated as a model case of successful reform that reflects well on the Chinese penal system. It remains one of the longest accounts of the 'remoulding' process by a former prisoner to have been officially published in China. In other words, this is how the system is supposed to work.

We can also read it as what it purports to be: P'u Yi, with whatever help he had from his co-writers, telling us with a convert's enthusiasm how under the firm but fair guidance of the prison authorities he came to see the error of his ways and become a new man with a new world-view and a place among the working people. It will be evident that he is extremely eager to take up correct positions and condemn himself in the right tones, expressing penitence where it is expected of him and gushing about how all was for the best in the best of all possible prisons.

One of the required occupations of prisoners in China is the endless writing of autobiographies and self-criticisms, as is clear from many independent accounts of the experience. Undoubtedly large parts of these and other chapters are rewordings or re-creations of some of the autobiographical writing he had to do in gaol, and however many other hands may have reworked it since, the chapters have the authentic tone of a prisoner writing what he thought the authorities would want to hear.

What we do not have in these two chapters is anything that conflicts with the official view of 'remoulding'. But even if it is all too good to be the whole truth it may well be a genuine expression of what P'u Yi wanted to be on record as saying.

The special consideration shown P'u Yi and other high-ranking Manchukuo, Japanese, and Nationalist officials cannot be regarded as typical of Chinese prison conditions. These were all people of potential value in winning over others in future, and political considerations saved them from the harsh justice that many lesser figures received.

The move of the prisoners from Fushun to Harbin during the Korean war may well have been connected with fears of an American-led invasion of Northeast China. This would explain why they were able to return to Fushun later, when the scare was presumably over.

I Expect to Die

On July 31, 1950 the Soviet train carrying the "Manchukuo" war criminals arrived at the station of Suifenho on the Sino-Soviet frontier. The Captain Asnis who was responsible for escorting us told us that we would be handed over to the Chinese authorities the following morning, and advised us to sleep peacefully.

After boarding the train at Khabarovsk I had been separated from the members of my household and put in the same carriage as the Soviet officers. They had beer and sweets for me, and told me funny stories during the journey; but for all this I felt that they were taking me to my death. I thought that I would be doomed from the moment I set foot on Chinese soil.

From the opposite berth came the even breathing of Captain Asnis. I lay with my eyes wide open, kept awake by the fear of death. I sat up and silently recited some Buddhist scriptures, and was just going to lie down again when I heard the tramp of soldiers coming along the platform. I looked out of the window, but I could not see anyone. The marching boots were growing fainter, and all I could make out were some ominously flashing lights in the distance. I sighed, hunched myself up in the corner of my berth, and gazed at the empty bottles on the table. I remembered something Asnis had said while we were drinking the beer that had been in them: "At dawn you will see your motherland, and returning to one's motherland is an occasion for congratulations. Don't worry, Communist political power is the most civilized on earth, and the Chinese Party and people have great generosity."

"Liar," I thought as I looked across at Asnis, who was now snoring. "Your words, your beer, your sweets — they're all a trick. My life will last no longer than the dew on the outside of the windowpane, but there you are sleeping like a log."

I did not believe that Communists could be "civilized". To me they were still the "raging floods and wild beasts" that I had been told they were for decades while I was living in Peking, Tientsin and Changchun. I attributed the humane treatment I had received from the Soviet Union, a Communist state, to the fact that it was one of the Allies and thus restricted by international agreements. I thought that China would be quite different. There the Communists had overthrown Chiang Kai-shek, and would presumably hate me a hundred times more bitterly than he had done. I thought that once I was in the clutches of these notoriously cruel men I could not even hope for a comfortable death.

I spent the night thinking such terrifying thoughts. When Captain Asnis told me the next morning to come with him to see the representative of the Chinese Government my only thought was whether I would have the courage to shout "Long live Emperor Tai Tsu" before I died.

With my mind numb I followed Asnis into another compartment where two Chinese were sitting. One was wearing blue civilian clothes and the other was in a khaki military uniform without any badges of rank and with a patch reading "Chinese People's Liberation Army" on his chest. They stood up and exchanged a few words with Asnis, then the one in civilian clothes looked me up and down and said, "I have come to receive you on the orders of Premier Chou En-lai. You have now returned to the motherland."

I lowered my head, waiting for the soldier to handcuff me. But he sat there motionless, just looking at me.

"He knows I can't run away," I thought as I got out of the train and stepped on the platform over an hour later. Two rows of armed soldiers were drawn up there, one of Soviet troops and one of Chinese troops with the same patch on their chests as the officer in the train. I walked between them and boarded the train opposite. I remembered that Chiang Kai-shek's eight million strong armed forces had been wiped out by men wearing this patch, and reflected that in their eyes I must be lower than a worm.

In the carriage I saw a group of former "Manchukuo" officials and the members of my own household. They were all sitting up straight, and none of them were shackled or bound. I was taken to a seat near the end of the carriage, and a soldier put my case in the luggage-rack. I tried to look out of the window but found that it had been papered over, and I saw that at each end of the carriage was a soldier with a submachine-gun. My heart sank. Surely this meant that we were being sent to the execution ground. The faces of all the criminals around me were deathly pale.

A little later an unarmed man who looked like an officer walked into the middle of the carriage. "Good, now you have returned to your motherland," he said as he surveyed us. "The Central People's Government has made arrangements for you, and you have nothing to worry about. There are medical personnel on the train, so if any of you are sick you can ask to see the doctor."

What ever could he mean, talking like that? Presumably he was trying to reassure us and prevent anything untoward happening on the journey. Then some soldiers came in and gave each of us a pair of chopsticks and a bowl, telling us to look after them carefully as they could not be replaced on the journey. This must mean, I thought, that the journey to the execution ground would be a long one.

Breakfast consisted of pickled vegetables, salted eggs, and rice porridge. The flavour of this home cooking after so many years abroad whetted all our appetites, and we soon finished a big bucket of porridge. When the soldiers saw this they gave us the bucket of porridge that they had been going to eat themselves. I could not understand this. I knew that as there were no cooking facilities on the train they would have to wait till the next station before they could cook some more. I reached the same conclusion: they must have some evil intentions towards us.

After breakfast some faces did not look nearly so worried. When my companions discussed this later they said that the generosity of the soldiers showed that they had been very well trained and disciplined and would not mistreat us on the journey. My views were completely different. I thought that the Communist Party hated me bitterly and might well murder me on the journey for the sake of revenge. Indeed, they would be bound to do so, and almost certainly today or tonight. Some of the others went to sleep after breakfast, but

I was feeling most uneasy and had to have someone to talk to. I wanted to make my escorts know that I ought not to be killed.

Sitting opposite me was a young security soldier, and he seemed the most likely person to have a conversation with. I looked at him carefully, and then found a subject of conversation in the patch on his chest. "You are a member of the Chinese People's Liberation Army (this was the first time I had ever used the respectful form of the word 'you'), and the meaning of the word 'liberation' is very good. I am a Buddhist, and in the Buddhist scriptures there is the idea of liberation. Our Buddha is compassionate, and has sworn to liberate all living beings. . . ."

The young soldier stared at me wide-eyed, listening without a sound as I prattled on. When I said that I had never killed any living thing and did not even swat flies, his expression was incomprehensible to me. My spirits sagged and I stopped talking. How was I to know then that the young soldier found me as incomprehensible as I found him?

My despair was now even deeper. The sound of the wheels on the rails made me feel that death was getting ever closer. I got up from my seat and wandered along the passage between the seats to the other end of the carriage. After standing outside the door of the lavatory I turned back. Half-way down the carriage I heard my nephew Little Hsiu talking to someone in a low voice. Hearing the words "democracy" and "monarchy" I stopped and shouted at them, "Still talking about monarchy these days? If anyone thinks that democracy is bad I'll fight him."

Everyone was dumbfounded by this outburst, but I continued to shout hysterically, "What are you all looking at me for? Don't worry, they'll only shoot me."

A soldier came up and pulled me back to my seat, advising me to take it easy. I clung to him as if I had been bewitched and whispered, "That one is my nephew. His ideas are very bad and he is against democracy. The other one is called Chao and used to be an officer. He said many bad things in the Soviet Union."

I went on like this after returning to my seat. When the soldier asked me to lie down I had no choice but to do so, but I still continued to talk as I lay on the seat with my eyes shut. Finally I dozed off, probably because I had not slept for several nights.

When I woke up it was the next morning. I wanted to know the fate of the two men I had reported. I stood up to look, and saw that they were both sitting in their old places. Little Hsiu's expression was normal, but Chao looked a little odd. On closer examination I saw that he looked depressed and was gazing at his hands closely. I concluded that he knew that he was about to die and was pitying himself. Then I remembered the stories about avenging ghosts and was frightened that his ghost would come to settle accounts with me. I went over and kotowed in front of him. Having thus averted disaster I walked back to my seat muttering an incantation for the souls of the dead.

The train slowed down and came to a halt. Someone muttered "Changchun". I jumped up like a spring and searched in vain for a chink in the papered windows through which to look. I could hear a lot of people singing nearby. I thought that this must be the place where I was going to die as I had been emperor here. Everyone was here, waiting for my public trial. While in the Soviet Union I had read about the struggle against local despots and knew about the procedure of the trials: first of all the accused was escorted to the platform by militiamen. Just then two soldiers came in through the carriage door, which gave me an awful fright. In fact they were only bringing the rice porridge for breakfast, and after their arrival the train started to move again.

When the train reached Shenyang I was convinced that I would die here in the place from which my ancestors had arisen. Soon after the train stopped a stranger came into the carriage with a piece of paper in his hands. "As it's so hot today," he announced, "the older ones among you are to follow me and come for a rest." He started reading out names from the list in his hand. It seemed odd to me that the list included not only myself, who at forty-four might just be considered older, but also my nephew Little Hsiu, who was only in his thirties. Clearly this was a trick. I was an emperor, the others were ministers, and Little Hsiu had been reported by me. We all climbed into a large car which was followed by soldiers with guns. "This is it," I said to Little Hsiu. "I'll take you to meet our ancestors." His face suddenly blanched. The man with the list laughed and said, "What are you afraid of? Didn't I tell you that you were coming here for a rest?" I paid no attention, and went on telling myself that this was a trick.

The car stopped in front of a large building with more armed soldiers at the door. A soldier without any weapon came up to greet us, and led us inside. "Upstairs," he said. I now had the courage of desperation and had decided that if I was to die I might as well get it over with quickly. I rolled my coat into a bundle, tucked it under my arm, and went upstairs. I went so fast that I overtook the soldier who was leading the way and forced him to hurry to get in front of me again. He showed me into a large room with chairs and tables on which was spread fruit, cigarettes and cakes. Throwing my coat on a table I grabbed an apple and started eating it, convinced that this was the banquet always laid on for condemned men, and that the sooner I ate it the sooner it would all be over. By the time I was half-way through the apple the room was full.

A man in civilian clothes started speaking near me, but I was too busy with my apple to pay attention to what he was saying. When I had finished the apple I stood up and cut him short.

"Stop talking. Let's go."

Some people in civilian clothes laughed, and the speaker said with a smile, "You're in too much of a hurry. Don't worry, when you get to Fushun you'll have a good rest and then do some proper study."

I was flabbergasted. Weren't they going to kill me? What did this mean? I went up and grabbed the list of names from the man who had brought us here. Although this made people laugh, I was now certain that the list was not an order for execution or anything of the kind. Then Chang Ching-hui's son Little Chang came in. He had returned to China earlier with another group of war criminals, and he told us about how they were now; he also passed on some family news. When we heard that the earlier group were all alive, that our families were all right and that the children were either studying or working our faces all lit up. Tears came into my eyes.

My relief only lasted for the hour or so it took to get from Shenyang to Fushun, but it saved me from going mad, as I had been thinking of nothing but death for the five days since we had left Khabarovsk.

Arriving in Fushun

Before our train reached Fushun all kinds of views about our rosy prospects were being voiced. The atmosphere had changed completely, and conversation was animated as we smoked the cigarettes we had brought with us from Shenyang. Some said they thought that we would be put up in a luxurious club they knew there; some thought that we would be allowed home after resting there and reading Communist books for a few days; some said that they were going to cable their families to get things ready for their return; and others thought that we might be able to bathe at the Fushun hot springs before we left. We spoke of the fear that we had all shared earlier and roared with laughter. But when we got out of the train and saw that we were surrounded by armed sentries, there was not a smile to be seen on our faces.

We were escorted by the soldiers into some large lorries. My mind went blank, and the next thing I remember was that I was somewhere surrounded by a high, dark brick wall surmounted with barbed wire and with watchtowers in the corners. I followed the others until we stopped in front of a row of single-storeyed buildings. All of the windows were barred. I realized that this was a prison.

The soldiers escorted us along a narrow passage and into a large room where we were searched. Then we were led away by unarmed soldiers. I and a few others followed a soldier some way along the passage until we came to a cell. Before I had taken a look round the room the sound of a heavy iron bolt being pulled across the outside of the door jarred on my ears. The cell contained a long wooden bed, a long table, and two benches. I did not know the former "Manchukuo" officers who were in the cell with me at all well, and I did not talk to them, so I did not know whether they too were frightened or whether they were inhibited by my presence. They stood to one side with their heads lowered and did not make a sound. Then I heard the bolt being pulled. The door opened and a warder came in to take me to another cell, where I was surprised to meet my three nephews, my brother Pu Chieh and my father-in-law Jung Yuan. So we were to be allowed to stay together. They had just been issued with new quilts, mattresses, and washing kit, and they had brought a set for me.

I was reassured by what Jung Yuan told me. "This is a military prison, and everyone here wears army uniform. It doesn't look as though we are . . . in danger for the moment as otherwise they wouldn't have given us towels and tooth-brushes. When we were searched just now they kept our valuables but gave us receipts for them, which isn't like the way . . . ordinary criminals are treated. And the food isn't bad."

"Perhaps the good food is an execution banquet," suggested my nephew Little Ku bluntly.

"No. That sort of meal includes wine and there wasn't any wine here. Let's see if the next meal is as good. If it is, then we know that it's not what you think: I've never heard of a condemned man being given several banquets."

I began to believe my father-in-law the next day, not because the food was still as good but because some army doctors gave me a physical examination. They were very thorough, asking me what illnesses I had previously suffered from, what I normally ate, and what I could not eat. They gave me a pair of new black trousers, a coat, white underclothes, and, what was even more surprising, cigarettes. This was certainly not the way that condemned men were treated.

A few days later a short, squat man of about forty came into our cell. He asked each of us our names, what books we had read in the Soviet Union, and whether we had been sleeping well for the past few nights. When he had heard our answers he nodded and said, "Good. You will be given books and newspapers at once to do some serious studying." They came a few hours later, along with some board games and playing-cards. From that day on we listened to the radio twice a day, once to the news and once to music. We were allowed to walk in the yard for half an hour every afternoon. The first time we went out for a walk Little Ku told us that he had heard that the man who had told us to "do some serious studying" was the governor of this prison for war criminals. We later learnt that the man who had brought us the books was a section head named Li.

In those days we called all the prison staff "Mister" as we knew no other way to address them. Mr. Li brought us three books: *On New Democracy, A History of Modern China,* and *The History of the New-Democratic Revolution.* He said that as there were not enough books at the moment we would either have to take it in turns to read them or have them read aloud for everyone to hear. Many of the terms used in these books were strange to me, but the strangest thing of all was asking us prisoners to read books.

The first of us to take an interest in them was Little Ku. He read them faster than anyone else and immediately asked the rest of us to help him with his problems. When we could not help he asked the prison staff. Jung Yuan mocked him: "Don't think this is a school — it's a prison." "Didn't the governor tell us to study?" asked Little Ku. "Whether you study or not this is a prison," replied Jung Yuan. "It always has been a prison and it still is one, books or no books." Pu Chieh said that he had heard of prisoners being given books to read in Japanese jails, but never of a "civilized prison" like this in China. Jung Yuan shook his head. "A prison is a prison whether it is civilized or not. You would do better to recite Buddhist scriptures than learn that stuff." Little Ku was going to argue with him, but Jung Yuan shut his eyes and started intoning scriptures in a low voice.

When we came in from our exercise that afternoon Little Ku passed on a piece of news that he had heard. Someone had tried to give his warder a watch, and had been told off for it. This started some of the younger men talking. Hadn't the hot water for our last baths been brought by the warders, asked Little Hsiu. "I've never heard of warders carrying water for prisoners before." Little Jui said that the warders here were not at all like the traditional idea of warders: they did not curse or beat us. Jung Yuan, who had finished prayer as a preparation for his supper, murmured:

"You youngsters are too inexperienced; you're making a big fuss over nothing. The fellow who tried to give the watch probably did it when someone else was looking. How could the warder possibly accept it then? Just because they don't curse or beat you, you imagine that they don't hate us. Just you see, we'll get our punishment later."

"Is bringing us our bathwater a punishment?" retorted Little Ku.

"Say what you like," murmured Jung Yuan, "the Communists can't like us." He felt in his pocket. "I left my cigarettes on the windowsill outside," he said angrily. "What a pity, it was the last packet I had left from Shenyang." He opened a packet of low-grade cigarettes he had been issued with and grumbled, "The warders here nearly all smoke. I've made them a present of that packet for nothing."

Just when he had finished saying this the cell door opened and in came a warder named Wang with something in his hand. "Has anyone in this room lost some cigarettes?" he asked. We all saw that what he was holding was Jung Yuan's packet of cigarettes from Shenyang.

Jung Yuan took the cigarettes and thanked him profusely. When he had gone he lit up one of them, and after smoking it quietly for a while he struck his thigh as if he had suddenly seen the light. "These warders must have been specially picked. Of course they could choose some comparatively civilized ones to outwit us."

We were all silent, awed by Jung Yuan's judgement of experience.

A few days later Jung Yuan's explanation was made to look very unconvincing. Pu Chieh was impatient to see the day's paper after our exercise one afternoon. He told us with excitement that he had heard there was an article in it which revealed why New China wanted us to study. We crowded round him, eager to see the article. He read it out to us, and it included a passage which said that as New China needed talent of all sorts it was necessary to train and select large numbers of new cadres. He had heard that in the opinion of the other cells the government was letting us study and giving us favourable treatment because it intended to use us to help make up for the lack of talent in New China. Ridiculous as it sounds today, we were nearly all convinced that this was the case. Only Jung Yuan expressed his doubts.

We began to study seriously. Previously all of us except Little Ku had found the books uninteresting and had only read them for the sake of the warders in the passage. But even now our study only amounted to learning the new terms. Jung Yuan, of course, did not take part, and recited his scriptures with his eyes closed while the rest of us studied.

My blind optimism did not last long. Soon afterwards the prison authorities reorganized the cells and separated me from my family.

Separated from My Family

Why was I separated from my family? It took me a long time to realize that this was a most important step in my remoulding. When it happened I thought that it was because the Communist Party was implacably hostile towards me, and reckoned that they intended to question the members of my household about my past activities so that they could condemn me later.

While in the Soviet Union I had said that all my traitorous actions were carried out under compulsion, completely concealing my collaboration with the Japanese imperialists and my attempts to win their favour. My relations had helped me in this and covered up for me. Now that we had returned to China I needed them to keep my secrets more than ever. I felt that I had to keep a good eye on them and make sure that they did not let slip any careless words. I had to be particularly careful with Little Hsiu.

During the first day at Fushun I had noticed that Little Hsiu's attitude had changed as a result of the incident on the train. I had felt an insect crawling up my neck and asked him to look at it. In the past he would have come at once, but this time he pretended not to hear and did not move. On top of this, when Little Jui came and took the caterpillar off my neck and threw it on the floor, Little Hsiu snorted and said, "He's still saving life, saving that insect so that it can harm someone else." I felt weak all over.

When Little Jui was folding my bedding for me a few days later I asked him to shake out my quilt. This was an unpopular thing to do as it made the atmosphere in the cell unpleasant. Little Hsiu grabbed the quilt and threw it down on my bed. "You two aren't the only people in this room," he said. "Your lack of consideration for others won't do at all." "What do you mean by 'you' and 'us'?" I asked. "Have you no sense of manners?" He turned away without answering, sat down by the table and started writing, his lips pursed. I went over to look, but he snatched the paper away and tore it up, only leaving me time to see the words "we shall see".

I bitterly regretted what I had done on the train. Ever since then I had done my utmost to be friendly to him, and had even explained that I had meant no harm by it and had always been very fond of him. I took every opportunity to explain to my three nephews that the principles governing human relationships could not be cast aside, and that in times of difficulties it was essential that we should be loyal to each other and stand together. When Little Hsiu was not present I warned the others to be very careful with him, to make sure he did not do anything wrong, and to try and win him over.

As a result of our efforts Little Hsiu did nothing dangerous and I felt that there could be nothing wrong with him after all. But just when I had stopped worrying about him a warder told me to move to another cell.

The others packed for me and moved my bedding and case to the other cell. When they went away, I was left by myself amid a crowd of strangers. I felt so awkward that I did not know whether to sit or stand, and the eight people who were already in the cell were clearly inhibited by my arrival and said nothing. After a while, probably as a result of some agreement, my bedding was put on a bed by the wall. Later I realized that this was a good place as it was near the heating in winter, while being cool in summer because it was by the window. But at the time I was too worried about the dangers involved in separation from my family to notice this or their respectful expressions. I sat down, but the wooden bed seemed extraordinarily hard, so I got up and started walking to and fro. Then I had an idea and went and knocked on the cell door.

"What is it?" asked the stocky warder as he opened the door.

"May I ask, sir, if I can have a talk with the governor?"

"What about?"

"I want to explain that I have never been separated from my relations before, and I'm not at all used to it."

He nodded and told me to wait. Soon afterwards he came back to tell me that the governor had given permission for me to move back. I was delighted, and gathered up my bedding while the warder took my suitcase. In the corridor I met the governor.

"Out of consideration for you older men the authorities have decided to give you food of a higher standard," the governor said. "We thought that if you were living with your relations but eating different food it might have a bad effect on them, so we. . . ."

I saw what he was getting at, so without waiting for him to finish I interrupted, "That doesn't matter. I can guarantee that it won't have any bad effect on them." I almost added, "They have always had to be used to that."

The governor smiled. "Your ideas are too simple. Have you never thought that you must learn to look after yourself?"

"Yes, yes. But I should learn gradually, step by step."

"Very well," said the governor with a nod, "start learning then."

When I went back to my old cell I felt that I had been away for a year. They were all pleased to see me, and I told them what the governor had said about learning to look after myself. Everyone was happy to infer from this that the government was in no hurry to deal with us.

They did not let me practise looking after myself, and I had no inclination at all to do so. I was preoccupied with the governor's implication that we would be separated later and was trying to think of some way of preventing it. But ten days later, before I had found a solution to this problem, a warder told me to pack.

While Little Jui got my things together I took the chance to give some instructions to my relations. I could not do this by word of mouth for fear that the warder would hear, so I wrote a note for Pu Chieh to pass round to the others. As there were two outsiders in the cell, former officials in the puppet government of Wang Ching-wei, I had to be rather vague. I wrote that we had got along well, that they should continue to be loyal and stand together after I had gone, and that I felt a deep concern for each of them. I hoped that they would understand that what I really meant was that they should watch their words.

My nephews carried my baggage and took me along to the cell I had been moved to the previous time. Here I was given the same good bed, and once more I could not sit still. I paced up and down, then knocked on the door again.

The same squat warder opened it. I knew now that he was called Liu, and felt friendly towards him because he had brought us some extra *baozi* (steamed dumplings with minced meat filling) when he saw how much we enjoyed them when we ate them for the first time a few days previously.

"Mr. Liu, there's something. . . ."

"Do you want to see the governor?"

"I wanted to discuss it with you first. I . . . I. . . ."

"Aren't you used to it yet?" He laughed, and I seemed to hear other people laughing behind me. Blushing, I tried to explain.

"It's not that I want to move back again, but I wonder if I could be allowed to see my family members once a day. I would feel much happier if I could do this."

"Won't you be able to see them when you take exercise in the yard? There's no problem."

"I'd like to be able to talk to them. Would the governor give permission?" There was a rule then that people in different cells were not allowed to talk to each other.

"I'll ask for you."

Permission was granted, and from then on I was able to talk to the members of my family every day. Some of my nephews told me what happened in their cell and what the authorities had said to them. Little Ku still seemed not to be worried, Little Hsiu was the same as before, and Little Jui continued to wash my clothes and mend my socks for me.

With one worry off my chest new problems arose. For the past forty years I had never folded my own quilt, made my own bed, or poured out my washing water. I had never even washed my own feet or tied my shoes. I had never touched a rice-ladle, a knife, a pair of scissors, or a needle and thread; so now that I had to look after myself I was in a very difficult position. When other people were already washing in the morning I would only just have got into my clothes. When I was getting ready to wash someone would remind me that I should first fold my quilt; and by the time I had rolled up my quilt into an untidy bundle everyone would have finished washing. When I put my tooth-brush into my mouth I would find that there was no tooth-powder on it, and when I had finished cleaning my teeth the others would be almost through with their breakfast. So it went on all day.

Being slower than the others was not nearly as bad as having people laughing at me behind my back. My cellmates were all former "Manchukuo" officers who would never have dared to raise their heads in my presence in the old days; when I first came into the cell they did not venture to address me as "you", so they either called me "sir" or else showed their respect by using no word of address to me. But now I found their sniggers very hard to bear.

But this was not the worst thing. On our first day in Fushun a rota of duties had been made for each cell by which everyone took it in turn to sweep the floor, wipe the table and empty the chamber-pot. I had never had to do any of this when I was in my old cell, but the problem that faced me now was what to do when my turn came. Was I to empty the chamber-pot for others? I felt worse about this than I had about the secret agreement between "Manchukuo" and Japan: I thought that I would be humiliating my ancestors and disgracing the younger members of my clan. Fortunately a member of the prison staff came the next day to say that I was ill and could not take my turn. I was as happy as if I had been saved from certain death, and felt grateful for the first time in my life.

With this danger past another cropped up. The governor appeared as usual when we were taking our afternoon exercise in the yard. He always talked to one of us prisoners while we took our exercise, and this time he seemed to have picked on me. He looked me up and down, and must have seen that I was terrified.

"Pu Yi," he called. I had never been addressed by my personal name before my return to China and was still not at all used to it. I preferred people to call me by my number (981) as the warders had done when we first arrived at Fushun.

"Yes, governor," I said as I went over to him.

"You were issued with the same clothes as the others, so why don't you look like them?" he asked quietly in a friendly voice.

I looked down at my clothes and then looked at the others. Their clothes were neat and clean, whereas mine were creased and filthy. One of my pockets was half torn off; my jacket was missing a button; there was an ink-stain on my knee; my trouser-legs seemed to be different lengths; and my shoes had only one and a half laces between them.

"I'll tidy myself up," I murmured. "When I go back I'll repair my pocket and sew a new button on."

"How did your clothes get so creased?" he asked with a trace of a smile. "You should notice how others do things. If you are able to learn from the good points of others, you will be able to make progress."

Although the governor had spoken very kindly I was furious. This was the first time that my incompetence had been pointed out publicly, and it was the first time I had been in the public eye not as an image of majesty but as "rubbish". I turned away from the gaze of my former "ministers" and "generals", wishing that night would fall. "They want to use me as a specimen for everyone to study," I thought in my misery. I looked at the high, grey wall. All my life I had been surrounded by walls, but in the past I had been treated with respect and enjoyed a special position within them, even in Changchun. But within these walls all that was gone. I was treated the same as anybody else, and even had difficulty in surviving. I was miserable not because of my incompetence but because others regarded me as incompetent, and because I had lost my natural right to have others wait on me. The gratitude I had felt for being let off the cell chores had completely vanished.

That night I discovered that when the others undressed for bed they folded their clothes neatly and put them under their pillows, while I just dropped them in a heap at my feet as I took them off. The governor's remarks seemed to have some sense in them. If I had known about learning from the good points of others I would not have got into the wretched situation I was in now. Why had my fellow prisoners not told me before? What treachery.

In fact those former puppet officers were still too inhibited by my arrogant manner to point any of this out to me.

We spent two months in Fushun, then at the end of October we all moved to Harbin.

Move to Harbin

Some of the younger men among us felt like chatting on the train to Harbin and were willing to play cards with the warders, while the rest of us said little and spoke very quietly when we did. The atmosphere in the carriage was gloomy most of the time, and quite a few of us could not sleep at night or eat during the day. Although I was not as terrified as I had been when I first returned to China, I was still more worried than any of the others. It was soon after the entry of the Chinese People's Volunteers into Korea, and U.S. forces were close to the Yalu River. One night I and Pu Chieh had been unable to sleep, and I had quietly asked what he thought of the military situation. He answered in a flat voice, "Entering the war is asking for trouble. We'll be finished in no time." I took this as meaning that China would be defeated and the U.S. troops would occupy at least the Northeast; and also that the Communists might finish our group off to prevent us from falling into their hands. I later found out that this was what all we prisoners thought then.

My despair deepened when I saw the jail in Harbin. It was a former "Manchukuo" prison, and the sight of it made me realize what it meant to be paid back in one's own coin. It had been designed by the Japanese specially for imprisoning people who had been found guilty of "anti-Manchukuo and anti-Japanese activities". It consisted of two fan-shaped two-storeyed cell-blocks round a watch-tower in the centre. There was a grille of iron bars an inch thick in front of and behind the cells, which were separated from each other by concrete walls and could hold seven or eight men each. My cell was comparatively uncrowded with only five of us in it, but as it was designed in the Japanese manner we had to sleep on mats on the floor. I spent about two years here, and I have heard that it was later demolished. Although I did not know when I first came that very few of those who had been incarcerated here during the "Manchukuo" period had survived the experience, the sound of the iron gates being opened or closed was more than enough for me. This noise always made me think of torture and the firing squad.

We were treated as we had been in Fushun. The warders were as kind, the food was as good, and the papers, broadcasts, and recreations continued as before. This reassured me to a certain extent, but it could not calm me completely. I remember how the mournful sound of a practice air-raid warning went on and on in my head one night long after it had really stopped. Before I believed that the Chinese and Korean people's forces were really winning victories in Korea I was convinced that even if the Chinese did not kill me, I would die in an American air raid. I was sure that whatever happened China would be defeated and I would die.

I remember clearly that none of us believed the newspaper reports of the first victory of the Chinese People's Volunteers on the

Korean front; and we were very suspicious of the news that in the second successful campaign the Chinese and Korean people's forces had driven the Americans back to near the 38th Parallel. Some time after New Year 1951 one of the administrative cadres read out the announcement that the Chinese and Korean troops had taken Seoul, and clapping burst out from all the cells. Even then I only half believed it. When the "Regulations for the Punishment of Counter-Revolutionaries" were announced in the press that February the prison authorities stopped us from reading the papers for fear that we would be alarmed. We did not know this and thought that the reason must be defeats in Korea. We were more suspicious than ever of the earlier victories, and I was convinced that my doom was at hand.

I was woken up in the middle of one night by iron gates opening and I saw some people taking one of the prisoners out of the next cell. I started to shake all over, convinced that the U.S. forces were approaching Harbin and that the Communists were going to get rid of us at last. After a wretched night I found the next morning that I was completely wrong. In fact one of the men in the next cell had been having trouble with a hernia, and the warder had reported this to the governor, who had brought an army doctor and nurses along to examine the invalid. I had seen them taking him to hospital, but I had been so terrified that I had seen only their army trousers and failed to notice their white coats.

But this did not bring me much relief. I still thought that every motor vehicle I heard was coming to take me to a public trial. All day I watched and listened to everything that went on outside the bars, and I often had nightmares at night. My cellmates were not in a much better state than I was. Their appetites, like mine, were shrinking and their morale sinking. Every time we heard a noise on the stairs we would all turn our heads to look, and at the appearance of a stranger a silence would fall over the cells as if we were all facing our last judgement. When we were all in the depths of despair we were given new hope by a talk a security chief gave us on behalf of the government.

The security chief stood in front of the watch-tower and addressed all the cells for about an hour. He told us that the government had no intention of killing us, but wanted us to examine ourselves and study, and thus remould ourselves. He said that the Communist Party and the People's Government believed that under the people's political power the majority of criminals could remould themselves into new men. He said that the ideal of Communism was to remake the world, and that to do this it was first necessary to remould humanity. When he had finished, the governor spoke. I remember that his speech included a passage that went something like this:

"You are only thinking of death, and imagine that everything is a part of the preparations for your death. Why don't you ask yourselves this: why is the People's Government making you study if it plans to kill you?

"You have a lot of strange ideas about the Korean War. Perhaps some of you think that the People's Volunteers cannot possibly beat the American forces and that the Americans are bound to invade the Northeast, so you are worried that the Communists will kill you first. Some of you may have a blind belief in the might of the U.S.A., and believe that it is invincible. Let me assure you, the Chinese and Korean peoples are certainly capable of defeating U.S. imperialism, and the Chinese Communist Party's policy of remoulding criminals will definitely succeed. Facts have proved that the Communist Party never makes empty claims.

"Perhaps you will say that if we are not going to kill you, it would be a good idea to let you go. No, it wouldn't. If we were to release you before you had been remoulded, you might commit other crimes. Anyhow, the people would not approve and would not forgive you when they saw you. So you must study properly and remould yourselves."

Although I did not understand or believe all of this speech, I did see that there was some justification for claiming that the government did not want to kill us. This was the only possible explanation of why they had extended our bath-house in Fushun, saved the life of the invalid, and given special food to the older men among us.

Later I found out that such things were nothing unusual in the prisons of New China, but at the time they seemed all very strange to us, and we regarded them as marks of special consideration. So when we heard these government officials telling us formally that the government did not want to eliminate us we felt much more relieved at once.

None of us paid much attention to the references to studying and remoulding. I thought that we were given books and papers to pass away our time and keep us from wild thoughts. It seemed absurd to me that reading a few books could change one's thinking. I was even less prepared to believe that the American armed forces could be beaten. The four ex-officers in my cell, who regarded themselves as military experts, maintained unanimously that even if America did not have the nerve to flout world opinion and use atom bombs, she could still dominate the globe with her conventional weapons; her power was unrivalled, and it was nonsense to say that she could be defeated. Later we realized that the Communists were not the sort of people to talk nonsense, and before long we began to notice that the news about Korea did not seem to be faked. My military cellmates told me that while the casualty figures for both sides could be fabricated, it was very hard to keep up lies about territory won or lost. The news that the American commander was willing to hold talks would have been even harder to invent. If the American troops were willing to discuss a ceasefire, how could they be invincible? The ex-officers were mystified, and I was too.

The development of the Korean War showed how wrong our original expectations had been, and proved that America was not a real tiger but a paper one. I now felt much calmer, for if the Communists were not being defeated they would not be in such a hurry to get rid of me.

Our studies, which had previously been haphazard, were now directed by a cadre from the prison authorities. He gave us a talk on feudal society and then let us discuss it. We all had to write notes.

One day this cadre said to us: "I have already said that before you can reform your thought you have to understand what kind of ideology you already have. Your ideology is inseparable from your personal background and history, so you must start by examining them. For the sake of your thought reform, each of you must write an autobiography."

This sounded to me like a trick to make me write a confession. Were the Communists going to finish us off even though the military situation had been stabilized?

Writing My Autobiography and Presenting My Seals

I regarded writing my autobiography as the prelude to my trial and was determined that I would make the most of this chance to save my life. I knew what line I would take. When we had climbed out of the lorries and were about to enter the Harbin prison Little Ku had whispered in my ear, "If they ask any questions, we'll stick to the story we used in the Soviet Union." I had nodded.

This story covered up my collaboration and represented me as a good, innocent patriot. I realized that I would have to be more careful here than in the Soviet Union and not leave a single loophole in it.

Little Ku had spoken on behalf of all my nephews and my personal attendant Big Li. It meant that they were prepared and were as loyal to me as ever. But loyalty would not be enough to prevent loopholes; I had to give more instructions to them all and to Big Li in particular, as he was the witness of a key part of my story — how I had gone from Tientsin to the Northeast.

I could only talk to him during the rest periods when I was allowed to see members of my family. The younger criminals, including all the members of my household (except Jung Yuan who was dead by now and my "imperial physician" Dr. Huang who was ill) had now started doing such jobs as carrying water, serving food and helping in the kitchen. It was not so easy for me to see them as it had been. But this new development had its advantages in that they could move fairly freely and pass messages for me. I sent for Big Li and reminded him to say that he knew nothing about how I had left Tientsin, and that he had only packed my things on Hu Sze-yuan's instructions after I had gone. Big Li nodded to show that he had understood and went away.

The next day Little Jui passed on a message to me from Big Li. Yesterday evening he had been talking to Section Head Chia of the prison staff and had told him that in the Northeast I had treated those under me with great kindness and had never cursed or beaten anyone; and that when in Lushun I had locked my door and refused to see the Japanese. This alarmed me: why had he mentioned Lushun? I asked Little Jui to tell him not to say too much, and to pretend he knew nothing about what had happened in Lushun.

Having satisfied myself of Big Li's loyalty and given instructions to my nephews I started writing my autobiography. I described my family background and my childhood in the Forbidden City. I said that I had been forced to go to the Japanese Legation and maintained that I had stayed out of politics while in Tientsin; I kept up the fiction that I had been kidnapped and led a wretched existence in Changchun. I ended by saying:

> When I saw the suffering of the people but could do nothing about it I was overwhelmed with grief. I wished that Chinese troops would fight their way into the Northeast, and longed for some international development that could bring about its liberation, a hope that was finally realized in 1945.

After careful revision I wrote out a fair copy and handed it in. I believed it would convince any reader that I had thoroughly repented.

After handing in the autobiography I tried to think of some other way of convincing the government of my "sincerity" and "progress". Clearly it was not enough to have Big Li and the others praising me. I needed some practical achievements. But my achievements since starting to take my turn on prison chores did not even satisfy me, let alone the prison authorities.

After hearing the speeches of the head of the security organization and the prison governor we were nearly all trying to think of ways to show how we had raised our "political consciousness" in the hope that we could save our lives this way. It seems laughable now, but we thought then that efficient hypocrisy would fool the government. My great sorrow during the time I was under this illusion was that I could not make as good a showing as the others.

We all tried to win the confidence of the prison administration through our study, our chores, and our daily life. The member of our group whose "achievements" in study were most outstanding was our group leader, Old Wang, a former "Manchukuo" major-general who had studied law for some years in Peking. As the most educated man among us he picked up the new theoretical terms fast. The other three ex-officers, like myself, found it hard to sort out the difference between "subjective" and "objective", but they made more "progress" than I did. They always had something to say in the discussions. The worst thing was that we each had to write an essay explaining in our own words what we had learnt about the nature of feudal society. I could manage to say something in the discussions, but writing the essay was more difficult. I did not see much point in study, and I was frightened by the explanations of feudalism I read in books. If, for example, the emperor was the chief landlord, then I was doomed because of this as well as for my betrayal of the nation. This thought so terrified me that I had difficulty in writing a single word. When I eventually put a piece together by cribbing passages from here and there I saw that it was not as good as those of the others. My achievements in study were clearly not going to satisfy the authorities.

The only evidence I had given of progress was to take my turn on the rota of cell duties after the move to Harbin. This was made easier because there were water closets in the corner of every cell so that there was no question of emptying chamber-pots. The work was light enough, consisting only of receiving the three meals and the hot water that were sent over every day and wiping the floor mats. This was the first time I had ever served others, and things went wrong when I spilt some vegetable soup on somebody's head. From then on one of the others would always help me when my turn came round, partly from kindness and partly to avoid another scalding.

My clothes were as untidy as ever, and Little Jui continued to wash and mend them for me. This embarrassed me, but when I had tried to do my own washing after the governor spoke to me in Fushun I had soaked myself in water without mastering the art of using soap and wash-board. Soon after handing in my autobiography I resolved to make a second attempt to do my own washing to prevent the authorities from despairing of me. I washed a white shirt, but when it was dry it looked more like a water-colour than anything else, and Little Jui took it away, whispering to me that this was not a thing for "Above" to do. I agreed with him, racking my brains for some other way to impress the authorities.

As I paced up and down thinking, I heard one of my brothers-in-law, Old Wan, and some of his cellmates talking about the donations that were being made by all sections of the Chinese people to buy aircraft and heavy artillery for the Korean War. We were not allowed to talk to prisoners in different cells, but there was nothing to stop us listening to their conversation. One of them was a former "Manchukuo" minister whose son had repudiated him and was now, he thought, fighting in Korea. He said that if his property had not been confiscated he would like to contribute it for Korea. The others laughed at him for thinking that he might still have his property or that his son might be allowed to fight; then one of them said that the only ones among us whose property was really worth anything were the emperor and the former premier.

This woke me up. It was true that I had far more jewellery than any of the others. Apart from the things hidden in the bottom of a suitcase I had some very valuable items that I had not concealed, including a priceless set of three seals exquisitely carved out of three interlocking pieces that had been made for Chien Lung after he retired from the throne. I decided to hand these over as a proof of my "political consciousness".

Some of the prisoners had tried to join the Chinese People's Volunteers to fight in Korea. When their requests were refused I was jealous of the way they had shown their "political consciousness" at no serious risk to themselves. I was not going to lag behind. By a piece of luck a government official was making a tour of inspection that day, and when I saw him coming I recognized him as the man who had told me not to worry in Shenyang. I could see from the manner of the prison governor, who was accompanying him, that this man was his senior. I thought that it would be more effective to make my offering to this high official. When he entered our cell I bowed low and said: "I beg to announce, sir, that I wish to present this object of mine to the People's Government."

He did not take it, but nodded and said, "Aren't you Pu Yi? You'd better discuss this with the prison authorities." He asked a few other questions and went. I told myself that if he had taken a good look at my seals he would not have been so casual about them. I wrote a letter to the prison authorities and handed it over to Warder Liu together with the seals.

I heard nothing more about the seals for many days and began to suspect that the warder had stolen them. One evening when the others were playing chess or cards I was brooding over the seals, convinced that my suspicions were well founded. Just then the stocky Warder Liu stopped outside the cell and asked me why I was not playing cards like the others. When I told him that I could not, which was true, he went off to fetch a pack, then he sat on the other side of the bars and shuffled it. I, meanwhile, was hating him.

"I'm sure you can learn to play," he said as he dealt. "Besides, when you become a new man and start a new life, you won't have much fun if you can't enjoy yourself."

I was amazed at his duplicity. When another warder, who was devoted to his pipe, came along and gave one of my cellmates some of his own tobacco to roll a cigarette, I was convinced that all the warders were trying to deceive us. But I was not going to be taken in.

In fact, of course, the one who was trying to fool others was myself. Soon afterwards the governor said to me in the prison yard:

"I have seen your letter and the seals. We have also got the things you presented in the Soviet Union. But what matters to the people is men, remoulded men."

Changes in My Household

I did not understand the implication of what the governor said until many years later. At the time I just took it as proving that I must be in no danger for the moment if they wanted me to reform. But just when I was not expecting it, danger came.

One day one of the side-pieces of my spectacles came loose and I asked the warder to take them to Big Li to be repaired. Big Li was skilful at repairing delicate things like spectacles, watches and fountain pens. He often mended them for people, and he had always done my glasses before. This time was different.

In that prison one could hear upstairs what was happening downstairs and *vice versa*. Soon after the warder had gone I could hear Big Li grumbling indistinctly, and I did not like the sound of it. A moment later the warder came back and asked if I could think of some way of doing it myself as Big Li said that he was unable to mend them. I was furious at Big Li's effrontery. "If I could repair them myself I wouldn't have asked him to do it," I replied. "Please speak to him again, Mr. Chiang." Warder Chiang was young, slim and silent, and all my cellmates said that he was a decent fellow. He must have been, because he did as I asked and went down again.

This time Big Li did not refuse and mended them. But he did a rough job, only tying the spectacles together with a thread. The original screw seemed to have disappeared.

I thought the matter over carefully and decided that Big Li had changed. I remembered that a few days ago I had sent Little Jui to fetch him as I had not seen him for some time. Little Jui had come back to tell me, "Big Li says that he's busy and hasn't got time." I could now imagine that he must have said something like, "I haven't got time to be always at his beck and call."

Soon after the affair of the broken spectacles came the new year of 1952. We were allowed to have a New Year party, and we put on a little show, using the empty ground in front of the watchtower as our stage. One of the acts gave me a warning of disaster.

Little Hsiu, Little Ku and Big Li had written a recitation in dialogue form, and all the men in their cell except Little Jui came on to perform it. They poked fun at the unpopular behaviour of some of the prisoners, such as the former "Manchukuo" minister of justice Chang Huan-hsiang, known as "Big Mouth". Big Mouth had a foul temper. He would disturb all his neighbours when he was quarrelling, and when he was once told that he was dropping rice on the floor he deliberately spilt even more. The satirists then directed their fire at the prisoners who read at the tops of their voices when they saw a warder come past.

I had found all this as funny as the rest of the audience, but then the superstitious prisoners came under attack. The performers jibed that these people did not realize that their divinations and prayers had not saved them before, and were still secretly praying. The targets of this attack clearly included me, as I still recited spells and prayed sometimes. While I was prepared to admit that there was truth in their claim that prayers had done me no good, it was quite intolerable that I should be publicly satirized. This was gross disrespect.

That was not the end of it. The next victim was the type of man who was put in a jail where he learnt what was right and was treated as a human being by the government, but "still acts as the slave of another". Obediently serving that certain "other person" would not help him to reform and would only make the other go on behaving as if he were the lord and master. It was only too clear to me who was being attacked and who was the "other person". I now understood why Little Jui had not taken part in the performance; I felt sorry for him, and was worried that he would not be able to hold out.

In fact, Little Jui had changed as well. Big Li, Little Hsiu and Little Ku had not appeared in the courtyard for some time, and I rarely saw Little Jui, so that my dirty clothes had piled up for days. After the New Year party he did not come for my washing any more, and it was not long before there was another major development.

On a day when it was my turn to do the cell chores, I was squatting by the bars waiting for the food to arrive when Little Jui brought it along. When he had handed it all to me he put a little ball of paper into my hand. I was astonished, but I quickly hid it and turned round to hand out the food, trying hard to act naturally. After the meal I retired to the lavatory that was behind a low wall in the corner of the cell and unfolded the note.

> We are all guilty and should confess everything to the government. Have you yet reported the things I hid for you in the bottom of a case? If you take the initiative and hand them over the government will certainly treat you leniently.

Rage welled up within me, but a moment later it gave way to the chilly realization that my subjects were rebelling and my family deserting me. I flushed the note down the lavatory and reflected that these young people had changed. This was beyond my comprehension.

Big Li's father had been a servant of Tzu Hsi's in the Summer Palace, and it was because of this that Big Li had been able to get a job as a page in the Forbidden City after the expulsion of the eunuchs. He was then fourteen. He had followed me to Tientsin, where he studied with some other pages of mine under a teacher of Chinese. He was made a personal attendant of mine, and I regarded him as one of the most reliable of my servants. I chose him to accompany me when I left Talitzukou in my attempt to flee to Japan in 1945, and when we were in the Soviet Union he had once punched a Japanese for not getting out of my way. He had always been respectful and totally obedient to me, and had faithfully carried out my instructions to destroy some of my jewellery without leaving a trace of it. I could not think why such a man as this should have changed and lost his respect for his "superior".

Little Ku was the son of Pu Wei, the second Prince Kung. As the "Great Ching Emperor" I had allowed him to succeed to his father's title and had brought him up to be one of the mainstays of a future restoration. In the Soviet Union he had written poems to express his loyalty to me. My upbringing had made him a devout

Buddhist, and at one stage he spent whole days deep in "White Bone Meditation" before a picture of a skeleton. He had still shown loyalty to me even after our arrival in Harbin. That such a person should have written an attack on me made it clear that this loyalty had disappeared.

The most surprising change was that which had taken place in Little Jui. He came from a fallen princely family, and I had summoned him to Changchun when he was nineteen to study with the sons of other impoverished noble houses. I had regarded him as the most obedient and honest of the court students. He seemed less gifted than the others, but he served me better than his cleverer companions. He showed his loyalty to me throughout our five years in the Soviet Union. I once tested him by asking if he had ever had a disloyal thought, and he confessed that he had once felt that he had been wronged when I made him kneel on the ground for an hour as a punishment. When I told him that I would pardon him he kotowed to me, looking as happy as if he had just gone from hell to paradise. Just before my return to China I nominated him as my "successor" in the event of my death, and his joy at this can be imagined. From then on he did everything for me. But now he of all people was trying to teach me that I was guilty.

If I had been more observant I would have noticed some warning signs of these inconceivable changes. At the New Year party Little Ku had recited a ballad to the accompaniment of clappers describing the way that their thinking had changed. In this he described how having been brought up from childhood in "Manchukuo" they had been indoctrinated with reactionary propaganda. They had been taught to believe that Japan was the most powerful nation on earth; that the Chinese common people were incapable and needed to be governed; that it was natural for men to be divided into different grades; and so on. Their return to China had shown them that these were all lies. On their first day back they had been astonished to see that their engine-driver was Chinese, and similar discoveries had followed almost every day. What had most surprised them had been the attitude of the prison authorities and the victories in the Korean War.

At the time I had thought of this ballad as no more than a curtain-raiser and had paid no attention to it. I was unable to understand that Little Ku was explaining why they had rebelled: they now saw that I had been deceiving them.

I understood least of all that in their contacts with the prison staff since being separated from me they had all been deeply struck by the change in their status. Although they were prisoners, they were treated as individuals with their own characters, whereas before they had been nobles in name but slaves in fact. Now they had heard about different kinds of young people from themselves — about Chao Kuei-lan who had lost a hand to save a factory, and about the exploits of the People's Volunteers in Korea. They had started to ask themselves why they had never heard about such people before. Why had they only known how to meditate and kotow? Why had they been expected to be grateful for curses and beatings while others had covered themselves with glory? Why had they been so ignorant while others had achieved so much?

Thoughts like these had made them change and started them studying seriously and telling the prison authorities all about their pasts.

After destroying the note I sat by the wall gloomily reflecting that the Communists were really dangerous if they could change my nephews and Big Li like that. My only consolation was that my brother and brothers-in-law were still acting normally. But my big worry remained: would Little Jui report on me to the authorities?

I did not know what to do. I had a total of 468 pieces of jewellery hidden in the bottom of the case: platinum, gold, diamonds, pearls and other gems that I had carefully chosen to keep me for the rest of my life. I was sure that without them I would be unable to support myself if I were ever released, as the idea of earning my own living had not occurred to me. If I were to hand them in after hiding them for so long it would prove that I had been deceiving the authorities. But if I did not hand them over, Little Jui was not the only one who knew about them, and the others were even more likely to give me away than he was. If that happened I would really be in a mess.

"If you hand them over voluntarily the government will treat you leniently." This sentence floated through my mind and then gradually disappeared. I thought that the words "Communists" and "lenient" were incompatible, despite the way I had been treated in jail and the accounts I had read in the papers of the lenient treatment of offenders exposed in the Five-Anti and Three-Anti movements.[1] Soon after the beginning of these movements I had read of the executions of some monstrously corrupt men. Later I had seen reports of the crimes of capitalists who had been guilty of stealing state property and economic secrets, of graft, and smuggling, and of tax evasion, and had compared them with my own record. I had my own interpretation of the motto, "The ringleaders will always be punished; those who were forced into cooperating will not be punished; and those who perform meritorious deeds will be rewarded." I thought that even if the accounts of leniency were true they could not possibly apply to me: I was a ringleader and therefore bound to be punished.

"If you confess you will be treated leniently." I smiled bitterly to myself. I was convinced that the moment I told the governor about the jewels he would be furious at having been deceived and punish me. He might even go on to find out if I had been engaged in any other kinds of deception. That, after all, was how I had treated those under me in the old days.

No, I could not confess. Surely Little Jui and the others would not be so heartless as to report me. I put the matter aside.

A week later it was again Little Jui's turn to bring food to our cell. I saw that his expression was very serious and that he was not looking at me at all. He stared at my case for a moment and then slipped off. I was worried. What was he up to? Less than two hours later he suddenly appeared again at the beginning of our study period. He paused outside the cell for a moment, looked at my case, and went off again.

---

[1] The Five-Anti (Wu Fan) movement was a campaign against bribery of government workers, tax evasion, theft of state property, cheating on government contracts, and stealing economic information from government sources. The Three-Anti (San Fan) movement was a campaign against corruption, waste and bureaucracy.

I was sure that he had gone to see the prison governor. Torn by worries, I decided to hand the jewels over voluntarily before he reported me.

I took the hand of Old Wang, the head of our group, and told him that I had something to confess to the government.

Confession and Leniency

"I am no good. The government has treated me so humanely, but I hid all these things in contravention of the prison rules, no, the law of the country. These things do not really belong to me, they belong to the people; I have understood this at last, which is why I have confessed and handed them over."

I was standing in the governor's office with my head bowed before him. My 468 pieces of jewellery lay gleaming on a table by the window. "Let them shine if I can save myself by handing them over, and if the policy of leniency applies to me," I thought.

The governor looked at me carefully and nodded. "Sit down." His tone of voice made me feel that I had grounds for hope. "Did you have much of a mental battle over this?"

I avoided mentioning Little Jui's note. "I was afraid that if I confessed I might not be leniently treated."

"Why?" asked the governor, with a smile on his lips. "Because you were an emperor?"

"Yes," I replied after a moment's hesitation.

"That is not surprising. As you have a peculiar history it is only natural that you should have some peculiar ideas. Let me repeat, then, that the Communist Party and the People's Government are as good as their word. They are lenient to those who confess, they lighten the sentences of those who reform, and reward those who distinguish themselves, irrespective of social status. It all depends on your conduct. You broke the prison regulations by failing to hand these things over at once and by hiding them for so long, but now that you have confessed and admitted your guilt this shows that you have repented. For this reason we shall not punish you."

He told the warder outside the door to fetch the member of the staff responsible for looking after valuables. When he came, the governor told him to take that pile of stuff and give me a receipt for it.

I was astonished. Leaping to my feet I protested: "No, I don't want a receipt. If the government will not confiscate them I want to donate them."

"No, we will look after them for you. Will you please check them through?" The governor got up and was about to go. "I have told you before that remoulded men are far more valuable to us."

I went back to my cell with the receipt. My cellmates were holding a discussion on *How China Became a Colony and a Semi-Colony*, a book we were studying, but when I came in they stopped talking about that and welcomed me with a warmth they had never shown before, congratulating me on my progress.

"Old Pu, we admire you." They had stopped calling me Mr. Pu and changed to this informal way of addressing me. When I had first heard this "Old Pu" I had not liked the sound of it, but today it made me feel good. "Old Pu, your action has shown me the way." "Old Pu, I had never realized you were so brave." "Old Pu, I must thank you for giving me more confidence in the policy of leniency to those who confess."

Here I should add that I was more untidy than ever now that I was washing and mending my own clothes. My cellmates' respect for me had decreased by at least half when they were calling me "Mr. Pu". Some of them had even been calling me "Rag Market" behind my back, and they often laughed at me for my incompetence in study. In contrast to all this, their present praises exhilarated me.

In the rest period that day I heard Old Yuan, the former "Manchukuo" ambassador to Japan, talking about what I had done. Old Yuan was a very intelligent fellow who could think of more in the twinkling of an eye than others do in a day. What he said gave me something to think about.

"Old Pu is a wise man, not a bit stupid. He was absolutely correct in seizing the initiative and admitting that he had those jewels. Of course, he could not have deceived the government, as the government has more information on us than you imagine. Remember the newspaper reports of the Three-Anti and Five-Anti movements. Millions of people gave information to the government. The government even knows about things you forgot years ago."

I realized that I could not get away with the lies I had told in my autobiography. If I were to admit to them, would I go scot-free as I had over the jewels? This would be a political, not an economic question, and I did not know whether it would be dealt with in the same way. The governor had said nothing about this. But then economic crimes were just as criminal as political ones, and the principles that the governor had spoken of should apply to them too.

I could not make up my mind. I started to look more carefully into the examples of leniency in the papers. The Three-Anti and Five-Anti movements were reaching their conclusion, and more and more cases were being dealt with, all of them leniently. I examined them with Old Wang, the former legal official, comparing what I read about with my own record and wondering whether the policy of leniency would help me.

When the government was preparing to deal with the cases of the Japanese war criminals the prison authorities told us to write down what we knew about the crimes of the Japanese in the Northeast. One of the prisoners asked if we were allowed to write about others besides the Japanese. He was told that this was, of course, permissible, but that we should concentrate on the crimes of the Japanese. This worried me. Who else did he want to write about? "Others" clearly referred to Chinese, and the biggest Chinese criminal was undoubtedly myself. Would any of the members of my family write about "others"?

The "Manchukuo" war criminals wrote about the crimes of the Japanese with great enthusiasm. Our group wrote several dozen accusations on the first day alone, and Old Wang said with satisfaction, "We haven't done badly, and I'm sure we can produce as much again tomorrow." "Who knows how much the people of the Northeast could write if they were asked to," put in somebody. "Of course the government will carry out investigations among them," replied Old Wang. "What do you think, Old Pu?" "I'm sure it will," I answered, "but I wonder whether it will ask about others besides the Japanese." "Some people will be bound to write about us even if they are not asked to. The common people hate us just as bitterly as they hate the Japanese."

Big Li brought us our supper that evening. He seemed to be in a very bad temper, putting the food on the floor and going away without waiting for me to take it from him. I remembered at once that he had helped me to get into the luggage compartment of the car when I had left the Quiet Garden.

We spent the next day too writing about the Japanese. As I did not know much I could only write a little, but Old Wang was still satisfied as the others had written a lot. "Just imagine," he said, "how much information the people of the Northeast will be able to give the government. As a former legal official I can tell you that if you have evidence you can get anyone to talk in the end. In the old days we used to think that the most difficult thing was to get evidence, but things are quite different for the People's Government, with the ordinary people all providing information." My heart turned over. I thought of the case I had read about of the man who had executed a leading Communist in 1935 and had recently been caught by the security authorities in his hiding place deep in the mountains. Probably the Communists had been keeping a file on him since 1935.

The next day, when I was writing my last report on the Japanese, I heard a voice on the stairs. I turned to look and saw a stranger near the watch-tower followed by the governor. I guessed that this must be someone from a higher body come to inspect. He looked at each cell in turn, and revealed no emotion as the governor told him the name of each prisoner. Although he was not in uniform I guessed from his stern expression that he must be a military man. He looked as though he was under fifty.

"What are you doing?" he asked me as he looked into our cell. I was surprised by the mildness of his voice and the hint of a smile on his face. I stood up and told him that I was writing about the crimes of the Japanese. He was interested. "What crimes do you know about?"

I told him about the slaughter of the labourers on the construction project, the story that Tung Chi-hsu had told me. Perhaps I imagined it, but the smile seemed to disappear from his face and his expression became very severe. I had not expected that the story would produce so strong a reaction.

"I was shocked by it at the time as I did not realize that the Japanese were so cruel."

"Why didn't you protest to them?"

"I. . . . I didn't dare."

"Because you were frightened?" Without waiting for my answer he went on to say, "Ugh! What disgusting things fear can do to a man." He was speaking calmly again.

"This was all my fault," I said in a low voice. "I must confess my guilt to the people; I could not atone for it even if I were to die ten thousand times."

"Don't put all the blame on yourself. You must take only your share of the responsibility and keep to the facts. You will not be able to evade the guilt that is yours, and you will not be held liable for the crimes of others."

I went on to say that I had been moved by the way the government had treated me, and that I recognized my great guilt and was determined to reform. I do not know whether the official was listening as he examined the cell and asked another prisoner to bring the tooth-mug for him to inspect. When I had finished he shook his head and said, "You must stick to the facts. If you really acknowledge your guilt and show repentance you will certainly be treated leniently. What the Communist Party says counts, and it attaches great importance to facts. The People's Government is responsible to the people. You must show that you are making progress by what you do, not just with your tongue. Try hard." He glanced at what I was writing and then went to the cell next door.

My heart was very heavy. As I looked through the pile of material I had just written, it seemed that only today had I realized how serious were the events described in them. From then on those severe eyes haunted me and his words echoed through my brain. I realized that I was up against an irresistible force, a force that would not rest until it had found out everything. This force had caught the executioner of 1935 although he had been hiding deep in the mountains, and I realized that it would make a full account of the crimes of the Japanese in the Northeast, and that the crimes of the big and little puppets in "Manchukuo" would be unable to escape its attention.

It was a Sunday, and as I was hanging my washing out to dry in the prison yard I saw Big Li, Little Jui and a member of the prison staff approaching from the distance. After standing by the flower beds for a while, the three parted. Little Jui walked over in my direction, but just when I was going to greet him, he went straight past without so much as a look in my direction. I suspected that he had done something irrevocable.

I went back to my cell and re-examined the items about the Three-Anti and Five-Anti movements in the old newspapers. Old Wang came over and said, "What are you doing? Studying the Five-Antis?"

"No." I put the papers down and announced my decision. "I have been thinking about some events of the past. Previously I did not see their true nature, but now I see that they were crimes. Do you think it would be all right if I included them in my study essay?"

"Of course." He lowered his voice and added, "Anyhow, the government has got so much material on us that it is much better to speak up."

I took up my pen. The general outline of my essay was that the feudalists and compradors were indispensable to imperialism in its aggression against China, and that I was a typical example. For the sake of their dreams of restoration the feudal forces had used me as their signboard and collaborated with the Japanese imperialists, while the Japanese had used me as a signboard when they turned the Northeast into their colony. I wrote out the details of my activities in Tientsin and of the relations that I and my clique had with the Japanese, including my meeting with Doihara.

Two days later Old Wang told me that the prison authorities had read my essay and thought that I had made great progress, for which my group ought to praise me.

"A piece of real evidence is worth more than ten thousand empty words," said Old Wang, the former legal official.

Making Boxes

At the end of 1952 we moved out of the barred building into a new and spacious block. Here there were new beds, tables and benches, as well as windows that let in plenty of light. As what the governor had said about "reform" seemed to be true, and as I had been praised instead of punished for writing that piece of personal history, I began to study seriously. In those days I thought that there was nothing more than reading involved in remoulding oneself, and imagined that once I had mastered the ideas in the books my remoulding would be complete. It never occurred to me that reading was not enough, or that reading alone would not enable me to understand the meaning of the books. In late 1950 and early 1951, for example, I had read *What Is Feudal Society?* but it was only in the spring of 1953 that a period of labour — making boxes — taught me what feudalism really meant.

The prison authorities arranged with a Harbin pencil factory that we prisoners should make some of the cardboard boxes in which the pencils were packed. From then on we spent four hours every day studying and four working. The prison staff told us that this would vary our routine, while a spot of manual work would be good for us as we had never done any before. I did not realize then what special significance these words had for me.

I had, of course, never stuck a pencil box together in my life, and for that matter I had never even sharpened a pencil. All I knew about pencils was what I could remember about the trade-marks on them — Venus pencils had an armless woman on them, and there were German ones with cocks. I had never noticed the boxes they came in, and had no idea that making the boxes was so much trouble. Before I had been pasting for long the novelty had worn off and I felt as if my whole mind was sticky with paste. By the time that the others had all made several I had not finished my first one, and it did not look much like a box or anything else for that matter.

"How on earth did you make that?" asked Old Hsien, a former head of a "Manchukuo" military hospital, taking my creation in his hands. "Why won't it open? What the hell is it?"

Old Hsien had been brought up in Japan, where he studied medicine, and as the brother of the notorious female agent Chin Pi-hui (whose Japanese name was Kawashima Yoshiko) and son of Prince Su he came from a leading family of pro-Japanese traitors. He was a foul-tempered man, and particularly liked to vent his spleen on me as I was too timid to stand up to him.

My feelings were a mixture of jealousy, disappointment, and fear of being mocked at, and that busybody Old Hsien had drawn the others' attention to me. They crowded round my box and laughed unpleasantly. I grabbed the box from Old Hsien and threw it on the waste pile.

"What? Are you deliberately throwing it away?" Old Hsien glared at me, his eyes popping.

"I'm not throwing it away. It's not so bad as to be completely useless," I muttered as I took the box from the rubbish heap and put it on the heap of finished goods. But this was clearly wrong.

"Rejects are rejects wherever they're put."

This ambiguous insult infuriated me. Almost trembling with rage and unable to control myself, I retorted: "You are very brave with me. You bully the weak and are scared of the strong." His face went red and he shouted: "Who do I bully? Who am I scared of? You still think that you're an emperor and that everyone has to wait on you, don't you?" Fortunately the others were ignoring him, and the cell chief came and made him keep quiet.

But this was not the end of the matter. Old Hsien was not prepared to give up that easily, and the next day he chose to sit in the place next to me for pasting. He kept giving my work critical looks, so I turned round and sat with my back to him.

Although I did not do as well as the others I did make some progress that day. In the evening the prison authorities bought some sweets for us with the money that we had earned for our work. This was the first time I had enjoyed the fruits of my own labour, and although my efforts had been the least successful my share of the sweets tasted better than anything I had ever eaten before.

"Pu Yi, you didn't do so badly today, did you?" said Old Hsien.

"No, no rejects today," I said, counter-attacking.

"Hm, you'd do better if you were a bit more humble," replied Old Hsien, smiling coldly.

"What's proud about saying that none of my boxes were rejects?" I was getting angry, and my sweet no longer tasted so good. One of the things about Old Hsien that I found most objectionable was his knack of choosing the moment when I was feeling happy to start picking holes. "If I make any more rejects, you can call me what you like." With that I ignored him. But he went over and picked out one of the boxes I had made and held it up for everyone to see. "Look."

I looked up, and my sweet almost choked me. I had stuck the label on upside-down. I was furious and I wanted to throw the box into his ugly face. Restraining this impulse I muttered, "Think what you like."

"Temper! Still acting the stinking emperor," he raised his voice. "I only criticized you for your own good, but you won't realize it." He heard a warder coming along outside the cell, so he shouted louder still, "You are still dreaming of being emperor again."

"You're talking nonsense," I retorted angrily. "I'm stupider than you, and I'm not as good at talking or doing things, and I was born that way. Will that do for you?"

The others came over to break up the argument. Ours was a big room, and there were eighteen of us in it. Apart from myself there were three former puppet ministers and fourteen ex-officers.

One of the ex-ministers was Chang Ching-hui, who was now senile, did not usually study or work and was very silent. That evening all of us except Chang Ching-hui held a discussion on the "boxes affair". Some of them said that even if Old Hsien had meant well in criticizing me he need not have shouted, and some said that I was wrong not to admit that I had made the boxes badly. The Mongol Old Kuo said that it was not surprising that I had lost my temper as Old Hsien had taken such a bad attitude, and a former regimental commander who was a friend of Old Hsien's objected that Old Kuo was looking through tinted spectacles. Another view was that the matter should be discussed at the criticism meeting on Saturday. Everyone was talking at once. Then I saw that the regimental commander was tugging the coat of Old Hsien, who was shouting so much that the corners of his mouth were covered with foam. Everyone fell silent, and when I turned round a prison official called Li who was in charge of study had come in. He asked the cell chief what we were quarrelling about, and Old Wei said: "I report, sir, that this started over a reject cardboard box."

The prison officer picked up the box on which I had stuck the label upside-down and said: "Why quarrel over such a trifle? Why not just stick another label on the right way up?" We were flabbergasted.

But the matter was still not yet over. Some days later Little Jui told us when he brought the materials for our work that some of the other groups were going to hold a competition, and he wanted to know whether we would take part or not. We said we would. Little Jui then told us that Little Ku in their group had invented a way of pasting boxes that was at least twice as fast as the old method. We realized that we would have to raise our efficiency if we were to take part in the competition. Taking our cue from the reports of technical innovations that we had read about in the press, we started a production line in which each of us did one process. I liked this idea as it would make my work easier and might, I thought, cover up my incompetence. But before long there was a bottleneck at my stage in the line, and Old Hsien was the one who noticed it.

"One man's shortcomings are affecting the work of the group. What should we do about it?" He feigned an embarrassed expression.

I did not argue with him this time and stood there facing the pile of half-made boxes, just like the people who used to stand outside the Mind Nurture Palace in the old days waiting to be summoned to my presence. When the man who did the next process to mine pointed out that my work was not up to standard and was thus raising the rate of rejects for the whole team, I realized that nobody, however fair-minded, could refute Old Hsien's unkind criticism. I left the production line and went back to working by myself.

Once again I knew the misery of loneliness. Having been rejected by the group I felt that the contrast between me and them was as great as if I were standing there naked in front of them. I almost burst with rage when Old Hsien deliberately coughed as he walked past me, his pitted face revealing his delight in my misfortunes. I needed some sympathetic person to talk to, but the others were all far too busy. Then I caught flu and felt completely wretched.

That night I had a nightmare in which the face of Old Hsien was right on top of me saying evilly, "You are a reject. You're only capable of becoming a beggar." In my dream I saw myself squatting by a bridge like one of the "monkeys guarding the bridge" that the eunuchs had told me about when I was a boy. I felt a hand pressing on my head and woke up with a start. I saw an indistinct figure in white standing in front of me and feeling my chest. "You're running a high fever as your flu has got worse. There's nothing to worry about. Just let me take a look at you."

My head was aching and my temple throbbing violently as I took hold of myself and realized what was happening. The warder had heard me talking deliriously in my sleep, and when he could not wake me up he sent for a doctor. The doctor took my temperature, the nurse gave me an injection, and I drifted back to sleep.

I was ill for a fortnight, and I gradually got better under the daily attentions of the doctor and nurse. I spent most of my time in bed, doing no work or study. I thought a lot more in those two weeks than I had in the previous few years. My thoughts ranged from the cardboard boxes to the terrifying face of the Empress Dowager Tzu Hsi as I had seen it as a child.

Her dim memory had only seemed frightening to me in the past, but now I hated her. Why had she picked on me to be emperor? I was an ignorant and innocent child, in every respect at least as well endowed as Pu Chieh, but because I had been chosen to be emperor I had led a completely enclosed existence. I had not even been taught the most basic practical knowledge, with the result that I now knew nothing and was completely incapable. My knowledge and skills were less than those of a child, to say nothing of Pu Chieh. I was mocked and bullied by Old Hsien and his like, and if I were ever allowed to live by myself I would be incapable of surviving. Was not my present state the fault of Tzu Hsi, the princes and the Ching ministers?

Whenever I had been laughed at previously or been shown to be incompetent I had resented it bitterly, hating those who found fault with me and the People's Government that was incarcerating me. But now I saw that this was wrong of me. I really was laughable, incapable and ignorant. Previously I had resented the disrespect in which my nephews held me, but now I saw that there was no reason why they should respect me. I could not even recognize leek when I ate it, and I had acknowledged a foreign deity as my own ancestress.

What, after all, was so divine about me? The Mongol Old Cheng told me that when his father Babojab rebelled in the early years of the Republic the whole family had sworn to be prepared to die in support of my restoration; his mother had worshipped me as nothing less than a god. He observed that it was a great pity that she was now dead, as otherwise "I could have told her that Hsuan Tung is just a piece of rubbish". Could I blame people for saying things like this?

I only blamed the Empress Dowager and the rest of them, and hated the Forbidden City with a new intensity. I thought of it as an even bigger enemy than Old Hsien.

When I was nearly better the governor sent for me. After asking about my health he went on to inquire about the quarrel between me and Old Hsien. He asked if I had been shocked. After giving him a brief account of the affair I ended by saying, "I was very shocked at the time, but now I am not particularly angry. I only hate my own incompetence and all those people in the palace in Peking."

"It is good that you have recognized your own shortcomings; that shows progress. There is no need to be miserable about your inability, which can be overcome if you are willing to learn. It is even more important that you have recognized the source of your incompetence. You ought to ask yourself why those princes and court officials brought you up that way."

"They were only concerned about their own interests. They didn't care about me, only about themselves."

"I'm afraid you're not quite right there," the governor replied with a smile. "Can you really say that Chen Pao-shen and your father intentionally worked against you? Did they deliberately try to harm you?"

I could produce no answer.

"You should give this question careful thought. If you are able to find the answer, your illness will have been well worth while."

I continued to think about this after returning from the governor's office, and I went over my past life many times before the first criticism meeting I took part in after my illness. My failure to find an answer made me angrier and angrier.

At this criticism meeting someone criticized Old Hsien for his malevolence, saying that he was always deliberately attacking me. Most of the others expressed similar views, and some even put the blame for my illness on to Old Hsien and showed that he was having a bad effect on the remoulding of all of us. Old Hsien turned grey with panic and made a faltering self-criticism. I said nothing throughout the meeting although I was seething with hatred. When someone suggested that I speak Old Hsien turned paler than ever.

"I have nothing to say," I said in a low voice. "I only hate my own incompetence."

Everyone was astonished, and Old Hsien's jaw sagged. I started to shout, "I hate the place where I grew up. I hate that evil system. What is feudalism? Feudalism means ruining people from childhood."

There was a convulsion in my throat and I could not go on. The others were muttering something, but I could not hear what it was.

The Investigators Arrive

From the end of 1953 onwards we studied *Imperialism* for three months, and after this we moved back to Fushun in March 1954. Before long the working party from the investigating organization arrived and began to question the prisoners.

We later found out that the government had made the most thorough preparations for investigating the crimes of the Japanese and "Manchukuo" war criminals, and had mustered strong forces for the job. A batch of Japanese war criminals was transferred to Fushun. The government had been collecting material for several years, and about two hundred investigators had been assembled and given special political and technical training.

The investigation of the "Manchukuo" war criminals began with a big meeting at the end of March. As far as we prisoners were concerned the investigations consisted of reporting others' crimes and admitting our own, and they were more or less finished by the end of the year.

The head of the group of investigators told us at the meeting that after our study and reflection over the past few years it was now time for us to acknowledge our guilt. The government had to examine our crimes, and we had to recognize the past for what it really was, confess our crimes, and report the crimes of the Japanese imperialists and the other Chinese traitors. Whether confessing our own crimes or reporting those of others we had to be honest, neither exaggerating nor minimizing. The decision that the government finally took on how to deal with us would depend on our crimes and our attitude, and its policy was one of leniency to those who confessed coupled with severity to those who resisted.

At the meeting the prison governor announced some new rules. We were forbidden to exchange information on our cases, to send notes to other cells, and so on. From that day on each group took its exercise in turn, so that it would be impossible to meet prisoners from other cells.

After this meeting each group returned to its cell for a discussion. Everyone said that they were going to make thorough confessions and reports, and intended to admit their guilt humbly in order to obtain leniency; but some of them, like Old Hsien, were visibly anxious about it.

I caught his alarm, and my belief in the policy of leniency gave way once more to doubts. If a former hospital director had grounds for fear, surely I, an ex-emperor, had far more. As I had already confessed my main crimes my principal worry was how to convince the investigators that I was being truthful. I therefore decided to rewrite my life history in greater detail, while bringing in all I knew about the crimes of the Japanese war criminals. I promised to do this at the meeting of our group.

Carrying out this promise was not easy. When writing about the end of the "Manchukuo" period I came to the declaration of war against Japan by the Soviet Union. I had been terrified that the Japanese might suspect me and kick me aside in that time of crisis, and had racked my brains for some way to ingratiate myself with them. On the night after hearing of the Soviet declaration of war on Japan I had sent for Chang Ching-hui and Takebe (the head of the "General Affairs Office of the State Council of Manchukuo") on my own initiative. I gave them an oral "edict" ordering them to mobilize speedily and do everything possible to support Japan against the attacks of the Soviet Red Army. What was I going to say about this now? I had to mention it as there was a chance that other people knew about this edict; but if I did mention it, then would not this one action I took without prompting from the Japanese make the investigators suspect that I had not, after all, been completely under the control of Yoshioka? If they did that, the whole of my autobiography would be invalidated.

I decided that I would not say too much about the matter. It could do me no harm to be a little reticent about some of the bad things that I had done. I put the blame for this edict on Yoshioka, then wrote the confession out again, going into greater detail about the things I dared to mention, and writing all I could about the crimes of others. I handed all this in and waited for the summons of the investigators.

I wondered what the questioning would be like. Would the interrogator look like an ordinary human being or like a monster? Would he use torture on me, as I had tortured offending servants and eunuchs in the Forbidden City and Changchun? I was sure that he would be cruel. I was more terrified of torture, or even a slap in the face, than I was of death. I had been in a Communist prison for three years and had seen that people were not beaten or cursed but were treated with the dignity due to them as human beings. This should have been enough to show me that my earlier fears of cruelty were groundless, but I was convinced that an interrogator was bound to be suspicious and use violence on his subject.

I spent ten uneasy days tormented by such thoughts. Then the dread moment came when a warder told me to go and see the investigators.

I was taken to a room that was about ten metres square. In the middle was a large desk, in front of which was a small table set with tea-bowls, a teapot and an ash-tray. Behind the desk sat two men, one middle-aged and one young. They indicated to me that I was to sit on a chair beside the table.

The older man asked me my name, age, place of origin and sex, and the younger man's pen scratched across a piece of paper as he wrote down my answers. "We have read your confession," the older man said, "and we would like to have a talk with you. You may smoke."

The older man asked me about a number of things from my childhood to the time of my capture. He nodded at my answers as if he were satisfied. "Very well, we'll leave it at that for the moment. Interrogator Chao may have some more questions to put to you later."

The atmosphere of the questioning, which had come as a complete surprise, ended my worries about torture.

I was a little disappointed at my next interrogation to find that only Chao was in the room. As I sat in front of this young interrogator I wondered if he would be any good. Would he be able to understand that I was telling the truth? Would he have a young man's hot temper? Whose word would he believe if others had written lying reports about me?

"There is a question I would like to ask you," he said, interrupting my train of thought. He wanted to know about the procedure for issuing imperial decrees and rescripts in "Manchukuo", and I replied truthfully. When he mentioned one decree, he asked me how long before its promulgation I had seen it. I was not sure and replied, "Probably one or two days beforehand, but it may have been three or even four."

"There is no need to give a reply at once. You can tell me when you remember. Let's go on to another question now." I could not think of the answer to that either, and got stuck. I wondered whether the interrogator would think that I was deliberately concealing something and lose his temper. Instead he said: "Let's put that one aside too. You can tell me when you remember."

I had to take my hat off to that young man in the end.

At one session — I can no longer remember which — he produced some of the materials I had written and laid them before me.

"You have written here that the Japanese invaders took sixteen million tons of grain from the Northeast in one year, following a plan made by Furumi Tadayuki, the war criminal who had been deputy chief of the 'General Affairs Office of the State Council of Manchukuo'. This is too vague. Which year was it? How do you know the figure of sixteen million tons? Please give me more details."

I had, in fact, overheard two former puppet ministers in my cell talking about it, but I could hardly admit this, so I said that the Japanese robbed the Northeast of all its wealth, and took all the grain that was grown. The interrogator interrupted me again at this point: "Do you know the annual grain production of the Northeast?"

I could say nothing.

"On what do you base the statement in the material you wrote?"

I saw that I could not bluff my way out of this situation, so I admitted that my only authority was gossip.

"So do you believe what you have written or not?"

"I. . . . I don't know."

"Hm. You don't even believe it yourself." The interrogator looked at me, his eyes wide open. "So why did you write it?"

I did not know what to say. He put the cap on his fountain pen and tidied up the thick *Manchukuo Yearbook* and *Government Report* on his desk. It was obvious that he did not want any more answers from me, and he closed the interrogation by saying, "Whether you are referring to yourself or to others you must always stick to the facts."

I looked at him silently, acknowledging to myself the truth of what he had just said. I was, after all, frightened that others might tell lies or exaggerate about me. I went out of the room wondering if all interrogators were as conscientious as this young fellow. What would happen if an incompetent one were to read some lies about me?

This question was soon answered when my cellmate Old Yuan told us about an experience of his. He had written down a figure he had worked out for the amount of iron and steel taken from the Northeast by the Japanese. The interrogator had not believed it and had given him a pencil, asking him to work out how much ore would be needed to produce so much iron and steel, and how much ore was actually mined in the Northeast each year. Old Yuan ended by telling us that the interrogator had files on the natural resources of the Northeast.

Now I understood why Interrogator Chao had all those reference books on his desk. To verify all the written evidence several hundred investigators had spent more than a year travelling all over the country and reading through files by the ton, as I found out when I signed the general conclusions on me written by the investigators.

The reason why I ran into trouble with that young investigator was because he was so conscientious in his search for the facts, and because I was stupidly worrying that he would think I was not being honest. I therefore hurriedly wrote out a self-criticism and sent it to him. With this done I felt that the situation was not too serious.

The Sufferings and Hatred of the People of the Northeast

I never knew or cared much about the calamities that the Japanese had inflicted on the people of the Northeast, and I never thought they had anything to do with me. But when I attended a study meeting on the crimes of the Japanese war criminals in the Northeast I realized how serious they were. This meeting, in which the Japanese war criminals participated, made a very deep impression on me. The most striking testimonies were the confessions of Furumi Tadayuki, the former deputy head of the "General Affairs Office of the State Council of Manchukuo", and of a former "Manchukuo" gendarmerie commander.

Furumi had been a favourite of the Japanese military, and one of the real rulers of "Manchukuo". Acting on the orders of the Kwantung Army he and his superior Takebe Rokuzo had planned and carried out the rule and the looting of the Northeast. He spoke in great detail about the policy of forcibly seizing the land of the peasants in the Northeast for the resettlement of Japanese immigrants; about the "Five Year Plan for Developing Production" that was designed to plunder its natural resources; about the use of opium to poison the people; and about many other policies, including squeezing grain and other commodities out of the people as part of the preparations for the Pacific War. He told us about some of the results of these policies, and every example he cited was an atrocity. In 1944, for instance, over fifteen thousand labourers from all over the Northeast were conscripted for military construction at Wangyemiao in the Khingan Mountains. So bad were the conditions under which they were forced to work that more than six thousand of them died.

Furumi also had a lot to say about the Japanese opium policy. This was initiated in early 1933, when the Japanese Army was short of funds before its invasion of Jehol. As it did not then control the production of opium in the Northeast it imported over two million ounces of foreign opium and scattered leaflets by air all over Jehol encouraging the cultivation of the opium poppy. Around 1936 the Japanese Army greatly extended the area under opium cultivation in "Manchukuo", did all they could to expand production, and later gave themselves a legal monopoly of the sale of opium. The Japanese founded "Societies for the Prevention of Opium-Smoking" everywhere, set up opium dens with "hostesses", and made great efforts to spread the addiction among young people. In 1942 the Japanese "Asia Revival Council" held a "Conference on the Opium Needs and Production of China" which passed a resolution stating that "Manchukuo and the Mongolian border regions are to meet the opium requirements of the Greater East Asian Co-Prosperity Sphere"; after this the area under opium in the Northeast was increased to 3,000 hectares. According to Furumi's calculations, "Manchukuo" produced over 300 million ounces of opium before its collapse. The profit from it made up one-sixth of the revenue of the puppet government; in 1944 it reached a total of 300 million dollars, over a hundred times higher than it had been at the beginning of "Manchukuo", thus providing Japan with one of her most important sources of finance for her aggressive war. There were about 300,000 addicts in Jehol alone, and in the Northeast as a whole one person in twenty was an opium-smoker.

The gendarmerie officer testified that the gendarmerie often perpetrated mass slaughters, after which the local people would be assembled to see the corpses. Sometimes they would arrest a number of people they regarded as suspicious, line them up, select one of them at random, and then split him open with a sword in public. He had killed over thirty victims this way. Those the gendarmerie arrested had to undergo all kinds of tortures: they were beaten; they had cold water, peppery water and paraffin poured down their noses; they were burned with incense sticks or red-hot pokers; and were hung upside-down, to mention but a few of the torments.

Apart from what the people of the Northeast suffered directly from the Japanese invaders, it is not difficult to produce facts and figures about what they underwent at the hands of the puppet government and the Chinese traitors. Through various orders and grain policies, and through the system of supplying grain to Japan, the people of the Northeast were robbed of practically all the grain they produced every year, and at the end of the "Manchukuo" period they could only keep themselves alive by eating the "compound flour" they were supplied with that was made out of maize husks, bean-cake and acorn flour. The grain that was taken from them was either kept for military use or sent off to Japan. The amount sent to Japan annually steadily rose to 3,000,000 tons by 1944; and the total for the last six years of the "Manchukuo" period was over 11,100,000 tons.

As a result of the legislation controlling grain, cotton cloth, metals and other commodities the people found themselves being made into "economic criminals". Ordinary people were, for example, absolutely forbidden to eat rice, and they could be punished as "economic criminals" if the remains of rice were found in their vomit. In the year 1944-45 alone 317,100 people were punished for "economic crimes".

At the same time as their grain was being taken from them, the peasants of the Northeast were losing their land. In the last two years of "Manchukuo" 390,000 Japanese immigrants were moved into the Northeast, and the puppet government took 36,500,000 hectares of land from the people of the Northeast to give to them.

As they wanted to plunder the Northeast of its natural resources and turn it into their economic base, the Japanese used the puppet government to enslave the people of the Northeast through a variety of devices. After the "Labour Control Law" was issued in my name in 1938, 2,500,000 men (excluding those who were conscripted south of the Great Wall) had to do forced labour without payment every year. Most of them worked in mining and military construction, and they died in great numbers because of the terrible conditions under which they worked. Thus in 1944, during the "Flood-Prevention Project" in Liaoyang city 170 out of a force of 2,000 young labourers died of their sufferings.

Peasants, ordinary workers, clerks, students and young men who failed to pass the medical examination for the army all had to participate in this slave labour which was officially called "voluntary labour".

Those who suffered the worst were the inmates of the "reformatories". At the end of the "Manchukuo" era the savagery of Japanese rule neared the point of madness. The "Thought Rectification Law" and the "Security and Rectification Law" were proclaimed in 1943 in an attempt to solve the shortage of labour and curb the growing resistance of the people, and concentration camps were set up all over the Northeast under the name of "reformatories". People who had been reduced to destitution or who were dissatisfied were thrown into these institutions on charges of "vagabondage" or "bad thoughts" and forced to do hard labour. Sometimes the authorities stopped passers-by and labelled them as "vagabonds" without even bothering to question them, then threw them into a "reformatory" from which they would never emerge.

The inmates who had survived until the collapse of the "Manchukuo" regime were now telling the People's Government with bitterness and hatred about what the puppet rulers had done to them. A peasant of Hokang city was arrested in 1944 and taken to the police headquarters on a charge of anti-Manchukuo and anti-Japanese activities. There were seventeen others there with him, and after being viciously beaten they were moved to the Hokang Reformatory and forced to mine coal in the Tungshan mines. They had to work twelve hours a day, were only given a tiny ball of *kaoliang* at each meal, had no clothes or bedding, and were frequently and savagely beaten.

My mother heard that I was in the reformatory and she came to the place where I was working to see me through the barbed wire. When the police saw her they grabbed her by the hair and kicked her until she could not get up from the ground. Later they beat me with spades, so that I was covered with wounds and lay unconscious for seven days. Once, when we were not given any vegetables to eat with our meal, a fellow-prisoner called Sung Kai-tung bought some scallions from a passer-by with some money of mine. He was seen by the traitor Section Head Wang, who called the two of us over, took five dollars off me, and had me beaten up so badly that I bled from my mouth and nose. Then he forced me into a sack by hitting me on the head when I refused, and when I was in the sack they picked it up and dropped it three times, by the end of which I was unconscious. People died there daily, and every three or four days seven or eight corpses used to be carried out. Nine of the seventeen men who were arrested with me died there. I caught T.B. there, and I am still unable to work. My mother was driven mad, and my three sisters, of whom the oldest was only eleven, had to go out to beg for their food every day.

The oppression of the people of the Northeast by the army, police, law courts and prisons of "Manchukuo" was a story of bloody atrocities too numerous to enumerate. The sixty-one-year-old peasant Huang Yung-hung had been arrested for sending a letter to the Anti-Japanese Allied Army, and had witnessed a mass murder.

On the 26th day of the 2nd month by the lunar (Chinese) calendar the puppet police took over thirty of us prisoners to go and dig a pit outside the western gate of Chaoyuan. We returned to the prison after nightfall. On the 27th I and Wang Ya-min, Kao Shou-san, and Liu Cheng-fa were taken in one group and twenty others were taken in a second group to outside the west gate, where the group of twenty men were all shot. Then they brought along another batch of twenty-two men and shot them too. After shooting them the police poured petrol over their bodies and set them on fire. One of the men was not dead, and when he caught fire he tried to run away, but the police shot and killed him. When the bodies had all been burned they told us to bury the forty-two men. This grave is still there outside the west gate of Chaoyuan, and I could find the place again.

This hell on earth was the "paradise of the Kingly Way" that I had ruled as "Chief Executive" and "Emperor Kang Te". All these atrocities had been carried out in my name. No wonder that all of the testimonials of the victims of the "Manchukuo" regime ended with such expressions as:

"I demand that the People's Government avenge us. We want the Japanese and the Chinese traitors to repay their blood debt."

"Avenge our murdered families. Punish the Japanese and the traitors."

"You Can Never Escape the Consequences of Your Sins"

The problem was even more serious than this.

The confessions and revelations of the Japanese war criminals and the accusations of the people of the Northeast stirred us "Manchukuo" war criminals. The reaction of the younger ones among us was particularly strong, and I was exposed by my nephews, my brothers-in-law and Big Li. I found myself surrounded by hatred, even within my own family. It was as if I were standing within a circle of mirrors, and wherever I looked I saw my own unpleasant image.

After attending the study meeting of the Japanese war criminals we were assembled and asked to talk about it. Some were still so moved that they swore to confess their own crimes and report those of others. The main target of accusations was Chang Huan-hsiang, the former puppet minister of justice, who had gone to great lengths to ingratiate himself with the Japanese in the old days and was now very unpopular in the prison because he deliberately spoiled the food, broke prison rules, shouted at warders and so on. Some people warned him that if he did not behave properly in future the government would not be able to forgive him. As I was afraid of being treated this way myself, I was worried that the others might think I was not behaving properly. As we were not allowed at the time to tell each other anything about the confessions we had made and the information we had given, I was frightened that others might not know that I had already confessed, so I decided to speak at the meeting. When I had told the meeting about everything I had confessed and was just coming to my conclusion, Little Ku jumped to his feet and asked me, "You've said a lot, haven't you, but why didn't you mention that note?"

I was struck dumb for a moment.

"The note, Little Jui's note." Little Hsiu was standing up too. "You said just now that you handed over those jewels on your own initiative. Why didn't you say that Little Jui prompted you?"

"Yes, yes, I was just going to mention it. Little Jui was the one who enlightened me. . . ." I hastily filled in this gap in the story, but the glares I was getting from Little Hsiu and Little Ku made it clear that they were far from satisfied. Fortunately the meeting was then brought to a close.

Back in my cell I wrote out a self-criticism and handed it to the prison staff. I was sure that the governor would be angry with me, and was furious with Little Jui for having told the others about the note. Little Ku and Little Hsiu, members of my own family, were really heartless to do this to me. They were not even as loyal to me as Big Li. Not long afterwards I saw the reports on me that they had written, and then I realized that the change in my own family had been even more terrible than I had imagined.

There was a rule that every report had to be read by the person accused in it, and Interrogator Chao brought me the pile of ones about me. "When you've read them," he said, "sign the ones with which you agree. If you disagree, raise your objections."

The first ones I looked at were written by some former puppet ministers, and as they only referred to well-known facts about the "Manchukuo" regime I signed them all. But when I started reading the ones written by the members of my family my palm was soon sticky with sweat.

My brother-in-law Old Wan's report contained a passage that read:

On the evening of August 8, 1945 I went to the palace to see Pu Yi. He was writing something, and Chang Ching-hui and Takebe were waiting outside his room for an audience. Pu showed me what he had written and its general import was that all the "Manchukuo" armed forces were to fight alongside the Imperial Japanese Army and smash the invading enemy (the Soviet Red Army). He said that he was going to give this order to Chang Ching-hui and Takebe, and he wanted to know if I had any suggestions to make. I said that there was no alternative.

This was a disaster, as I had put the blame for this on Yoshioka. Big Li's testimony was even more terrifying. He described my departure from Tientsin, and told how I had made an agreement with him about sticking to the old story before I wrote my autobiography. This was not all. He exposed my daily conduct in great detail, showing how I had behaved with the Japanese and how I had treated the members of my household. If there had been only one or two cases of this sort mentioned in their reports that would not have mattered much, but as it was there was an enormous list of charges against me.

Old Wan, for example, had also written:

> When films were shown in the palace we had to stand up if the Japanese emperor came on the screen, and clap any shots of Japanese soldiers making an attack. This was because the projectionists were Japanese.
> There was a drive to economize on coal in 1944, so Pu Yi gave orders that there were to be no more fires in the Yi Hsi Lou (a building in the palace) in order to impress Yoshioka, but he used an electric fire in his bedroom without letting Yoshioka know.
> When Pu Yi fled to Talitzukou he put the Japanese goddess and the picture of Hirohito's mother in his carriage on the train, and he made a ninety-degree bow whenever he walked past it. He ordered us to do likewise.

Little Jui's report included a passage about the orphans I employed as pages, and revealed how badly they had been treated and what cruel and unjust punishment I had so frequently inflicted on them. He also reported the death of the page who had tried to escape.

The wording of Big Li's accusations made no secret of his hatred.

> This person Pu Yi was cruel, frightened of death, and extremely suspicious; he was also very cunning and thoroughly hypocritical. His

treatment of his servants was inhuman. When he was in a bad temper he cursed them and had them beaten even if they had done nothing wrong. If he was feeling at all unwell or tired the servants suffered for it, and they were lucky if they got away with cuffs or kicks. But when he was with strangers he behaved as if he were the kindest man on earth.

In Tientsin he used to have people beaten with wooden rods or horsewhipped, and in the "Manchukuo" era many other new kinds of floggings and tortures were added. . . .

He made everyone act as his accomplice. When he wanted someone beaten, he suspected collusion if anyone refused to do the beating for him or did not hit hard enough. If that happened, the beater would be beaten himself, and several times harder. All of his nephews and attendants flogged people for him at some time or other. One page of twelve or thirteen called Chou Po-jen (an orphan) was once beaten so badly that he had wounds a foot long on his thighs which took two or three months to heal under the attention of Doctor Huang. While this boy was recovering Pu Yi told me to take milk and other things to him and say: "How kind His Majesty is to you! Did you get such good things to eat in the orphanage?"

By the time I had read this last accusation I began to have doubts about the self-justification I had resorted to in the past. Previously I had thought that everything I had done had been justified. I had only submitted to the pressure of the Japanese and done their bidding because I was forced to; and my treatment of the members of my household, even the torture, had always seemed to be my right. To cringe before the strong and bully the weak had seemed both natural and reasonable to me, and I had imagined that anyone else would have done the same in my position. Now I realized that not everyone was like me, and that my self-justification was completely void.

Nobody, after all, was weaker than prisoners stripped of all rights, but the Communists who held power did not beat or curse us, or regard us as less than human. As for power, the American troops with their first-rate equipment could be regarded as "powerful", but the Communist troops had not feared them despite the inferiority of their own equipment, and had dared to fight them for three years until they forced them to sign an armistice.

More recently I had seen new examples. From the accusations of the masses I had learnt that many ordinary people had not followed my creed in the face of violence and oppression. A peasant from Payen county called Li Tien-kuei had put his hopes in the Anti-Japanese Allied Army when he could stand the oppression of the Japanese and the traitors no longer. At the Chinese New Year in 1941 he had sent the anti-Japanese fighters ten catties of millet, 47 fried twists, 120 eggs, and two packets of cigarettes. This was later found out by the puppet police, and he was arrested. He had been hung up and flogged, and given electric shocks. Bloody corpses of men who had died under torture were put beside him to frighten him. All this was in an attempt to make him reveal some clue about the anti-Japanese forces. His tortures continued until he was freed after the Japanese surrender.

In 1943, when he was still a child, Li Ying-hua of Chinshan village had taken eggs to some passing anti-Japanese fighters, and when this was discovered by police spies he was taken to the police headquarters. First of all they had given him tea and cigarettes and invited him to eat *jiaozi*, saying: "You're only a kid and don't understand things, so if you talk we'll let you go." Li Ying-hua smoked the cigarettes, drank the tea, and ate the *jiaozi*. Finally he said: "I'm only a farmer and I don't know anything." The agents then suspended him upside-down and beat him, gave him electric shocks, burned him, stripped him naked and hit him with spiked rods, but they got nothing out of him.

I now knew that not all the people on this earth were weak. The only explanation for my past actions was that I bullied the weak and feared the strong, and that I feared death and was greedy for life. My basic justification had been that my life was the most valuable and that I was more worthy of preservation than anyone else. In the past few years I had learnt something of my true worth from my attempts at washing my clothes and making boxes, and now I had an even clearer idea of it from the accusations of the common people and the members of my household.

In the mirrors that surrounded me I saw that I was a guilty man, completely lacking in glory, and with no possible justification for my conduct.

I signed the last accusation against me and walked along the corridor, my mind full of remorse and sorrow.

"You can never escape the consequences of your sins."

CHAPTER NINE

◫◫◫◫◫◫◫◫◫◫◫◫◫◫◫◫◫◫◫◫◫◫◫◫◫◫◫◫◫◫◫◫◫◫◫◫◫◫

I ACCEPT REMOULDING

In this final chapter the positive and enthusiastic approach is unrelenting. By 1955, when it opens, the authorities had evidently decided that P'u Yi was by now useful for propaganda purposes. For the first time in five years he was allowed visits. His fourth wife, Li Yü-ch'in, who despite the remarks in this book about the good treatment of P'u Yi's relatives had been given a hard time first by the family and then by the authorities, was finally allowed in that year to know where he was being held and to visit him.

Her view of his reform is not as glowing as his own. According to her published account, she found his mouthing of progressive clichés hard to take when he showed hardly any interest in how she had coped during the intervening ten years, and she was bitter at the pressures put on her not to ask for a divorce. The prison authorities seemed concerned only with P'u Yi's reform and the help she could give him, and not with her plight. After she finally and reluctantly insisted on an end to the strange marriage, he showed his displeasure at her disloyalty by refusing to see her when an outing from the prison took him to Changchun, where she worked. As late as 1961, when she had remarried and had a son, there was still pressure on her to drop everything and start looking after P'u Yi again, as he was incapable of looking after himself.

The chapter does not bring out just how privileged his treatment was after his release. His monthly salary of 200 yuan was very high by the standards of the day, his free accommodation and medical care were excellent, and his work was not onerous. Even his much-publicized labour in the Botanical Gardens outside Peking was something of a ritual. His fifth and final marriage was arranged for him by the Chinese People's Political Consultative Conference and the Communist Party's United Front Department. Li Shu-hsien, a nurse from Hangchow, was evidently well qualified to look after him. Her picture of him is of a man very much concerned with her well-being and terrified of losing her. He received something approaching VIP treatment from his release till his death from kidney failure in 1967. He was even protected from the Cultural Revolution by Chou En-lai's intervention, and the local police kept Red Guards away. He was thus spared the raids on his home, beatings, struggle meetings, and other humiliations that someone with his background would otherwise have had to endure.

P'u Yi's presentation to foreigners as a living advertisement for the People's Government and the Communist Party began in 1956, while he was still in prison; and after his release he was often required to meet foreign visitors to China.

In 1980 an odd final touch was given to his life story when his ashes were solemnly transferred to the First Hall of the Revolutionary Cemetery at Papaoshan in the outskirts of Peking.

How Shall I Be a Man?

"A new year has begun. What do you think about it?" This was the question that the governor asked me on New Year's Day, 1955.

I said that I could only wait for my punishment. The governor shook his head and disagreed strongly.

"Why be so pessimistic? You should take a positive attitude to your remoulding and try hard to make a new man of yourself."

These words calmed me, but they did not eradicate my gloomy pessimism. I fell deep into a pit of self-contempt, which now played a bigger part in my thinking than the worries I had about my sentence.

While we were in the prison yard during a recreation period one day a reporter came with a camera to take pictures of us. As the period of accusations and recognition of our guilt was over we were allowed to take our recreation in the yard together, and an extra half-hour had been added to it. The yard was very lively, with some people playing volleyball and pingpong while others talked to each other, sang, and did all sorts of things. After putting all this on film the reporter finally got round to taking a picture of me. A former "Manchukuo" official who had been standing beside me watching a game noticed what the reporter was up to and hurried away with the words, "I'm not going to be photographed with him." Immediately afterwards all the others who were standing near me went away.

During March a group of Liberation Army generals came to inspect the prisons for war criminals that were under the control of the Shenyang military district, and the governor sent for me and Pu Chieh to go and see them. When I saw the room was full of gold epaulettes my first thought was that this must be a military tribunal, but then I discovered that the generals wanted to know how my studies were going. They were very friendly and showed a great

397

interest in what I had to say, and they asked me about my childhood and my life in "Manchukuo" days. Finally one bearded general said, "Study well and remould yourself. In the future you will be able to see the building of socialism with your own eyes." As I went back to my cell I thought that he must be a marshal, and Pu Chieh told me that he was not the only marshal among them. I was greatly impressed. The Communists, whom I had not expected to show the least tolerance for me, actually treated me as a human being, whether they were marshals or warders. But my fellow-prisoners were not even prepared to stand beside me, as if I were something less than human.

Back in my cell I told my cellmates what the marshal had said. Old Yuan, a former "Manchukuo" ambassador to Japan and the quickest man in our cell, said: "Congratulations, Old Pu. If the marshal said that you will be able to see socialist construction, that means you're safe."

This cheered all the others up greatly. If the number one traitor was safe, they would certainly be all right.

After the end of the period of accusations and acknowledging guilt, many of us had been most concerned about the future. Old Hsien, for example, had not smiled once since the beginning of this period, but now his face broke into a broad grin and he patted me warmly on the shoulder. "Congratulations, Old Pu, congratulations."

The ban on talking during the rest period had now been lifted, and during the day our cells were no longer locked. Someone happened to come into our cell just at this moment, so the good news was immediately spread round the whole prison. It was still being discussed at rest time. I thought of my nephews and Big Li, who had been ignoring me since the period of accusations and acknowledging guilt; I was sure that this news would have cheered them up, so I took this as an excuse to go and talk to them. I saw Little Ku and Little Hsiu beside a tree in a corner of the yard. But before I got there they went away.

In April the prison authorities made us elect a study committee as the Japanese war criminals had done. This committee, which was under the supervision of the authorities, enabled us prisoners to organize our own study and daily life; it was responsible for passing on to the prison staff any problems that arose, and for reporting on discussions and criticism meetings. It could also make suggestions on its own initiative. It had five members, who were chosen by election and had to be approved by the prison authorities; there was a chairman, and four other members responsible for study, daily life, sport and recreation respectively. The study head and the daily life head of each cell had to report to the responsible committeeman every day. This innovation stirred the prisoners, and we regarded it as proof that the authorities were confident we would re-mould ourselves. Some of us realized more clearly than before that remoulding was up to ourselves. Facts later proved that this com-mittee did a lot to help our remoulding. But at first my feelings about it were not the same as those of others. This was because two of the five members were the relations of mine who had made the most unflinching accusations against me. One was Old Wan, the chairman, and the other was Little Jui, the member responsible for our daily life.

Soon after its creation the study committee decided that we should build a sports ground. We had been using one that had been made by the Japanese war criminals, but now we were going to level a piece of land for ourselves. Little Jui was in charge of the job, and he gave me a dressing down in public when we were about to start work on the very first day. I was late for the roll-call because of some trifle, and as I ran to my place in the ranks hastily buttoning my clothes I heard my name being shouted.

"Coming, coming," I replied, hurrying to the end of the line.

"You're late every time we assemble," shouted Little Jui with a grim expression on his face. "You keep all the rest of us waiting just for you. You haven't the least consideration. Just look at yourself, you're a complete mess. You can't even button your jacket up properly."

I looked down and saw that my buttons were all in the wrong holes. Everyone turned round to look at me as I fumbled ineffec-tively.

I was worried that now they kept the records of the weekly criticism meetings, they would put a most unfavourable light on my actions. The weekly criticism meetings in our group were different from before, when we had either shouted at each other or else exchanged only polite remarks. Now we talked much more sensibly and seriously. This was partly because some of us had thrown off our ideological burdens or learnt something about remoulding, and thus took a more positive attitude. Another difference was that the irrelevant speeches we used to make would not get past the study committee. One reason why I felt that the weekly criticism meetings had changed was because when other people spoke about me they no longer did so with any reservations; and another more important one was that among the new members who had been moved into our group was Big Li, who knew me only too well and was in charge of our daily life. When others spoke about my shortcomings his introductions and analyses would enable them to go to the root of the trouble and hit me where it hurt. When the explanations of Little Jui and Old Wan on the study committee were added to all this, I would scarcely seem human.

When in the past some external shock reduced me to the depths of despair I would sometimes blame myself and take it as the retribution for my own actions, but at other times I would feel indignant with fate and with others for deliberately making things difficult for me. At the beginning I also used to be angry with the Communist Party, the People's Government and the prison authorities. Now I had no reason to complain about the last three, and felt more strongly that things were my own fault, but I still tended to blame my troubles on others. When I read the reports that had been written about me and realized that all the things I had wanted to keep secret had now been revealed, so that the government knew everything, I had thought that it would only be natural if they either took their revenge on me or at least abandoned their hopes of remoulding me. But the interrogators, the prison governor, and the marshal had all said that I should study, remould myself, and become a new man. All the prison staff shared that view, as they showed in many practical ways.

After we built the sports ground the study committee decided that we should make our prison yard more beautiful in preparation for May Day by planting flowers and trees, weeding, and levelling the ground. We all set to work with enthusiasm. At first I was helping to fill in a big pit, but Warder Chiang said that as my eyesight was so bad there was a danger that I might fall into it, so I was transferred to weeding a flower-bed. After I had been working there for a while the Mongol Old Cheng came up to me, snatched the plant I had just uprooted from my hand and shouted, "What's this you've pulled up? Eh?"

"I was told to weed, wasn't I?"

"Do you call this a weed? Can't you see that all the things you've pulled up are flowers?"

I was the focus of attention once more as I squatted there, not daring to raise my head. I wished that all the flowers and weeds would disappear.

"You really are a reject," Old Cheng went on shouting as he held the plant in his hand. Warder Chiang came up, took the plant from Old Cheng, looked at it, and threw it on the ground. "What's the good of laying into him like that? You should help him by teaching him to weed properly so that he won't do it wrong next time."

"I'd never imagined that there were still people who didn't know the difference between flowers and weeds," replied Old Cheng offensively.

"I'd never imagined it either, but now that we know differently, we must work out how to help him."

Previously the words "I'd never imagined" had always been connected in my mind with unpleasant remarks, such as "I'd never imagined that Pu Yi was so stupid — he isn't worth saving", or "I'd never imagined that Pu Yi was so hypocritical or so evil — you could never remould him", or "I'd never imagined that Pu Yi was hated by so many people — he can't be saved". But now "I'd never imagined" was actually followed by "but now that we know we must work out how to help him".

One day my glasses broke again. After some hesitation I had to ask for Big Li's help once more. "Please help me," I asked in a weak voice. "I've tried to do them myself several times, but I just can't. Nobody else can do it, so please could you mend them for me?"

"You still want me to wait on you," he replied with a glare. "Haven't you been waited on long enough?" He went off angrily to another place at the table. I stood there helplessly, wishing that I could dash my head against the wall. Less than two minutes later Big Li came back and took the glasses from me, snorting angrily.

"Very well then, I'll mend them for you. But let me tell you this, I'm only doing it to help you reform. Otherwise I wouldn't have time."

When it was time for the break I went to the new reading-room to relax by myself, and there I met Pu Chieh. I told him what was on my mind, and mentioned that I had sometimes spent sleepless nights because of the hostility of the members of my household. He asked me why I didn't talk it over with the prison authorities. "Why?" I asked. "I made them suffer in the old days, so it's only natural that they should hate me." Pu Chieh replied that he had heard the prison staff telling them to forget old grudges and help me. Only then did I understand why Big Li had swallowed his temper and come back from the other side of the table.

I divided the help that I received into two categories. One was practical, such as Big Li repairing my glasses and the others helping me to stitch up my quilt and mattress after washing them; without this assistance I would have wasted a whole day on the job and thus hindered collective activities. The other kind of help was verbal, and this was the category into which I put the criticisms of me that others made. The prison staff often said that we should help each other through criticism, self-criticism and the exchange of opinions. I gave very little of this kind of help to others, and I was not at all willing to accept it from them either. So although Big Li had told me that his aim in mending my spectacles was to help me remould myself, and although the governor had told me that criticism was one of the ways of helping each other reform our thought, I was still unable to see any connection between any of these forms of help and my thought reform and remoulding. I thought that the practical help that others gave me only proved my own incompetence and showed their contempt for me; and I regarded criticism as being no more than a way of re-opening my wounds and causing me pain. I would have preferred no help at all.

Whenever government officials talked about becoming a new man they always linked it with reforming one's thought and changing one's outlook. But what worried me was the question of face. I wondered how I would be treated by society and my family, and whether I would be rejected or not. Even if the Communist Party and the People's Government were to allow me to survive, society might not tolerate me, and even if I was not beaten I was afraid that people would abuse me and spit on me.

Whenever the prison authorities talked about thought reform they pointed out that a man's actions were always supported by a particular ideology, so that it was necessary to analyse the ideological roots of a man's crimes in order to prevent him from committing them again. I, on the other hand, was convinced that I could never repeat what I had done in the past. If the people of New China were prepared to tolerate me I could guarantee this. What need was there to go into my thinking?

I thought that the key to becoming a new man lay not in myself but in the way others treated me. The governor said that if we reformed properly the people would treat us leniently, but they would not tolerate any refusal to remould ourselves. It was, in fact, up to myself. I only began to understand this because of a little thing that happened to me after many days of distress.

It Is Up to Me

One Sunday I was washing my clothes as usual. When I had finished it was time for recreation, and what I felt like doing was going to read by myself in the reading-room. I had just sat down when I heard voices outside.

403

"Can't any of you play tennis?"

"I can't, but Pu Yi can. You should ask him."

"Even if he can he'll never have time for it. Goodness knows when he'll finish washing his clothes."

"He's much quicker now."

"I don't believe you."

This infuriated me. I had undoubtedly finished washing them, and I'd done just as many as the others, but there were still people who would not believe it, as if I were fundamentally incapable of making any progress. I fetched my racket and went out into the yard, not so much because I wanted to play as to show the others that I had finished my washing. When I reached the court the people I had heard talking a moment ago were no longer there, so I played with some others who wanted a game. Some spectators gathered to watch. I played with spirit, sweating heavily.

When I went to wash my hands at a tap afterwards I met the governor, who often spent his Sundays in the prison.

"You've made progress today, Pu Yi."

I was pleased to hear this. "I haven't played for a long time."

"I was talking about that," he said, pointing at my washing drying on the line. "As you can now do your washing as quickly as the rest you can enjoy the same amount of rest and recreation as they do."

I nodded and walked round the yard with him.

"In the old days you were too busy to enjoy rest and recreation like everyone else, so you were not equal with them and resented it. But now that you are equal, you are much happier when it comes to washing clothes. So you see, you hold the key to the problem yourself. There is no point in worrying about how other people treat you."

A moment later he went on: "The Second World War turned you from an emperor into a prisoner. At present there is a great battle going on in your mind, a battle to turn an emperor into an ordinary worker. You've already learnt something about what an emperor really is, but this battle is not yet over, and you still don't think of yourself as the equal of others. You must get a better understanding of yourself."

I thought about what he had said for a long time. While I agreed that I held the key to the question, I could not see that I was still giving myself an emperor's airs. But as time went on life gradually taught me that this was true.

When our group had returned to the cell after removing the rubbish one day the member of the study committee who was responsible for daily life criticized us. "You didn't turn the tap off after washing your hands, and the water is still running. This was irresponsible, and I must ask you not to do it again."

Big Li immediately asked me if I had been the last to wash, and when I admitted that I had probably forgotten to turn the tap off, he said that this was an example of the way I still behaved as I had done when I was an emperor. "In those days you never even touched a door handle as you always had others to open and close doors for you. Even now you only open doors and never close them behind you. You haven't stopped behaving like an emperor yet."

"Now I think of it," said Old Yuan, "you often cover the door-handle with newspaper when you open the door. Why do you do that?"

"It's because you're afraid it's dirty, isn't it?" interrupted Big Li.

"Everyone touches it, so of course it's dirty," I replied.

This brought an avalanche of attacks down on me. "Why are you the only one to mind dirt?" "Is it a dirty door you're worried about, or dirty people?" "Doesn't this show that you think you're a cut above everyone else? You think we're all lower than you, don't you?"

I protested vigorously that I entertained no such feelings, but I could not dispel my own doubts. Did I really do this? Did I really have such thoughts? Later someone pointed out to me that when we bathed I was always the first to get into the bath and always got out when the others followed me in; and another fellow-prisoner reminded me that I had always taken the first bowl of *jiaozi* in the

Soviet Union. I had to admit to myself that Big Li was right when he said that I had still not got rid of all my emperor's airs.

When I look back today I see that Big Li was a teacher to me, albeit a stern one. Whatever his motives may have been, he was always·making me see things that I had never thought of for myself, and I finally came to understand that I had only myself to blame for most of my troubles.

Once I lost our group a number of points in a hygiene inspection because I had made a splash on the floor when cleaning my teeth and only rubbed it with my feet instead of cleaning it up properly. Big Li came up to me with a rag and asked me why I had not used a cloth.

"I didn't think of it."

He laid into me for this reply, accusing me of only thinking of myself. "You can only think about your rights, never about your duties." He was on the point of doing it himself, but he flung the cloth on the floor and told me to wipe up the mess myself. I obediently did so.

From the time of the discovery that the Americans were using germ bombs in Korea and the Northeast and the consequent nation-wide patriotic hygiene movement there were several campaigns in the prison at fixed times each year to eliminate pests. Among my many memories of these campaigns is the fly-swatting affair.

Big Li brought in some new fly-swatters one day. There were not enough to go round, and the others were all asking for them. I made no effort to get one, but Big Li handed the first one to me. This was the first time I had ever handled a fly-swatter, and I felt rather awkward as I had, to tell the truth, never killed a single fly in my life.

There were not many flies in the prison, and by the standards of the "New Capital" of "Manchukuo" they were virtually extinct. I hunted for a fly and when at last I found one on the sill of an open window I waved my swatter to drive it out.

"What do you think you're doing?" shouted Big Li from behind me. "Are you killing pests or saving life?"

This may have sounded like a joke to the others, but I knew what he was getting at. I blushed and said in a forced voice, "Of course I'm not saving life." At the same time I wondered why I had let the fly go.

"You won't kill because you're afraid of retribution. Isn't that it?" As he glared at me I felt guilty but put on a bold front.

"What are you talking about? The fly got away, that's all."

"Think it over."

At the criticism meeting that evening nobody mentioned the affair at first, but then Big Li told everyone how I had forbidden the killing of flies in Changchun and even directed people to rescue a mouse from the jaws of a cat. Everyone roared with laughter, then they criticized me for my superstition. While I had to admit to myself that they were right, I heard myself saying: "I'm certainly not superstitious. Didn't I kill flies last year?"

Old Yuan could not restrain his guffaws. "I remember — thanks for reminding me. You gave your swatter to someone else and fanned all the flies away with a newspaper to let them escape."

Amid the peals of mocking laughter that followed only Big Li kept a straight face. "I don't know what it means when other people save life, but in your case I'm sure that it's complete selfishness. You do it to get the blessing of the Buddha. It doesn't matter if everyone else is killed provided that you stay alive. You think that you're the most valuable person on earth."

"That's an exaggeration," I protested.

"Pu Yi does sometimes humble himself," put in Old Yuan.

"Yes," I added, "I don't regard myself as at all superior to anyone."

"Perhaps you do humble yourself sometimes," said Big Li, "but sometimes you still think of yourself as higher and more important than everyone else. I've no idea how you got that way."

Later I gradually came to understand. After forty years of living as a very superior being I had been suddenly brought down to earth. This explained why sometimes I disagreed with the others, lost my temper, and nursed grievances. On the other hand, I was constantly seeing that I was inferior to others, and this made me dispirited, full of hatred, self-abasing and miserable. In short, I had lost my emperor's airs but I still kept my old standards. I realized this later when I discovered that it was impossible to judge some people by these standards. While I was in the same cell as Big Li before I came to understand this, I could only see what the governor had been talking about. I realized that I did not treat others as my equals in my relations with them, which aroused their resentment and prevented them from treating me as an equal or respecting me. It was only when I encountered the generosity of people who could not be measured by my yardstick that I found out what sort of person I really was.

Why So Magnanimous?

One day soon after the Chinese New Year of 1956 the governor made an announcement at the end of a talk on the growth of the national economy:

"You have already studied documents on the First Five-Year Plan, agricultural co-operation, and the socialist transformation of handicrafts and privately-owned industry and commerce. You have also read in the papers about the appearance of joint state-private enterprises in some of the big cities. But all you know about socialist construction is what you have learnt from books. You need to see the present state of the country with your own eyes to be able to link your studies with reality. For this reason the government will arrange for you to make visits outside in the near future. You will see Fushun first, and later you will go to other cities."

That day the atmosphere in the prison was much more cheerful than it had ever been before, and some of the prisoners even saw this as a sign that we would soon be released. I did not share their hopes, convinced that I would certainly not be released even if they were. I was even alarmed about the prospect of showing my face in public on a visit. That afternoon I heard some of the others talking about the problem that was on my mind.

"What do you think the people will do when they see us?"

"Nothing will happen as we'll be taken by government personnel. Otherwise they wouldn't let us go."

"I'm not so sure. What happens if they get excited?" asked Old Fu, minister of agriculture of "Manchukuo". "My goodness, I used to be a petty official, and I've seen the masses when they get worked up. If they turn nasty, surely the government will do what the people demand."

"Don't worry, the government wouldn't let us go if it wasn't quite sure of what it was doing."

The new head of our cell's study group, a former official in the Wang Ching-wei puppet government, came over and said, "I don't think that the government will reveal who we are."

"Whether they reveal it or not, people will know," said Old Yuan with a laugh. "Do you think it will be all right just because the Northeasterners won't recognize you? Once they spot one of us, which they're bound to do, they'll know what sort of people we are."

I thought of the pictures of me that the people of the Northeast had been forced to bow to in the past, and was sure that they would have no difficulty in identifying me. How could the government prevent them from getting worked up and demanding my public trial? As Old Fu had suggested, wouldn't the government do what the people demanded?

In those days I still thought of the common people as completely ignorant and barbarous. Surely they would deal with me, their hated enemy, with ferocious cruelty, ignoring the government and Party policy of leniency and remoulding. I doubted whether the government would be able to prevent this, and suspected that it might be prepared to "sacrifice" me to win popular support. But I was quite wrong.

I shall describe many amazing things I saw on the visit in the next section, but first I want to describe the astonishing people I met.

The first was an ordinary young woman. She had survived the Pingtingshan massacre, and was now the head of the kindergarten of the Fushun Open-cast Mine. Some of the mine staff told us about the history of the mine and the massacre.

In the eastern part of the mining area was a village of about a thousand households called Pingtingshan. Most of the inhabitants were destitute miners. After the Japanese occupation of the North-east, anti-Japanese fighters appeared in this district as they did elsewhere. One night in the autumn of 1933 the South Manchurian Anti-Japanese Volunteers clashed with the Japanese at Pingtingshan, killing a Japanese official and about a dozen Japanese guards, and burning a Japanese store.

The next day, when the resistance fighters had gone, about 190 Japanese guards and some Chinese quislings surrounded Pingtingshan and drove the whole population — men, women and children — at bayonet point to the hill outside the village. Here all three thousand of them were machine-gunned, and then the soldiers bayoneted all the bodies to make sure they were dead. After this they soaked the corpses in petrol, burnt them, and bombarded the hill with heavy artillery to cover the remains. Finally they surrounded the village with a fourfold barbed-wire fence and allowed no strangers in. A warning was issued that anyone who harboured fugitives from Pingtingshan would be killed with his whole family. Thus it was that Pingtingshan was turned into a desolate hillside covered with bones. A popular lament was sung in the Fushun area that went like this:

> Pingtingshan used to be full of life,
> But now it's covered with blood and weeds.
> Gather some bricks,
> Pick up a bone,
> The Japanese have slaughtered our parents and cousins,
> The sea of blood is deep; our hatred will never die.

But the Japanese were unable to slaughter all of the villagers or to cow the workers of Fushun. A little girl of five called Fang Su-jung had escaped from the pile of bloody corpses and had been looked after secretly by a disabled old miner. Thus a witness of the atrocity had survived.

After we prisoners had seen the mine it was time for us to look over the welfare facilities, and so we went to Fang Su-jung's kindergarten. As she was in Shenyang at the time the kindergarten staff told us about her meeting with the Japanese war criminals the previous day.

The kindergarten staff had at first refused to let her meet them as it might be too much of a shock for her. The Japanese criminals discussed the matter and then begged to be allowed to see her as they wanted to apologize to her. After the hesitation of the kindergarten staff had been overcome she finally came in to see them. The war criminals bowed low to her as an expression of their guilt and asked her to tell them about the massacre.

She told them how her father had led her out while her mother carried her baby brother. "The Japanese soldiers and the traitors were shouting that we were to go for a photograph. I asked granddad what a photograph was and he gave me a windmill he had just made and told me not to ask any questions." Thus she had gone with all the other villagers to the execution ground. When the machine-guns started firing her grandfather had covered her with his own body, and she had passed out without even crying. When she came round she found herself surrounded by blood and gore; smoke blotted out the sky.

She was in terrible pain from the eight bullet and bayonet wounds in her body, and was suffering even greater agonies of terror. Her grandfather was silent and she could not see her mother or brother. She climbed out of the pile of corpses and went back to the village, only to find that it had been reduced to smoking rubble. She climbed through the barbed wire and crawled across a field of *kaoliang* stubble, covering her face with her hands. An old man found her and wrapped her in his jacket, after which she had passed out again.

This man was an old miner, crippled after a life of hardship and suffering, who was now reduced to selling cigarettes to keep himself alive. He kept her in a sack, only opening it at night to feed her. Realizing that he could not go on like this for long he had smuggled her in his sack past the Japanese and taken her to the house of an uncle of hers. This uncle had kept her outside in a straw rick, tended her wounds, and fed her at night. When winter approached he took her to some other relations in a more distant village, and she lived with them under a different name.

Wounded in mind and body, Fang Su-jung had grown up nursing the deepest hatred. But when at last the Japanese surrendered they were only replaced by corrupt and venal Kuomintang officials, and to her hatred of the murderers of her family was added loathing for the Chiang Kai-shek troops, who killed, burnt and looted just as the Japanese had done. Finally her village was liberated, and light came into her life. The Party and the government supported and educated her. Later she found a job, married and had children. Now she was a well-known Fushun model worker.

What did this woman say to the criminals who had committed such appalling crimes against China when she met them face to face?

"Even if I were to bite you to death my hatred of you would not be sated. But I am a member of the Communist Party, and the great cause of socialism and changing the world means even more to me than my private feelings. Our Party had made all kinds of policies to achieve these ends, and I believe in them and will carry them out. For the sake of this cause I have put my private hatred to one side."

This amazing forgiveness struck the hundreds of Japanese war criminals dumb for a while, and then they began to weep for shame and kneel before her, asking the Chinese Government to punish them.

Fang Su-jung's magnanimity was astounding enough, but then as a Party member and a cadre she was obliged to take such an attitude. What was even more unimaginable was the magnanimity shown me by an ordinary peasant of Taishanpao.

Taishanpao is a village on the outskirts of Fushun that then formed an agricultural co-operative. We went there on the day after we visited the kindergarten, and my heart was pounding with fear on the way. I remembered the accusations written by peasants that I had read and wondered how I would be treated, convinced that the "crude" and "ignorant" peasants would be incapable of behaving as Fang Su-jung had done. In fact we had met a number of workers and members of their families the previous day, but I had attributed their behaviour to an ignorance of who we were. The previous evening we had visited the home for retired miners. Old men who had worked in the mines all their lives or who had been kicked out by the Japanese after suffering some incapacitating injury had been saved from destitution immediately after the formation of the People's Government, and a former Japanese luxury hotel had been turned into a home where they could end their lives in peace. They spent their time playing chess, growing flowers, reading the papers, and in any other way that suited them. When I visited one of them with a few other prisoners he told us about the wretched life of miners in "Manchukuo" days. I felt ashamed and frightened, hiding in the corner and saying nothing for fear of being recognized. I noticed that instead of the family snapshots that we had seen on the walls of the workers' quarters he only had a picture of Chairman Mao, who was clearly dearer to him than his relations — that is, if he had any relations left alive. I wondered if he understood Chairman Mao's policy of remoulding criminals.

During the first day of our visit we had all tried to make ourselves inconspicuous. Big Mouth, who had once been in charge of building a Japanese Shinto shrine in Fushun, was ashen-faced, and tried all the time to hide in the middle of our group. When we reached Taishanpao not one of us dared to raise his head. In this uneasy state we listened as the chairman of the co-op told us about the co-op's past and present. We went round and saw new tools, poultry, hothouses full of vegetables, livestock, granaries and other things. Everyone we met was kind to us, and some people stopped the work they were doing to stand up and greet us. I congratulated myself on going unrecognized for so long. But when I was in the house of a co-op member at the very end of the visit I was unable to conceal my identity any longer.

The house that I and a few others visited was that of a family named Liu. The parents both worked in the fields, the eldest son was a book-keeper for the storage pits, the second son was at middle school, and the daughter worked at a hydro-electric plant. Only Mrs. Liu was at home when we arrived. She was cooking, and when she saw the commune cadre leading us in she took off her apron and asked us to sit in the north room, which was newly built of concrete. She treated us as real guests, asking us to come right inside and sit on the *kang* in the Northeastern manner. There was a chest of drawers by the wall, and on it stood a large clock, a gleaming tea-service, a number of vases, and a tea-caddy.

The cadre who had brought us did not tell Mrs. Liu who we were, just saying that we were visitors who had come to see the co-op. Then he asked her to talk to us. Although she was not a good talker she told us that they had originally been a family of seven tilling seven *mou* of land (a little over an acre), and that during "Manchukuo" they had lived almost like beggars. "We grew rice, but we had to eat acorn flour. We had to hand over all the rice we grew, and if they found a single grain of it in the house we were 'economic criminals'. Once a man was arrested when he was sick in the road and the police found rice grains in his mess. We all dressed in rags. Some families were even worse off than we, and grown-up girls only had sacking to wear. . . . One New Year the kiddies had nothing to eat, and I can't tell you how cold it was, so my old man said we should secretly have a meal of rice. The police came to the village in the middle of the night, and that really gave us a fright. In fact they had come to seize men for forced labour, and they sent them out to fell trees and build defences. They said it was for protection against bandits, but really it was because they were scared of our Anti-Japanese Allied Armies. My old man was dragged off. Hardly any of the men who were taken off from our village for forced labour came back alive. . . ."

Her son came in while she was speaking. He was very short, and on closer examination we could see that he had been born a cripple with stunted legs. In answer to our questions he told us that in the old days his deformity had forced him to lead a dog's life, whereas he now worked as the book-keeper for the storage pits with as much dignity as everyone else. His eyes were full of hatred for the past, but when he talked of the present his voice and manner became cheerful and confident, just like his mother. He told us

414

about all the vegetables that had never been grown in the village before, and his mother showed us the large crock of rice in the corner. "Who wants to look at rice?" her son asked with a laugh. "There's nothing to it these days," she riposted, "but how often did you see it in the time of Kang Te?"[1]

This last remark stung me to the quick.

I had been frightened when we first came into this house that they would ask me my name, and now I felt that it would be unforgivable dishonesty if I did not tell them who I was before I went. I stood up and said with my head bowed, "The Kang Te of whom you speak is Pu Yi, the traitorous puppet emperor of 'Manchukuo'. I am he. I owe you my apologies."

Before I had finished speaking the former puppet ministers and generals who were with me rose to their feet and told her who they were. One had been the minister responsible for forced labour, one had been in charge of sending grain to Japan, and one had been a military commander who forced men into the puppet army to fight for the Japanese.

The old lady was dumbfounded. Although she had guessed we were "Manchukuo" war criminals she had clearly not known who we were, nor had she imagined that we would ask her to deal with us.

How in fact did she deal with us? She did not curse or weep, nor did she call in the neighbours or the widows and orphans of men killed in the old days to vent their wrath on us. Instead she said with a sigh that wrung my heart, "It's all over now. Don't let's say any more about it." She wiped away her tears. "As long as you're willing to study, do what Chairman Mao says, and become decent people, you'll be all right."

We had been weeping silently before, but with these words we broke into sobs.

"We know what sort of people you are," said her son in a low voice. "Chairman Mao says that the great majority of criminals can be remoulded, and what he says can't be wrong. If you reform and acknowledge your guilt the common people will forgive you."

---

[1] The reign title used when I was "Emperor of Manchukuo".

Such was the magnanimity of the peasants whom I had thought crude, ignorant and liable to take their revenge without caring about the policy of leniency and remoulding.

They were now their own masters, and behind them they had a powerful government and army led by the Communist Party. Yet when faced with prisoners who had committed the most appalling crimes against them they were able to show such generosity. It was on this visit that I learnt the answer why.

The Changes Explain Everything

Our mood at the end of our three-day visit was in sharp contrast to that in which we had set out, lively conversation replacing grim silence. For our first two days back in prison we talked all the time, and the topic was always our trip. The recurrent theme was, "Things have changed, society has changed, all Chinese have changed." Of course, the theme of change was one we had often read about in the papers and in family letters or heard about from the prison authorities during the past few years, but some of the more worldly-wise among us had wanted to check on this at first hand. One of these was Old Yuan in our cell, and this time he too was convinced.

One evening we were talking about the cakes we had tasted ourselves in the workers' canteen. One of us said that while we had seen the food provided at work it was a pity that we had not seen any meals being cooked on the gas rings in the workers' flats. Then Old Yuan told us what he had discovered. While the rest of us had been looking at the workers' rooms he had gone behind the building to look in the dustbins, where he had found fishbones, eggshells and other food remains.

Old Fu, who had been a supply officer with the old Northeastern army before becoming the "Manchukuo" minister of agriculture, was normally a taciturn fellow, but today he was rather animated. "In the days of 'Manchukuo' you wouldn't find fish or meat in workers' houses, and even before that they were a rare sight. I ought to know — I started out in life as a petty official."

Old Cheng, who had been brought up by the Japanese, said frankly: "When I read the papers and studied political documents in the past I was sometimes convinced and sometimes suspicious, and I used to think that this Northeastern industrial base was something left by the Japanese. But at the factory attached to the Industrial School I saw that the old Japanese belt-driven lathes there had been replaced with brand-new Chinese-made equipment; now I believe that the Chinese have indeed stood up. They really have changed."

I certainly agreed that they had changed, and I had other feelings about the visit as well.

The astonishing magnanimity that the people had shown me during the three days of our visit had made me wonder whether this could be real. Were they prepared to ignore the crimes that traitors had committed against them? Did they really have such faith in the policy of remoulding criminals? How could this be?

The changes explained everything. From the late nineteenth century onwards Fushun had been famous for its mineral wealth, but those who had benefited from it had not been the wretchedly poor miners. In 1905 the open-cast mines had come under Japanese control after the defeat of tsarist Russia, and in the four succeeding decades it is estimated that between 250,000 and 300,000 miners died of their sufferings in the mines.

The miners, who were mostly destitute peasants from Shantung, Hopei and the Northeast, came in droves every year. They worked over twelve hours a day. Most of them lived in "big houses" with one or two hundred men to a room, and wore rags all the year round. Some of them could not afford clothes for their new-born babies, and when the children died of starvation, they were forced to bury them naked. Low as their wages were, they had to pay a proportion of them to the managers and the gangers. What was left was not enough for adequate food and clothing. Few of them could afford to marry, and before liberation 70 per cent of the men in the Lungfeng Mine were bachelors.

There was no question of safety precautions in the mines, and explosions and cave-ins were common events. As the workers used to put it, "If you want to be a miner, you have to risk your life." After a gas explosion in 1917 the Japanese owners sealed off a mine to prevent losses of coal, leaving 917 men inside to be burnt alive. A flood in the same mine killed 482 miners in 1928. According to "Manchukuo" official statistics, 251,999 men were killed and injured in these mines between 1916 and 1944. A mountain valley was filled with the bodies of those who were not buried inside the pit, and was called the "Ten Thousand Men's Grave".

The Japanese opened a place they called the "Pleasure Garden" where there were over a thousand whores, gambling houses, and opium and morphine dens.

In old Fushun there were luxury homes for Japanese and the towering head-gear for the mines, but there were also beggars and dead cats and babies beside the Yangpai River and floating in the sewers. In winter new corpses were found every day by the Yangpai bridge. Fushun also had a "reformatory" during the "Manchukuo" period, a concentration camp for the workers who opposed "Manchukuo" and Japan.

There had been enormous changes since then. On the remains of the shacks with 3,500 square metres' floor-space that the Japanese had built for the workers in thirty-one years, new workers' quarters of 170,000 square metres had been erected in the seven years since liberation. We visited one worker's home here, probably belonging to one of the 80 per cent of the miners who had married since liberation.

In these rooms I saw the blue flames of a gas ring.

The head of the mine office told us something about gas as we walked along one of the underground roadways of the Lungfeng Mine. The Lungfeng, Shengli and Laohu collieries had been exceptionally bad for gas, the great enemy of miners all over the world. The three mines were in a terrible state immediately after liberation, particularly the Lungfeng, whose roadways had been obstructed by falls as a result of sabotage first by the Japanese and then by the Kuomintang. It was also so full of gas that blasting and electrical equipment could not be used in it.

In the autumn of 1949 one of the mine's engineers proposed to the Party committee that the gas should be piped to the surface and put to good use above ground, which would also end the gas danger in the mine. The committee gave the engineer their full support, and the workers, particularly the older men and their dependants, said that they were willing to do anything to make this plan succeed. An experimental project was organized. The workers who were members of the Party were in the forefront of the struggle that was waged day and night in the gas-filled underground roadways. At first they met with difficulties. They were often surrounded by dense gas and attacked by cowards and conservatives; but on July 1, 1950 the experimental project was completed, and a blue flame shot from the nozzle of the pipe bringing the gas up from underground. The old workers wept, and the youngsters shouted, "We've won again."

This story made me think of a song I had heard some chubby youngsters singing in a kindergarten that morning:

> Without the Communist Party
> There would be no New China.

As we walked along the underground roadway we came across a brightly-lit shop selling fruit, sweets, towels, handkerchiefs and so on. We stopped here, and our guide explained that a filthy and rat-infested stream flowed here in "Manchukuo" days. "No one dared to touch the rats as supersitition was widespread and people said that they were the horses of the Taoist god Laotzu. The miners used to worship him in the hope of getting some security in their lives. Nowadays they have all thrown the pictures of Laotzu out of their houses." Pointing at the clean concrete floor he told us that the miners used to walk barefoot in the filthy water here in the old days, and that at some faces they used to work stark naked.

We walked on past electrically-drawn wagons that were carrying the coal away.

"In the old days there were roadways where trains went but people couldn't. Men were often run over, but of course the number killed that way was nothing compared with those who died in explosions. The miners used to say that they were 'lumps of flesh stuck in the coal-face'. They would return each night from their long labour underground thankful that they had survived another day. There was always a crowd of women and children waiting at the pithead when the miners came off, and if a man was missing they knew he was dead. Often the bodies weren't even recovered." He pointed to the wall. "I saw four men buried alive there. I first came down the pit when I was fourteen, and I wouldn't like to say how many times I've brushed with death since then."

He told us how terrified the workers used to be of sickness. Their resistance was low as their shacks were unheated, they had rags for clothes and sacks for bedding, and their food ration was only eight tiny corn buns a day. If the Japanese found that a man was sick they would put him into a heavily guarded isolation centre and give him only a bowl of rice porridge at each meal. Some of the inmates were incinerated before they were dead, or buried alive in "Ten Thousand Men's Grave". Our guide told us that the father of the man we had just seen driving the train had been buried alive.

After a moment's silence he went on to tell us that once he had almost suffocated in the foul atmosphere there used to be down the mine. He had been ill when he went up, but the ganger had threatened to flog him if he did not go down the pit again. As he was the youngest miner in the shack in which he lived the others came and chased the ganger away. He said that the workers most feared by the Japanese and the overseers were the Eighth Route Army prisoners, who were prepared to kill their oppressors if they caught them underground. This meant that the Japanese were forced to treat them better. Although these prisoners were rigidly segregated from the other miners, their resistance showed the rest of the miners that the gangers and the Japanese were no more formidable than the mine rats, and that their days were numbered.

I was conscious of the contrast between this self-confident miner and myself as I was in those days, sick of eating meat, taking my daily injections and medicine, overcome with feelings that my end was near, and with all my human dignity lost. In those days he would have thought of me and my kind as no more than rats. What was his view of us now?

I thought of the tears shed by the older workers when the gas was first successfully piped off and the confident victory cries of the younger men. In their eyes all secrets had been revealed and everything and everybody could be remoulded. What did they care about an emperor when the future was theirs? This was another reason why they were able to be so forgiving towards me. Everything had changed, and the most basic change was the one that had taken place in people. Without the Communist Party all these changes and the magnanimity extended to us would have been impossible.

Meeting Relations

I learnt from this visit that if the people were to forgive me I would have to become a real human being. I had learnt other things too. On the first day of the visit I had looked at the new government through old-fashioned spectacles, refusing to believe that any regime could be on terms of mutual confidence with the masses, as I had read in books. I thought that the reason why the Communist Party had such powerful armed forces and so strong a government was because of its great cunning and its demagogic skill. This was why I had feared that they might sacrifice me to the wrath of the masses. Now I knew that the reason why the people supported and trusted the Party was because of the unprecedented benefits it had brought them, benefits that I had seen with my own eyes during our visit. No previous regime had even wanted, let alone been able, to bring about such progress.

I had also thought that even if the poor did well in the new society, those who had been rich or important in the old days, people closely connected with myself, and members of the minority national groups would not be at all satisfied. Soon after our trip I was visited by some of my own relations, and I learnt that this view was as absurd as the other. In fact an unprecedentedly large proportion of all social strata was pleased with the new state of affairs.

We prisoners had started to exchange letters with our relations in the summer of 1955. We found out from them that they were not being discriminated against because we were criminals. Some of the children were at school and some at work; some had become specialists and some had joined the Communist Youth League or the Party. Many of us were greatly encouraged by our family letters, and realized a little more clearly what the changes in society meant to ourselves. Some of the more suspicious of us were only half convinced, and a few were so biased as to put the most fantastic interpretations on them. When Old Chang, a former puppet general, received the first letter from his son he found that it began "Mr. Chang, I am sorry, but I cannot address you in any other way. . . ." Old Chang went almost mad with grief, and many other prisoners sympathized with him. "So this is how the new society brings up the young," some people muttered. "Because the father's in jail the son wants no more of him." I could not help remembering how Chen Pao-shen had said that the Communists were heartless and unjust. Old Liu, another former general who was in the same cell as Pu Chieh, was very fond of his daughter and was deeply worried that she might be the victim of discrimination. Previously he had been thoroughly sceptical about New China, but now he read in a letter from her that she was well provided for and had been admitted to the Youth League. Her organization was taking good care of her, she had plenty of friends, and had been sent by the state to an art school, which was the fulfilment of her old ambition. Old Liu shook his hoary head over the letter, saying, "Even if every word in it is true I won't believe it until I can see her with my own eyes." From 1956 onwards all our questions were answered, and I learnt that the problems that had been solved were not just those of single families but those of a whole nationality and a whole younger generation.

On March 10, three days after our trip, the warder told me, Pu Chieh, my two brothers-in-law and my three nephews to go to the governor's office. We went into his reception room, and to our astonishment we saw my uncle Tsai Tao and my third and fifth sisters. We had been separated for over ten years.

When I saw my uncle looking as fit as ever and my sisters in their cotton-padded clothes I felt as if I were dreaming.

Tsai Tao was the only surviving close relation of mine from the previous generation. In 1954 he had been elected to the National People's Congress as the representative of China's two million Manchus. He was also a member of the National Committee of the Chinese People's Political Consultative Conference. He told me that he had met Chairman Mao a few days back at the second meeting of the Congress. Premier Chou En-lai had introduced him to the Chairman as Mr. Tsai Tao, the uncle of Pu Yi. Chairman Mao had shaken him by the hand and said, "I have heard that Pu Yi's studies are going quite well; why don't you go and visit him?"

As my uncle told us this his voice shook so much with emotion that it was almost inaudible, and I was unable to hold back my tears. We all wept, and my nephew Jui finally sobbed out loud.

In this meeting with my relations I learnt that not only had I myself been saved but that the entire Aisin-Gioro clan and Manchu nationality had been rescued.

My uncle told me that while there had been only 80,000 registered Manchus before liberation the present figure was thirty times as high. I understood the significance of this change. I knew what a wretched state the bannermen had fallen into under Peiyang warlord rule and the Kuomintang government, when they had found great difficulty in getting jobs unless they pretended to be of the Han nationality. Many of the members of the Aisin-Gioro clan had changed their surnames to Chin, Chao or Lo; my father's family in Tientsin, for example, had taken the name Chin. After liberation more and more Manchus acknowledged their nationality, and when all of them registered after the proclamation of the Constitution the total of 2,400,000 surprised even the Manchus themselves.

I remembered my anger at the time of the robbery of the Eastern Mausolea and the vow I had sworn before the tablets of my ancestors that I would avenge them. In fact all I had done had been to speed the destruction of my own people and clan; and it was only after the collapse of my clique and the Japanese who claimed to support me that the Manchus and the Aisin-Gioro clan had found a secure future. The proof of this was the change from 80,000 to 2,400,000.

This historic change affected not only the younger Aisin-Gioros but also the *beileh*[1] Tsai Tao and my own sisters. My uncle was now 69, but such was his mental and physical vigour that I could see little of the old man about him. I noticed that his customary way of talking to me was unchanged. He explained that after liberation he had worked for a department of the People's Liberation Army that was in charge of horses, and he was very pleased to tell me that he had spent some time in the steppes of the Northwest. At the moment he was planning to make a trip to inspect the work of the national minorities as a part of his duties as a member of the National People's Congress.

Immediately after the entry of the People's Liberation Army into Peking many of the old Manchus had been worried, particularly those of the Aisin-Gioro clan, and they did not lose their doubts even after reading the Proclamation of the People's Liberation Army.[2] Most of these old Peking Manchus had not been members of the "new nobility" of the "Manchukuo" or Wang Ching-wei puppet regimes, but some of them had not yet lost their superstitious respect for my person and were more alarmed than ever when they heard that I had been imprisoned. The combination of this, the ever diminishing number of Manchus, and their destitution meant that they had no "illusions" about the People's Liberation Army. Their first surprise came when they learnt that the Northeastern People's Government had opened a special school for Manchu children. Later on they saw representatives of the Manchu nationality take part with representatives of all other circles in the meetings of the Chinese People's Political Consultative Conference that discussed the Common Programme.[3] Then cadres from the People's Government visited the homes of quite a few of them to invite them to be representatives in

---

[1] A Manchu noble title.

[2] This was made public in April 1949. It contained an eight-point covenant, promising, among other things, to protect the lives and property of all the people except counter-revolutionaries and saboteurs.

[3] The Common Programme served as a provisional constitution before the adoption of the Constitution by the National People's Congress in September 1954.

local political consultative conferences. The cadres asked them to make suggestions on behalf of themselves and the Manchu people and to contribute their efforts to the building of a new society. In Peking all the descendants in my generation of my great-grandfather the emperor Tao Kuang and of Prince Tun, Prince Kung and Prince Chun were over sixty except for a few cousins of mine who were a little younger. My second cousin Pu Chin (also known as Pu Hsueh-chai), an outstanding painter, calligrapher, and player of the *ku chin* (an ancient Chinese stringed instrument), was now over sixty, and to his surprise he was able to take his *ku chin* down from the wall again and go once a week to the banks of Peihai Lake in Peking to indulge his passion for this ancient art with his old and new friends. He saw a bright future for Chinese classical music in the youngsters who were his students. In addition to this he had been elected vice-president of the *Ku Chin* Research Association and president of the Calligraphy Research Association; he had been invited to attend a district political consultative conference; and he had become a teacher at the Academy of Chinese Painting. His brother Pu Chien was also teaching Chinese painting. His cousin Pu Hsiu had been a "Companion of the Chien Ching Gate" in the Forbidden City and looked after my Tientsin property while I was in Changchun, but had since lost his eyesight and been unable to earn his living. After liberation his experiences and the historical materials that he carried in his brain were valued highly by the new society, and he was asked to become a member of the Institute for Classical and Historical Studies. These institutes have been founded all over the country, and their members include scholars who passed the imperial examinations of the Ching Dynasty, witnesses of the events of the warlord and Chiang Kai-shek periods, participants in the Revolution of 1911, members of the early revolutionary organization, the Tung Meng Hui, and even people who had seen behind the scenes at the last feudal court. Pu Hsiu was full of confidence in life, and he recounted what he remembered about Ching history for others to write down on his behalf.

These phenomena, that already seemed normal to the new society, were fresh to me and made a deep impression. But what made the deepest impression was the change I could see in my sisters.

Some six months previously I had exchanged letters with my brothers and sisters in Peking. I had realized from what they wrote that big changes were taking place in my family, but I had never given the matter much serious thought. During the "Manchukuo" days all of my brothers and sisters except Fourth Brother and Sixth and Seventh Sisters had lived in Changchun and accompanied me in my flight to Tunghua. After my capture I had been worried that they might be discriminated against as traitors. Second Sister's husband was the grandson of the "Manchukuo" premier Cheng Hsiao-hsu, while Third Sister was married to the younger brother of my first wife; and Fifth Sister had married the son of the chief of staff to Chang Hsun, the monarchist general who had put me back on the throne in 1917. These two husbands had both been "Manchukuo" lieutenant-colonels. The father-in-law of my fourth sister had been the Manchu official who was notorious for having killed the outstanding woman revolutionary Chiu Chin in 1907. All of my sisters' husbands had been either military officers or civil functionaries of the "Manchukuo" regime. Sixth and Seventh Sisters alone had been regular students, but I was still worried that they might have suffered because their eldest brother was a leading traitor. Such anxieties were shared by all of us prisoners, but mine were worse than those of the others. Later my family correspondence showed me that my fears were groundless. My brothers and sisters enjoyed the same right to work as other people and their children could go to school and receive scholarships in the normal way. Fourth Brother and Seventh Sister were still primary school teachers, Sixth Sister was a freelance painter, Fifth Sister was a seamstress, and Third Sister was a social activist who had been chosen by her neighbours as a member of the street committee responsible for security. Although they were doing their own cooking and looking after their own children, their letters showed that they were satisfied and happy. I stopped worrying. Now that I had seen these two sisters again and heard what they said to their own husbands, I started to think about them even more.

I can still remember how Old Wan, the husband of Fifth Sister, stared wide-eyed as he asked her, "Can you really ride a bicycle?

Can you sew too?" These were things that had astonished him in her letters, and he wanted to ask her about them in person. He had good reason to be surprised. As a child she had not even dared to run, and when she grew up she had been surrounded by maids and waiting women. She had never even entered a kitchen or touched a pair of scissors; could she now ride a bicycle to work and use scissors to make clothes? Was she really a self-supporting seamstress?

What was even more amazing to him was the way she answered quite naturally, "What's so strange about that? There's nothing to it."

Third Sister had been through rather more than Fifth Sister. As her son was ill she had not gone straight back to Peking after the Japanese surrender but had stayed at Tunghua with two nurses. She had no property, and as she was afraid of attracting attention because of her origin and her fine clothes she set up a cigarette stall in Tunghua. She was nearly forced to leave by Kuomintang agents and was swindled by a merchant who sold her some matches that would not strike. After a few years of this insecure life she returned to Peking in 1949. Since liberation she had regularly taken part in meetings of the street committee. She had known something about the policies of the government as she had been in contact with the People's Liberation Army and the People's Government in the Northeast; and as she enjoyed the confidence of her neighbours she had been elected to work for the street committee. The part of her job that she spoke about with the greatest enthusiasm was explaining the new Marriage Law.

This would not have been particularly fascinating to other people, but it gave me rather a surprise. She had been even more the "refined young lady" than Fifth Sister in the old days, and was always asking me about the presents I gave to other people. Who would have expected that this spoilt, lazy girl, capable only of asking me for things, was now a social activist? It sounded incredible at first, but this change made sense. I came to understand why she was an enthusiastic propagator of the new Marriage Law and why she

427

sometimes burst into tears when reading the papers. I knew she meant it when she said, "In the old days I was nothing but an ornament."

Although she was quite well educated and a noblewoman, her life in the old days was futile and jejune. When she and her husband were staying in Japan I once wrote and asked her to tell me about everyday life in that country. Her reply read like this: "I am sitting in a room with my maid ironing my clothes beside me. Outside the window an old servant is watering flowers, and a puppy is sitting on the floor gazing at a box of sweets. . . . That's all there is to it." Now her life had much more meaning because her neighbours were so eager to hear her read the papers to them.

Later she told me about an experience of hers when she was in Tunghua after the Japanese surrender. "One day the people's militia came for me and said that the common people were holding a meeting at which they wanted me to tell them about my past. I was scared stiff of struggle meetings against traitors and said that I would do anything they liked if they let me off. Then I saw some cadres who told me not to be frightened as the masses were very reasonable. I had no choice and had to go on the platform, shivering with terror as I was, and tell the meeting about my life. There were huge crowds of people there including some who had come just to see the princess. When I had finished speaking a whispered discussion started. Finally someone got up and said, 'She hasn't done anything wicked herself, so we don't have anything against her.' Everyone agreed with this and the meeting ended. Then I realized that the common people are very reasonable."

This last point was something that I had just come to understand myself.

On the second day of meeting the family I happened to receive a letter from Second Sister in which she said that her eldest daughter was in the second year at a physical training college and had become an outstanding spare-time driving instructor. She had recently ridden a motor-bicycle all the way from Tientsin to Hankow. My sister wrote happily that her daughter, an aristocratic young lady 12 years ago, had become an athlete, and her other children were also doing well at school. When I mentioned this to Fifth and Third Sisters they wiped the tears from their eyes and told me about their own children. This convinced me that the fate of the Aisin-Gioro clan had really changed.

I once made a calculation on the basis of the "Jade Register" of the imperial family compiled in 1937 and the information provided by my brothers and sisters about the rate of infantile mortality in my branch of the Aisin-Gioro clan. Thirty-four per cent of the children had died in the Ching Dynasty, 10 per cent during the Republic, and none in the ten years since liberation. The figures for the whole Aisin-Gioro clan would be even more staggering, with something like 45 per cent of the boys and girls of my and my father's generation dying in childhood, mostly under the age of two.

I had not made these calculations when I met my uncle and sisters, but the early death of so many of the children of my family in the old days occurred to me then. And those who grew up were capable of nothing except carrying a bird-cage around; there were no other possibilities open to them. Apart from strolling in the Hou Men district with their bird-cages in their hands, the older generation would drink tea every day from dawn until lunch, when about ten dishes of cheap food would be laid out for show, and after that they would throw their weight around at home. That was all the older generation was capable of, while the youngsters were rarely aware of the need to learn anything but how to serve and imitate their seniors. Even if they were driven by penury to look for work or tried to find some job in which to use their talents they never found anything. I had known so many cases of this during the Republic.

But things had changed completely. The fate of my juniors was something that I could never even have hoped for in the old days. My brother and six sisters in Peking had twenty-seven children between them, and all of them who were of the right age were in school or university. My uncle Tsai Tao had sixteen grandchildren and great-grandchildren, of whom one was a technician at a hydro-electric station, one had distinguished himself with the People's Volunteers in Korea, one was an army cultural worker, and the others (except for those who were below school age) were all studying or working. In the eyes of this generation the idle life of their elders was just a joke.

One member of the younger generation had met with a different fate. Pu Chieh's wife had written to him from Japan telling him that their elder daughter, a girl of eighteen, had killed herself in a suicide pact with a young man because of a love affair. I have since heard many different versions of this story, and I am convinced that the boy was as unfortunate as my niece. Such are the contrasts in the fate of young people in different periods and societies.

From that year onwards there were continual family visits to the prison. It is worth mentioning the meeting between Old Liu, the most resolute sceptic of us all, and his daughter who was studying to be an artist. She brought her future husband along with her.

"Don't you believe it yet, Dad?" she asked him. "I'm at art school, and this is my fiancé."

"I believe it now," her father replied.

"Do you understand that I would have been unable to go to art school if it were not for the leadership of Mao Tse-tung?"

"I understand."

"If you understand that, you should study properly and reform."

Previously Old Chang had almost gone out of his mind when he received a letter in which his son addressed him as "Mr.". But now his daughter came to visit him with a letter from her brother. Old Chang showed this letter to almost everyone in the prison.

Dear Father,

I now see that I was too "leftist". The teaching that I have been given by the Youth League and the criticisms of my comrades are right: I should not have taken such an attitude to you. . . . What difficulties are you having with your studies? I thought that you were bound to be using a pen in your studies, so I have bought one and asked Sister to bring it to you. . . .

The Japanese War Criminals

In June and July I went with some other prisoners to appear as a witness at the military tribunal hearing the cases of the Japanese war criminals at Shenyang.

I had read in the press that over a thousand Japanese war criminals had been in captivity in China, some in Fushun and some in Taiyuan. They had all committed crimes during the Japanese invasion of China. In June and July of 1956 forty-five of them were sentenced at Shenyang and Taiyuan, while the rest were not put on trial but were repatriated with the help of the Chinese Red Cross. Thirty-six prisoners from the Fushun group were tried at Shenyang in two groups. I had known about some of them during my "Manchukuo" days, and had heard others of them speaking at a meeting in the prison at Fushun. One of these was Furumi Tadayuki, the former vice-head of the "General Affairs Office of the Manchukuo State Council". It was against him and his superior Takebe Rokuzo that I and four former puppet ministers were to give evidence. Furumi was the first to be tried by the court, and he was later sentenced to eighteen years' imprisonment.[1]

As I went into the courtroom I thought of the victory in the Korean War, the successful signing of the Geneva Agreement, and China's position in the world since the founding of the People's Republic. The trial of Japanese war criminals on Chinese soil was unprecedented.

When the Chinese People's Volunteers and the Korean People's Army won in Korea I had thought that there was no hope for me except to acknowledge my guilt and throw myself on the mercy of the Chinese people. Now that the Japanese war criminals were being tried I was not worried about my own future and was instead filled with national pride. In addition I thought about many other problems.

---

[1] He was released in February 1963 before serving his full sentence.

In the last part of the speech he made before his judgement Furumi said something like this:

There is not a square inch of land in the whole of the Northeast that bears no trace of the barbarity of Japanese imperialism, and the crimes of imperialism were my crimes. I most deeply acknowledge that I am a war criminal who has openly violated international law and humanitarian principles by committing the gravest crimes against the Chinese people, and I sincerely apologize to them for this. Over the past six years the Chinese people have treated me with kindness although I am so horrible a criminal, and they have given me the chance to reflect coolly on my crimes. Thanks to this I have recovered my conscience and my reason, and I have learnt which road men should take. I do not know how I can possibly repay this gift of the Chinese people.

I remember that after I had given my evidence the judges asked him what comments he had to make. He bowed deeply and said that every word of my testimony was true.

My thoughts went back to the International Military Tribunal in Tokyo. There the Japanese war criminals had used lawyers to make trouble and attack the witnesses. In the hope of lightening their sentences they had used every conceivable method to cover up their crimes. But at this court all the war criminals admitted their guilt and submitted to punishment.

My brother and brothers-in-law told me a great deal about the Japanese prisoners. They had helped in translating the confessions of the Japanese prisoners and the letters that some of them had sent from Japan after they were repatriated. When my brothers-in-law were released this work was done by Pu Chieh, Old Pang, and others. From 1956 onwards I heard quite a few stories about the Japanese war criminals.

One of them had been an army general, and when the investigating body began its work in 1954 he told them almost nothing. But at this military tribunal he admitted that he had directed his men to perpetrate six different massacres of civilians in Hopei and Honan. In October 1942, for example, a unit under his command had butchered over 1,280 residents of Panchiatai Village and burnt down some thousand houses. After being sentenced to twenty years' imprisonment he said to a journalist that he deserved to have been sentenced to death and told him how fairly he had been interrogated and tried. He had even been provided with a lawyer. "When I remember how many Chinese people I have killed and how difficult I made life for their dependants, my heart is cut to shreds at the thought that it is those very relations who are now looking after me."

A former Japanese colonel was interviewed by journalists on the Japanese boat in which he was being repatriated without having been tried. As he had been very angry when his former subordinates had questioned him in prison about his crimes they were hoping that he would have something uncomplimentary to say about China. When he failed to give them what they wanted, one of the journalists asked, "Why do you go on talking that way? Are you still frightened of China?" "I'm on board a Japanese boat," the colonel replied, "so why should I be afraid of China? I'm telling you the truth, that's all."

Third Sister's husband had been head patient in one of the sick-rooms. There was one Japanese war criminal who always made trouble for the nurses and warders and disregarded the prison regulations; but at a farewell party after his release was announced he burst into tears and made a speech about his mistakes. There was another invalid who, although not as troublesome as the previous one, refused to see his guilt. He was sent to hospital for two emergency operations on a malignant rectal cancer, and the doctor gave some of his own blood to save his life. After leaving the hospital he told a large meeting how he had butchered and tortured the Chinese people in the past, and he compared this with the way the Chinese people had saved his life when he lay dying. Both he and his audience were in tears throughout his speech.

Once when we were levelling the ground to make flowerbeds we dug up a bone with a bullet hole in it. Old Yuan and Old Hsien, who had studied some Western medicine, said that it had belonged to a young girl. Later on my brother-in-law Old Wan translated an article by a Japanese war criminal, who had been the governor of this prison in the old days, describing the hellish life of the patriots who had been incarcerated there. The place rang with the screams of the tortured and echoed with the clanking of chains. It was stinking and filthy; in winter the walls were covered with ice and in summer it was swarming with flies and mosquitoes. The prisoners were only given one small bowl of *kaoliang* a day and had to do heavy labour from dawn to dusk. Many were beaten or worked to death. This article went on to describe the changes in the prison since then and the sharp contrast between the conditions in the old days and those he had experienced as a prisoner himself.

Many of the war criminals wrote in letters and articles that they 'had felt fear and hatred when they were sent back to China by the Soviet Union. Some of them, like myself, had tried to understand things in terms of their old ideology, and had failed to see why the Chinese people were treating them as they did. When they saw the boiler-room being built they imagined that it was going to be a death house and when they saw medical facilities being provided they assumed that they were going to be used in experiments as prisoners had been in the time of Japanese rule. Others saw in their lenient and humane treatment a sign of weakness, but the victories of the Chinese People's Volunteers in Korea showed them that the people who were reasonable to them were certainly not weak, whereas the true sign of weakness was cruelty.

Even before these stories came out nearly everyone except me knew about the changes that had taken place in the Japanese war criminals; I was too preoccupied with my own problems to think about them. In fact the changes had become more and more obvious ever since 1954 or thereabouts. In his diary for 1955 Pu Chieh described plays and performances of music and dancing put on by the Japanese prisoners. One play was about the horrible effects of the atom bomb explosion at Nagasaki. He also mentioned sports meetings the Japanese prisoners held on the ground they had levelled themselves.

Now I look back on it the changes that took place in them are very clear. Why did these prisoners become so happy and high-spirited? Why was it that after their release they took with them the musical instruments they had been given by the prison authorities and played with tears in their eyes as they looked back towards China from the Japanese boat that was taking them home? Why were they so fond of singing "Tokyo-Peking"? Why was it that even those who had served sentences said, "We are grateful to the Chinese people and are ashamed of. . . ."

Letters sent back from repatriated Japanese war criminals often contained such sentences as: "I learnt in China how one should live"; "Now I know what life is"; and "As I take the first steps along the course of a human life I wish to say, Mr. Governor, that I shall never forget the warmth of your handshake as you wished me good health".

Some prisoners read in the Japanese press about girls who went around with the American troops like the "jeep girls" of pre-liberation China, and they roundly condemned these women. One prisoner wrote a letter to his wife asking her if she was doing this. When the letter was checked by the prison authorities they took it back to the writer and asked him with great patience to reconsider it. "Is it proper to write a letter like this to your wife? Even if you had any grounds for asking such a question — and you don't — whose fault would it be? Not hers, surely." The prisoner said nothing, crumpled the letter into a ball, and threw it on the floor. Then he put his head into his hands and burst into tears.

They were grateful to the Chinese people for teaching them to recognize the truth as well as for treating them leniently. Just as I had learnt what in fact emperors were, they had come to see what militarism and Japan were really like. In letters written from Japan they described the startling increase in juvenile delinquency.

In the U.S. bases American tanks were rolling over their land; U.S. military aircraft were soiling their skies; and G.I.s were debauching their women. One letter from a man who had returned to his village was full of the changes that had taken place among the youth there. "Some have become gangsters, others kill because of women, and some have joined the Self-Defence Force and are living a depraved life, besotted with liquor and girls." The young people did not obey their parents, and culture was decadent and full of violence.

The released prisoners spoke about the new China and Japanese militarism, opposing the restoration of the latter and pleading for independence, peace, and democracy. They did this in spite of surveillance and restrictions that they avoided with great ingenuity. When reactionaries did not allow them to perform Chinese dances themselves, they taught them to professional dancers, so that they spread throughout the whole of Japan. They were asked to speak about their life in prison and about New China. They spoke about the friendship of the Chinese people for the people of Japan, of their attitude to war now that they were strong, and of their hopes and ideals. Some people doubted, some had their reservations, and others were convinced. The pro-American government disliked them more and more, while the people's belief in what they said grew.

They published a book called *The Three-All Policy*[1] in which men who had themselves participated in the savageries committed by the Japanese army in China described how they had exterminated the populations of whole regions, used the Chinese people as the subjects of experiments in bacteriological warfare, dissected people alive, and so on. The first printing of 50,000 sold out in a week.

When a number of retired generals heard a former fellow-soldier of theirs describe his experiences in China they were silent for a long time before one of them said, "Our instincts and what we know of you are enough to convince us of the truth of every word you have told us. But we can only say so behind closed doors."

When one ex-soldier went back to his village the local people came to greet him with a banner reading "Eternal Victory". But when he got off the train the returning soldier made a very painful speech, after which the local people understood the causes of the Hiroshima disaster and wept. The banner was dropped to the ground.

Many of the dependants of the war criminals were simple working people and men of goodwill. Quite a few of them had written to the Chinese government in the past asking for the release of their "innocent" husbands and sons. Later some of them were allowed to come to China to visit their imprisoned relations. When they heard what their menfolk had to say and listened to recordings

---

[1] The policy of "burn all, loot all, and kill all" carried out by the Japanese invaders in China.

of the accusations made by the Chinese people before the court they wept with the prisoners. They understood now that the men were guilty and had been deceived by militarism.

The changes among the Japanese war criminals, like those that took place in my family, shook me to the core. One fact stood out clearly in my mind: the Communist Party used reason to win people over.

"The World's Glory"

From the second half of 1956 onwards I was often interviewed by foreign journalists and visitors, and other foreigners wrote to me asking for my picture. In February 1957 I received a letter from a Frenchman in which he asked me to autograph a picture of myself. In addition to some photos of my past there was an article, though what the point of it was I do not know. It read as follows:

THE IMPRISONED EMPEROR OF CHINA

The world's glory is meaningless: this sums up the life of a political prisoner now awaiting sentence in Red China's Fushun Prison. As a child he wore precious silks, but now he is dressed in tattered clothes of padded cotton as he walks alone in the prison yard. This man's name is Henry Pu Yi. Fifty years ago his birth was marked with a lavish display of fireworks; now he lives in jail. When he was two, Henry became the emperor of China, but six years of civil war threw him off his imperial throne. 1932 was an important year for this "Son of Heaven": with Japanese support he became Emperor of Manchukuo. After the Second World War he was not heard of again until the present, when this striking photograph revealed his tragic fate. . . .

Had he sent me this two years earlier I might have shed a few tears over it, but it was too late now. In my reply I wrote: "I am sorry, but I am unable to agree with your interpretation. I cannot sign the photograph."

Not long before that I had been asked a number of similar "sympathetic" questions in interviews with some foreign journalists: "Don't you feel sad at having been the last emperor of the Ching Dynasty?" "Don't you feel that it is unfair that you have not been tried after so long a time? Don't you find this surprising?" I replied that what was sad was my past life as Ching emperor and puppet emperor, and that when it came to surprises, I was astonished by the leniency with which I was being treated. The journalists did not seem to understand me, and I imagined that the French gentleman who had written to me would doubtless share their incomprehension when he read my reply.

In my view what was truly glorious was the magnanimity of Fang Su-jung, the girl who survived the massacre, the simple words of the Taishanpao peasants, the great changes that had taken place among the younger members of the Aisin-Gioro clan, the gas jets in the kitchens of the Fushun miners, the Chinese lathes that had replaced Japanese ones in the industrial school I visited, and the peaceful life of the retired workers in the old people's home. Was all this "meaningless" to me? Was it meaningless that others had put their hopes and trust in my becoming a real man? Was this not the most valuable judgement that could have been passed on me?

I am convinced that my feelings were shared by many of the other criminals, and that some of them had come to this conclusion before me. Indeed, so many of us were now determined to remould ourselves through our own efforts that the New Year of 1957 was quite different from previous ones.

At New Year and other festivals we had parties at which the talented ones among us would perform. The corridor where the parties were usually held would be hung with lanterns and decorations, and this combined with the good food we were given for the occasion to give us a sense of well-being. But some time before the New Year of 1957 we felt that this was not enough, and we wanted to hold a big party in the hall as the Japanese war criminals did. The prison authorities told our study committee that if we thought we could manage it we could go ahead, and could have the newly-arrived Chiang Kai-shek war criminals to fill the hall as our audience. When the study committee passed this news on to the cells we all set to with great enthusiasm.

We prisoners were all pleased because we reckoned that we would have a happy New Year, and the prison authorities gave us their backing because this method of enabling prisoners to educate themselves had been very successful with the Japanese war criminals. The Japanese prisoners wrote plays themselves on the basis of what they read in the Japanese press. One of them was on the horrors of the nuclear explosions in Japan and the crimes that Japanese militarism had committed against the people of Japan and the rest of the world. They had a great educational effect on writers, performers, and audience alike. Our study committee therefore decided to include plays of this sort in our show. This proposal was generally supported, and two plays were soon outlined. One was a "living newspaper" called "The Defeat of the Aggressors" about the repulse of the British invasion of Egypt; and the other was to be about the transformation of a "Manchukuo" traitor. They were written by Pu Chieh and a former official of Wang Ching-wei's puppet government.

As the work on the plays went ahead all kinds of other performances were in preparation. Our conjurer Old Lung, for example, announced that he was going to do some bigger trick than producing eggs from a hat or swallowing ping-pong balls. The busiest man was Old Wan, the head of the study committee, who was in charge of all the arrangements. Little Jui was responsible for the decorations, and Big Li, now an accomplished electrician, looked after the lighting.

In previous years, I had not performed in the corridor parties and had been thought too clumsy to be of much use in the preparations. This time too I expected that the others would not want me to get in their way, but then to my great surprise our cell-chief, Old Chu, discovered that I could sing passably well and signed me up for the choir. I was deeply moved, and I sang with gusto. Just when I had learnt my songs Old Wan, the chairman of the study committee, sent for me.

"Pu Yi, there's a part for you in the first play. It's not too difficult and there aren't many lines to learn. Anyhow you can improvise if you feel like it. This is a worthwhile job and a part of our mutual education. . . ."

"You don't have to persuade me. As long as you think I'm up to it, I'm game."

"Of course you can do it," grinned Old Wan. "You're certainly up to it. You have a strong, clear voice. You. . . ."

"Take it easy. What do you want me to play in?".

"We've called it 'The Defeat of the Aggressors', and it's about the British invasion of Egypt and the uproar it caused. It's based on press reports. Old Jun is playing the main role — the Foreign Secretary Selwyn Lloyd. You will be a left-wing Labour M.P."

I went to see Pu Chieh to read the script, hear his explanation of it, and copy down my lines. Then I had to choose my costume. As I was playing a foreigner I would naturally have to wear Western clothes, of which there was no shortage in the prison as the suits of many of the prisoners were kept there. I went back to my cell with the blue suit I had worn at the International Military Tribunal in Tokyo, a shirt, a tie and other clothes. As nobody else was in the cell I dressed up by myself. Just when I had put on a white shirt Old Yuan came in and asked me with astonishment what I was doing.

As I was excited and my shirt collar was too tight I could not answer at first. Finally I panted, "I'm going to be in a play. Come and loosen the belt at the back of my waistcoat."

He did this for me, but the waistcoat was still too tight. I realized that I must have put on weight. My leather shoes from England pinched my feet, so I asked Old Yuan in irritation whether I would need to wear leather shoes to play a British Labour M.P.

"You certainly will. Some British Labour M.P.s even use scent, so of course you can't wear padded cloth boots. Don't worry, your leather shoes won't pinch after you've worn them for a while, and the waistcoat can be altered. Go and learn your lines. It's great news that you will be acting." He ended with a laugh that still rang in my ears as I went out into the corridor. I was in very high spirits: Old Wan had said that this would be self-education and a kind of mutual help. This was the first time I had been in the position of helping other people instead of just being helped. After all, I had my abilities just like everyone else, and was on equal terms with the rest when it came to helping each other.

From then on I recited my lines incessantly. As Old Wan had said, they were very short, and my part was probably the smallest in the play. At the very end of the play Selwyn Lloyd made a speech in the House of Commons trying to justify the failure of the invasion, and some opposition members started to question him and then joined in an attack on him. At this point I was to stand up in their midst and say to Selwyn Lloyd, "There is no need for you to continue to defend your actions. They are disgraceful, disgraceful, and, I say it again, disgraceful." The chamber was then supposed to be filled with angry insults and demands for Lloyd's resignation, during which I was to shout "Get out! Get out!" This play had a very simple plot, in which the most important element was this parliamentary debate which only lasted some fifteen minutes. I spent many dozens of fifteen minutes preparing my part for fear I would forget my lines or say them wrong and thus disappoint the hopes that had been placed in me. In the past I had suffered from insomnia or talked in my sleep because I was worried or frightened. This was the first time that excitement and nerves had kept me awake.

When New Year came and I went into the hall for the party the festive atmosphere and the magnificent stage made me forget my nerves. Our show compared well with the parties of the Japanese war criminals: choral and solo singing, Mongol songs and dances, crosstalk, ballads sung to the clappers, conjuring, the living newspaper "The Defeat of the Aggressors", and the play "From Darkness to Light". When we saw how impressed the Chiang Kai-shek war criminals were we winked at each other in our excitement.

The other acts went off successfully, drawing plenty of applause, and the first item after the interval was the living newspaper. The debate began. Old Jun had dressed himself up to look just like

Selwyn Lloyd. As he had a naturally big nose he was the only "M.P." who looked like an Englishman, and his acting was outstanding: in his anger, fear, desperation and arrogance he was the living image of a defeated Foreign Secretary. After about ten minutes Old Yuan whispered to me (an action that was in the script), "Don't be too wooden. Put some movement into it." I peered forward and looked at the audience. I had the feeling that the attention of all of them was focused on me, the left-wing M.P., and it made me very nervous. Nobody had noticed me when I was singing in the choir, but now all their eyes were on me. Before I could recover my calm Old Yuan nudged me: "Say something; say something to refute him." I stood up in a panic, turned towards Old Jun, who was still spouting away, and realized that I had forgotten my words. Inspiration came to me in my despair, and I shouted "NO! No! No!" in English. My outburst cut Old Jun short, and then I remembered my lines. When I had said them I heard a burst of applause from the audience and cries of "Get out! Get out!" from the stage. The Foreign Secretary scuttled off stage in confusion.

Old Yuan was the first to congratulate me after the show: "You didn't do at all badly. Although you were a bit nervy, you weren't at all bad." Then others expressed their satisfaction and roared with laughter at the words I had improvised.

The hall gradually calmed down and the play "From Darkness to Light" began. This took us into a different world. The first scene showed how two down-and-out Northeastern officials became leading traitors. In the second scene they tried to get in with the Kuomintang after the Japanese surrender but were captured by the Soviet Red Army. In the third they attempted to deceive the authorities after being sent back to China but without success, and they finally responded to the education they received from the government and its policy of leniency: they acknowledged their guilt and accepted remoulding. Although the play was nothing wonderful in itself, all of us war criminals could see ourselves in it. It reminded us of our own pasts, held our attention, and made us feel more and more ashamed of ourselves. In one part of the play some traitors forced the people to work on the building of the Emperor Jimmu Shrine. Big Mouth saw that this was his story, and he was heard to mumble, "What's the point in showing that disgraceful business?" In another scene a group of traitors were sitting round in a room fawning on the Japanese and making suggestions about how to steal grain from the people of the Northeast. I heard someone next to me sighing and saying "How filthy!" I felt that the filthiest thing was not any of the characters in the play but the curtained niche in the corner of the room in which hung the "True Imperial Image" of the traitor emperor. When the characters in the play bowed to it every time they came on stage I realized that it was the dirtiest thing in the world.

The climax of the evening came in the last scene, when government personnel explained the policy of remoulding criminals. The applause and shouting of slogans was louder than anything I had ever heard before. This was due not so much to the play itself as to the combined effects of family letters and visits, our trips outside, the confessions of the Japanese war criminals at the military tribunal, and other factors. Amid the ear-splitting shouts and applause could be heard muffled sobs. Old Liu, who had not believed that his daughter was being looked after until he saw her with his own eyes, was shaking with sobs; and Old Chang, who was on good terms with his son again, was crying out loud as his fountain pen shone from his breast pocket.

The emotions stirred up at this meeting showed us what kind of "glory" was still possible for us in the present world, a "glory" that was shining ever clearer. Soon after the New Year thirteen prisoners were released without trial, and they included my three nephews and Big Li. After seeing them off we had an even better party to celebrate the Spring Festival with a play about a Northeastern village in "Manchukuo" days and after liberation. Then four more prisoners were released, including my two brothers-in-law. This was the time when I received the letter from the Frenchman about "the world's glory".

Another Visit

In the second half of 1957 we went on another trip, this time to Shenyang, Anshan, Changchun and Harbin. We saw the Tahuofang reservoir project near Shenyang, eighteen factories, six technical organizations and schools, three hospitals, two exhibitions, and a sports palace. In Harbin we visited the area that had suffered disaster from the Japanese 731 Bacteriological Unit and the Hall of the Northeastern Martyrs. This trip made an even deeper impression on us than the previous one.

The great majority of the enterprises we visited were newly built, the exceptions being a few that were left from the time of the Japanese. These Japanese factories had been almost completely wrecked when they were taken over. The Anshan Iron and Steel Works and the Shenyang Machine-Tool Plant, for example, had been sabotaged both by the Japanese and the Kuomintang. After they were taken over by the People's Government they were rebuilt, and expanded to their present gigantic size. Many of the former "Manchukuo" ministers who had seen these plants in the old days were astonished by their growth. What surprised me most was the amount of equipment with trade marks and specifications in Chinese on it. Even I, inexperienced as I was, thought of "Made in USA", "Made in Germany" when machinery was mentioned, but now I saw whole sets of equipment made by China herself. Some of the products of these plants were even going for export, and all of them bore the proud words: "Made in the People's Republic of China".

At the Anshan Iron and Steel Works I stood in front of the enormous iron and steel structures and tried unsuccessfully to think how all this could have grown out of a heap of scrap. But that was what had really happened. When the Japanese left Anshan they said: "Give Anshan to the Chinese to grow *kaoliang* on. Even if they want to start it up again they'll need twenty years at a calm estimate." But the Chinese people had taken not twenty years but three to start it up and reach an annual output of 1,350,000 tons, far above the highest figure ever obtained in the "Manchukuo" period. Five years later annual production was up to 5,350,000 tons, more than the total output for the whole thirty-one years from the foundation of the Showa Steel Works by the Japanese in 1917 to the final withdrawal of the Kuomintang in 1947.

I saw many other things like this on the trip, and they all told me that the Chinese people had stood up. Not only could they win military victories, but they could triumph on the economic front as well. If I had not seen this with my own eyes, or if someone had predicted it ten years earlier, I would have been as sceptical as the Japanese who advised the Chinese to plant *kaoliang*.

During the previous forty years I had forgotten that I too was Chinese. I had joined the Japanese in praising their nation as the most splendid one on earth; I had shared Cheng Hsiao-hsu's illusions about using "foreign officials" and "foreign strength" to develop China's resources; and I had often sighed with Pu Chieh over the stupidity of the Chinese as compared with the intelligence of the white races. Even after going into prison I had still refused to believe that the new China would be able to keep its place in the world. So far from being elated when the Chinese and Korean people's forces won battles in Korea I had been terrified that the Americans would drop atom bombs. I had not been able to understand why the Chinese Communist Party dared to expose U.S. imperialism at the rostrum of the United Nations or why the delegates of the Sino-Korean side dared to warn the Americans at the Panmunjom talks that they would not be able to gain at the conference table what they had failed to win on the battlefield. In short, I had suffered from a very bad case of "soft bone disease".

After the Korean armistice was signed and China played a new role in world affairs at the Geneva Conference I had thought about China's international relations since the Opium Wars: from the time of my great-grandfather Tao Kuang to the Kuomintang and Chiang Kai-shek they had been a continuous record of "soft bone disease". During those 109 years the bringers of cannons and opium, the pseudo-missionaries — the foreigners who thought themselves so civilized and superior — had come to China and burned, killed, plundered and cheated. The foreign invaders had stationed their troops in China's capital, ports, big cities and forts, and had all regarded the Chinese as slaves, savages and targets. They had caused China so many days of national disgrace, and made China sign so many treaties turning her own people into slaves. So many humiliating terms had appeared in the diplomatic history of the period: equality of opportunity, the open door, most favoured nation treatment, leased territories, mortgaged tariffs, consular jurisdiction, garrison rights, railway-building rights, mining rights, river transport rights, air transport rights, and so on. The foreigners had even once enjoyed the special privileges of paying one hundred U.S. dollars as compensation for killing a donkey, eighty dollars for killing a man. They had not been liable for trial by Chinese courts if they raped Chinese women.

But this shameful period was now gone for ever. The Chinese people had stood up and were now confidently building their own country, making the foreigners who had laughed so insultingly shut their mouths.

I heard an anecdote in the Changchun Number One Motor Works. When the factory had just started production some children from a primary school wanted to visit it. The factory planned to send an imported bus to fetch them, but the children insisted on a Chinese-made lorry.

Their country must have meant a lot to those children, but for forty years it had been nothing to me.

Whether in one's own society or on the world stage one could now be very proud of being Chinese.

I had always been curious in the past about how other people lived — with the exception, that is, of the late "Manchukuo" period. The first time I had gone out to satisfy this curiosity was to visit my father's mansion, and the second time was when I used the excuse of Chen Pao-shen's sickness to go and see him. I had been most impressed by the freedom of their lives. When I moved to Tientsin I felt that the "top Chinese" I saw in Western restaurants and foreign amusement parks were more free than I was but not so well born; for this reason I did not admire them much, but I was still curious about them. In "Manchukuo" I was too worried about my own position to be very curious. After my repatriation I took no interest in such matters at first, feeling that other people's lives were no concern of mine, but as I took a rosier view of my future these things meant more to me. On this trip I paid a great deal of attention to the way people lived, and what I found out brought back memories and caused me great pain.

Harbin made the deepest impression. The children's railway in the Children's Park there reminded me of how I had played with ants in my own childhood. The survival rate of new babies at the children's hospital and the general level of health would have been beyond the imagination of the Ching imperial family. Sitting on a bench on Harbin's Sun Island as I looked at the pleasure boats on the river and listened to the youngsters singing and playing accordions made me think back to the first part of my life. I had never sung for joy nor had I ever known the pleasure of sunning myself on the grass, to say nothing of being able to walk about as I pleased. In those days I had been worrying whether the kitchen was cheating me and frightened that the Japanese were going to kill me. But here people seemed to be carefree. On an island a few yards in front of me a young artist was painting from life. He was sitting with his back to me, and he did not turn round once although his bag and canvas were leaning against a chair with nobody looking after them. He seemed to be quite confident that nobody would take them. This would have been inconceivable in the old society, but now it was a fact.

Here was another fact: there was a wooden box inside a telephone booth in the park with a piece of paper stuck on it: "Please put four cents in the box for each call made."

One of my fellow-prisoners told me that there used to be a club on Sun Island in the old days in which you had to give a tip every time you visited the lavatory. But now letters from home told us that the staff in any restaurant, hotel, bath-house or other such place would be insulted if you tried to tip them. This was another fact.

Two visits we made in our last days in Harbin showed me the difference between two kinds of people in the world. The first place was where the Japanese 731 Bacteriological Unit had committed its atrocities and the second was the Hall of the North-eastern Martyrs.

A book called *731 Bacteriological Unit* was published in Japan after the Second World War by a man called Akiyama Hiroshi who had been a member of the unit. According to this book there was a group of buildings about four kilometers in circumference, and the main one was four times the size of the Marunouchi Building in Japan. There were about 3,000 personnel, and they raised tens of thousands of rats. In addition they had 4,500 Ishii style incubators in which they reared astronomical numbers of fleas and produced 300 kilograms of bubonic plague germs a month. There was a prison there where up to four or five hundred prisoners of war or anti-Japanese patriots were kept to be used in experiments. Some were Chinese and others were citizens of the Soviet Union or the Mongolian People's Republic. They were referred to not as men but as "logs". At least six hundred of them would be tortured to death there every year, and the experiments performed on them were of indescribable cruelty. Some men were skinned alive; some were put into refrigerators for experiments and the bones of their hands would go on shaking after the flesh had been frozen off; others were laid on operating tables like frogs while white-coated personnel dissected them; some were tied to stakes in nothing but their underpants while germ bombs were exploded in front of them; and others were fed well and then infected with germs, and if this did not kill them the experiment was repeated until they died.

When he was in this 731 Unit the author heard that the germs bred there were more powerful than any other weapon and could kill 100,000,000 people, a claim on which the Japanese Army prided itself.

When the Soviet Red Army was approaching Harbin this Unit tried to cover up all trace of its crimes. The Japanese poisoned all the surviving prisoners, planning to burn them to ashes and then bury them in a large pit. As the executioners were in a panic they did not burn the corpses thoroughly and could not get them all into

448

the pit. They pulled out the half-burned corpses and divided the flesh from the bone. The flesh was then burned to ashes and the bones were put through a pulverizing machine. Finally the main buildings were destroyed with explosives.

Not long after someone from a nearby village was walking past the ruins when he saw some fleas jumping around in a broken pottery jar. One of these fleas bit him. Little did he realize that it had infected him with the bubonic plague that the murderers had left behind them. Plague broke out in the village, and the local people's government at once sent an army of medical workers to deal with it, but for all their efforts 142 lives were lost in this village of only a hundred or so families.

This shocking event had been witnessed by Chiang Shu-ching, a co-operative member and model worker we visited. After telling us about the crimes that had been committed against this village during the "Manchukuo" days she said, "The Japanese surrendered and laid down their arms and the people's government let us live happily. We had our own land and kept the crops we harvested for ourselves. We were all so pleased and saying that everything was just fine because life was going to be good with the people's government leading us. We didn't know that we hadn't seen the end of the evil caused by the Japanese, or that they had left this behind after they went. The bastards."

I noticed one thing that was the same both in Chiang Shu-ching's spick-and-span little house and in the spacious offices of the agricultural co-operative: whenever the members of the Gold Star Co-operative talked about the past they said little and spoke slowly, but the moment the subject turned to the present or the future the atmosphere change completely. When they talked about the harvests they were now getting, particularly the vegetable crop, they spoke with animation and went into great detail. To back up what they had said they took us to see their hothouses and the new things they had bought: drainage and irrigation equipment, heavy lorries and various kinds of chemical fertilizer. We saw a newly-built school and clinic as well as new electric power cables. When they talked about the targets for the next year they became even more excited. The co-op head pointed to some rows of new tiled houses and chose his words with great caution: "After next autumn I think we might be able to build a few more." None of us believed that "a few" meant only ten or a dozen.

As we were leaving this village the co-op members brought baskets of cucumbers and radishes to give to us. "Take them with you. We've just harvested them, and although they're not worth anything they're very fresh." The co-op head ignored our protests and thrust them into our coach.

I gazed through the windows at the rapidly receding tiled roofs of the Gold Star Co-op and thought of the extraordinary impression that the co-op head's very ordinary words "After next autumn I think . . ." had made on me. Ordinary men like him, whom I had despised in the past as being thoroughly uncivilized, toiled diligently with their own two hands, doing a job that was both ordinary and great. They turned thatched cottages into brick houses to give the people a better life. The Japanese imperialists, on the other hand, whom I used to regard with fear and trembling as the representatives of an outstanding nation, had used modern science and technology to create plague and death. They too had had their ideal: the enslavement and elimination of an oppressed nation.

The rubble of the germ factory at Pingfangchu showed the meaning of evil, while each relic of the martyrs in the Hall of the Northeastern Martyrs showed what was meant by good. Each exhibit told how its former owners had shed their last drops of blood for the sake of the finest human ideals, thus covering themselves with glory. Both the ruins of the germ factory and the bloodstained clothes and last messages of the martyrs were mirrors in which we visitors could see our own ugly past.

The Hall of the Northeastern Martyrs is a majestic building in the Roman style that was used as the Harbin police headquarters during the fourteen years of "Manchukuo". Countless numbers of the bravest Chinese were interrogated, tortured or sent to the execution ground from here in that bloody era. The martyrs whose photographs and relics are exhibited here are only a tiny proportion of the total. All the exhibits and the details about times and places brought back shameful memories. On September 21, 1931, three days after the outbreak of fighting in Shenyang, the Manchurian Committee of the Chinese Communist Party held an emergency meeting which called upon all Party members and all patriotic soldiers to take up arms and fight against the enemy. Pictures of this resolution and the house that was the committee's headquarters reminded me by contrast of my days in the Quiet Garden over twenty years previously. To save the nation in its hour of danger the people of the Northeast had risen under the leadership of the Party and fought, not heeding the obstruction put in their way by Chiang Kai-shek. I, however, had intensified my treachery. I remembered Doihara, Itagaki, Cheng Hsiao-hsu and his son, and Lo Chen-yu; I also recalled my stay in Tangkangtzu and Lushun.

When the guide told us about the life of Yang Ching-yu I thought of my various "imperial progresses" to Tungpientao — the region where the First Allied Anti-Japanese Army under Yang Ching-yu, Li Hung-kuang and other generals operated. I had seen the peaks of the Changpai Mountains as the sun rose above the morning mist. But I had not been moved by the beauty of my motherland as my attention had been on the Japanese gendarmes and the puppet troops and gendarmes on both sides of the railway tracks. The Japanese-run papers always said that the "bandits" in this district had been cleared up, but when I went there the Japanese were worried and gave the appearance of being faced with a mighty foe. When I fled to Tunghua and Talitzukou right at the end of "Manchukuo" I was told that this area was "unsafe". The Allied Anti-Japanese Armies fought there right down to the Japanese surrender, when it was not they who were destroyed but the Imperial Japanese Army that had so often pronounced itself victorious. The anti-Japanese forces had been faced by the powerful Kwantung Army and the "Manchukuo" troops who were better equipped than themselves, and the difficulties that surrounded them were almost unimaginable; but by looking at the cooking pots, water bottles, home-made knives and well-worn sewing machines that the resistance fighters had used I seemed to see the smiling faces of their owners — faces like that of the young director of the Lungfeng Mine, lit up with the smiles that come only from confidence and determination. As I looked at a pair of shoes made from birchbark a song echoed through my brain:

> Birchbark shoes,
> Chinese goods,
> We make them ourselves from our own materials,
> The straps are from the wild hemp,
> The soles from the birch trees.
>
> With birchbark shoes,
> Top-rate shoes,
> Soldiers can climb to mountain peaks.
> Fashionable girls can't buy them.
> Rich old ladies aren't lucky enough to wear them.
>
> Birchbark shoes
> Are really good.
> Soldiers in them run across the hills,
> Scaring the devils out of their wits,
> Chasing lorries honking in terror.

The Japanese had made me approve batch after batch of laws. With these in their hands they had herded families and villages together, instituted grain controls, blockaded mountain areas, and used every conceivable means to cut the economic links between the resistance fighters and the outside world. In this way they succeeded in surrounding General Yang Ching-yu and some of the anti-Japanese troops, but despite their desperate shortage of food they fought on — so long in fact that the Japanese began to doubt their own intelligence reports and common sense. How could these men go on fighting without grain? What were they eating? After General Yang Ching-yu laid down his life the Japanese cut open his stomach to solve this riddle, and all they found was grass and leaves.

I remembered the sighs of Yoshioka, the "Imperial Attaché": "The Communists are terrifying." In the eyes of the Imperial Japanese Army, equipped as it was with aircraft and tanks, even grass was frightening.

452

When General Yang Ching-yu and his comrades-in-arms were singing that song about birchbark shoes I had been terrified that the Japanese would leave me, and scared by my nightmares; and while they were eating grass I had been sick of eating meat and spent all my days practising divination and reciting sutras.

The maps, seals, bloodstained clothes and childhood compositions of Yang Ching-yu swam before my eyes. From behind me came the sound of my Chinese and Japanese fellow-prisoners weeping, a sound that grew louder and louder. As we looked at the photograph of one martyr called Chao Yi-man someone pushed his way forward and knelt before the picture sobbing bitterly as he kotowed to it.

"I was the puppet police chief. . . ."

He was Yu Ching-tao, who had been Harbin police chief before becoming "Manchukuo" minister of labour. When the martyr Chao Yi-man was held in this police headquarters and questioned in this very room Yu Ching-tao had been one of her interrogators. But now the interrogator had been judged by history and imprisoned. Needless to say, Yu Ching-tao was not the only man who should have cried.

Labour and Optimism

After this visit I was firmly convinced that the gates to the new society stood wide open to me and that the only remaining problems lay within myself.

I began 1958 full of hope. This optimistic attitude had first revealed itself when we were carrying coal in the autumn of 1957. Every autumn the prison authorities moved in large quantities of coal, some for keeping us warm and some for making briquettes for the hothouses in which we grew our winter greens.

This was the first year we had taken part in the work of moving the coal in and making briquettes. I was by now far more capable than I had been in the past. In my cell there were four of us who did most of the heavy work: Old Wang, the Mongol Old Cheng, myself and a fairly young former "Manchukuo" general. The exercise was very good for me. I got much stronger and my old ailments all disappeared. When we were making briquettes I took the fairly heavy job of carrying the coal. As the prison governor and some other cadres were helping the work went with a swing. Just before we finished the job Old Hsien and I brought in three more basketfuls.

As we were handing in our tools I heard Warder Wang saying to one of his colleagues, "I see Pu Yi's working seriously. He doesn't try to show off."

Old Hsien and I put down the basket of coal that we had been carrying with a pole over our shoulders and took our clothes from the tree on which they had been hanging. The governor asked me with a smile how my shoulder was. I looked at it and replied, "It doesn't hurt and it isn't swollen. It's a bit red, that's all."

"How's your appetite these days?"

"Three large bowls of rice or thirty big *jiaozi*."

"Insomnia?"

"I go to sleep as soon as my head hits the pillow. There's nothing wrong with me at all now."

All the others laughed, but no longer with the mocking laugh of the old days. I would not be hearing that laugh any more.

I had also made progress in other fields. I did not find it nearly as much of an effort to study *Political Economy* and *Historical Materialism* as I had before, and my clothes were now very nearly as clean as everyone else's. But what I had most confidence in was labour. As long as I was not asked to do such delicate jobs as making paper flowers I was always first-rate, and even those who were better at theoretical study than me had to take their hats off to me in this respect.

The admiration of my companions and the growth of my own confidence were due not so much to the implanting of a proper attitude to labour as to the new enthusiasm for labour that existed throughout society. From late 1957 onwards we noticed this from the press, family letters, and the prison staff themselves. It seemed that everyone was striving to participate in physical labour, which they saw as something glorious. Tens of thousands of government personnel went to the countryside, schools added periods of labour, and all kinds of voluntary short-term labour units appeared. In the prison itself the staff helped to make briquettes, prepared vegetables in the kitchen, looked after fires, and even brought the food to our cells. Before we were out of our beds in the morning we heard the sounds of wheelbarrows loaded with picks and shovels. This meant that the governor and staff had already set off to clear waste land outside the prison. All this showed us that in the new society labour was the standard by which men were measured. Those who were being remoulded could clearly be no exception. I forget who it was who told me that many people were under the delusion that labour was a punishment that God had inflicted on the human race, and that only the Communists saw it correctly as one of the human rights. I had by then lost all interest in gods or Buddhas and failed to see any connection between God and labour. We could all see that from the Communist point of view labour was something natural. I remember that once when we were clearing out a pile of rubbish the intellectual Section Head Li happened to come past. He picked up a shovel and set to, working more quickly and efficiently than we did and not thinking that there was anything odd in what he was doing.

The importance attached to labour and the enthusiasm for it in 1958 made a still deeper impression on us. I learnt many amazing new things from the letters I received from Peking. Second Sister, who had always stayed at home and taken no interest in anything else, now took part in the activities of her street committee by helping to set up a nursery for the children of working mothers. Fourth Sister, who worked in the former imperial palace, joined in a voluntary lake reconstruction project outside the Te Sheng Gate of Peking and was named as a "five good" activist. Third Sister and her husband participated in political studies organized by the committee of a district people's political consultative conference. Old Jun worked on the Ming Tombs Reservoir together with some other old men of the district people's political consultative conference and they were praised for a technical innovation they made. Fifth Sister and her husband Old Wan told me with pride that their eldest son, who had studied geology at university, was doing research on the uses of snow and ice and was now with an expedition exploring the mountains of the Northwest. Some of my nephews and Big Li were working as team leaders on a state farm on the outskirts of the capital. Everywhere was work and enthusiasm, and the war drums were pulsing for the attack on nature. In this historic campaign to lift the country out of backwardness everyone was doing his bit. My fellow-prisoners all got the same impression from their family letters. When we heard that Chairman Mao, Premier Chou and government ministers all took part in the building of the Ming Tombs Reservoir we could no longer be held back. We asked the study committee and the prison authorities to organize us for productive labour.

The prison authorities met our request. First they set up a workshop to manufacture electric motors, but as we were too few for the job it was given to the Chiang Kai-shek war criminals from other sections of the prison. We were then given other work that would train us in productive skills. We were put into five groups according to our abilities: animal raising, food processing, horticulture, market gardening, and medicine. I and four others formed the medical group. We combined labour with study. We had to clean up the clinic every day, do all the odd jobs, and help with auxiliary medical work; we also spent two hours a day reading up medicine and held discussions under the direction of Dr. Wen of the prison staff. My four colleagues had all been doctors before, and three of them revised their Western medicine while the other studied Chinese medicine with me. In addition we all did a course on acupuncture and moxibustion. This period of working in a small group gave me new confidence.

I was not as good as the others at helping with the medical work at first. The surgical cotton-wool swabs I made looked like lumps of worn cotton padding; when I took blood pressures I would concentrate on looking at my watch and forget to listen to the stethoscope, or else listen and forget to look; when I was learning to use the electrical equipment for treating blood pressure I was always in a muddle and could not do things right. I was only better than the others when it came to odd jobs and manual labour. I made up my mind to master my medical work. When the doctor or nurse had taught me something I would ask my fellow-students to go over it again with me and then practise it endlessly myself. Thus I gradually learnt to master my job as a medical assistant. One of the Japanese war criminals used to come in every day for electrical treatment, and he would always bow low to me afterwards and say "Thank you, doctor" to my great delight. As I wore a white coat and spectacles it was not surprising that he made this mistake; it also showed that my technique was good enough to win the patient's confidence. At the end of the first course Dr. Wen examined us, and I got full marks as well as the others.

When we were trial-producing electric motors I had been frustrated in my attempts to get any but the simplest jobs given me and I had regarded this as prejudice against me. But now I had learnt to be a medical assistant, had been mistaken for a full-fledged doctor, and had got full marks in my first exam. I was confident that I was not a complete idiot and would be able to master this skill; I would no longer need my 468 pieces of jewellery to support myself.

One day I asked to see the governor. As the old governor had been transferred to another post in which he had other responsibilities apart from our prison he did not come regularly, so I saw a deputy governor by the name of Chin who was now running the prison.

"The government ought to accept that jewellery formally," I said. "Anyhow, I lost the receipt for it ages ago."

I thought that I would have to explain about the jewellery to the deputy governor, but to my surprise he replied at once with a smile:

"I know all about it. Well then, are you confident that you will be able to support yourself through your own work?"

I spent the rest of that day giving information about each of the 468 pieces of jewellery while a secretary wrote it all down. When this was over I went into the courtyard with a feeling of relief, thinking that the words of the deputy governor were proof that I had made good progress. Was the day in sight when I would be a real man?

The Test

I had rated myself too highly, as I found out when I was faced with a test.

At the time when the Great Leap Forward was taking place throughout the country, the prison governor put it to us that we needed to review our thoughts in order to clear away the ideological obstructions to our progress. The method used was for each of us to discuss in our study meetings the changes that had taken place in our thinking and the questions that we still did not understand.

When my turn came I had trouble. After I had spoken about my old ideology and the changes in many of my attitudes someone asked me: "A person with your background must have had very close ties with Japanese imperialism, and you may still hanker after it in your private thoughts and feelings. Your connections with it were no looser than ours, so why are you the only one not to mention this? Don't tell me that you have no such feelings."

"I have no feelings for the Japanese besides hatred. I differ from you on this."

This provoked a storm of protest. "Why aren't you more humble? You still think you're a cut above the rest of us, don't you?" "What sort of feelings for them do you have now? Are you more advanced than the rest of us?" Someone cited many examples from my past, such as the poems I had written when I went to Japan and the way I had helped the Japanese empress dowager up some steps, to show that in those days I had been more grateful to the Japanese than anyone else; he found my complete denial hard to accept. I replied that in the past I and the Japanese had made use of each other, so that there was no question of gratitude. I was not trying to cast aspersions on the others when I made this denial that was completely true, but nobody was prepared to accept my explanation. When I described my terror during my flight to Talitzukou I was asked:

"When the Japanese were going to send you to Tokyo they sent you three hundred million yen for your preparatory expenses. Didn't that make you grateful to Japanese imperialism?"

"Three hundred million yen?" I was astounded. "I don't know about any three hundred million yen."

This was not in fact a great mystery. When the Kwantung Army took the last gold reserves from the "Manchukuo" treasury it had announced to the world that they were being transported to Japan for the "Emperor of Manchukuo". I had never seen a cent of this money, and everyone knew this, which was why it had not been held against me. The only reason it had been brought up now was because they wanted to know about my state of mind at that time. Had I thought back calmly or humbly listened to what others had to say I would have been able to remember about it; but instead I asserted with confidence that I knew nothing whatever about it.

"You don't know about it?" Many of those who did know about it started shouting. "This business was handled by Chang Ching-hui and Takebe Rokuzo. Are you trying to repudiate your responsibility because Chang Ching-hui has died recently?" Someone else asked, "Didn't you write about this in your confession?" When I said that I had not they were even more incredulous: "But everyone knows about it." "This isn't a matter of three hundred or three thousand but of three hundred million."

That evening I cast my mind back and recalled that Hsi Hsia had told me in Talitzukou that the Japanese had taken all the gold of the "Bank of Manchukuo" with them on the pretext that it was to be used to support me in Japan. This must have been the three hundred million yen the others were talking about. But at the time I had been too worried about the immediate threat to my life to pay any attention to the matter. The next day I asked whether this was the money in question and was told that it was. I therefore told my study group about it.

"Why did you conceal this before?" asked several of the others in chorus.

"I didn't conceal it. I forgot about it."

"Do you still maintain that you forgot about it?"

"I've remembered about it now."

"Why didn't you remember about it before?"

"I've told you: I forgot. It's only natural to forget things sometimes, isn't it?"

This stimulated another storm of objections. "The further back you go the better your memory is, and the nearer things are the more you forget them. Most peculiar." "It's quite obvious that you were too scared to admit to it before." "If you haven't got the guts to admit your mistakes you'll never be remoulded." "None of us believe you. I can guarantee that the government will not fall for your stories again." "You're a word-twister and a liar." "How can as dishonest a man as yourself ever be remoulded?"

The more I tried to defend myself the less the others believed me. I was worried: obviously they all thought that I was lying. If they were unanimous would the governor take my word against theirs? These thoughts rushed through my brain, possessing me like devils, and I went silly. I had never been worried about this before, but I was now. At the thought that my word was not likely to be taken against all of theirs my courage melted away and I fell back into my bad old ways; I was prepared to forget about my principles so long as I could weather this storm. Wouldn't I be able to muddle my way through this crisis if I made a confession? Very well then. I said that I had not dared to mention this before as I was frightened that the government would punish me, but now they had all persuaded me to overcome my fears.

Although I had really forgotten about the three hundred million yen it seemed as if something that had been hidden in the bottom of my soul had now been exposed.

The members of my group showed no more interest in my problem after that, but I could not put it out of my mind. The more

I thought about it the uneasier I became, convinced that I had made a mess of the whole business. Although there was no shadow of doubt but that I had forgotten about the money, I had said that I had concealed the fact. For fear that the government would think me dishonest, I had told a lie. This affair had given me a sick conscience, and I was now suffering for what I had done.

In the past when I had suspected that every act of the prison staff implied their hostility towards me, I had been tortured by the fear of execution. Now I knew that the government did not want to kill me and was even helping me to become a new man. But just when I was full of hope I had encountered this new tribulation, and the more encouragement I received from the prison staff the worse I felt.

One day a warder told me that the governor wanted to see me. I assumed at once that it would be about the three hundred million yen, and I reckoned that he would probably be angry with me for continuing to try and conceal my crimes despite the way I had been treated. The other possibility I thought of was that he might be pleased with me for owning up to my crimes and writing a confession; he might even praise me for it, and that would be even worse. I went to the governor's reception room in fear and trepidation, only to find that he wanted to talk to me about something completely different.

This interview with the governor plunged me into still deeper gloom. The old governor had not been in the prison for a long time, and today there was another senior official with him. After inquiring about my studies and manual labour they asked what I was doing in the campaign to eliminate pests. The governor said he had been told that I had made some progress in killing flies and done my duty, but he did not know how successful I had been in the current campaign against rats and mice. I replied that I had not yet made a plan, but I thought that everyone in our cell would destroy at least one.

"What about you?" asked the senior official sitting next to the governor. I then recognized him to my horror as the man who had asked me in Harbin why I had not protested at the massacres committed by the Japanese. Without waiting for me to answer he asked another question: "Are you still against killing?" He roared with laughter and his guffaws calmed me down. I replied that I had long given up such ideas and was planning to destroy at least one mouse during this campaign.

The governor shook his head. "Your plan is too conservative. Even the children in primary schools plan to destroy more than one each."

"I'll do my best to kill at least two."

The governor interrupted to say that he would not set a limit for me and would let me kill as many as I could. With this he sent me back to my cell.

I returned to my cell with a heavy heart. This was not because I was alarmed at the prospect of catching mice, a thing I had never done in my life, but because of the thoughts that this conversation had aroused. I remembered how the governor had specially inspected my plan during the anti-fly campaign and how he had encouraged me when I had learnt to wash my clothes. The prison authorities had devoted so much effort to teaching me how to become a man; but now I felt that even if I caught a hundred mice I would not be able to atone for my wrongdoing.

When Warder Chiang, who had just come off duty, saw me sitting in the club by myself he asked me if I had thought of any way of catching mice and offered to help me make a trap. In my total ignorance of how to catch them I did not even know where mice lived. I gladly accepted his offer, and as I was learning to make mouse-traps my worries came back to me.

We talked as we made the traps, and Warder Chiang told me about his childhood. Thus it was that I chanced to hear about the sufferings he had endured. I had never imagined that this calm and kind young man had suffered so much injustice in the days of "Manchukuo". He had been a typical victim of the policy of combining households and villages. After his family had been compulsorily moved several times they spent the winter in a shack and all caught typhoid fever. His seven brothers all died, leaving him as the only survivor. The dead brothers had to be buried naked.

His story ended when we finished making the mouse-traps. He took me to find some mouse holes, and I followed silently, wondering how a young man whose brothers had all been killed by the "Manchukuo" regime could today be helping me. Had all the other warders, who were so kind to us prisoners, suffered like him in the past? I asked him, "Did Warder Wang and Warder Liu suffer such injustice under 'Manchukuo'?"

"Everyone was ground down in those days. Warder Wang was taken for forced labour three times, and Warder Liu was left with no choice but to join the anti-Japanese army."

I realized without having to ask again that all the members of the prison staff who were of Northeastern origin had suffered in the days of "Manchukuo".

The guidance of Warder Chiang enabled me to kill six mice. When Warders Wang and Liu heard that I had caught some mice they came in to see my "captives" as if this were a marvellous achievement, and they praised me for my progress. Their congratulations made me feel most uneasy: while these former victims of the "Manchukuo" regime were attaching such importance to my progress I was still deceiving them.

I went to work in the clinic every day as usual, sweeping the room, taking blood pressures, giving electric therapy and studying Chinese medicine; and the short Japanese war criminal continued to bow to me. But now I did not hear what he was saying, the *Outlines of Chinese Medicine* became hard to understand, and I often had to take people's blood pressure several times over. My sisters and brothers-in-law wrote about their new triumphs in their letters and expressed the hope that I would soon be remoulded and able to share their happy life. I now read such words as a rebuke.

When autumn came round we did a crash job of making coal briquettes, and the deputy governor and cadres all lent a hand in preparing the fuel to be used in the hothouses in the winter. I put all my energies into carrying coal while avoiding drawing the attention of the governor. If he had praised me then it would have been worse than a dressing down.

One day I had been busy with something else and by the time I came round to giving electric therapy there were two people waiting. One was the Japanese who always bowed to me, and as he was a regular patient I decided to treat him first. To my surprise he gestured to the other man and said in Chinese, "Please be first. I'm in no hurry."

"You came first, so you should be treated first," said the other man, a Chiang Kai-shek war criminal.

"Thank you very much, but I'm in no hurry. I can sit here and wait. I'm going to be released shortly," he added as an explanation.

I had not known before that he spoke such good Chinese, and as I arranged the equipment for the Chiang Kai-shek war criminal I cast several glances in his direction. He was looking gravely at the wall opposite. A moment later his gaze turned to the ceiling.

"This room was a torture chamber in the 'Manchukuo' days," he said in a low voice. I did not know whether he was talking to himself or to us. "Who knows how many patriotic Chinese were tortured here?"

After a pause he pointed to the ceiling. "In those days chains used to hang from there and the walls were covered in blood." His eyes swept the walls and settled on the glass-fronted cabinet. After another period of silence he spoke again. "When the Chinese gentlemen were repairing this building we thought that it was being restored as a torture chamber where revenge would be meted out to us. Later on, when we saw white-coated doctors we thought that we were going to be dissected in experiments. We never imagined that a clinic was being built to cure our illnesses." His voice was choked with sobs.

The Chiang Kai-shek war criminal had gone now, so I asked the Japanese to come over for his treatment. He stood up and said respectfully, "No, thank you. I came to look at this room. As I have missed Dr. Wen, would you please tell him that while I have no right to thank him, I would like to thank him on behalf of my mother. Thank you too, doctor."

"I'm not a doctor; I'm Pu Yi."

I do not know whether he replied or not. He bowed, turned, and went out of the room.

I could not hold out any longer. No matter how hard it might be for the governor to understand, I had to put an end to my lie.

It happened that the old governor was in the prison at the time, and he asked me to come for a talk. I opened the door of his reception room and saw the familiar grey-haired figure behind the desk looking at a pile of papers. He asked me to sit down, and a moment later he put the papers away and looked up.

"I've been looking at the record of your cell. How are things? Have you been having any ideological problems recently?"

Now that the vital moment had come I hesitated. I looked at the minutes of our cell's meetings and thought of the unanimity with which the others had attacked me. I could not help wondering whether there was any point in telling the truth as it was my word against all of theirs. But I could not keep the deception up any longer.

"Tell me what the meetings of your group are like."

"They're good. They have summarized our thinking correctly."

"Hm?" The governor raised his eyebrows. "Give me more details."

I realized that I was breathing unnaturally. "I spoke the truth when I said that," I replied. "The conclusion that I had been too worried to mention things was quite true. But there were one or two cases. . . ."

"Go on. You know how much I want to understand your thinking."

I knew that I had to speak out now, and with my heart pounding I poured out a breathless account of the whole business. The governor listened with close attention. When I had finished he asked:

"Why was it so difficult to say that? What were you frightened of?"

"I was scared because it was my word against all of theirs."

"If you speak the truth you have nothing to fear," said the governor with the utmost gravity. "Do you think that the government can't investigate the matter for itself and reach its own verdict? You still don't really understand that to be a real man you need courage. You must have the courage to speak the truth."

I wept. I had not imagined that he would be able to see everything so clearly. What else was there for me to say?

Special Pardon

PROPOSAL OF THE CENTRAL COMMITTEE OF THE COMMUNIST PARTY OF CHINA TO THE STANDING COMMITTEE OF THE NATIONAL PEOPLE'S CONGRESS

The Central Committee of the Communist Party of China proposes to the Standing Committee of the National People's Congress that in celebration of the tenth anniversary of the foundation of the great People's Republic of China a number of reformed war criminals, counter-revolutionaries and common criminals should be granted special pardons.

We have won a great victory in the socialist revolution and the socialist construction of our country. Our motherland is flourishing, production and construction are forging ahead, and the living standards of the people are being steadily raised. The government of the people's democratic dictatorship is unprecedentedly consolidated and strong. The people of the whole country are more politically conscious and better organized than ever before. The political and economic state of the nation is excellent. The policy of the Party and the People's Government of combining punishment with leniency in dealing with counter-revolutionaries and other criminals, and the policy of combining reform through labour with ideological education have achieved great successes. The majority of the prisoners now under detention have been remoulded to a greater or lesser extent, and a considerable number of them have genuinely reformed.

In these circumstances the Central Committee of the Communist Party of China believes that at this time, when we are celebrating the tenth anniversary of the founding of the People's Republic of China, it would be fitting to announce and put into effect a special pardon for a number of war criminals, counter-revolutionaries and common criminals who have really reformed. The adoption of this measure will help to change negative factors into positive ones and be of great assistance to their further remoulding, as well as to that of the other criminals still in captivity. It will enable them to realize that under our great socialist system their future lies in reform.

The Central Committee of the Communist Party of China requests that the Standing Committee of the National People's Congress will consider this proposal and reach an appropriate decision.

Mao Tse-tung
*Chairman of the Central Committee
of the Communist Party of China*

September 14, 1959

A resolution on these lines was passed by the Standing Committee of the National People's Congress, and on September 17 Chairman Liu Shao-chi proclaimed the special pardon.

The delight with which Chairman Mao's proposal and Chairman Liu's order were greeted in the prison was unforgettable. After the announcer had read the last sentence there was a moment of silence around the radio followed by an explosion of cheers, slogans and applause. It was as if ten thousand strings of firecrackers had been let off at once, and it went on for a long time.

From that moment on the morning of September 18 onwards the whole prison was excited. All sorts of views were expressed: the Party and Government were always as good as their word; we now had a future and it would not be long before we were out; we would be pardoned in batches; we would all be let out at once. Who would be in the first group to be released? Most of us realized that pardon would depend on whether one had reformed or not, and some regretted their tendency to slack off recently. There were those who said modestly that they were not yet up to the standard while they discreetly packed their clothes, burnt their discarded notebooks and threw away their worn-out socks.

The yard was a hubbub of voices during the break. I heard Old Yuan asking Old Hsien, "Who's going to be in the first lot?"

"It's bound to be those who have done best in their studies recently. You've got a good chance."

"No, I'm not good enough; but I'm sure you are."

"Me? If they let me out I'd go to Peking and send you some Peking specialities. I'd fancy some Peking dates."

I heard Big Mouth's voice from another part of the yard. "They should either let all of us out or none."

"You've got no confidence in yourself," someone said to him. "You're scared of being left behind."

"Leave me behind? Unless they keep Pu Yi here they won't keep me."

Even I was quite sure that he must be right. On the following day, I think, the deputy governor asked me what I thought of the special pardon.

"I think that I am bound to be the very last — that is, if I can ever remould myself. All the same, I shall try my hardest."

For most of the prisoners pardon and release meant reunion with their families, but this did not affect me. My mother had died long ago, my father had been dead since 1951, and my last wife had divorced me in 1956. Even if they had still been alive none of them would have understood me as well as the people here. Nobody I had known before could teach me how to be a real man as the staff here did. One might say that release meant regaining freedom and light, but it was in prison that I had found truth and light, and won the freedom of knowing about the world. From my point of view pardon would mean that I was qualified as a human being and could begin a new life that would have real significance.

I had received a letter from Old Wan recently. He told me that the son of his who was studying to become a geologist had led a team of mountaineers in the conquest of the Chilien Mountains. After this he had gone on to Tibet just at the time when the serf-owners rebelled, where he and his fellow-students had fought on the side of the serfs. After the crushing of the rebellion they had gone on to assault new peaks. In his letter that was so full of pride and happiness Old Wan often mentioned how glad he was that his son had been brought up in the present and not in the accursed past.

468

Today his son had a brilliant future. Were it not for today he would not have had such a son, nor would he himself have been working alongside all other true Chinese citizens as a translator and a builder of socialism. He hoped that I would soon be sharing this happiness that we had never known before. He believed that I was heading that way.

A month after the proclamation of the special pardon we went on another visit, this time to the Tahuofang Reservoir near Shenyang. When we had last come here in 1957 we had seen an endless mass of people working in the valley, and I had learnt from a table-top model that it was going to have a capacity of 2,110 million cubic metres — enough to hold a flood that might only occur once in a thousand years — and would irrigate 80,000 hectares of land. When we made our second visit this mighty project had been completed for a year, and a vast man-made sea stretched before our eyes, bounded by a dam that was 48 metres high, 8 metres wide at the top, 330 metres wide at the base and 1,367 metres long. When Furumi Tadayuki, the Japanese war criminal who had been deputy head of the General Affairs Office of the "Manchukuo State Council", came back from this visit he told all of us about his impressions in the club. Part of his talk went something like this:

"As I stood on the dam at the Tahuofang Reservoir I was struck with its grandeur, beauty and peace. I felt that this was a victory that had been won over nature and a source of pride and joy to the Chinese people as they continue the conquest of nature. . . . The sight of this reservoir reminded me of when I stood on the dam of the Shuifeng Reservoir in the old days as head of the planning department of the General Affairs Office, deputy minister of economics, and deputy head of the General Affairs Office of 'Manchukuo'. In those days I thought with pride that the only people in Asia who could wage such struggles against nature and build so big a project were the Japanese; I despised the Chinese and thought them completely incapable of such a thing. The Chinese workers were dressed in rags, and I thought of myself as an entirely different kind of being from them: I looked down upon them with arrogance as if I were great, brilliant and exalted.

"But the men who worked on the Tahuofang Reservoir now had tremendous energy because they were full of confidence. They toiled selflessly. They were full of life, their faces shining with pride and happiness. I, standing on a corner of the dam and surveying the scene, was a war criminal who had committed the most serious crimes against the Chinese people. Who was right?"

On one side were the Chinese people, "their faces shining with pride and happiness", and on the other was a war criminal. In my mind I was leaving one side and crossing over to the other, the right side. This was the only solution I had found after ten years of thinking it out.

The past ten years had taught me the rudiments of the difference between right and wrong. The victory in the Korean War; the confessions of the Japanese war criminals; China's diplomatic successes and unprecedented standing in world public opinion; the changes in the country, society, my nationality, my own clan and myself — all this had happened under the leadership of that very Communist Party that I had viewed with hatred, prejudice and fear ten years ago. The events of these ten years and the history of the past century or so had taught me that the decisive force in history was the common people whom I had so despised. It was inevitable that the first part of my life should have ended in disaster, and that imperialism and the reactionary Peiyang power on which I had relied should have collapsed. I now understood that Chen Pao-shen, Cheng Hsiao-hsu, Yoshioka, the gods and the Bodhisattvas had been unable to tell me what my destiny was. I now knew that my fate was to be a man who supported himself through his own labour and brought benefits to humanity. The best fate was one that was linked with that of the people.

"One must take the side that is right."

This needed courage, and the proclamation of the special pardon gave me courage, as it did to all the others.

We put more effort into our work and study, and many of us were awaiting eagerly the next assessment of our studies. The food-processing team now made bean-curd that was both soft and white, the stock-breeding team had fattened up their pigs so that they were even finer than ever, and in the medical team we had stopped making mistakes. Even Big Mouth had started to behave himself and was not quarrelling any more.

More than a month passed. One evening the deputy governor came to talk to me about the special pardon. "What have you been thinking about for the past couple of months?" he asked me.

I told him what I have mentioned above and also said that some people seemed to me to have been remoulded quite well. I mentioned the food-processing and pig-breeding teams and some individuals who had been praised for their studies recently.

"You find it quite easy now to think of the good points of others," said the deputy governor with a smile. "What would you think if you were included in the special pardon?"

"It's out of the question," I replied, laughing.

Out of the question. That was what I thought as I went back to my cell. "But . . . if?" The very thought of this made me tense. Later I concluded that I might be pardoned in the future, but it would be bound to be a long time. My prospects were not so dim. I imagined myself, Old Wan, Little Jui and the others taking our place among ordinary people and doing ordinary things. In these daydreams I was given a job as a medical assistant in a hospital, the sort of job I had read about in the papers. But I was sure that it would be a long time before the people gave their approval and accepted me as one of them. At the thought of my future happiness I was almost unable to sleep.

The next day we were ordered to assemble in the club. Facing us was a broad strip of crimson cloth stretched across the stage that took my breath away. On it was written "Fushun War Criminals Prison Special Pardon Meeting".

A representative of the Supreme People's Court, the two governors and some other people were sitting on the platform. Below the platform all was silent except for the pounding of my heart.

After a few words from the prison governor the representative of the Supreme People's Court went to the middle of the stage and read from a sheet of paper. "Aisin-Gioro Pu Yi".

My heart leapt.   I went and stood in front of the stage and heard someone reading out:

NOTICE OF A SPECIAL PARDON
FROM THE SUPREME PEOPLE'S COURT OF
THE PEOPLE'S REPUBLIC OF CHINA

In accordance with the Special Pardon Order issued by the Chairman of the People's Republic of China on September 17, 1959 this Court has investigated the case of the "Manchukuo" war criminal Aisin-Gioro Pu Yi.

The war criminal Aisin-Gioro Pu Yi, male, 54 years old, of the Manchu nationality, and from Peking, has now served ten years' detention. As a result of remoulding through labour and ideological education during his captivity he has shown that he has genuinely reformed. In accordance with the stipulations of Clause I of the Special Pardon Order he is therefore to be released.

Supreme People's Court of
the People's Republic of China

December 4, 1959

Before I had heard this to the end I burst into tears.   My motherland had made me into a man.

A New Chapter

I was on the train.   Outside was a snow-covered plain, bright and vast, unfolding before me like my own future.   Inside the train I was surrounded by ordinary workers.   This was the first time in my life that I had sat with them or shared a train with them.   I was going to live with them and build with them; I was going to — no, I had already — become one of them.

Soon after boarding the train at Fushun something happened that showed me at once the quality of the society that I was coming into and of the people I was among.   A train attendant and a woman passenger came into our carriage looking for a place for a little girl they were carrying. There was an empty seat behind me, and the man sitting next to it vacated his seat as well for them. The woman laid the girl down on the seats while she stood over her, clearly most anxious. Another passenger asked her if the child was ill, and, if so, why she was out of doors. The woman's reply astonished us. She was a teacher in a primary school near the station, and the girl was a pupil of hers who had suddenly felt a bad pain in her abdomen during class. The school health worker had suspected appendicitis and said that she should be sent to hospital immediately. As the girl's parents both worked in a distant mine there was not time to ask them to come and take the child to hospital, and it would also have taken too long to send her to the mine hospital to be operated on. The teacher decided to put the girl straight on the Shenyang train. The platform staff had allowed her to pay for the tickets on the train itself and told her that they would tell Shenyang by phone to look after them. This incident made me think of the words of Tao Yuan-ming:[1] "From the time of our birth we are brothers, needing no kinship of flesh." This thought is shared by many people today. Then it occurred to me that what Mencius[2] had said about looking after the aged and young of other families as well as one's own had actually come about in the present day. Judging by such conduct, the society into which I was moving was even finer than I had imagined.

On December 9 I arrived in Peking, the home town that I had left thirty-five years earlier. On the platform of the magnificent railway station I saw Fifth Sister and Fourth Brother whom I had not met for over ten and more than twenty years respectively. As we took each other's hands I heard them call me "elder brother", a familiar form of address that my brothers and sisters had never used with me in the old days. I felt that a new life was beginning in my family.

I said goodbye to Section Head Li who had come with us and to Old Meng. Old Meng was one of the eight Chiang Kai-shek war

---

[1] A poet of the Eastern Tsin Dynasty who lived in the late fourth and early fifth centuries A.D.

[2] Thinker and educationalist (372-289 B.C.).

criminals in our prison who had received a pardon, along with Kuo Wen-lin, a former "Manchukuo" general, and myself. He went off with his wife who had come to meet him. Fourth Brother carried my black leather case as I walked off the platform with Fifth Sister and her husband Old Wan on either side of me. When we were off the platform I looked at the station clock and pulled out my pocket watch. Before leaving Fushun the governor had chosen this watch from the pile of things I had presented to the government in jail and told me to keep it. I protested that as it had been bought with money derived through exploitation I did not want it. The governor replied that the people were giving it to me now, so I should keep it. This watch was the French gold watch I had bought in the shop on the edge of the Legation Quarter in Peking when I was trying to shake off my father's chief steward on my way to the foreign legations in 1924. On that day my record of disgrace had started. Now this same watch was marking the beginning of my new life as I set it by Peking time.

On the day he gave me that watch the governor had said to the ten of us who were being released that when we went back home to our families and our neighbours we should apologize to them for the wrongs we had done them in the past. "I believe," he said, "that your neighbours and relations will forgive you, provided that you behave well and serve the people conscientiously." These words were fully borne out when I went to the home of Fifth Sister and Old Wan. Everyone in their compound was kind to me. The next morning I wanted to do something for the neighbours, and when I saw that some people were sweeping the lane I took a broom and joined them. When we had swept as far as the entrance to the lane I could not find my way back home and went into a stranger's home. They guessed what had happened and took me home. They said there was no need for me to thank them as we were all from the same street, and even if we had not been there was nothing odd about people helping each other in the new society.

I went to see my uncle Tsai Tao and his family. I learnt that our clan was flourishing. He had addressed the National People's Congress on his findings during his tour of the minority areas. I heard my cousin Pu Chin play his *ku chin* and watched while he did some calligraphy for me that was better than ever. I also saw a picture of flowers and birds that Pu Chien had recently painted. I went to visit Second Sister and found that she was now running a nursery. Her husband, a postal engineer, told me that she was so busy that the headaches she used to suffer from had disappeared. I also visited Fourth Sister, and Third, Sixth and Seventh Sisters and their husbands. Fourth Sister was working in the archives of the former palace, Sixth Sister and her husband were both painters, and Seventh Sister and her husband were teaching.

I was even more struck by the second generation. On the day of the Spring Festival countless youngsters with red scarves round their necks swarmed all over my uncle's house. Of the older members of that generation I met the former member of the People's Volunteers who had distinguished himself in action, the Peking woman motor-bicycle champion, the leader of the mountaineering team, the doctor, the nurse, the teacher, and the car driver. Most of the youngsters were doing specialized vocational training or studying in middle school. Some of them had joined the Communist Party and the Youth League, and all the rest of them were doing their best to attain these honours.

I also met many friends from the old days. Shang Yen-ying was now a member of the Institute of History and Literature. When I saw him he was lying on a couch; he was so old he could no longer speak clearly. When he saw me his expression became constrained and grave, and he tried to get up. I took his hand and said, "You are old and ill, so you should lie down and rest. We are members of the new society now, and we can enjoy a normal relationship. When you are better we will serve the people together." The formal expression vanished from his face and he nodded to me with a slight smile. "I'll go along with you," he said. "I'm going along with the Communist Party," I replied. "I will too," was his answer. I met some of my old friends who had been palace eunuchs and found out how they were doing. The local authorities ran a special home for them where they could spend their declining years in peace.

Practically everyone I met on the first day said: "Now that you're back you must have a good look around — you've never been able to wander round Peking before." I told them that the first thing I wanted to see was Tien An Men, the Gate of Heavenly Peace.

I already knew Tien An Men Square well from films, papers and letters. On the screen I had seen the parades being reviewed by Chairman Mao, and I had watched festival celebrations. I had seen pictures in the papers of traffic policemen taking kindergarten children across the road, and of Chinese-made Red Flag and East Wind cars parked there. I knew that the Great Hall of the People had been built in ten months, and I had heard about the reactions to the square of foreign guests from all over the world. At last I was here in the place I had dreamed about for so long.

The majestic Tien An Men Gate that stood in front of me was a witness of the motherland's change from misery to happiness, and of the change from the old Pu Yi to the new Pu Yi. On my left was the imposing Great Hall of the People in which the affairs of the nation were decided, including the special pardon under which I had been allowed to start a new life. On my right was the Rev-olutionary Museum and behind me was the Monument to the Rev-olutionary Heroes. They told me what a bitter struggle so many heroes and martyrs had waged for over a century to achieve the fruition of today, of which I too was a beneficiary.

It was in Tien An Men Square that I took my first walk feeling free, safe, happy and proud. I, Fifth Sister and my cousin Pu Chien strolled slowly to the west. When we reached the Cultural Palace of the Nationalities with its white walls and blue roof my sister asked me with concern: "Elder brother, are you tired? Is this the first time you've walked so far?" "I'm not tired," I replied, "for the very reason that this is the first time."

"The first time" were three words that constantly cropped up as I began my new life. "The first time" was always difficult, but I was too excited to feel uneasy about it.

I went to the barber's for the first time, or, strictly speaking, for the second time, as I had once been out to the Chung Yuan Company for a haircut thirty years ago in Tientsin. At any rate, what happened now happened to me for the first time. I sat in the chair and saw a mysterious object I had noticed in a Harbin department store. I asked the barber what it was that was making a humming noise at the next chair and he told me it was a hair-drier. "Do you dry or cut the hair first?" I asked. This question astonished him. "Haven't you ever had your hair cut before?" He thought I was trying to pull his leg. When I realized this I burst out laughing, and when I heard the hair-drier humming over my own head I felt more pleased than ever.

The first time I rode on a bus I gave my cousin Pu Chien a fright. As I was waiting in the bus queue I saw other people standing aside for old people and children to get on first, so I let a woman who was standing next to me get on before me. I did not realize that she was the conductress. Seeing that I was not getting on, she jumped aboard; then the door closed behind her and the bus moved off. A few moments later my cousin came rushing back from the next stop, and we started to laugh out loud at each other when he was still some way off. "Don't worry," I said with full confidence, "nothing can possibly happen." With so many people looking after me what had I to worry about? That very morning I had collected a leather wallet from a shop near Third Sister's place where I had left it by mistake. It was impossible for me to get lost.

The Peking municipal authorities organized a series of visits for a number of us who had come here after special pardon, including the former Kuomintang generals Tu Yu-ming, Wang Yao-wu, Sung Hsi-lien and others. This was to help us to know Peking better and get used to everyday life. We saw some new factories, all kinds of public utilities that had been expanded since liberation, some urban people's communes, and other places; these visits went on for about two months. Finally the others insisted that we go to the former palace with me as temporary guide.

What I found most surprising was that the air of decay and collapse I had known there when I left had disappeared. There was fresh paint everywhere. The curtains for the doors, windows and beds, the cushions, the tablecloths and everything else were all new. I heard later these were all made in the Palace Museum's own factory after the original patterns. Very little of the palace collection of jade, porcelain, calligraphy, paintings, and other *objets d'art* had been left after the depredations of the Peiyang warlord government, the Kuomintang government, and its various guardians, myself included. I did find, however, that quite a few things had been bought back by the museum or presented by collectors. The picture "River-side Scene at the Ching Ming Festival" by the Sung artist Chang Tse-tuan, for example, which had been stolen by Pu Chieh and myself, had now been bought back.

In the imperial garden I saw children playing in the sun and old men sipping tea. I sniffed the spring fragrance of the ancient cypresses and felt that the sun was shining brighter here than it had ever done before. I was sure that the former palace had taken on a new lease of life.

In March 1960 I was sent to the Peking Botanical Gardens of the Institute of Botany of the Chinese Academy of Sciences. Here I spent half my time working and half studying. This was a preparatory stage before I took up the post in which I was to serve the people. Under the guidance of the technical personnel I learnt how to plant seeds, look after seedlings, and transplant them in the hot-houses. I spent the other part of the day either studying or writing this book.

In the first part of my life I did not know what the world "family" meant, and I only began to have some family feeling in my last years in Fushun. Before I had been in the Botanical Gardens for long I felt that I had a second home, living as I was in a friendly and co-operative atmosphere. Once I realized when I came back from a walk that I had lost my watch; I was sadly convinced that I had gone too far to be able to find it again and I gave it up for lost. When Old Liu, my room-mate, heard that I had lost it he asked me in detail about the route I had taken, and set off at once although he was off duty. To my great embarrassment many of the others also found out what had happened, and all of them who were off duty went out to look for the watch. In the end Old Liu found it in front of the dining-hall of a brigade of the Evergreen People's

Commune and brought it back in the highest of spirits. I felt that I was being given back much more than just a watch.

That summer a militia unit was formed in the Botanical Gardens, and it drilled every day. I applied to join, but the others all said that I was over the age limit. "I am a member of the big family of the motherland," I protested, "so I too should be allowed to defend her." I made my point and was allowed to join in the training as an over-age militiaman. Soon I was able to achieve another ambition and demonstrate in Tien An Men Square. The occasion was the march in support of the Japanese people's struggle against the Japan-U.S. Security Treaty.

This was the time when I began to undertake social activities, which made me feel that I was on the same side as the people of the whole of China and the rest of the world who were fighting for peace, democracy, national independence and socialism.

On November 26, 1960 I received a voter's card with my name on it. It seemed the most valuable thing I had ever had in my life, and when I put the ballot-paper into the red box I felt that I was the happiest man on earth. I, along with my 650 million compatriots, was now the owner of our 9,600,000 square kilometres of land. The help that was being extended from this land to the oppressed peoples and nations of the world was great and reliable.

In March 1961 I completed my preparatory stage and took up the post in which I was to serve the people: I became a literary and historical worker for the Historical Materials Commission of the National Committee of the Chinese People's Political Consultative Conference.

In this job I worked on literary and historical material of the late Ching and Peiyang warlord periods. I often came across familiar names and historical events with which I was connected. Most of the authors of these materials were participants in or eyewitnesses of the events they described, and they and I were all witnesses of the history of this period. I gained a clearer view of the developments in the period from these rich source-materials. The lady Yehonala (Empress Dowager Tzu Hsi), Yuan Shih-kai, Tuan Chi-jui, Chang Tso-lin, and all those other figures who were cast aside by history had seemed in their day to wield overwhelming power; while the people, whom they butchered and oppressed, had seemed helpless. Writers of the type of Hu Shih had cheered such figures on; the old-timers had put their hopes of restoration on them; and they had inflated themselves to ever greater proportions in the belief that the powers who backed them would support them for ever. But they turned out to be only paper tigers when they perished in the flames of history, and history was the people. "In appearance, the reactionaries are terrifying, but in reality they are not so powerful. From a long-term point of view, it is not the reactionaries but the people who are really powerful." My own experiences had made me accept the truth of this, and I was going to proclaim it to the people through my work and in my capacity as a witness.

I also continued to write this book.

My office helped me in many ways and provided me with much valuable material, and with the enthusiastic help of many other friends I was able to use many books and documents from archives as well as information that had been specially hunted out. Some of this was hand-copied for me by friends I had never even met, some of it was checked by comrades in my publishing house who went on long journeys to do so, and some was recorded by old gentlemen who had witnessed the events with their own eyes. Much of the inaccessible material was provided by archives and libraries; I should like to mention in particular the National Archives, the History Museum, Peking Library, and the Capital Library, where the comrades made special searches and compilations for me. I was embarrassed by the amount of concern and support I received, but there is in fact nothing unusual about it in our country, where anyone who is doing something that will be useful to the people or is proclaiming the truth will find interest and help everywhere, apart from what he gets from the Party and government.

My book drew the interest of many foreign friends. I was visited by foreign journalists and visitors who asked me about my experiences, particularly my reform over the past ten years. One Latin American said that it showed him once again how great Mao Tsetung's thought was, and urged me to finish my book soon. An

Asian friend said: "I hope you will send me a copy of the English edition of your book as soon as it comes out so that I can translate it into my own language and let the people of my country read your amazing story."

In 1962 our bitter struggle against the difficulties originating at home and abroad was brilliantly successful, and that year brought me further happiness. I was invited to sit on the National Committee of the Chinese People's Political Consultative Conference and to hear the reports at the National People's Congress on the construction of the motherland. On May 1, I and my bride Li Shu-hsien started our own little home, and this ordinary home was, to me, something extraordinary.

This is the new chapter. This is how my new life began. When I think of my home, my voter's card, and the boundless prospects that stretch out before me I will never forget how I gained this new life.

There is another story I should tell about the policy of remoulding criminals, the policy that gave me a new life. As my nephew Little Jui said, I have to include it in this book.

In the summer of 1960 I went to Fragrance Hill Park with Little Jui, and we talked about the very first changes in each of our minds and what it was that first shook us.

Little Jui talked about Little Hsiu first. Little Ku had been shaken when he saw a Chinese train at Suifenho Station where only foreign trains had been seen before, and Little Hsiu had been made to feel that his past life had been futile by the welcome given to the girl worker who had lost a hand. Then Jui talked about himself. "There were many things I shall never forget. The first was when I broke a window-pane while cleaning it soon after I started work. The moment the pane hit the floor a warder came running in. I was terrified, but to my surprise he asked me if I had hurt myself. I said that I was all right, though I had smashed a pane of glass. He said that a piece of glass did not matter, but I had better be careful not to cause anyone injury."

"Things like that have happened to me," I replied. "At first I was most concerned about whether I would be killed or not and doubted whether the policy of leniency would apply to me. What made me see that I had some chance and thus gradually brought me round to a more optimistic view was the unexpected way I was let off scot-free after handing over the stuff I had been hiding in the bottom of my suitcase. Talking of that, I must thank you for the help you gave me then."

"My help?" asked Little Jui, his eyes wide open. "Didn't the prison governor tell you what really happened?"

"Yes, he did. During the time of accusations and acknowledging guilt I wrote a self-criticism about it to the governor after I owned up under Little Ku's questioning at the big meeting. After the New Year I told the governor that I had not mentioned the note you sent me for fear of getting you into trouble. He told me that he knew all about the business and had asked you to write the note in order to help me hand the stuff over on my own initiative. The governor was very conscientious, but you helped me too."

"So you still don't know the details. I didn't want to write that note and was in favour of searching you and confiscating the things to punish you. This is something I have to tell you, and you must include it in your book."

Only now did I learn the full story. Little Jui had divulged my secret to the governor some time previously and asked him to confiscate the stuff. The governor had refused: "It would be very easy to find it but it wouldn't help him in his remoulding. Be patient. It will be much better for him to take the initiative in handing the things over when he's more politically aware." A long time later Little Jui had asked the governor to make a search. The governor's reply had been that different people's thinking developed at different speeds and that it was no use being impatient. The Communist Party was sure that the great majority of criminals could be remoulded when they were in the power of the people, though the process varied. What mattered was not the jewels or the prison rules but how best I could be helped to remould myself. "You must understand," the governor had said about me, "that because of his unique background he finds it hard to believe immediately in the People's Government's policy of leniency to those who confess. If we were to make a search he would lose this chance of understanding the policy. Leave the initiative to him. Rather than make a hurried search you should think out some way of hastening his awakening." Little Jui then thought of writing me a note. When nothing happened for several days after he had passed it to me he grew impatient again and said to the governor, "Pu Yi will never wake up and he hasn't got a scrap of awareness. Why don't we search him?" "It is more important than ever not to be impatient at this point," was the governor's reply. In the end, of course, I had handed the jewels over in desperation; and from that moment on I began to see that there was a new way out for me.

"From then on I understood that the government really believed that the majority of criminals could be reformed," said Little Jui with emotion. "You know yourself that you were still trying to resist and deceive the government then, and the prison authorities knew all about it. Even before the investigators came we had told the government about everything. But from that time on the prison authorities believed that you could be remoulded and were anxious for you to study and reform."

We were standing on the slopes of Fragrance Hill looking towards Peking, which was bathed in sunlight. I thought of one thing after another that had happened in the past ten years. I recalled the grey hair of the old prison governor and the lively speech of the younger deputy governor. I thought of all the warders, doctors, nurses, and other members of the prison staff. When I tried to deceive them; when I used all kinds of shameful methods to resist them; when my ignorance, incompetence and stupidity were thoroughly revealed; when I was in total despair about myself and felt that I could not bear to live a moment longer — at those times these Communist Party members had held firmly to their belief that I could be remoulded and led patiently to becoming a new man.

"Man" was the very first word I learnt to read in my first reader, the *Three Character Classic*, but I had never understood its meaning before. Only today, with the Communist Party and the policy of remoulding criminals, have I learnt the significance of this magnificent word and become a real man.

Afterword

SIMON WINCHESTER

Among the pleasing fantasies that modern historians may occasionally enjoy in their baths—what if Bonaparte had won, for instance, or if Archduke Ferdinand had ducked—those involving the altered fates of this century's toppled monarchs, tsars, and emperors must be particularly compelling. What, one might wonder, if a Zog were to drive victoriously into Tirana, or a Romanov were to return in glory and ride the length of Nevsky Prospekt; and further, and more compelling yet, what if one of those magnificently double-barrelled Aisin-Gioros—the Manchurian despots who for three hundred years ruled China under the title of the Ch'ing dynasts—came back to Peking, and stood in triumph before the Gate of Heavenly Peace?

Well, for much of the late summer and autumn of 1986, it was more or less as though one had. The Italian film director Bernardo Bertolucci re-created, and transported to Peking—indeed, transported right into the heart of the 9,999-room Forbidden City itself, where the emperor had lived—one Mr Henry P'u Yi Aisin-Gioro, the last emperor of China, for the making of the film of the authorized 'autobiography' which precedes these final paragraphs.

Bertolucci clad him—or rather, he clad the four actors who played him at his various ages—in shining imperial yellow and arrayed him in jewels. He surrounded him with 1,000 backwards-walking, eyes-averted eunuchs: all drawn from the People's Liberation Army, their heads shaven for £2 extra daily pay, their queues stuck on with spirit gum, and, happily for them, uncastrated (the old firm that held the royal warrant for the operation having long since fallen victim to the Revolution). And he assembled no fewer than 19,000 extras to dance attendance on, or, depending on the stage in the 61-year-long story, to treat with, or capture, or subdue, the Son of Heaven and Lord of Ten Thousand Years.

So, surrounding the modest majesty of P'u Yi there were envoys and tutors, bannermen and cooks, wives and gaolers, advisers and entertainers and valets, tasters of food and drinkers of wine, and lots and lots of soldiers: soldiers of the Imperial Guard, soldiers of Chiang Kai-shek's Kuomintang army, soldiers from Japan and from Russia, soldiers of Mao's army, and Red Guards acting on the lunatic orders of the Gang of Four. This mighty cast was duly assembled, fed, watered, and made to act in front of the klieg lights and the magnificent Peking palaces—'the sets that Hollywood dared not build'—in order to realize the most expensive independent film ever conceived. And the film was duly realized, on time and within budget, in no small part because everything was done (incredibly, for a film about the Chinese Imperial leadership) with the full co-operation of the present Chinese Communist regime.

The film, which at one level presents a complex panorama of all those aspects of modern Chinese history connected by that single, almost invisible, skein of the life of the last Manchu emperor, took a year to make. For six months the crews were in China, filming under the unblinking scrutiny of the Communist Party bureaucrats and before throngs of the curious Pekingese. And by all accounts everyone—Italian director and lighting men, English producer and sound recordists, wardrobe masters, Party bosses and, above all, the great masses of the Peking streets—everyone found it a drama and a circus that was fascinating, unprecedented, and hugely enjoyable.

But once the camps had been struck and the costumes packed and the trucks and the planes had departed for the Italian studios and the producers' European homes, one was minded to wonder why. What exactly was it that the Chinese, and in particular these unreconstructed masses in whom Mao and Lenin had so accurately placed their faith, had all so clearly enjoyed, and why had they so enjoyed it?

As the final fragments of imperial yellows and scarlets were scrubbed away, and Peking was returned to its customary leaden sludge of greys and browns, people began to ask: What exactly do today's Chinese think of their old emperors? What knowledge have they—what is their received wisdom of the decadent glories of the Ch'ing—the glories and the ghastliness that Signor Bertolucci tried so assiduously to capture? And why, given that the making of such a film would demand the asking of such awkward questions, did the Party authorities allow Bertolucci and his colleagues to make it in the first place?

The answers to these questions are necessarily complicated, and sometimes ambiguous. They are bound up in the imperturbable continuity of that mightiest of global entities that we call China, whether it is called a Celestial Kingdom or People's Republic, and whether its rulers are styled Sons of Heaven or General Secretaries of the Communist Party. The important thing is that, despite the vicissitudes of history, China remains, her borders much the same, her people much the same, her self-knowledge and her self-confidence much the same, and, crucially, her people's attitudes much the same. The answers to the questions raised by the widespread acceptance of the film lie deep within the character of the Chinese, a group of races who, though they have undeniably been profoundly altered by the fervour and the zeal of their two twentieth-century revolutions, are bound by an uncanny intimacy to the verities of their long history.

If one accepts this view, then it follows that it matters less than one might expect to the average Chinese how terrible were the decadent excesses and the unbridled terror of the Manchus, or of anyone else who had ruled them. Maybe the Manchus—who dined on Goat Nipples and Bear's Paw, and who insisted on inferiors performing the full nine *kowtows*, and who were reputed by some fabulists to beat a servant to death every day just for fun, and whose court stranglers could keep a victim living on the verge of death for half an hour with their deft handling of the cheese wire—were rightfully destined to be violently overthrown and disgraced. But they were, by the same token, rulers: cruel and despotic rulers maybe, but also figures of undisputed authority who, to the Chinese Confucian mind, needed to be respected, bowed down before, and obeyed. They were awesome creatures, and the Chinese are a great people for a proper appreciation of the nature of awe.

A friend in Hong Kong recalls her grandmother—she had bound feet, and teetered painfully around Peking in her old age—telling her stories of the last emperor. When he visited the village where she lived, she and all her neighbours would feel obliged (no one would order them) to flatten themselves to the dust, and turn their heads away from the face of their lord. But she never objected—either then, or, more importantly, now. She told her grandchild of the imperial visits with affection, and awe. Her behaviour, she said, was what emperors expected of their subjects.

The simple existence of an emperor—even a foreigner, a Manchu—gave a certain integrity and certainty to life and country. To so huge and chaotic a country as China, the existence of so unchallengeable a figure as an emperor gave to the masses below an impression of stability, of national oneness. Emperors were not necessarily good, but they were *there*, they ruled, they were obeyed—and without them China might crumble and decay.

Would the Indians be much more than curious if the Mauryan kings, or the Moguls—or their filmic equivalents—came back to Delhi? And the Italians, and the Romanians—would they not merely shrug their shoulders if their heaven-sent leaders were paraded before them once again? Somehow it seems that to many Chinese, all their leaders, be they Ch'ing or Sung, Tang or Ming—or even Yuan, who, with Kublai Khan, were Mongols every bit as foreign as the Manchu Ch'ings—are supremely a part of the great sweep of Chinese history, perhaps to be condemned as individuals, or even as dynasties, but to be revered in their entirety.

As to why the Communist leaders permitted Bertolucci to make the film—the answer to that is more difficult to give, and may have less validity in the immediate aftermath of the filming than when the agreements to permit it were first signed. Thus while the film teams were in Peking in the summer of 1986, arresting the attention of the millions, so they, and we, all praised Teng Hsiao-p'ing (Deng Xiaoping) for open-mindedness. We breathed admiringly the fresh air that seemed to be sweeping away the outdated doctrines and dogmas of the Maoist era. But then Signor Bertolucci went away, and almost immediately (though quite coincidentally) the Shanghai students rioted, the police reacted, Mr Teng expressed his displeasure, the reformers were purged, the secretary of the Party was sacked, and a new campaign was started against bourgeois Western liberalism.

One is tempted to wonder whether Bertolucci would so readily be given permission to make his film today. In the climate of 1987, it is perhaps a little less than prudent for the average Pekingese to make much display of affection for history and curiosity about empire. China, it must be remembered, is still passing through an exceptionally volatile phase of its history.

*   *   *

In a gritty suburb of northwest Peking, in a *hutong* busy with jangling bicycles and vegetable sellers, lives an old man who, had the revolutionary events of 1912 and 1949 never taken place, would probably have been the present emperor of China. P'u Chieh, the younger brother of P'u Yi, was created heir apparent by the Japanese during Manchukuo days. P'u Yi died, childless, in 1967, and had history taken another turn P'u Chieh and his Japanese wife would now be sitting in luxury and splendour on the Dragon Throne.

Instead the old, frail man lives in his half-dozen rooms grouped round a dusty courtyard, and tends to his plants, and his pets. He has five cats, and a companion—a minder—from the Communist Party. He makes a modest living as a calligrapher, and by representing the Manchu people at the National People's Congress. He says, whenever he meets an enquirer, that he has been thoroughly, and voluntarily, converted to the wisdom of socialism—'I am but a drop of stagnant water that has been purified in an ocean of one billion people', he will say, with a glance at his companion, almost as if to ask whether he had uttered the phrase correctly. He talks little about—and without affection for, or even interest in—the life he once led, other than to mention with studied distaste the eunuchs, the food-tasters, and the afternoons spent hunting grasshoppers with his brother.

But then, if you appear interested, and sympathetic to his curious plight, the man who could have been emperor will take his jade chop of majesty from a drawer in his desk, dab it in scarlet ink, and affix a seal in your notebook. The characters read simply *Aisin-Gioro P'u Chieh*—the stylized signature and seal of the senior surviving member of one of the most powerful families in the pre-revolutionary world. 'Take good care of that seal', he says. 'One day it may be very valuable again. We never know what will happen in China.'

China, so huge, so ancient, so unwieldly, so crammed with people—we never know, as the should-be emperor said, just what will happen next.

There is just a simple certainty that it will remain, eternally, Chinese, with a uniquely proud people, for whom all its leaders, from Kublai Khan to Mao Tse-tung, from Henry P'u Yi to Chiang Kai-shek, are to be respected for the parts they have played in one of the oldest continuous nation-stories in the world. The tragic drama of P'u Yi is a part of that story, and as such will continue, in its own minor and peculiar way, to give to the Chinese still more of that pride and self-assurance which has set them apart from the rest of the world for the last three thousand years.

Index

A

Academy of Chinese Painting, 425
"Administrative Committee for the Northeast", 240
Aisin-Gioro clan, 3, 17-18, 129, 196, 228, 275-276, 423-424, 429, 438
Akiyama Hiroshi, 448
Aldrovani, Count, 268
"All-Manchurian Assembly", 253
Alston, Beilby (British minister), 107
Ama-terasu-o-mi-Kami, *see* Heaven Shining Bright Deity
Amakasu Masahiko, 234-235, 237-239, 254
America, 13, 83, 157, 187, 189, 190-191, 210, 242, 267, 269, 293, 324, 435
Amur River (Black Dragon River), 205
An Te-hai (eunuch), 5
Anhwei, 88, 98, 184
Anhwei clique, 105
Anshan, 444
Anshan Iron and Steel Works, 444
"Anti-Communist Autonomous Government of Eastern Hopei", 283
Anti-Japanese Allied Armies, 288, 320, 387, 392, 414, 451
Anti-Japanese National Salvation Society, 288
Antung, 309
Arita Hachiro, 206
"Army of Pacification", 176, 183
Articles for Favourable Treatment, 36, 37-38, 79, 85, 96, 123, 157, 165, 175, 228
Ashikaga Takauji, 219
"Asia Revival Council", 384
Asnis (Captain), 333-334
"Autonomous Military Government of Inner Mongolia", 283
Awaji Maru, 233

B

Babojab, Prince, 86-87, 97, 376
"Bank of Manchukuo", 459
"Big Mouth", *see* Chang Huan-hsiang
Black Dragon Society (Black Ocean Association), 197, 203-206, 225, 275
"Boxers", *see* Yi Ho Tuan
Britain, 4, 13, 108, 115, 189-190, 197, 210, 221-222, 268, 293, 302, 324, 439-440
Buddhism, 110, 266
Bungei Shunju, 232
Burnell-Nugent, F. H., Brigadier, 222

C

Calligraphy Research Association, 425
Capital Library, 480
Central Committee of the Communist Party of China, 466-467
Chang Chieh-ho, 63-67, 69, 77, 79, 84
Chang Chih-tung, 59
Chang Ching-hui, 105-107, 240, 254-256, 283, 286-287, 292, 317, 319-320, 324, 338, 374, 379, 389-390, 459
Chang Hai-peng, 224, 255-256
Chang Hsueh-liang, 139, 184, 186-188, 194, 218, 226, 229, 268
Chang Hsun, 87-92, 94-100, 105-107, 120, 142, 145, 162, 180, 192, 426
Chang Huan-hsiang ("Big Mouth"), 360, 388, 413, 443, 468, 471
Chang, Little, 338
Chang, Old (former puppet general), 422, 430, 443
Chang Pi, 146
Chang Tso-hsiang, 220
Chang Tso-lin, 105-108, 120, 123, 145, 153-154, 156, 158, 163, 175-177, 179-188, 190, 192, 194, 197, 225, 246, 284, 479

497

New Army (Peiyang Army), 12, 19
New China, 342-343, 353, 403, 419, 422, 435-436
New Fourth Army, 314
Niuhuhu (Eastern Dowager), 5
Nomanhan campaign of 1939, 314
North China, 33, 229, 274, 283-284, 313
North China Daily Mail, 104-105
Northeast China, 72, 86, 97, 107, 123, 129, 158, 182-184, 186-190, 193, 197-198, 209, 215, 217, 219, 220-230, 233-234, 238-240, 244-245, 253-254, 266-268, 272, 274, 284, 286, 288, 294, 297, 299-300, 304, 312, 324, 328-329, 350, 352, 354-355, 367-368, 370, 381-388, 406, 409-410, 417, 427, 432, 443, 451
Northeastern army, 416
Northern Expedition, 176, 187, 200, 217
Northeastern People's Government, 424
Northwest China, 424, 456
Notice of a Special Pardon from the Supreme People's Court of the People's Republic of China, 472

O

Ohira Kihachiro, 86
Okamura (Japanese general), 183, 293
Oki, 218
On New Democracy, 341
Opium Wars, 445
Organizational Law of "Manchukuo", 258
Osugi Sakae, 234
Oudendijk, W. J., 129-130, 150
Oxford University, 110, 116

P

Pacific War, 293, 312, 383
"Pagoda of the Loyal Souls", 278
Pai River, 199, 230-232
Palace Museum (Peking), 477
Panchiatai Village, 432
Pang, Old, 432
Panmunjom talks, 445
Panpitien, 6
Pao-chia system, 288
Pao Hsi, 150, 256, 277
Paris, 267

Payen County, 392
Peace Preservation Army, 284
Pearl Consort of Kuang Hsu, 16
Pedigree of Ching House, 249
Peihai Lake, 425
Peiyang (Northern) Army, 12, 16-17, 20, 33
Peiyang warlords, 95-101, 105, 184, 313, 423, 478-479
Peking, 3, 5, 10, 12, 14-15, 17, 34, 37, 54, 59, 73, 80, 83, 92, 97-98, 102, 105-107, 111, 119-120, 122, 125, 127, 134, 143, 145-146, 151-154, 163, 166, 168-169, 175, 178, 181, 185-186, 188, 196-197, 207-210, 212, 217, 229, 273-276, 290, 292, 300, 310-311, 328, 334, 356, 377, 425-427, 429, 435, 455, 468, 473-477, 483
Peking Botanical Gardens of the Institute of Botany, 478-479
Peking Daily, 166
Peking-Fengtien Railway, 187
Peking-Hankow Railway, 194
Peking Leader (English-language newspaper), 106
Peking Library, 480
Peking Police School, 144
Peking-Tientsin region, 196-197
People's Government, Chinese, 334-335, 352, 358, 365, 368-369, 376, 386, 388, 400, 403, 412-413, 424, 427, 436, 444, 466-467, 480, 482-483
People's Liberation Army, Chinese, 334, 336, 397, 424, 427
People's Political Council of the Kuomintang, 34
People's Republic of China, 325, 431, 444, 466, 472
Pingfangchu, 450
Pingtingshan (massacre), 409-410
Prince Regent (Pu Yi's father), 16-24, 26, 28, 31, 33-36, 147, *see also* Chun, 2nd Prince
Prison governor, 345, 355, 357-359, 366, 397, 400, 402-404, 435, 461, 465, 474
"Proclamation of the Chief Executive", 255
Proclamation of the People's Liberation Army, 424
Property Control Law, 289

OXFORD

MORE OXFORD PAPERBACKS

Details of a selection of other books follow. A complete list of Oxford Paperbacks, including The World's Classics, Twentieth-Century Classics, OPUS, Past Masters, Oxford Authors, Oxford Shakespeare, and Oxford Paperback Reference, is available in the UK from the General Publicity Department, Oxford University Press (JH), Walton Street, Oxford OX2 6DP.

In the USA, complete lists are available from the Paperbacks Marketing Manager, Oxford University Press, 200 Madison Avenue, New York, NY 10016.

Oxford Paperbacks are available from all good bookshops. In case of difficulty, customers in the UK can order direct from Oxford University Press Bookshop, 116 High Street, Oxford, Freepost, OX1 4BR, enclosing full payment. Please add 10 per cent of published price for postage and packing.

SETTING THE EAST ABLAZE

Peter Hopkirk

Peter Hopkirk's book—the last in his trilogy set in Central Asia—tells for the first time the story of the Bolshevik attempt between the wars to set the East ablaze with the new gospel of Marxism. Lenin's dream was to liberate the whole of Asia, but his starting-point was British India. A shadowy, undeclared war followed, in which the British and their allies were determined to wreck Moscow's plans.

Among the players in this new Great Game were British Indian intelligence officers and the professional revolutionaries of the Communist International. There were also Muslim visionaries and Chinese war-lords—as well as a White Russian baron who roasted his Bolshevik captives alive.

Pieced together from the intelligence reports of the day, and the long-forgotten memoirs of eye-witnesses, here is an extraordinary tale of intrigue and treachery, barbarism and civil war, whose echoes continue to be heard in Afghanistan and elsewhere today.

SOE IN THE FAR EAST

Charles Cruickshank

The whole course of the Second World War in the Far East might have changed if the activities of Special Operations Executive had been given a free rein by the military and politicians. This is the startling conclusion of Dr Cruickshank's official history, based on secret files and the accounts of surviving agents.

'admirably vivid . . . a pleasure to read' *Listener*

'full of Cruickshank's dry wit and tales of startling bravery' M. R. D. Foot, *Times Literary Supplement*

'The author is as diverting as Le Carré.' *Glasgow Herald*

MACARTNEY AT KASHGAR

C. P. Skrine and Pamela Nightingale

This book describes the life of Sir George Macartney who, for almost thirty years at the turn of the century, was Britain's representative in Sinkiang, one of the most remote posts ever maintained by the British government. The book's appearance will be especially welcomed by those who enjoyed the memories of wild Kashgar and its strange peoples in Lady Macartney's *An English Lady in Chinese Turkestan*.

THE TIBETAN BOOK OF THE DEAD

Edited by W. Y. Evans-Wentz

The Tibetan Book of the Dead—the *Bardo Thödol*—is unique among the sacred books of the world as a contribution to the science of death and of existence after death, and of rebirth. It is used in Tibet as a breviary, and is read or recited on the occasion of death, but it was originally conceived to serve as a guide not only for the dying and dead, but also for the living. For this revised and expanded third edition of Dr Evans-Wentz has written a new preface.

'Dr Evans-Wentz, who literally sat at the feet of the Tibetan lama for years in order to acquire his wisdom . . . not only displays a deeply sympathetic interest in those esoteric doctrines, so characteristic of the genius of the East, but likewise possesses the rare faculty of making them more or less intelligible to the layman.' *Anthropology*

BAYONETS TO LHASA

Peter Fleming

With an introduction by Brian Shaw

China has recently opened Tibet to foreign visitors, creating renewed interest in a land that was, for much of its history, isolated and inaccessible. In modern times, that isolation first came to an end (albeit temporarily) with the Younghusband Mission to Lhasa of 1903–4, one of the stranger episodes in British imperial history.

Thanks to the patience, force of character and flair of Colonel Francis Younghusband, a treaty was signed and the foundations of Anglo-Tibetan friendship laid.

A SUPERFICIAL JOURNEY THROUGH TOKYO AND PEKING

Peter Quennell

Introduced by Geremie Barme

First published in 1932, *A Superficial Journey* resulted from a year spent in Japan, much of it in Tokyo and Kyoto, and a visit to Peking. The book is, as Quennell states, 'a kind of travel film, a sequence in which image suggests image'. Kabuki actors and the puppet theatre; Tokyo's Joy Quarter and the arid and tomb-ridden vistas of north China; grotesquely shaped goldfish, the 'Bourbons or the Hapsburgs of their breed', and political gossip in Peking—these are some of the images that Quennell records.

ON A CHINESE SCREEN

W. Somerset Maugham

Introduction by H. J. Lethbridge

This remarkable book resulted from Maugham's travels in China between 1919 and 1920 and was first published in 1922. It presents in a sequence of vignettes and brief sketches an extraordinary range of the European types then resident there: missionaries and their wives, Catholic priests and nuns, consular and diplomatic officials, taipans and business men, soldiers and seafarers, and all the flotsam and jetsam of European communities in the East. There are Chinese among the portraits as well, including an official who was supremely sensitive to beauty in all its forms and yet grossly venal in his public life and a Chinese professor of comparative literature who made wonderfully bizarre evaluations of foreign writers.

Since Maugham visited China the treaty ports have gone, the privileged expatriate communites have vanished, and the visitor is no longer free to wander at will. *On a Chinese Screen* is now an important historical document.

FOREIGN DEVILS ON THE SILK ROAD

The Search for the Lost Cities and Treasures of Chinese Central Asia

Peter Hopkirk

During the T'ang dynasty the towns of the Silk Road, the great trans-Asian trade route linking China with Imperial Rome, became famous as centres of Buddhist art and learning. But as the Silk Road declined the towns were devoured by the encroaching desert sands, and their great riches became no more than the subject of local legend. This is the story of their rediscovery at the turn of the century by international adventurers and explorers.

THE SIEGE AT PEKING

Peter Fleming

Introduced by David Bonavia

Peter Fleming, brother of Ian—creator of James Bond—and the epitome of the enlightened English gentleman adventurer and explorer, was for many years the *Times* correspondent in China. His account of the Boxer Rebellion in 1900 is a brilliant work of historical journalism.

'provides a fascinating glimpse of the last days of the Mancho dynasty which ruled China from 1644 to 1911. Crisply written, meticulously researched. It is not hard to see why the Chinese have never been very keen of foreigners.' *Tribune*

THE CHINESE FESTIVE BOARD

Corrine Lamb

The Chinese Festive Board presents a delightful picture of Chinese manners and dining etiquette that is as accurate today as it was when the book was first published in 1935. There are chapters on the conventions of Chinese food, on wine, cooking methods, ingredients, and on how to order a meal. In addition there is a selection of recipes gleaned by the author from twenty years of hospitality at the table of princes, generals, peasants, inn-keepers, and even cameleers. All this is complemented with Chinese proverbs and illustrated with photographs and line-drawings.

The book reflects the Chinese belief that eating is an affair involving pleasant anticipation, careful thought, meticulous selection, and, finally, a wholehearted, if somewhat noisy, gusto during the process itself.

CONFUCIUS

Raymond Dawson

Has any individual ever shaped his own country's civilisation more thoroughly, or been set up as an example to more of his fellow countrymen, than Confucius? But what we know about the man himself is vague and shadowy, and the sayings attributed to him may often seem—to the Westerner—obscure, trivial, or banal. Raymond Dawson resolves these paradoxes, showing the contemporary applicability of the sayings, and giving reasons for the strength of their influence throughout the two and a half millennia of their currency.

'This work is to be commended for its quiet and straightforward approach. It is pleasing to have this lucid treatise to recommend to students, and more mature scholars will also find it stimulating.' *British Books News*

Past Masters

TRESPASSERS ON THE ROOF OF THE WORLD

The Race for Lhasa

Peter Hopkirk

Hidden away behind the protecting Himalayas and ruled over by a God-king, Tibet has long been the stuff of travellers' dreams. This book tells for the first time the dramatic story of how foreign powers (including Britain) raced to be the first to unravel the mysteries of this medieval land.

'well told, elegiac story with a very unhappy ending' *Sunday Times*

'This is a marvellous book, well researched and beautifully written—a treat for armchair explorers everywhere.' *New Statesman*